The Reference
Assessment Manual

Compiled and Edited by the

Evaluation of Reference and Adult Services Committee
Management and Operation of Public Services Section
Reference and Adult Services Division (RASD)
American Library Association

The Pierian Press
Ann Arbor, Michigan
1995

ISBN 0-87650-344-X

THE PIERIAN PRESS
Box 1808
Ann Arbor, Michigan 48106
1-800-678-2435

TABLE OF CONTENTS

PREFACE — v

The Research Process vii

PART I: OVERVIEW

Chapter 1: Assessing Library Services:
The Reference Component 1
Marjorie E. Murfin

Chapter 2: What Reference Services Should Be Offered? 16
Marjorie E. Murfin

PART II: USERS AND QUESTIONS

Chapter 3: Library Users and Reference Patrons 23
Marjorie E. Murfin

Chapter 4: Question Classification 42
Jo Bell Whitlatch

PART III: MATERIAL RESOURCES

Chapter 5: Reference Environment 47
Anna M. Donnelly

Chapter 6: Reference Collection Use 50
Anna M. Donnelly

Chapter 7: Electronic Databases and Reference Assistance . . . 53
Ralph Lowenthal and Marjorie E. Murfin

PART IV: HUMAN RESOURCES

Chapter 8:   Worklife and Morale 57
          Ralph Lowenthal and Marjorie E. Murfin

Chapter 9:   Reference Duties and Responsibilities 64
          Ralph Lowenthal and Marjorie E. Murfin

PART V: REFERENCE PROCESS

Chapter 10:   Reference Training 67
          Beth S. Woodard

Chapter 11:   Communication and the Reference Interface 76
          Helen M. Gothberg

Chapter 12:   Reference Librarian Knowledge and
          Search Strategy 82
          Jo Bell Whitlatch

Chapter 13:   Reference Volume, Staffing, and Accessibility . . . 86
          Marjorie E. Murfin

PART VI: RESULTS

Chapter 14:   Costs and Outcomes 93
          Marjorie E. Murfin

Chapter 15:   Reference Effectiveness 99
          Frances Benham

ANNOTATED BIBLIOGRAPHY   113

SUMMARIES OF INSTRUMENTS   255

Secondary Author Index 347

Title Index 355

Preface

With the publication of this manual, a wide range of instruments useful in assessing reference services will be available to the profession. In the past, evaluations and research in libraries tended to be conducted only in a single library with an instrument developed especially for that study and seldom utilized in other libraries. Also, librarians attempting to assess reference services have reported difficulty in identifying reliable and appropriate assessment instruments.

To meet these needs, this work attempts to provide practicing librarians, reference managers, and researchers with access to a wide range of evaluation instruments useful in assessing reference service effectiveness. A secondary aim of this publication is to encourage library administrators to support and promote evaluation of services. Easy access and identification of appropriate evaluation instruments should encourage people to replicate and build upon previous studies, thereby improving existing evaluation instruments and enhancing knowledge of how to assess reference services.

Reference service assessment instruments for both public and academic libraries are included. Specific topics included are users and questions, material resources, human resources, the reference process, and results. The assessment manual does not cover evaluations of bibliographic instruction, reference service by appointment, and database searching for a fee. One topic that was considered for inclusion in the instrument manual but later dropped was reference personnel performance management. While there is great interest in the topic of performance evaluation, there is also a plethora of material published on this topic. On the other hand, there appear to be few instruments designed specifically for reference librarians.

Each chapter describes the scope of the topic, its importance, the state of the field, and research needs. The *Manual* also includes an annotated bibliography of selected works. Each instrument that has been selected for inclusion has been fully described. Instruments have been included in the *Manual* whenever possible. When an instrument cannot be included, information on how to obtain it has been provided.

Most of the instruments included in the *Manual* can be easily adapted for assessment of reference service in an electronic environment. Assessment of on-site reference services also continues to be essential if we are to improve our understanding of and ability to provide effective service utilizing new electronic reference sources. We encourage librarians, reference managers, and researchers to use the instruments provided in the *Manual* in order to conduct additional assessments of reference services and enrich our knowledge of how to improve the quality of reference services.

The *Manual* began as an idea expressed by Marcia Myers during her term as chair of RASD's Evaluation of Reference and Adult Services Committee (1985/86). It was encouraged by Charles Bunge during his tenure as president of RASD. Myers put out a call for instruments that might be included but received little response. During her tenure as chair and at intervals over subsequent years, the Evaluation of Reference and Adult Services Committee provided well-attended programs on reference evaluation at annual meetings of the American Library Association. Under the leadership of Marjorie Murfin, the committee continued to discuss the potential of the *Manual* and to recognize widespread interest in the proposed project. Frances Benham, chair in 1988/89 and 1989/90, called again for instruments through many library publications, announcements to relevant ALA groups, and committee member contacts. These efforts, spurred by the increasing interest in the profession, resulted in the identification and collection of numerous evaluation instruments. An outline was developed and writing assignments were agreed upon. Organization and writing continued under Anna Donnelly, chair in 1990/91, who selected for committee appointment several *Manual* contributors. Jo Bell Whitlatch, who served as committee chair in 1991/92, agreed to edit the *Manual*. Beth Woodard, current chair in 1992/93 and 1993/94, guided efforts leading to publication. Chapter authors met in New Orleans at Loyola University prior to the 1993 ALA annual meeting to review chapters and to accept final assignments in preparation for publication.

Many people active in the American Library Association provided important support, encouragement, and advice, especially James Sweetland, Andrew Hanson, and Herbert Bloom. The committee particularly appreciated the detailed editorial advice and assistance provided by Mary Jo Lynch.

The Research Process

This overview of the research process outlines the steps essential in planning and implementing a successful assessment program. In addition, concepts vital to research, such as validity and reliability, are defined.

Conducting an effective assessment of reference services requires careful planning and development of the evaluation project. The authors of the *Manual* advise planning assessment projects through use of the following steps:

1) Define the purpose or goal of the assessment and obtain the agreement of staff involved in the project. A good way to proceed is to attempt to provide the answer to this question: What are the problems to be studied and how will the information be useful in planning, managing, or improving reference services? The **Scope** and **Importance of Research** sections in each chapter of the *Manual* will assist librarians in determining the type of information they can expect to obtain from the use of the various instruments.

2) Provide concise statements of assessment goals (broad purpose) and objectives (specific measurable standards) and the information needed. Objectives should be stated in specific terms. Specific statements include, for example, providing correct and complete answers to 80 percent of all factual questions; providing all information needed to 80 percent of all user queries; providing courteous service to 90 percent of all users; or ensuring that 90 percent of users wait two minutes or less for reference assistance. Specific written goals and objectives statements will assist users of the *Manual* in selecting the instruments most suitable for their particular assessment situations. Each potential instrument should be evaluated carefully to determine whether it will be able to supply the specific information needed.

3) Select appropriate methodologies related to study objectives. The **State of the Field** section in each chapter of the *Manual* informs the reader of the methodologies employed in studying the topic. The summary that accompanies each assessment instrument also addresses strengths and weaknesses of that instrument. An important reason for publishing the *Manual* is to encourage use of the instruments selected; however, the annotations in the bibliography also provide additional alternatives.

4) Collect and analyze the data. Information on data collection and analysis is often included in the instrument summaries. The extensive bibliography contains detailed information on results of previous studies using an instrument. These annotations also provide readers with examples of the types of data they can expect to obtain from an assessment project that employs the instrument. Networking and identifying assistance is important to the success of all projects, and it is particularly helpful to people beginning their first assessment project. Authors of assessment instruments are generally delighted to work with others interested in using their instruments. Statistical expertise is available from a wide range of places: library school faculty, research centers, state libraries, and faculty in many disciplines on the local college campus.

5) Communicate the results of the assessment. Unless the results of the project are communicated both within and beyond the participating institution(s), much of the value of the project will be lost. Effective communication of the results is important because the data should be useful in improving reference services; the report will contribute to the general body of knowledge concerning reference evaluation; and the report will stimulate further evaluation projects. Possibilities for communicating the findings include posting initial findings on electronic mail, presentating papers at conferences, poster sessions at conferences, publication in ERIC, research notes or articles in journals, and, for extensive projects, publication as a book.

Many specific terms are defined within the **Scope** section of the chapter dealing with the topic. However, in this overview the authors of the *Manual* have included a few definitions of common research terms that are vital to understanding all assessment projects:

- **Attitudes** are opinions about relatively simple phenomena. Data on attitudes are most commonly collected through questionnaires.

- **Behaviors** are information on what people actually do. Data on behaviors are most commonly collected through observation. Observation can be obtrusive, where subjects are aware they are being observed, or unobtrusive, where subjects do not know their behaviors are being observed. Observation can include self-observation, such as keeping diaries; reference interview recording devices; and physical traces, for example, papers in books which record use if the papers are moved.

- **Case Studies** usually study a single situation but employ a variety of methods, such as interviews, structured and unobtrusive observations, and existing documents and records.

- **Climate** concerns the prevailing standards, norms, and attitudes of a group or organization.

- **Effectiveness** is a measure of the quality of service. There is no right way to measure effectiveness because assessments of effectiveness depend upon values and are essentially subjective. Measuring the effectiveness of a service requires assessing performance against a standard. Some of the common standards used in assessing effectiveness are 1) economic, such as productivity (reference questions answered per hour); 2) process, such as user satisfaction (with reference services); 3) acquisition of valued resources (number of online bibliographic and full-text databases available); and 4) quality of outcomes (accuracy of answers, users receiving all the information they need).

- **Environment** is defined as social, cultural, and physical forces shaping a group or organization. Environment may also be viewed as those elements over which the reference staff can exercise little or no control when providing service.

- **Input measures** are measures of what goes into a library, or, more often, measures of the ability to acquire resources. Examples of input measures related to reference service are number of electronic databases acquired or accessible, number of reference materials acquired annually, salary funds available to hire reference staff, reference staff size, and number of questions received.

- **Output measures** are measures of the result, the outcome, or end product of a service activity. Output measures are often concerned with the quality of the reference product, for example, accuracy of answers or users' reports on whether they received the information needed. Another outcome measure relevant to reference service is cost of answering the question.

- **Qualitative measures** have been more commonly used in the social sciences than quantitative measures. Common qualitative methods are observation, structured or unstructured interviews, and case studies. Qualitative measures typically capture the detail, depth, and complexity of human behavior in a natural setting (an uncontrolled environment). Results from qualitative studies tend to be descriptive with categories difficult to categorize and summarize.

- **Quantitative measures** have been most commonly used in the sciences. Experimental research determines the effect of a change in one variable (the independent variable) upon another variable (the dependent variable). Change is made in only one variable at a time in a highly controlled environment, which is typically a laboratory setting. In the social sciences, quantitative measures are more frequently used in field studies, where it is not possible to control all of the variables.

- **Reliability** refers to measures that are stable and dependable. Reliable measures secure consistent results with each repeated use. Pretesting instruments, adequate sample size, and good sampling selection procedures are important to ensure reliability of measures. Some of the instruments included in the *Manual* have been used repeatedly; others have been tested for internal consistency. However, many of the instruments in the *Manual* need much more extensive testing. Use of instruments in other settings will help the reference field develop a core of reliable instruments that have been tested in a variety of settings.

- **Validity** means that measures accurately reflect the concept being studied. Valid measures must reflect common agreements as to meaning and mental images associated with a particular measure. Does the variable measure what the evaluator intended to measure? If the evaluator intends to measure the accuracy of information provided, asking people how satisfied they are with the service is probably not a valid measure. How satisfied people are with the service may have more to do with the courtesy, friendliness, and promptness of service than with the accuracy of the information provided.

Chapter 1

Assessing Library Services:

The Reference Component

Marjorie E. Murfin

SCOPE

This chapter focuses on the reference component of the general library surveys which cover all services. Because reference is one of several library services, it is useful to first consider assessing these services together. The chapter shows how general assessments can provide data useful in assessing reference. The merits of various types of library surveys are discussed in light of obtaining data useful for evaluating reference services. The chapter does not discuss the general library survey as a vehicle for evaluating the effectiveness of the library as a whole.

IMPORTANCE OF RESEARCH

It is necessary to assess reference in the library setting due to the fact that today many new as well as older library services must compete for scarce resources. Library administrators need to be able to place each service in perspective in the overall library setting. Reference librarians need to be able to step back and see themselves in the larger picture of the library, and gain knowledge of the nature and extent of their contribution.

STATE OF THE FIELD

Overview

The librarywide survey, based on patron report, is the method that is most commonly used to obtain information on reference performance in the context of all library services. Other methods, such as experimental studies of patron information-seeking behavior (Taylor, 1966-67), user diaries (Oldman and Wills, 1977), and materials availability studies (Saracevic, Shaw, and Kantor, 1977; Whitlatch, 1978; Palais, 1981) have also been used to add to the total picture.

Perhaps the greatest advantage of the general library survey is that it is often the *only* way to gain answers to questions such as the following: Are library users asking the right questions in the right places? How successful are those who consult reference for information needs as opposed to those who have information needs but *don't* consult reference? How is reference regarded and used by library patrons in relation to other services? What are the conditions and circumstances surrounding reference use and nonuse? How do patrons, who do not ask for reference assistance, use the reference collection?

The methodology of assessing reference service in the overall library setting is not generally well developed. Although many user surveys with items or portions on reference service have been done and many instruments exist, the information that can be gained from any one of them about specific services, such as reference, is limited.

A major disadvantage of general library evaluation surveys in regard to reference is that they often do not succeed in obtaining certain facts vital to a meaningful evaluation of reference. This is because there are so many aspects of library service for the patron to consider that sufficient space cannot always be allotted to reference items. Such survey instruments may not identify where or of whom a question was asked or whether that question was reference or directional. Without this information, results may not evaluate the work of the reference department or even analyze information-seeking behavior of patrons in a way useful to reference departments.

A further disadvantage is that, in the past, inadequate scale construction often produced results extremely biased in the positive direction. Little research was available at that time and scale construction was not examined as a possible source of positive bias. Instead, ability of users to rate services was sometimes questioned, which led to a lack of confidence in the general library survey as a vehicle for assessment. Much is known by psychologists about designing test items to reduce response set and positive bias. The problem of positive bias is not insoluble and can be overcome fairly easily if scales are constructed by those knowledgeable in techniques for controlling positive response set.

Another disadvantage of general surveys is the difficulty of securing a good return rate for academic libraries. One study indicated that the best return rate was secured when forms were passed out to those *leaving* the library (Fisher and Alexander, 1976). However, there are instances of surveys being passed out at the beginning of a visit with good return rates being secured (Carnegie Mellon, 1978; Murfin and Gugelchuk, 1987). Return rates of mailed library surveys are generally unacceptable, but they might be improved with intensive follow-up. In-class surveys, administered by library representatives, done on the spot, and retrieved immediately, can have good return rates (Whitlatch, 1980). Telephone interview surveys require more time, effort, and expense in order to secure adequate sample sizes.

The Survey Population

In administering the librarywide survey, a basic choice must be made between collecting data in the library from samples limited to library users and collecting data from samples that will include nonusers as well. In academic settings, classroom administration can provide an excellent way to collect both user and nonuser data, while securing a good return rate. A disadvantage is that the more objective present-visit-only data cannot be obtained this way. However, present-visit-only data could be obtained, with non-user data being obtained in a separate survey. One public library has obtained data from non-users through a telephone interview survey (Yocum and Stocker, 1980).

Types of General Library Surveys

Some survey instruments concentrate on exploring information-seeking behavior, while others focus on evaluating the work of particular library departments. A few manage to combine both purposes successfully. Whichever type of survey is used, however, the problem of a clear identification of the reference department remains difficult.

Evaluating particular library departments or services in the same terms is difficult to accomplish, and most general surveys do not attempt to do this. In order to evaluate the work of particular departments, each of those departments must be clearly identified by location so that the work of one department will not be confused with that of another. If this difficulty can be overcome, this method has the advantage that we can learn something about the relative success of various approaches, units, and services.

However, rather than evaluating library departments, most survey instruments attempt to explore patron information-seeking behavior by asking about library activities engaged in and the success of those activities. They may also explore the services, approaches, and resources used and patterns of use, but do not often provide a clear identification of the work of the reference department.

Reference Locations

User success in identifying the best place to ask questions is a particularly difficult problem in large library buildings with many service desks. Following are some questions that might be raised: Are things working the way they should in the library with regard to the role of reference? Are people obtaining the right help in the right place? What percent of those who are helped in various locations succeed in finding what they want?

Although extremely difficult to investigate, a promising approach is a survey that identifies locations and asks how satisfied the patron was in regard to that location (University of California at Riverside, 1984). Another approach has been to ask users if they had ever been misdirected from one location to another (University of California at Riverside, 1981). A third survey asks the user if he or she requested help in the library. If so, the user is asked to check locations where requests for help were made. (University of Colorado Libraries, 1975). Although these methods provide some helpful information, no one overall library evaluation instrument has been found that does a more than adequate job of answering this question.

Reference Collection Use

Public and academic libraries have gained valuable information about how many users report having used the reference collection (University of British Columbia, 1981; Yocum and Stocker, 1980; Rodger, 1984a; New York University, 1981). Generally reported use of the reference collection is greater than use of reference service itself. In one academic library it was the fourth most used collection after the general stacks, periodicals and newspapers, and reserve (New York University, 1981). Other methods of studying reference collection use are discussed in Chapter 6, "Reference Collection Use."

Importance, Need, and Use

Importance, need, and frequency of use of reference service appear to be separate but related concepts. Importance appears to be the broadest concept, followed by need and use. For example, if something is *not presently needed* it might *still* be considered important. In regard to need and use, a need may be felt for something but, for a number of reasons, may not always be acted upon.

Importance and need have sometimes been inferred by use, that is, a service that is more heavily used than another should be considered of greater importance to patrons. Importance, however, can be much greater than use would indicate as shown in one library where only 56% reported being reference users, but 97% considered it important (Yocum and Stocker, 1980). Use figures should not be taken to represent the *importance* or need for a service also because use of a labor-intensive service such as reference, interlibrary loan, or online searching may be curtailed due to lack of personnel to provide these services.

Importance

Importance has usually been investigated in general library surveys by use of a scale of five (Marchant, 1970) or seven categories (Chwe, 1978). It has also been investigated by asking users whether or not they were willing to do without a service (Yocum and Stocker, 1980), or by asking them to rank services in order of importance in selecting a particular library branch (Yocum and Stocker, 1980). Other importance rankings are available (University of California at Los Angeles, 1979). All seem to yield results that could be of use to reference departments in helping define the place of reference in the library and the value it has for its users.

Importance of various services within the reference department can also be measured by the same methods described above. The more complex method of conjoint analysis has also been used to determine the trade-offs users might make in regard to retaining services. For more on conjoint analysis and ranking, see Chapter 2, "What Reference Services Should Be Offered?" Importance can also be measured on the level of the *individual reference transaction,* as has been done in some surveys. For more information on this, see Chapter 3, "Library Users and Reference Patrons."

Need for Help

Total need for help in the library includes both *perceived* and *unperceived* need. No estimates of total need have been found as part of a general library survey. Instead, perceived need has been measured in a variety of ways, but unperceived need is considerably more difficult to measure and has been investigated less often.

Perceived need for assistance begins when an individual seeking library information or materials encounters a problem situation that prevents him or her from achieving desired goals. The user then perceives a lack in his or her understanding of the situation, and that someone else might know how to resolve the problem.

Perceived need has been measured in general surveys where users report whether or not they were aware they needed any kind of help during their library visits. One researcher, using the interview method, found that 41% of those in the library needed help but that only 35% of that total would ask a librarian (Swope and Katzer, 1972). One academic and one public library found that about 29% to 36% of users reported needing help; 21% of the academic library patrons and 28% of the public library patrons actually asked for help (Carnegie Mellon, 1978; Rodger, 1984a). The same academic library also asked users the type of materials sought, if they needed help, and for what materials they needed help. Results were revealing and useful.

Perceived need for help can also be measured indirectly by asking users how difficult it was to use the library (Van House, Weil, and McClure, 1990). Surveys have also asked how difficult it was to find special types of materials such as periodicals (University of Cincinnati, 1984), or how difficult it was to use sources such as the microcatalog (University of British Columbia, 1981). In these three libraries results of "very easy" plus next-highest category vary from 74% for the library as a whole, to 82% for locating periodicals, to 94% for the card catalog. Ease of using the library as a whole and of finding periodicals was measured on a 5-category continuum scale (University of Cincinnati, 1984; Van House, Weil, and McClure, 1990). Generally, these results appear somewhat high in view of success rates of library activities (Saracevic, Shaw, and Kantor, 1977; Carnegie Mellon, 1978; Whitlatch, 1978; Palais, 1981). High results in regard to ease of use may be due to the tendency of some users not to realize that they have made errors. Instead, they believe that the library was easy to use, and that they failed to find what was wanted simply because it was not owned by the library. High results might also be due to possible inflation in the second category of the scale or to a combination of both factors.

Another approach has been to word the question where difficulty is defined for the user in terms of the user's perception of his or her own ability to find materials and information successfully and *efficiently* in the library. In one library only 31% reported that they were usually able to find what they searched for without wasting time and effort (New York University, 1981).

The problem of unexpressed needs for help has been investigated by asking patrons in a general survey whether they *needed* help, and if so, whether they actually asked for it. When this question was asked in an academic library and a public library, the percentage of those needing help but *not* asking for it was not large—some 8% to 9% (Carnegie Mellon, 1978; Rodger, 1984a). However, researchers, using the interview method, found that 41% of those interviewed needed help, but that 65% of that total would *not* ask a librarian (Swope and Katzer, 1972). This tends to suggest that the interview method will draw out more cases of need and more cases involving unasked questions.

Why do patrons, perceiving that they need help, not ask for it? At the point after the need has been perceived, a number of outcomes are possible: users may ask for help, try other approaches, return at another time, or give up the search. This question in its broadest form has been investigated by asking patrons what they would do if they encountered a problem in the library (White, 1971; University of British Columbia, 1984; University of California at Riverside, 1984). Responses of those who would *first* try to solve the problem themselves *without* help include 74% (White, 1971), 58% (University of British Columbia, 1984), and 20% of undergraduates and 34% of graduates (University of California at Riverside, 1984). In the second library, the most frequent response was to check other sources; next was to ask for help, followed by returning another time, and finally giving up on the search. In the latter library, by far the most frequent response was to ask for help, followed by searching on one's own or seeking answers from library brochures.

Some users, even *after* they have made attempts to solve their problems and have failed, still do not ask for help. Among the reasons that have been given are lack confidence in the reference librarian's ability, not wanting to appear ignorant, feeling that it is wrong to ask for help in the library, and previously unsatisfactory encounters at the reference desk. They may fail to ask for help because they can't locate the reference desk or because reference staff are too busy. Finally, they may succeed in asking their questions some place *other* than the reference desk because they don't know *whom* to ask or because reference service is closed. Combinations of the above have been used in a variety of library surveys (Swope and Katzer, 1972; Kent State University Libraries, 1976; University of British Columbia, 1984; Rodger, 1984a; Westbrook, 1984; University of California at Riverside, 1984).

Insights into this have also been provided by Kuhlthau (1988b), who studied the student search process using the longitudinal case study method. Her results, which tend to agree with those of Swope and Katzer (1972), find negative user attitudes based on past experiences, miscommunication, and the perception that librarians are ineffectual.

Unperceived need is that portion of total need where the best information or materials are *not* found, because the patron fails to realize that with help they could have been found. Total need for assistance is defined here as seen from an expert viewpoint and exists whenever a user fails to find, or is incapable of finding, the best information or materials available to meet his or her purposes in a reasonable amount of time. Naive users believe the library to be much simpler than it actually is and their own abilities to be much greater than is actually the case. In consequence, these users attempt to carry out procedures and reach false conclusions, failing to recognize their own errors. They conclude, if they cannot find what they want, that it is not there, and they report that no help was needed.

What are the dimensions of this problem? A number of studies on extent of user error have been done. One study indicates that one-third of those failing due to user error did not ask for help (Whitlatch, 1978). Other availability studies showed rates of user error at the catalog to be from 18% to 20% (Saracevic, Shaw, and Kantor, 1977; Palais, 1981). Another study also sheds light on user error in searching for subjects in the card catalog (Van Pulis and Ludy, 1988). The user with unperceived need would probably maintain that he or she knows how to find what is needed in the library without help. One study, however, indicates an unreasonably large number of patrons report knowing how to find what they need in the library (Kent State University Libraries, 1976). For the most part, many users who do not find what they want probably do not perceive that they might have made errors in their searches, or that what they wanted might have been found with help.

A second problem arises when users search for materials and/or information, fail to find exactly what they want, and go on to find something else with which they make do. These users may believe that what they have found is all that was available. They also fail to realize that they might have found more and better material with assistance.

One study on end-user searching demonstrated that when users reported partial or unsatisfactory searches and these same searches were redone by a trained searcher, some 60% of users reported their searches to be better and more satisfactory than their own (Kirby and Miller, 1985). More studies of this type are needed. Actual unperceived need for reference service is difficult to measure, but it can probably be best done when user errors are studied along with data on how many of those who made errors believed that they did not need reference assistance.

Methods of Measuring Reference Use

There are three methods by which frequency of reference use is usually estimated: 1) by asking users how often they use reference in general, 2) by asking users in the library whether or not they used reference on their *present* library visits, and 3) by keeping records of questions at the reference desk. These data are then used to infer patterns of reference desk use.

These three methods appear to yield differing results, with studies in academic and public libraries showing that 45% to 55% reported they were reference users, regular to occasional (Kent State University Libraries, 1976; University of California at Los Angeles, 1981; Yocum and Stocker, 1980; New York University, 1981); 21% to 28% reported that they asked for help on their *present* library visits (Carnegie Mellon,

1978; Rodger, 1984a); and reference desk records indicated that some 2% to 7% of users in academic libraries asked reference questions at the reference desk (Murfin, 1983). Can these differing figures be reconciled?

If the reasonableness criteria are applied, few reference departments in academic libraries with, for example, turnstile counts of 20,000 weekly could handle the 3,400 questions this would amount to weekly (if 17% of those in the library asked questions at the *reference desk*). According to reference desk records (which appeared to be correctly reported in an academic library), 2% of users in the library asked reference questions, but 17% reported they asked a "reference librarian" (as opposed to a "circulation librarian") for help (Carnegie Mellon, 1978). Even adding to the reference question record to allow for directional questions does not reconcile these figures in this library. A possible explanation is that this library had very limited reference hours and help must have been requested in other areas from other personnel and that users could not clearly make a distinction between reference, circulation, and other personnel (Durrance, 1989).

Is reported use of reference on a particular library visit a valid measure? Reports employing the present-visit-only method should be more objective than frequency-of-use reports because they are closer in time and refer to only *one* library visit, which is reported soon after it takes place. It appears in this case to lack validity as a measure of *reference desk* volume, but it may be valid in terms of volume of those who ask for *some* kind of help somewhere in the library. To know how many actually used reference desk service, the question should be framed as precisely as possible with location given. "Reference librarian" or "reference question" may not be able to be interpreted by patrons as intended by framers of questionnaires. Many patrons appear to have difficulty distinguishing who is and is not a librarian or to designate the functions of those persons whom they ask for help in terms of "reference" or "circulation" without a clear location being given. They may also have difficulty in distinguishing what is or is not a reference question. The high figures for reference use in general might be because this is a subjective report of perceived tendency, rather than a precise report of actual use. On one hand, use estimates can be made somewhat more objective when specific time periods (weekly, for instance) are given; on the other hand, it is more difficult for users to estimate in time periods because, to arrive at the number of times reference was used, one must first estimate the number of times the library was used. Reference use is also difficult to estimate because it is irregular rather than regular in nature. All in all, reported frequency of reference use probably still remains an expression of tendency rather than a precise count. The user's specific purpose at the time may be *more* important in determining actual use than his or her tendency to ask for help. The total who report themselves as reference users should probably be looked at as *potential* users, only a *portion* of whom will use reference at any one time (as their purposes dictate) while in the library.

D'Elia (1980a) has studied frequency of *library use* and found a number of interesting and significant relationships. In addition, two studies of frequency of both library and reference use suggest the possibility that in academic libraries infrequent library users have a *greater* tendency to ask reference questions than frequent library users. (Kent State University Libraries, 1976; New York University, 1981). In this sense, reported frequency of reference use may be a valid measure of tendency and perhaps, in turn, of the degree of need behind the tendency.

Presently, few patron reports of reference use in a particular library are available to be compared to reference desk records. As the ACRL General User Survey comes into use, there should be more such records available (Van House, Weil, and McClure, 1990). On the basis of library survey records available now, it appears that the measure may lack validity as a measure of volume of *reference questions* asked at the reference desk or even of reference questions as they are defined in reference desk recording. It may, however, be valid in terms of those who ask for *some* kind of help *somewhere* in the library. If viewed as a measure of user requests for help within a library building, this measure should be helpful. If a relatively large percent of users request help in the library as compared to recorded questions at the reference desk, then it may indicate that reference service is not sufficiently accessible. In regard to recording of questions at the reference desk, see Chapter 13, "Reference Volume, Staffing, and Accessibility."

Frequency of reference use data can also be useful in studying patron search strategy. Findings from an academic library (present-visit-only) and a public library (period-of-time) agree as to the search strategy reported most frequently by patrons. Consulting reference was the fourth most popular approach after use of the catalog, browsing in the stacks, and unaided use of the reference collection (Carnegie Mellon, 1978; Yocum and Stocker, 1980). These data might be helpful for comparison with other libraries.

User Success

How many people coming to the library have information needs for the type of help that reference service is designed to give? Of those having such needs, how successful are those who consult reference as opposed to those who do not?

Most library surveys attempt to determine how many users are in the library for the purpose of using library information or materials, as opposed to using the library only for study, returning books, using equipment, and so on. This group might be assumed to be potential users of reference. The success rate of this group might be compared to those of reference users. This comparison might be lacking in validity, however; users who consulted reference might have done so *because* they had more difficult problems than the reference nonusers; with this greater difficulty, the likelihood of success would be *less* for reference users. Unless we can know that reference users and nonusers had the *same* kinds of information needs, such comparisons should be made with care. With this understanding, this method might be a useful first step in addressing the question, and should be possible with a number of current survey instruments that ask for the user's purpose in the library. For more information on studies of patron information-seeking behavior and success, see Chapter 3, "Library Users and Reference Patrons."

Measures for Evaluating Quality of Reference Services

One or more quality or success rating scales are essential to any general survey that is intended to be more than a description of use. If these are not included, all other data are much more difficult to interpret (risk of misinterpretation is increased) and much of the usefulness of the survey is lost. A quality or success scale is particularly useful for determining the effectiveness of patron information-seeking behavior and of particular library departments.

Unobtrusive observation, a commonly used method for judging quality of reference service, cannot easily be used to compare the quality of reference with that of other services. For this kind of comparison, user feedback of the kind obtained in a general library survey is essential. A number of methods have been used to measure quality by patron report; some surveys use the word "success" (Carnegie Mellon, 1978; Van House, Weil, and McClure, 1990) and others use "satisfaction" (University of British Columbia, 1981; Whitlatch, 1981). Another library defines success in terms of finding what was wanted (University of California at Riverside, 1981). Chwe (1978) uses the "present condition" of a service. Marchant uses the word "quality," while D'Elia (1980b) advocates the academic method of grading on a scale A-F. Durrance (1989) suggests the "Would you use this service again?" type of response. Yocum and Stocker (1980) express quality in terms of the degree of need for improvement.

Satisfaction with a particular service or department differs from success in that it is an emotion or feeling growing out of one's particular encounters and experiences. However, success and satisfaction are closely related and success is probably the major ingredient in satisfaction. Evidence indicates that the percentage of users who reported being fully successful in finding what was wanted, and who were nevertheless dissatisfied, was very small (Bunge and Murfin, 1987). On the other hand, a majority of evidence indicates that the percentage of *satisfied* users will almost always be greater than the percentage of *successful* users. (Strong, 1980a; Bunge and Murfin, 1987; Whitlatch, 1989; Ankeny, 1991). This is because many of those who find only *approximately* what is wanted will still be satisfied.

Dissatisfaction, when not tied to the information or materials found, may cover other aspects of patrons' experiences, including the quality of the interaction, ease of obtaining service, and so on. For these reasons, an overall measure of satisfaction with reference service, such as that gathered in some general surveys, is difficult to interpret. For example, users may like the staff but be dissatisfied with the collection, or like the collection but be dissatified with the staff. Or there may be dissatisfaction with organization of materials, maintenance of equipment, or the hours. Satisfaction can best be interpreted if the patron is given an opportunity to relate it to information or materials found, staff, resources, equipment, and facilities.

A variety of types of scales have been used in previous library surveys. Research has indicated that the power of discrimination of scales can be improved by use of more categories and by anchoring (Cuadra, Katter, Holmes, and Wallace, 1967). On the other hand, general library surveys include so many services and areas which must be considered that the task for the patron can become formidable, and some compromise must be made. One study was successful in obtaining discriminating responses by use of shorter scales with three anchored categories, "mostly successful, partly successful and unsuccessful." (Carnegie Mellon, 1978). This may indicate that anchoring is the most vital factor. If so, scales can be made quicker and easier for the patron to mark by being shortened to three categories and still remain discriminating if each response category is properly anchored. In 3-category scales, the midpoint should be completely neutral, not, for example, like in the scale "good, satisfactory, and poor," or "very successful, successful, and unsuccessful," both of which obtain results biased in the positive direction.

Cronbach (1950) found the 5-point scale on a continuum of high to low to be prone to bias in responses and recommends anchored items in test design. Ankeny (1991) studied success ratings on such a scale as compared to a fully anchored 6-point scale, and found that the highest category was relatively free of bias, but that the next highest category was extremely biased in the positive direction. In a survey done by one library measuring reference success on a 5-point continuum scale (using "agree-disagree" categories), results combining the first and second categories gave a success rating of 82%. Another study one year later on a 6-point anchored scale gave a success rating of 56% (Binkley and Eadie, 1989). Further research is needed on anchored and unanchored continuum scales in library and reference measurement.

All in all, the use of the 3-category anchored success scale with a *truly neutral midpoint*, as used by Carnegie Mellon (1978), appears to have better power of discrimination than the sum of the first and second category of the 5-category continuum scale, and is probably an easier judgment foi the patron to make and easier for the evaluator to interpret later. It is certainly a possible choice for experimental use in the general survey where many judgments must be made. For more on success and satisfaction, see Chapter 15, "Reference Effectiveness."

Selection of Instruments

Instruments selected here are intended to form a representative sample of library survey instruments containing items or sections on reference service and/or information-seeking behavior in general. The instruments have been selected because they meet one or more of the following criteria:

1) They address questions important to reference service, answers to which must essentially be obtained through a general library survey;

2) They appear to be successful in solving problems in overall library evaluation of reference, such as identifying of whom the question was asked, where it was asked, and whether it was reference or directional;

3) They have been used previously or pretested and results appear to show that the items of interest to reference in particular have power of discrimination. Phrasing of questions is precise and designed to reduce uncertainty in respondents. Selection of questions and wording demonstrates practical knowledge of the reference process and reference patrons;

4) Two-category "yes-no" scales are avoided (unless there are only two *possible* dimensions to the answer). Research indicates that 2-category scales lack power of discrimination because they cause respondents to feel uncertainty. Under conditions of uncertainty respondents tend to mark the *highest* alternative thus leading to inflated ratings (Cuadra, Katter, Holmes, and Wallace, 1967; Cuadra and Katter, 1967). This has been supported by another researcher who found in two studies of the same end-user service that on a 2-category "yes-no" scale 78% of users reported finding what was wanted. Later,

when a 6-category anchored scale was used, only 43% reported finding exactly what was wanted (Ankeny, 1991).

RESEARCH NEEDS

Many aspects of reference require further investigation in the overall library setting. Foundations have been laid, but much work remains. Characteristics of library users and circumstances and conditions of library use should be related to need for and use of reference service. A method needs to be developed to enable patrons to report with some accuracy at which library service point questions were asked and whether or not they were reference or directional in nature.

How many and what kinds of questions are being asked in a library building (in addition to those asked at the reference desk), and where they are being asked? How successful are those users who do *not* consult reference as opposed to users who do so, on the *same* kinds of questions? More in-depth investigation is necessary concerning the following issues: the relationships between need for and use of reference service, patrons who do not seek help because they are unaware that they have made errors, whether the right questions are being asked in the right places in large complex systems, and number and effectiveness of referrals. Further research needs to be done on scales in library and reference measurement. Finally, a library survey instrument should be developed that would give a maximum of the kinds of useful information needed by reference departments, as discussed in this section.

INSTRUMENTS

Instruments included cover information-seeking behavior and satisfaction (Bundy), information-gathering behavior (Carnegie Mellon University Libraries); Rodger and D'Elia; Strong), present condition and importance of services (Chwe), use and importance of services (Yocum and Stocker), outcomes of user searches (New York University; University of California at Riverside), awareness, use of, and satisfaction with library services (University of California at Riverside), and success, ease of use, and satisfaction with library services (Van House, Weil, and McClure).

Bundy—Public Library Use Study
Carnegie Mellon University Libraries—Student Users Survey
Chwe—Model Instrument for User-Rating of Library Service

New York University; University of California at Riverside—Selected
   User Survey Items
Rodger and D'Elia—User Study
Strong—Patterns of Information Requests Survey
University of California at Riverside—UCR Library Services Survey
Van House, Weil, and McClure—General Satisfaction Survey
Yocum and Stocker—Survey of Public Library Users

Chapter 2

What Reference Services Should Be Offered?

Marjorie E. Murfin

SCOPE

This chapter will be concerned with methods that can help in making decisions about type, level, and amount of reference services to be offered. Methods will be discussed for determining user preferences, and other methods will also be considered for reconciling user preferences with management and library constraints. Because studying user preferences is one method of determining what services should be offered, cost preference studies will be included. However, cost analysis as a whole will be considered in Chapter 14, "Costs and Outcomes."

IMPORTANCE OF RESEARCH

A primary problem faced by any reference department is deciding what services should be offered and the mix and blend of these services. For example, shall research consultant service be offered? If research consultant service is offered, many issues must be addressed: Should another service be eliminated, and if so, which one? How much of the research consultant service should be made available? Should user education services be increased at the cost of traditional reference desk services? Limited resources require setting priorities, making trade-offs between one service and another, and determining the appropriate balance between quantity and quality of services offered.

Overall decisions on types and amounts of services offered involve the highest level of planning and decision making and can have serious impact on library and reference patrons. To make informed judgments, answers to the following questions are needed: What are the needs of users for information, materials, and assistance? What is the relative effectiveness of different reference services in helping users to plan and carry out the library search process, and in helping them to find the information and materials they are seeking? What services do users want and prefer? What trade-offs would they make if reductions or changes in services were necessary? Is it better to offer fewer services of greater quality or more services of lesser quality? What are the benefits gained by each of the services reference offers? Considering all factors, are the right services provided for users?

Advantages of this type of assessment are that, if it is done well, services of most value to users can be provided at the least cost. Mixes or blends of services that do not meet the actual needs or preferences of users can be avoided. For example, libraries may avoid disproportionately stressing certain reference services of lesser value to users over others of greater value to them. Failures that result from inadequately considered reductions in present services or additions of new services may also be avoided. Such failures are costly to both patrons and the library.

Disadvantages of this type of assessment are that, with the exception of user preferences, methods for weighing and comparing alternatives are not well developed and few instruments are available. In addition, a wide variety of data gathered by using many different methods of assessment is essential for sound decision making, but it requires a great deal of effort. In particular, the cost-benefit methodology sorely needed to help in making such decisions is not well developed. Finally, even after such assessment is done, results are sometimes disregarded or ignored by decision makers because they conflict with library interests or financial constraints. In such cases, decisions about services are made on the basis of what will most benefit the library rather than the user.

STATE OF THE FIELD

Overview

Individuals' information needs, from broad, generalized *original* needs through narrowed needs for specific materials, have been studied by telephone surveys, library surveys, diaries, and experimental studies. Descriptive reference question records, another important source of data (Wender, 1977), are discussed in Chapter 4, "Question Classification." User needs are discussed in detail in Chapter 1, "Assessing Library Services: The Reference Component," and Chapter 3, "Library Users and Reference Patrons."

Use Statistics

Volume of use gives *some* indication of patron needs and preferences and is an important indicator of need. However, actual use of services may not always tell the whole story. For example, usage of a particular service may be low because need for this service is low. However, use may be low for other reasons: potential users cannot "get to" the service due to inadequate staffing and/or hours; patrons are disappointed in the general quality and/or emphasis of the service, or believe the service is too slow or too costly, and thus make only minimum use of it. It is not advisable to judge patron preference and need for a service *entirely* on the basis of the use of that service.

While usage data for *one* particular library may be difficult to interpret, *comparative* usage data can tell us something (Watson, 1986). If the usage of a particular service in a library is considerably lower than that of peer libraries with similar enrollments, reasons for low usage should be investigated, including barriers such as time, cost, and poor quality. Interpretation of volume of use data is a complex problem and Chapter 13, "Reference Volume, Staffing, and Accessibility," provides more information.

Frequency or *intensity* of use data is also important. For example, it is helpful to know the frequency of use (per week, per month) of the different services as reported by various groups of patrons. The general library survey can, by means of computer cross-tabulations, determine how heavily services are used by different groups of patrons (University of California at Riverside, 1984). For more details on frequency of use, see Chapter 1, "Assessing Library Services: The Reference Component."

Comparison of Different Types of Reference Services

What kinds of reference services do our library users want and prefer? If forced to choose from among alternatives, what services would patrons choose? What trade-offs would they make in regard to quantity, quality, and types of services offered?

Some research comparing the effectiveness of reference services has been done, primarily in general library surveys where users have been asked which service was most effective in helping them to use the library (University of California at Los Angeles, 1981; University of California at Riverside, 1984; University of British Columbia, 1984). In the UBC and UCLA studies, traditional reference desk service was reported as the most useful service for learning about the library. In the UC Riverside study, reference desk service was thought to be the second most useful service after brochures. This question could also be investigated by experimental studies comparing 1) traditional desk reference service; 2) user education programs; 3) CD-ROM service; and 4) brochures, as to how well they help users to make effective use of the library. In this area, a certain amount of research has been done and a number of instruments are available.

On the simplest level, users have been asked in general library surveys to indicate their preference for services by checking, from a list, those services that are important to them (University of California at Los Angeles, 1981) or by rating the degree of importance of each service on a scale from one to four (Cornell University, 1984). Other surveys *combine* ratings of frequency of use and importance (Yocum and Stocker, 1980; University of California at Riverside, 1984) or importance and quality (Chwe, 1978) for each service. For more on importance ratings, see Chapter 1, "Assessing Library Services: The Reference Component."

The method of simple ranking of library services has been used by a number of investigators (Halperin and Strazdon, 1980; Robertson, 1980; Yocum and Stocker, 1980), and has the advantage of providing information about the *relative* importance of each service, while avoiding the patron's tendency to mark almost all services as equally important when given a choice of ratings for each service. A disadvantage of rankings, when compared to the more complex methods, is that rankings do not give any indication of the *magnitude* of differences between rankings. Also, they will not tell what trade-offs patrons would make when considering a number of factors. Used along with other methods, rankings should give some very useful information.

Methods of weighing alternatives have been employed to compare preferences for types of services. One method of weighing alternatives involves users expressing their degree of agreement with each alternative, in terms of percentages; for example, 50% "yes" and 50% "no" would indicate a neutral attitude toward a particular alternative. Miller (1973) suggested this method be used with an additional refinement, where management's judgment of feasibility is factored in to arrive at the best alternative.

Trade-off analysis is another method that may be used. In one example, users were asked to balance costs and benefits and express their preferences at different budgetary levels (Raffel and Shishko, 1969). Conjoint analysis asks respondents to make trade-off judgments of the relative importance of various levels of service combinations. Conjoint analysis has the advantage of showing what trade-offs would be preferred by patrons under different service configurations. Their greatest disadvantage is the intellectual difficulty of the task for respondents because they must consider a number of different factors at the same time. For these reasons, return rate of questionnaires is generally low. For example, in an analysis done by one academic library, return rate was 40% (Raffel and Shishko, 1969). Halperin and Strazdon (1980) reported that completing forms could take as long as 30 minutes, and they devised a scheme of remitting library fines for all respondents, which worked well to secure full cooperation.

In using conjoint analysis, one should be aware of the possibility of a poor return that *might* result in a biased sample. Use of this method requires careful consideration of how users are to be motivated and how their cooperation will be gained. If this problem can be solved, the results of conjoint analysis can be very useful for decision-making purposes. User needs and user benefits are more difficult to take into account in regard to the trade-off between quality and quantity. The lacking element here is assessment of benefits, without which the picture remains less than complete.

Benefit Analysis

What is the ratio of library time and resources expended in relation to benefits gained for each service reference offers? Although some progress has been made, this question is difficult to answer at the present time. Benefit methodology in regard to reference service is poorly developed. When more research is done on user errors, efficiency, and effectiveness of *reference-aided* user searches, as opposed to *unaided* user searches, units of benefit may be able to be established. Kramer (1971) has used a benefit measure of 9 to 1 for reference service, based on unaided searches taking nine times as long as reference librarians to find certain information.

In regard to expenditures of library resources by different reference services, some groundbreaking work has been done where unit costs are given for 1) a reference question; 2) a library lecture; and 3) an online search (Cochrane, 1989). However, without the appropriate benefits to balance with costs, these figures should be viewed as only *one* aspect of the total picture. For more detailed information on benefits and costs, see Chapter 14, "Costs and Outcomes."

Best Type and Quality of Services

Should quality be increased and access to centralized reference desk service be expanded at the expense of the user education program? Or should quality be increased and the user education program expanded at the expense of reference desk service? These are extremely difficult questions to answer because it is necessary to know the demand, present quality, and relative benefits for every service users need. User preferences in this regard can be assessed by simple ranking or by conjoint analysis. The various choices can include levels of quality and quantity for each service. For example, Halperin and Strazdon (1980) found that when users were asked to choose, they ranked "quality of answer" as more important than a wait of 10 minutes.

No one instrument has been discovered that will determine whether the library is providing the right services to users. A wide variety of factors must be taken into account in regard to users, including the academic needs and abilities, purposes, needs for information and materials, perceived and unperceived need for help, information-seeking patterns, errors, and success and failure rates.

Certain other information in regard to types and varieties of services must be collected. The general library survey, using an instrument with a valid and reliable success scale, and using *computer cross-tabulations* for data analysis, can help to determine whether there are particular groups of users whose needs are not being met (see Chapter 1, "Assessing Library Services: The Reference Component"). It is more difficult to determine whether *enough* different services are being offered. There is some evidence that libraries offering a variety of services are preferred by patrons (Kernaghan, 1979). Are certain services *not* offered that are needed by users? In this respect, reference services presently offered and volume of activity can be compared to those of peer libraries (Watson, 1986).

A beginning has been made in developing a model for reference service that will consider a number of reference factors at the same time, and balance them so as to achieve optimum use of resources and predict outcomes under different configurations of service. The model does not consider user needs or information-seeking patterns. It does include value systems of upper management, costs, usage of services, and user satisfaction. This model is not practical at the present time because it applies only to special libraries, is in a computer language that is not easily transferrable, requires a library to supply a very large amount of data, and could not be utilized without the guidance of an expert. If further development and adaptation were done, it could be a useful tool for reference management (Elchesen, 1982).

RESEARCH NEEDS

Much research remains to be done in this area. Perhaps the biggest stumbling block is the lack of a benefit measure for various reference services, so that the problem of what services to provide can be seen in full perspective. In addition, research already done on user importance ratings and preferences for different services needs to be replicated and expanded in regard to different groups of users. Needs and preferences of various groups need to be determined and taken into account.

Instruments need to be developed to assess potential use of proposed or new services, to assess patron reactions to changes and reductions in service, and to determine how changes in services affect reference patrons. Information needs of different groups of library users must be related to their information-seeking behavior and to the asking of reference questions. Experimental studies of user error and unaided user searching for materials and reference information are needed. Finally, work on developing unit costs for reference questions, user education lectures, and online searches should be continued and expanded. These unit costs, however, will vary for different types of libraries and geographical areas.

The relative outcomes and benefits of the various reference services should be studied and compared. Finally, an instrument or computerized model needs to be developed which should take into account user needs, abilities, constraints, information-gathering approaches, and preferences, as well as outcomes for the user in terms of quality and quantity of service and benefits gained. Finally, it should consider costs to the library.

INSTRUMENTS

Instruments included cover service preferences of users (Cornell University; Halperin and Strazdon; Miller; Robertson; University of California at Los Angeles; University of British Columbia; University of California at Riverside; Yocum and Stocker) and service benefits to users (Raffel and Shishko).

Cornell University—Information Sources in Agricultural Research
Halperin and Strazdon—Patron Preference for Different Aspects of Reference Service
Halperin and Strazdon—Reference Service Preferences
Miller—Preference and Feasibility Measure
Raffel and Shishko—Benefit Survey
Robertson—Library or Technical Information Services Survey
University of California at Los Angeles; University of British Columbia; University of California at Riverside—Selected Items from Overall Library Surveys
Yocum and Stocker—Survey of Public Library Users

Chapter 3

Library Users and Reference Patrons

Marjorie E. Murfin

SCOPE

Knowledge of library users is one of the major areas of knowledge that can rightly be expected of reference departments. It is important to understand who they are, what they know, and what they think. Even more important is to know how users go about seeking information in the library, something about the experiences they have, and the problems they encounter in this process.

The reference department gains much of this kind of knowledge from its acquaintance with reference patrons, which could be of great value to library planners in developing and structuring library services to meet patron needs. However, reference department recommendations may often be disregarded because they represent only the experiences of *one* public service department and are based on what is considered anecdotal evidence, not supported and documented by formal assessment methods. For this reason, a thorough knowledge of assessment methods in the area of information-seeking processes of library users is vital if reference is to be able to support its recommendations in the best interests of library users.

IMPORTANCE OF RESEARCH

To acquire data about library users and reference patrons, one must answer such questions as the following: Who are reference patrons? What are their characteristics, perceptions, attitudes, abilities, and state of knowledge regarding the library? Do reference patrons differ from library patrons in general? What are the types of information needs of a library's target population? How many of these information needs are brought to the library? How many patrons come to the library *with* and how many come *without* specific titles or citations? How do they go about locating specific titles and/or subject information? What are the problems they encounter, and when in the process do they encounter them? What do they do when they encounter a problem? At what point do they seek help, and from whom do they seek it?

Advantages of assessing characteristics, perceptions, and information-seeking behavior of library users and reference patrons are many. Such assessment, when well done, can help in planning a user-oriented library. More specifically, it can help solve the problem often faced by reference departments of how decisions made at upper levels will impact on library users. The reference department is, in a sense, the expert on library users, on their knowledge, abilities, problems, and responses. It might be expected that the library would come to the reference department for answers in this area, and that support would be given to departmental recommendations. However, reference is often unable to produce or know how to obtain hard data to support its recommendations in regard to what would best serve patrons' interests. As experts in this area, and with knowledge of research findings and assessment methods, reference librarians must be able to substantiate experiences with supporting data about how patrons feel, how they use the library, and where, when, how, and why they experience failure. Also, methodology is available that can help provide answers to questions regarding specific aspects of the information-seeking process.

A disadvantage of this type of assessment is that, while data on characteristics of library and reference patrons are fairly easy to obtain, a meaningful picture of the *complete* information-seeking process in a particular library is difficult to obtain. Even if a general survey is done, it usually provides only a sketchy picture of the process. Without a thorough study of the information-seeking patterns from the beginning to the end of the process for different groups of users, it is difficult to obtain an overall understanding about how the parts of the process fit together and at what parts of the process failure occurs most frequently. While availability studies provide a method of studying success in locating *specific titles* in the library, there is no comparable, fully satisfactory method of studying the process of seeking in the library for *information* rather than materials, where the need has *not* yet been translated into specific titles. Studies following individual users through the entire search process in the library provide good information, but few have been done. Experimental studies also have good potential, but the few that have been done have focused only on *parts* of the information-seeking process (Gothberg, 1976; McMurdo, 1982). However, several researchers are studying the process as a whole (Nahl-Jakobovits and Jakobovits, 1988; Kuhlthau, 1988b; Kuhlthau, Turock, George, and Belvin, 1990). An integrated method is needed that would follow the information-seeking process *both* for users who come to the library with specific titles and for users who have information needs but do *not* have specific titles.

STATE OF THE FIELD

User's Motivation

Beginnings are being made on studying the relationship between the importance of the user's goal and the nature and outcome of information seeking (Goldhor, 1979; Nahl-Jakobovits and Jakobovits, 1988). It is logical to expect that the importance of the information need would vary for different groups of users and would affect their information-gathering habits. Several studies that have investigated the importance of the user's goal and purpose have shown that it varies with the type of information need (Bunge and Murfin, 1983; Rodger, 1984a). Importance of the question was shown to be an independent factor and to be associated with increased success (Bunge and Murfin, 1983). This would be expected if importance of question corresponds in some way to motivation. Methods used to investigate importance of the information need to the user have been general library surveys (Rodger, 1984a), reference-only surveys (Bunge and Murfin, 1983) and interviews with reference users (Goldhor, 1979). Analysis of undergraduate user searching patterns illustrates a failed search by a poorly motivated user (Taylor, 1967). Overall, this has been a much-neglected area of research. Theories of motivation in general are explored by Brehm and Self (1989).

Perceptions and Attitudes

Questions needing answers in this area are as follows: What are the attitudes of library users toward reference service and reference librarians? What are the expectations of our patrons in regard to reference service?

A substantial amount of research has been done on the image of the reference librarian in the eyes of both students and faculty. Methods used have been questionnaires (Hernon and Pastine, 1977; Bloch and Bloch, 1981; Budd and Coutant, 1981) and case studies (Kuhlthau, 1988b). Images have not been particularly flattering, with one case study of four users suggesting that reference librarians were sometimes perceived as lacking in competence and knowledge (Kuhlthau, 1988b). In another study undergraduates using the catalog were surveyed and a large percentage considered that reference librarians would not know any more about the catalog than they did (Westbrook, 1987). Yet after having been helped by reference staff, only 8% to 9% of patrons in public and academic libraries reported that the librarian was partly or not knowledgeable (Bunge and Murfin, 1983). This discrepancy illustrates one of the problems of image research. Nevertheless, image research adds to our understanding of how patrons feel and why they respond in certain ways. Some instruments and methods are available.

Recently, important work has been done in development of an instrument for measuring library anxiety in users (Bostick, 1992). Further use of this instrument in the future should increase our knowledge of how library anxiety affects user attitudes and success.

One study on patrons' expectations of library or reference service speculates that as service improves, patrons expectations also rise (Oldman and Wills, 1977). Difficulties encountered in measurement are that patrons will express expectations that they believe the library wants to hear, or that they believe are most socially acceptable, or that match the library's present level of service. One library surveyed expectations of reference service and found that patrons expected the exact kind of service they were already receiving. Later it was found that they were not highly satisfied with the same level of service they had previously reported as meeting their expectations. (Binkley and Eadie, 1988). Other problems are conflicting expectations and those which are impossible to meet. For example, one participant in a study expected little useful help from reference librarians and questioned their competence. At the same time, she expected that they would check frequently with her to see if she needed anything because the librarian should know it was embarrassing for students to have to ask for help (Kuhlthau, 1988b). Questionnaires on expectations must be carefully designed to avoid tipping the respondent toward seemingly desired answers. One way to avoid this might be use of open-ended questions, as is recommended by Westbrook (1987).

Tendency to Use Reference Service

Evidence indicates that reference users will be, in general, a representative cross-section of those library users *seeking information and/or materials*. Several public library surveys show about the same percentage of library and reference users in age, occupation, and subject interest categories (Bundy, 1968; Bunge and Murfin, 1983).

Allowing for this general similarity, there will probably be some differences, however, with certain groups being somewhat overrepresented and others somewhat underrepresented. The overriding factors in whether or not reference is utilized appear to be the user's purpose, the user's subject discipline, and the type and subject of information need.

In academic libraries the user's discipline seems to have an effect. Whitlatch (1980) found that students in science and technology courses reported that their course work required library use considerably *less often* than was reported by those in social science and humanities courses. Students in the social sciences and humanities had a tendency to use *more* library material (Whitlatch, 1980) and to ask more frequently for reference assistance (Slater, 1963) than those in science and technology.

This same tendency is shown in the public library, except that in *certain areas* of *applied* science—medicine, home economics, animals, plants—more reference questions are asked than might be expected in proportion to users looking for that type of subject matter (Bundy, 1968; Bunge and Murfin, 1983). Other research also supports the differences in information-gathering behavior between those in pure and applied sciences, especially in regard to asking for help (Herner, 1954; Krulee and Nadler, 1960). Herner (1954) states that "reference services furnished by the library were used more than twice as often by applied as by pure scientists."

Type of materials being sought also appears to make a difference. In one library, some 24% of users seeking books needed help, while 100% of users needing government documents needed help (Carnegie Mellon, 1978). Slater (1963) found that in special libraries users seeking facts and short descriptions in handbooks needed considerably more help than those reading journals.

Differences in regard to purpose for coming to the library seem evident. Substantially *more* of those who said they came to the library for job-related purposes asked reference questions than might have been predicted on the basis of their numbers. Students appeared to ask questions according to their numbers in the library, but those who said they came for reading, recreation, and personal projects asked substantially *fewer* reference questions than might have been predicted on the basis of their numbers (Bundy, 1968; Bunge and Murfin, 1983).

Level of education also appears to influence tendency to ask for reference assistance. Several studies in academic libraries showed a growing tendency to use reference, as class level rose from freshman to graduate (Kent State University, 1976; University of California at Riverside, 1983). This is supported by a public library study where library users gave the three most important reasons for using a particular branch library. Users selected a library on the basis of "helpful staff" in increasing proportions as user educational level rose (Yocum and Stocker, 1980). Also, a comparison of several studies showed that although more high school students than college students were in the library, considerably more reference questions were asked by college students than by high school students (Bundy, 1968; Bunge and Murfin, 1983). One might speculate that reluctance, embarrassment, or the desire not to appear ignorant may account to some extent for the reluctance of those with less education to ask for reference help. An academic library study found that 11% of undergraduate users admitted to a reluctance to ask, while the majority of graduate students refused to answer this item (University of California at Riverside. 1983). There is also evidence for this in a study of library anxiety (Mellon, 1986).

Age level has also been indicated as a factor in reference use in the public library, indicating that the 12-18 age group may be underrepresented in a reference sample, and the 40 and over age group may be overrepresented in proportion to their numbers in the library (Bundy, 1968; Bunge and Murfin, 1983). This is supported by a study in which public library users selected a library on the basis of "helpful staff" in increasing proportions as age rose. Indeed, those 60 and over valued this more than *any* other factor, except that of closeness of location (Yocum and Stocker, 1980).

Other factors that may affect tendency to use reference service and differentiate reference patrons from other library users are reported in Yocum and Stocker (1980), where a greater tendency to select a library on the basis of helpful staff was shown for lower-income persons, non-whites, and females.

Another factor is indicated by two academic library surveys, where a considerably greater percentage of *infrequent* library users reported themselves as reference patrons, while a considerably lesser proportion of *frequent* library users reported themselves as reference patrons (Kent State University, 1976; New York University, 1981). This has been found only for academic libraries and was not substantiated in one public library where it was examined as a factor (Rodger, 1984a).

Many of these possible overrepresentations and underrepresentations may cancel each other out. For example, comparison of two public library studies showed the exact same proportion of men and women library and reference users—40% to 60%. In one of these studies, women had fewer job-related questions, which may have cancelled out any possible increased tendency on their part to ask reference questions (Bundy, 1968; Bunge and Murfin, 1983).

Methodology in this area is fairly well developed. A general library survey that can identify those who asked reference questions (see Chapter 1, "Assessing Library Services: The Reference Component") can be done and *computer cross-tabulations* utilized to determine the number and composition of reference users as compared to all library users. Surprisingly, these particular cross-tabulations are seldom performed or, if performed, are not reported.

Knowledge of Library Services

Because individual libraries can differ so greatly, and because newly-developed technology results in constant changes, it is difficult to find a single instrument that would be useful in all libraries. However, a number of instruments evaluate the library knowledge of users. Patron state of knowledge has been assessed by paper-and-pencil tests, library exercises, telephone interviews, user surveys, and other methods described below.

Some questions to be answered in this area include the following: How does the amount learned in a user education session (*without* later consultation of reference) compare to that learned through *only* consultation with reference as needed? What are the relative benefits derived from each method? How much reference assistance is needed to equal one lecture in terms of bringing a class to successful completion of a library assignment? How does the time spent preparing and giving one lecture compare to time spent in reference assistance as to a particular assignment? Can a patron with only reference assistance function as well in the library on a particular assignment as one who has had a prepared user education session, or one who has used only library information brochures? Do patrons with different levels of library knowledge ask different levels of reference questions? Are people with more library knowledge more successful in the library? How can patrons' levels of library knowledge best be assessed? How much faster do those with greater library knowledge complete the same assignment than those with lesser library knowledge?

A number of paper-and-pencil tests exist to measure knowledge of library concepts (Bloomfield, 1974; Hardesty, Lovrich, and Mannon, 1979; Werking, 1980), but some feel that they measure a broad type of academic ability instead (Ford, 1973). Methods of assessing library knowledge of users can involve in-person or telephone interviews. Patrons may also be given search questions designed to test their library knowledge but they should be observed *while searching* so that reasons for errors can be noted.

A paper-and-pencil test can cover more areas of knowledge and can be carried out faster and more easily than is possible with an experimental test situation. However, users can possibly function *more* effectively in the actual library situation than scores on paper-and-pencil tests would indicate. Self-service aids such as signs, brochures, catalog cross-references, and point-of-use directions, as well as reference assistance may help them over barriers. For example, one study found that only 53% of the subjects that users entered into a computer catalog matched established subject headings, but 81% of users found what they were looking for through index displays and cross-references (Van Pulis and

Ludy, 1988). Also, prepared test questions may not represent the test subjects' real information needs, and motivation to find answers may be lower, so that with their own questions patron success might be somewhat higher due to greater motivation. In order to explore this, groups of students could be given comparable paper-and-pencil tests and in-library performance tests (with and without reference assistance) to see to what extent paper-and-pencil tests actually correlate with in-library performance.

Little has been done in regard to comparing the relative benefits of reference service and user education, and methodology is poorly developed in this area. With further research, some of the above questions can be explored.

Information-Seeking Behavior

The following questions need answers: How many and what kinds of individuals' information needs are actually brought to the library? What are the subjects and types of information needs of patrons in academic, public, and special libraries? If they are seeking specific materials, what type of materials are they seeking? Can library users mark question categories of information need validly and reliably?

Extensive research has been done on patron information needs through telephone surveys, with respondents being asked about previous information needs (Chen and Hernon, 1980; Dervin and Fraser, 1985). If a need resulted in a library visit, the respondent may also be asked about benefits derived from that visit (Dervin and Fraser, 1985). Students have also been interviewed about their information needs over a period of time (Kuhlthau, 1988b). Research on information needs of scientists, technologists, and special library users has been even more extensive, utilizing a wide variety of methods. (Herner and Herner, 1967; Martyn, 1974). In contrast, there is relatively less research on the needs of nonscientific or technical academic library users. However, several studies in academic libraries indicated that many information needs are brought to professors and friends in preference to the library (Taylor, 1967; Whitlatch, 1980; Kuhlthau, 1988b).

One of the most usual research methods is the record of reference requests. In an academic library, reference requests in a particular discipline have been shown to reflect the information needs of the discipline as a whole (Wender, et al., 1977). As to those having need for reference information in particular, the nature of the patron's information need is usually reported by the reference librarian who categorizes it by type and/or subject. This is preferred over categorization by the patron because the librarian is more aware of the distinctions between reference and directional questions and so is more able to classify requests. For more on this, see Chapter 4, "Question Classification."

Some experimentation in performance appraisal has been done in unobtrusive observation of reference where a patron is given a form on which he or she checks the category of question asked and notes the success of the outcome. Making decisions about individuals requires a greater degree of confidence than making decisions about groups. For this reason, use of question categories for individual performance appraisal may not be advisable until it can be shown that a set of categories has been developed that can be marked validly and reliably by patrons.

For all library users, the usual method has been to insert a question in a general library survey regarding the user's purpose on this library visit or in general. Sometimes patrons are asked about the subject areas and types of materials used in the library (Bundy, 1968; Carnegie Mellon, 1978; New York University, 1981) or in their work (Cornell University, 1984).

Little has been done to explore information needs in more detail, that is, going *beyond* the broad subject such as education or broad types of materials such as books or periodicals. Except for broad subject, little is known about library users' needs for *information* as opposed to their needs for different types of materials. Several surveys asked users how great, over a period of time, their needs were for facts, and bibliographic or citation verification (University of North Carolina, 1976). Differences were found between students and faculty. Another asked faculty about the kinds of information needed in their work (Cornell University, 1984).

Information need or reference question categories have also been formulated. However, a set of question categories suitable for patron use is needed, by which patrons can reliably and validly indicate the nature of their information desires in sufficient detail to be useful. The types of information needs of *all* library users can then be reported in a general survey, and success determined. For example, how successful are users acquiring bibliographical information when they consult reference and when they do not?

Questions in this area are as follows: To what extent is the library *really* self-service? What are the stages of the information-seeking process as a whole? Where do those who come to the library with specific titles get those titles? Do characteristics of users influence the way the information-seeking process is carried out? What are the effects of the reference environment on the process? What are the steps in the *library* information-seeking process? How do patrons translate information needs into specific titles so that they can then search for and obtain library materials? How do they go about looking for specific titles, subject information, and factual information? What information sources do different groups of patrons use, and in what order? How does reference fit into this pattern? What search strategies do patrons use to find different types of information and with what success? What factors in reference communication and the reference environment create problems for patrons, and how can these conditions be improved? What are the experiences, problems, and responses of library users? What do library users see as the greatest problems with reference service?

Searching Patterns

Information is accumulating on how characteristics of users influence their searching patterns. Regarding scientists and technologists, Herner and Herner (1967) stated that it has been clearly demonstrated that subject field and type of work within that field have profound effects on information-gathering patterns. They also observed that pure scientists have a predilection for a small core of information media and methods. Another study of special libraries showed that different groups of users used different types of tools and behaved in different ways (Slater, 1963).

Such areas as preference for certain types of sources and persistence in searching probably do vary for particular types of users, as they do for reference librarians. For example, Weech and Goldhor (1984) found that some reference librarians followed a pattern of consulting many sources, while others followed a pattern of consulting few sources. Another study of four users' searching patterns showed that sources consulted varied from two for one person to more than 20 for another (Taylor, 1967). One study showed clearly different patterns of library use for graduates and undergraduates in an academic library (University of California at Riverside, 1983). Oldman and Wills (1977) identified two information-seeking styles: "information beaver" and "I don't want to know any more."

Aspects of the reference environment undoubtedly affect the way a search is carried out. For example, in one study a user, intending to consult reference but finding the reference desk unstaffed, embarked on a long futile search for a fact, beginning at the catalog and then going to the shelf to consult some 20 or more books (Taylor, 1967).

The observation and recording of users' searches and interviewing of users are both good methods for determining when, why, and how reference is consulted in the search process. There is evidence that some users consult reference before beginning their searches, and that others come at points during their searches when problems are encountered (Cole, 1946; Taylor, 1967; Lederman, 1981; Bunge and Murfin, 1983; University of British Columbia, 1984; Kuhlthau, 1988b). This area is covered in detail in Chapter 1, "Assessing Library Services: The Reference Component."

Differences in types of sources consulted have been shown to vary with type of information needed when reference librarians search. For example, the catalog is used significantly less often when factual information is wanted (Bunge and Murfin, 1983). In a study of four users, three used the catalog by a subject approach to choose exact titles to answer factual questions and were completely unsuccessful. On the other hand, use of the catalog to get a shelf area number and *then browsing among titles in that area* was successful two of three times (Taylor, 1967). A searcher reported going to the catalog for broad subjects in humanities and social sciences and to the "abstracts" for technical subjects (Kuhlthau, 1988b). Search patterns may be altered by format, as some users in a hurry may alter their searches to avoid microfilm (Kottenstette, 1969).

Pearson (1973) provides evidence that stage of the search process affects information-gathering behavior. Kuhlthau (1988b) has done a thorough study of the search process of students in preparing research papers, and, as part of the study, the stages of the search process have been differentiated: (1-2) task initiation and topic selection; (3) exploration; (4) focus; (5) collection of information; and (6) search closure. The student may use the library at any stages of this process, but heaviest use might be expected in stage 5.

The proportion of subject to author searches appears to have increased with the advent of the computer catalog (Matthews, Lawrence, and Ferguson, 1983; Lewis, 1987). Markey (1980) has also shown that the proportion of specific title searches *increases* and the proportion of subject searches *decreases* as academic level rises from underclass students to faculty.

Users may *come* to the library with specific titles obtained from books, professors, or other sources. They may also obtain specific titles by various methods *within* the library and return to the catalog to locate them. In the four cases mentioned above, two persons used five specific titles of their own. Out of 40 titles found by the four persons, the "specific title" response accounted for only 12.5% (Taylor, 1967). The immediate "specific title" response is considerably more prevalent in the case of reference librarians (Bunge, 1967; Murfin, 1970).

The subject of users who come to the library with specific titles has been thoroughly researched and a number of well-developed methods exist, including availability research (Kantor, 1984; Ciliberti, Casserly, Hegg, and Mitchell, 1987) and in-depth study of users at both computer and card catalogs (Tagliacozzo, Rosenberg, and Kochen, 1970; Markey, 1980; Lewis, 1987).

The Information-Seeking Process

Initially, in response to a stimulus, an individual feels a need to reach a goal and begins to formulate purposeful action. In the process it is realized that something is lacking, which prevents the purpose from being carried out. If information is lacking, then the individual decides whether or not to actively seek it out. If the decision to do so is made, then it must be determined *what* information would meet the purpose. In some cases, this step is bypassed when the user simply presents the purpose to the reference librarian, professor, or friend—"I have to write a paper and don't know where to start." Usually, however, a *broad* general picture of what is needed is formulated at this stage.

Once the individual has decided that information is needed to meet the purpose and that he or she will actively seek it out, then the following question may be asked: Do I know of a specific title that might have that information? If none comes to mind, the searcher usually translates his or her purpose or goal into a subject, *type* of information, or type of materials. The searcher then asks questions, not necessarily in the following order, which attempt to translate the purpose into library materials: Under what subject does my purpose fit? With what types of sources am I familiar with that might have that kind of information? Do I know of a shelving area in the library where I can go directly to find that type of material on that subject? Have I ever seen that kind of information before in a particular *type* of source, for example, an encyclopedia or atlas? What kind of information do I need *about* the subject? What group of people would write, want to know, or read about that kind of information? For a fuller discussion of search strategy, see Chapter 12, "Reference Librarian Knowledge and Search Strategy."

Translation of purpose into key subject words has been extensively covered in a variety of studies, and a number of excellent methods are available (Bates, 1977; Markey, 1980; Mandel and Herschman 1983; Van Pulis and Ludy, 1988). Translation of purpose into *type* of information wanted has been much less studied. This step may correspond to the "focus" step in the research process as described by Kuhlthau (1988b). One study of type of reference questions recorded by reference librarians indicates that *more* public and academic library patrons presented their questions in terms of the *type* of information wanted about the subject than presented it in terms of the subject *alone.* Examples of *types* of wanted information are statistics, criticism, analysis, relating of two subjects, and focus on specific aspect (Bunge and Murfin, 1983). An older study by Cole (1946) also supports this conclusion.

The step of translating subject and/or type of information wanted into a type of *source* is similar to the "specific title" response, except that the searcher does not have searchable names of specific works, and so must ask for help or locate them in a particular known shelf area or through the catalog. For example, "I've seen information like this before in an almanac." Two studies indicate that this response of asking for a type of source is less frequent and occurs more often in academic libraries. It may occur considerably more often when users go *directly* to, for example, encyclopedias, atlases, or indexes without asking for reference help. In the longitudinal study of four students, there was considerable evidence that students located and used common types of sources on their own without looking up specific titles. (Bunge and Murfin, 1983; Kuhlthau, 1988b).

Occasionally the subject and type of information wanted will be translated into an author or corporate author. One participant in a study (Taylor, 1967) found the answer after discovering an IBM serial while examining the shelves and realizing that "IBM might be interested in that kind of information." In Taylor's study of four searchers (1967), although some specific titles were brought to mind, all four had to make *additional* attempts to find specific titles. Three searchers used the subject catalog and also examined the shelves at the call number area. Two contacted professors, one asked a reference librarian, and one obtained a citation from a bibliography in a known item already in his possession.

As to providing sources for answering factual questions, Taylor (1967) found that consulting a reference librarian was 100% successful (one consultation only). Looking up the broad subject in the catalog, writing down the call number, and examining those *exact* books on the shelf was not successful in any of the cases used. However, *when other books in the call number* area were examined, success resulted in 75% of cases. Consulting professors was 25% effective in providing the complete answer. However, items given by professors when combined with library items resulted in success in one instance. In another instance, a citation from the searcher's own materials provided a full answer. One searcher who failed did so because of a failure in source consultation that included failure to use the book index and inability to pick out the correct chapter from the table of contents (Taylor, 1967).

Errors in catalog searching have been extensively studied (Perrine, 1968; Bates, 1977; Markey, 1980; Van Pulis and Ludy, 1988; Ciliberti, Casserly, Hegg, and Mitchell, 1987; Hunter, 1991; Peters, 1989). Errors in communication of reference librarians with patrons have also been studied (Kazlauskas, 1976) as have errors in CD-ROM searching (Puttapithakporn, 1990). Searching for subject information and/or facts at the shelf, and consultation of sources by users are areas where research is needed. Menzel (1958) emphasizes the value of unplanned discovery of information. Some research on the extent and value of browsing and consultation of books at the shelf has been done (Fussler and Simon, 1961).

Impact of Information

There are few studies on use and/or impact of information, except in regard to scientists and technologists and in special libraries. One measure of impact has been creative ideas and/or innovations on the part of information users. One study showed an increased amount of creativity and innovations after the introduction of online literature searching (Pitlack, 1980). Another study of award-winning firms, using special forms and interviews, showed that only about 4% of successful innovations originated from formal literature channels. However, an additional 13% came from the individual's stored knowledge, some of which may have also been obtained from formal literature channels (Langrish, et al., 1972). Another study of psychologists indicated that about 14% of creative ideas originated from formal channels (Garvey, et al., 1972).

Another way of looking at impact is to determine whether or not library materials met the purpose for which they were obtained. One study asked users who had checked out books what their purpose was and whether the books had met their purpose: 75% said the books had met the purpose (Raisig, Smith, Cuff, and Kilgour, 1966). In a study of public library telephone reference questions, users were called back at a later time and asked if they had actually made any use of the information they had obtained from the reference department (Goldhor, 1979). Other studies have examined decisions made and actions taken as the result of computerized literature searches (Wilson, Starr-Schneidkraut, and Cooper, 1989; Haynes, McKibbon, Walker, Ryan, Fitzgerald, and Ramsden, 1990).

A further way of studying impact is to look at the changes, presumably of value, that the information made in an individual's life. A study of public library users reports changes in the following terms: found a direction; learned skills; reached goal; secured ideas; gained understanding; planned, decided what, when, where; accomplished or finished something; got started or motivated; avoided or escaped from a bad situation; and confirmed own thinking (Dervin, 1985). While inventions or discoveries may not have often resulted, many other changes of value to individual users are clearly demonstrated here. Another excellent study examines all types of benefits derived from medical literature searches (Wilson, Starr-Schneidkraut, and Cooper, 1989). For more on this, see Chapter 14, "Costs and Outcomes."

Methods for Studying the Information Seeking Process

Book availability research has been developed to determine success rates of users at *each stage* of the search for specific titles. This method has been used in all types of libraries and appears to be effective. This same type of process might be applied to patron searching for subjects and factual information (Ciliberti, Casserly, Hegg, and Mitchell, 1987). Taylor's (1967) work is a promising approach to solving this difficult problem.

The entire information-seeking process is often explored in a broad way through a general survey given to a sample of all users entering the library. Various questions then pertain to the sources used, the areas visited, and the outcome of the visit. For more details on reference information from this type of survey, see Chapter 1, "Assessing Library Services: The Reference Component." Perhaps the most useful reference information from such a survey is the relative success of users, with similar information needs or activities, consulting or not consulting reference. Also useful are data on overall frequency of consultation of reference and reasons for nonuse of reference. However, information on patron search strategy obtained from such surveys is generally of limited use because not enough is known about the information need, *all* sources consulted, the order of consultation, and reasons for choice.

Sometimes library users are asked to provide detailed feedback about their thoughts, conclusions, and actions during each step of library searches of their own choosing. They may record this feedback on tapes or in written records. This method worked well in one case, produced extremely interesting results, and has become one of the most frequently cited items in reference literature (Taylor, 1967). In a broader version, individuals may record in a diary all of their information-seeking feedback, whether it occurs in the library or outside (Oldman and Wills, 1977). Self-recording is more economical than observation and appears to work well if the user records only *one* library search in detail and is highly motivated (Taylor, 1967). Problems with the diary method occur when users are asked to keep diaries of *all* information needs whenever they arise or when they are asked to keep diaries over too long a period of time (Herner and Herner, 1967; Oldman and Wills, 1977). If the diary procedure is too complex or goes on too long, recording decreases and becomes biased, with only the most important events being recorded. In a study of scientists' reading, participants saved their diaries until they had time to do some reading (Herner and Herner, 1967). In another, half of the participants dropped out at the 5-week period (Oldman and Wills, 1977).

Another diary method problem is that it is difficult to obtain sufficient numbers of highly motivated patrons for the sample to be large enough to generalize on the basis of results (Herner and Herner, 1967). Nevertheless, results can shed valuable light on the way users carry out various stages of the information-seeking process. A successful method of recording information needs of special library users is the use of random alarm mechanisms for reminding individuals to record their activities in the previous 15-minute period (Herner and Herner, 1967). This method has the advantages of lessening the time and onerousness of the task and of providing an obvious reminder to the individual to record.

Interviews of searchers have been praised by Kuhlthau (1988b) as being extremely revealing of users' perceptions and reasoning and for providing detailed data on mental processes. In this study interviews were supplemented with logs and diaries. A disadvantage of the interview method without other supporting evidence is that interviewees are not actually observed and reports are based on users' perceptions after the fact. Also, interviewees may omit or enhance certain activities due to the presence of the interviewer. On the other hand, information that might have been overlooked, detailed information, and previously unarticulated feelings may be drawn out by this method. Many users respond well to the personal attention of the interviewer and reveal much more than they would in an open-ended questionnaire. Feelings and problems are particularly well explored by this method. Another difficulty, however, is the time and effort required to obtain a large enough sample to be able to generalize from results. Despite its problems, if performed by highly-skilled investigators, interviewing remains an essential method for understanding perceptions and problems of those seeking information.

In Kuhlthau's study (1988b), users' narrative on how they usually carry out each stage of the research process is revealing: Four students were polled from high school through college to learn how their research is carried out and how it changes over time. This method has the advantage of the longer perspective in revealing the complex cognitive process that takes place over a period of time, involving the whole person, emotional and intellectual, and so offers a holistic view of the entire search process. Disadvantages of this method are its slowness, high cost, and small samples.

The observer method, (with the patron verbalizing as the search continues), even though extremely labor-intensive, probably generates more complete data because the observer can assure that adequate information, if not forthcoming, is furnished at each step of the process: for example, "Why did you look there?" A disadvantage is that patron behavior may be altered by the presence of an observer.

Unobtrusive observation has disadvantages related to observing the information-seeking behavior of users. It would be difficult to follow users through the library without being detected. Even if this could be done, without knowledge of what the user is seeking, a record of user behavior would not be useful. However, if unobtrusive following of the search could be done, information about the completed search might be obtained at a later point by interview or questionnaire. Ethical problems of following patrons without their knowledge raise concerns, and the limited amount of information obtained by this method is an additional disadvantage. An advantage is that patron search behavior would not be altered by the presence of an observer. In one study, users were observed and followed, the locations were visited, and time spent was recorded; the advantages and disadvantages of this method are detailed in Pings and Anderson (1965).

Patron searches may be observed if the patron gives permission. In such cases, patrons may verbalize their search strategies, which are then recorded by the observer. Disadvantages are that selection of patrons may be biased somewhat by including only those cooperative patrons or those not in a hurry.

This might also result in a sample of the most skilled in library research who are not embarrassed about having their search observed. A more representative group of patrons might be obtained, for example, in busy libraries by offering a small sum of money for participation.

Participants in an experimental test situation are given a list of test questions for which they must find answers in a certain period of time. They then search while being observed. A drawback is that these results should not be used to infer patrons' actual success in the library because the test questions may not be representative of their real information needs. However, this method could provide valuable data about *unaided* user information-seeking difficulties and ultimate success in locating certain types of information. This, in turn, could be compared to the same data for reference librarians, and the difference could represent a measure of the benefit in terms of time saved and answers found that otherwise would not have been found. Lederman (1981) has done a study of this kind, but with the purpose of studying communication apprehension rather than information-seeking behavior. Bates (1977) did an experimental study on subject searching in the catalog.

Reference question records can give some indications of the stage of the information-seeking process where users most often need help. One study of types of reference questions indicated that the great majority of users come to reference desks in academic and public libraries *without* specific titles and need help in translating a purpose, subject, or type of information into specific titles, or into a specific shelf area (Bunge and Murfin, 1983). They can then make contact with library materials by going to the shelf or being given or shown materials by the reference librarian.

Barriers Encountered in Information Seeking

Patron responses to barriers and problems in library searching can be discovered by observation or recording of the search process (Taylor, 1967). Problems and responses in the reference situation have been investigated in depth in experimental studies. Patron response to a busy desk environment (McMurdo, 1982) and also to negative communication behavior (Gothberg, 1976) has been investigated in an experimental test situation where patron responses to the negative situation were observed. This method is effective in exploring the effects of negative conditions on patron behavior.

Another method of exploring problems is the critical incident method where patrons are interviewed or given open-ended questions on overall library surveys. Patrons are asked to describe an incident or problem in connection with reference service (Westbrook, 1987; Wilson, Starr-Schneidkraut, and Cooper, 1989). Advantages are that patrons are not restricted by time or by quantitative categories, and the unstructured format leaves them free to express whatever is on their minds. Disadvantages are that the frequency of such incidents or their prevalence among different groups of users cannot be determined.

Problems with reference service and/or the library are sometimes investigated in special questionnaire studies (Hatchard and Toy, 1986). Questions have also been inserted in general library surveys asking how patrons felt about having to wait for service, and about problems they have experienced in the reference environment. For example, in one survey 35% of reference patrons responding to these same items reported at some time in the past having found the reference desk unstaffed, and 72% reported having found materials crowded on the reference shelves (Colorado State University, 1981).

RESEARCH NEEDS

Some questions about patron library knowledge have been addressed but results have provided only partial answers and much remains to be done. Other questions in this regard have not been addressed. There is an urgent need for research relating library knowledge to user success in the library, and research exploring the relationship between reference service and user education. A valid and reliable instrument should be developed that will measure those elements of library knowledge that enable a user to function effectively in the library.

As to patron attitudes, perceptions, and responses, a substantial amount of data can be pieced together from various surveys of academic and public libraries. But more definitive work still needs to be done over a cross-section of libraries as to how many users have information needs but do not use reference, and if not, why not. Surveys of patron perceptions of reference in a cross-section of libraries should be done.

Regarding patron information needs uniform categories should be developed, by subject, type, and purpose, with focus on developing categories that can be validly and reliably marked by both librarians and patrons. In the area of library and reference patron information-seeking behavior, some groundbreaking studies have been done. These studies need to be used as a base and built on with research more narrowly focused on patron error in choosing and searching information sources.

INSTRUMENTS

Instruments included cover information-seeking behavior (Bundy; Carnegie Mellon University Libraries), anxiety of library users (Bostick); success in locating materials (Ciliberti, Casserly, Hegg, and Mitchell), help libraries provide in the context of users' lives (Dervin), user effort and difficulties in library processes (Kantor), information search process (Kuhlthau), awareness, use of, and satisfaction with library services (University of California at Riverside), use and importance of services (Yocum and Stocker), and impact of search outcomes on decision making (Wilson, Starr-Schneidkraut, and Cooper).

Bostick—The Library Anxiety Scale
Bundy—Public Library Use Study
Carnegie Mellon University Libraries—Student Users Survey
Ciliberti, Casserly, Hegg, and Mitchell—Availability of Library Books
Dervin—"Helps" Users Obtain from Their Library Visits
Kantor—Measurement of Effort by Simulation
Kuhlthau, Turock, George, and Belvin—The Information Search Process:
    Process Survey and Perception Questionnaire
University of California at Riverside—UCR Library Services Survey
Wilson, Starr-Schneidkraut, and Cooper—Critical Incident Technique
Yocum and Stocker—Survey of Public Library Users

Chapter 4

Question Classification

Jo Bell Whitlatch

SCOPE

One of the most basic forms of measurement is to classify or categorize all objects or individuals into groups. Classifying structures human perceptions of the world by means of categorical types and may be a fundamental activity necessary to provide people with orientation to situations.

Construction of types remains an ever-present feature of research investigations. In libraries, classifications most commonly used for questions are reference versus directional and factual versus subject. Classifying permits researchers to seek and predict relationships between classified objects or individuals and other factors. However, classification must be used with caution because it emphasizes sharply defined discrete categories whereas experience may find process and continuity.

Classification assigns objects or individuals to different groups or subsets of the whole based on the possession of some observed characteristic, which distinguishes one group from another. Thus, the whole is divided into two or more categories. Classification schemes must be both comprehensive and mutually exclusive. Each object or individual must be assigned to one group only and all objects or individuals must be capable of being assigned to one group. The dimensions that make each group different from another must be explicitly stated and these dimensions should be of central importance for the study.

For libraries, an important consideration in classifying questions is *when* in the reference process questions are categorized. Should questions be categorized as they are asked by the user, after they are negotiated, or after the librarian has answered them? A question from a single reference transaction may not be assigned to the same categories both at the beginning and the conclusion of the reference process. Initial user questions are often somewhat different than questions that are asked because users may believe that the library does not have what is really wanted. Questions categorized after negotiation with the librarian may change significantly as they become focused on information available in the library.

IMPORTANCE OF RESEARCH

Seng (1978) notes that reference librarians should be able to improve the efficiency and effectiveness of their services by establishing personal databases of reference questions. Classification of the questions into different types and analysis of success rates associated with the different question types can be used to answer questions such as the following: Are there areas of the collection where the appropriate sources to answer questions successfully are lacking? Are there certain types of questions (for example, questions requiring statistical answers) where staff have lower rates of success in answering the question? Are staff with certain training or education more successful in answering specific types of questions? Is there enough repetition of similar questions that sample questions can be used in training new staff and to provide a database of frequently asked questions for ensuring that experienced staff with different backgrounds provide consistent and reliable answers to common questions?

STATE OF THE FIELD

Overview

This summary of the state of the art in reference question classification reviews five of the most common principles that have been employed in classifying reference queries: 1) Answer Characteristics; 2) Library Source Documents; 3) Users' Information Needs; 4) How User Intends to Use Information; and 5) Form of Answer Wanted by Users. The first two classification methods are based on librarian perspectives; the last three, on user perspectives.

Answer Characteristics

A common classification method is based upon the type of information required to answer the query. Questions that can be satisfactorily answered by clearly defined data have been widely referred to in the library literature as factual questions. Recent studies of reference queries have tended to focus on factual questions. However, studies by Woodard (1989), Whitlatch (1989), and Havener (1990) have compared success rates for factual questions and other types of queries.

When librarians classify questions as factual versus subject or instructional, they are contrasting questions with specific answers with questions that do not have specific, well-defined answers. Librarians have found that classifying questions as factual queries or subject or instructional is difficult because in reality many queries contain a mix of both elements. Therefore, classification schemes that categorize questions as factual or subject or instructional should let people select a category for mixed questions or develop a scale to measure the degree of specificity required in the answer. In fact, Buckland (1979) observes that specificity should be regarded as a continuous variable and one that is not easy to measure. Saracevic, Kantor, Chamis, and Trivison (1988) have scales that measure specificity as well as other question characteristics.

Instead of developing categories or scales to measure specificity, the characteristics of expected answers can be used to classify questions into categories and construct various indexes with combinations of characteristics. Jahoda's work (1977) provides a foundation for constructing an index of possible characteristics. Murfin and Bunge (1988a) have constructed an index to measure question complexity. Librarians answering the question assigned the attributes, which is not as objective a measure as classification by independent judges.

Library Source Documents

The typical approach to classifying reference questions has focused not on the question itself, but on matching questions to source documents. However, library documents cannot always meet the information needs of users. An implicit assumption of this approach to classifying questions and to teaching reference service is that for each question there is a correct or most appropriate answer or source. Research by Balay and Andrew (1975), Kesselman and Watstein (1987), Strong (1980a), and Cameron (1976) have all used this approach and noted the difficulties with consistent classification of questions and the problems with categories that are not mutually exclusive. Using schemes in which only librarians select these question types is not recommended because of evidence that librarian classification is not reliable (Kesselman and Watstein, 1987). Researchers should collect the actual questions asked and answers supplied and have expert judges classify questions. A form for collecting questions is the *Reference Transaction Slip* developed by Geraldine King and included in the instrument section of the *Manual*.

Users' Information Needs

The results of simple classification efforts have contributed a limited amount to knowledge useful in practice. Altman (1982) notes that reference questions have been analyzed by categories since the 1920s. In general the problem with these studies is that it is hard to know what to do with the data collected. Although knowledge of the percent of reference vs. directional can prove somewhat useful in determining staffing levels (St. Clair and Aluri, 1977), often the logical reaction is "so what?" If a library finds that 25% of its questions can be answered in encyclopedias, should the library spend 25% of its collection budget on more encyclopedias?

Perhaps the research agenda should be based on the structure of problems that produce questions as opposed to an agenda based on the content of questions (Swigger, 1985). Questions do provide evidence concerning the state of knowledge of the questioner and knowing that state of knowledge ought to prove useful in trying to find an answer. Problem definition and expectations of users have influenced the final evaluation of search results (Saracevic, et al., 1988).

Librarians may want to look at the study of information needs of particular social roles rather than particular individuals. Dervin (1976) has developed a content-analytic scheme that taps the universe of average citizen information needs and attempts to provide a set of mutually exclusive and exhaustive categories into which all citizen information needs can be classified. Dervin notes that citizen needs are often handled by sources for whom the topic area is only a tangential or unrelated concern and that people who attempt to seek help face a frustrating maze of obstacles. The situation is one of inefficiency and lack of communication among various information sources. Adopting Dervin's subject scheme and analyzing success in different areas might be very useful in assisting public libraries in analyzing how to coordinate their information services with other public agencies.

Academic libraries tend to analyze requests along subject lines related to the curriculum. Paterson (1979) has developed subject schemes for use in academic libraries.

How User Intends to Use Information

The questions are phrased as "Why do you want this information?" or "What do you intend to do with this information?" or "How do you intend to use this information?" Strong (1980a), Weech and Goldhor (1984), and Whitlatch (1987) have all developed classification schemes categorizing user intent. None of these studies have found that their categories of user purpose significantly influenced reference success.

Form of Answer Wanted by Users

Forms of answers (e.g., exact reproductions, short answers, lists of references) are thought to influence the usefulness of information provided. To get the right information to the right person at the right time, the information management or control process of the information delivery systems must have access to both appropriate information sources and appropriate information solutions (Dervin, 1976). Possibly information, as an independent concept, must be divided into types and successful information delivery may depend on the ability to deliver not just "information" but appropriate types of information. Hieber (1966) devised a question classification based on the format of answer that seemed to satisfy the user. However, some of the categories appeared to overlap (Brown, 1985).

RESEARCH NEEDS

The use of question categories in evaluating reference service has serious limitations. The major problem with all classification schemes is that data categories must be mutually exclusive (Brown, 1980). Those that have been devised tend not to be so. Because most categories devised are not mutually exclusive, future work should include further testing of scales to measure degrees of specificity and complexity.

Because recording questions is difficult at busy reference desks, researchers need to test the validity and reliability of various types of question categories and develop a set that gives valid and reliable results. However, based on current state of knowledge, libraries attempting to classify types of reference transaction for daily recording or research should record brief statements of questions which more than one person later classifies from the written statement.

INSTRUMENTS

Instruments included cover a form for collecting questions (King) and an index that measures question complexity (Murfin, Bunge, and Gugelchuk).

King—Reference Transaction Slip
Murfin, Bunge, and Gugelchuk—Reference Transaction Assessment
  Instrument

Chapter 5

Reference Environment

Anna M. Donnelly

SCOPE

Reference services operate at all times within a matrix of environmental factors which may, singly or in the aggregate, impact upon the quality of those services. Little attention has been given in the literature to the way in which effective reference performance is enhanced or impeded by such factors in the course of daily work. This section covers those environmental elements, whether physical or other-department dependent, in the working reference environment over which reference staff can often exercise little or no control at the points of service.

IMPORTANCE OF RESEARCH

Instruments or methodologies that attempt to analyze environmental elements may help answer such questions as the following: Is available space adequate to necessary functions? Do patrons have sufficient access to materials? Is equipment maintained properly? Are other library processes timely enough not to interfere with the reference process? Does the reference desk environment facilitate good communication? What components of the physical environment need improvement, either marginally or substantially? What factors in the reference setting impede successful transactions? Is there a solid basis upon which to make effective management decisions beyond felt impressions of the environment?

STATE OF THE FIELD

Overview

Until recently, the question of environmental effects specifically on reference performance has been addressed only peripherally in the library literature, which has looked at environmental issues mostly from the overall library environment perspective.

Related Methodologies

Recommendations on planning and designing the best physical environment address reference needs (Leighton and Weber, 1986; Fraley and Anderson, 1990) by touching upon some of the essentials. In-depth studies such as University of California at Santa Barbara's Report (1986) suggest more detailed appraisal procedures.

Larason (1975) dealt with reference service location in an academic library and considered means of alleviating environmental design problems encountered by library users. He examined the role of the reference service and environmental means of enhancing the usage of this service. He demonstrated that the use of the reference service could be changed by simply moving its location within an academic library environment, and developed a model to predict use of the service using environmental factors as the independent variables. His synthesis of relevant literature resulted in a general "passive systems" model; the concept of environmental programming developed as a logical extension of the passive systems analysis. A reference service desk as a stimulus was moved among three positions on one floor of an academic library. Three two-hour trials were conducted at each position in both of two semesters. Measurements of traffic patterns, area distributions of the user population, and usage at both the experimental desk and the prior service facility were taken to construct a model of service usage. The findings indicated that experimental environmental stimulus created use that would not have occurred otherwise, and that environmental programming is a promising design principle for libraries.

More recently Durrance (1989) noted the lack of investigation into the influence of the environmental setting on reference interview accuracy and conducted a study in this area (see Instrument section). White (1987) has also addressed the environment or interview question. Donnelly (1989) offered a means of determining and graphing staff perceptions of the reference environment. Environmental considerations were an important part of the study that preceded reference renovation at Oregon State University (Franklin, Knittel, and Maughan, 1991).

RESEARCH NEEDS

Almost no instruments and few methodologies are available in the area of reference environment. Most of the literature pursues one of two paths: physical structures or behavioral activities. More ergonomically oriented studies correlating these paths, such as those done in the Steffenson and Larason compilation (1978), would be welcome for reference service. Indeed, searching library literature under the word "environment" generally yields sources relating to the computer environment alone, or to preservation of natural resources. Libraries collect data on the natural environment but make little application to themselves. More ways of implementing global environmental evaluations for all library types and service levels are needed to shift from testing areas in isolation to assessment in context. Well worth developing is Samuel Rothstein's (1984) idea of a reference activities measure. Reference procedures and resources have been designed primarily for patron self-service (Rothstein, 1989). This fact actually hides all that reference librarians really do, while often the totality of conditions and influences under which they do it remain both unexplored and uncontrolled.

INSTRUMENTS

Instruments included cover user response to physical facilities (Colorado State University), staff perceptions of the reference environment (Donnelly), the influence of the environmental setting on the reference interview (Durrance), and innovation in reference arrangements (Franklin, Knittel, and Maughan).

Colorado State University—Questionnaire for Library Users
Donnelly—Reference Environment Problems Checklist
Durrance—Reference Interview and the Environment
Franklin, Knittel, and Maughan—Reference Arrangement Survey

Chapter 6

Reference Collection Use

Anna M. Donnelly

SCOPE

The *use* of *reference* collections (what kind of use, how much) has been only modestly explored in the literature. Although major changes are occurring due to the development of electronic full-text retrieval, this section is concerned primarily with use of nonelectronic reference materials. A "use" here may be considered as any examination of published or unpublished material for the purpose of seeking information, whether the information is actually found or not. Although use is related to collection development and evaluation, this section does not generally include studies that focus primarily on the latter two areas.

IMPORTANCE OF RESEARCH

Knowing how collections are used will help answer the following questions for better materials acquisition, management, access, and effective use: What levels of materials should be acquired for reference use? What should be relegated to general stacks or remote storage or discard? How can collections be better arranged physically to promote more effective use? What effect does closed or open stack arrangement have on reference use? How do reference use patterns vary: by patron, by level, by subject? What procedures are more effective in measuring reference use as opposed to general in-house use? What probability studies can be applied; how predictable is reference use? By what procedures can collection variables (such as size, language, or location) be isolated and correlated with actual use? How does aggregate use compare with individual title uses in a specific subject? How can the diagnostic tools and research techniques developed for measuring circulation or periodical use be adapted for reference analysis? What is the effect of the online catalog on reference materials use? What impact does current use have on reference collection development policies? What differences can be observed between using general stack and reference stack materials?

More broadly, use studies supply data for decision making on space and budget, and in developing goals and criteria for collection assessment. Relating to resource usage, Thomas Jordan (1989) suggests asking the following: What are the library policies for resource use? How much is the collection used? How well is the collection used? What is the fulfillment rate? What is the relationship between collection size, collection growth rate, and collection use? (82)

STATE OF THE FIELD

Because reference collections are generally noncirculating, past studies most applicable to reference are those which examine browsing or in-house use. Standard methods for collecting data on unrecorded uses include observation (obtrusive or unobtrusive), questionnaires, diaries, interviews, table or book truck or shelf counts. User surveys are reviewed in Chapter 3, "Library Users and Reference Patrons," and are therefore not repeated here, but should be considered in conjunction with any use studies undertaken. Few use studies concentrate on reference collections; they are either subsumed into the larger library collection study or not considered at all.

Browsing

Lawrence and Oja (1980) found that browsing could be an important way of accessing information by patrons, while Boll (1985) observed browsing was better for casual, but not research, purposes. Somewhat complex mathematical models have been offered for analyzing use (Morse, 1970). Ross (1983) noted that counting refiled books does not adequately reflect browsing activities in view of patron refiling. More recently, Frantz (1991) suggests browsing as a learning tool for staff. No doubt it has always been so for patrons.

In-House Use

The classic Fussler and Simon study (1961) estimated that from three to nine books were consulted for every one recorded (circulated) use. Broadus (1980) also found that in-library use parallels circulation, although this has been questioned by Selth and Briscoe (1992). A 1973-74 study in England showed, by using a book slip method, as many as 20 times more books were used in-library than as recorded by reshelving counts (Harris, 1977). Rubin's (1986) results suggested the need to supplement table counts because it misses patron reshelving. Baker and Lancaster (1991) offer a recent overview and practical methods for conducting this type of evaluation.

RESEARCH NEEDS

While there are many studies on collection use as part of overall collection development research, little has been done in depth on the specific characteristics of *reference* collection use, as confirming or refuting the anecdotal or impressionistic evaluations of use. As noted above, reference use is usually absorbed into "in-house" use studies or scattered in the broader investigations. Also, studies of reference collection use provide opportunities for joint projects involving library school faculty and librarians. Mosher (1984) pointed out the great need for collaboration between researchers and practitioners.

Use studies have had limitations. Lancaster (1982) summarizes these: they focus on present demand rather than on future need, nonusers are often overlooked, they don't reveal the need behind the demand, they may cover what is easily studied rather than what is significant, and the methodology may be obtrusive and costly. Despite such limitations, studies correlating reference collection use with other types of library uses would be of value in analyzing how well libraries integrate their resources and move users smoothly from a reference system to another internal library system, such as circulation. Quantitative statistics do not in themselves measure quality, but they may be used to develop qualitative indexes for reference use. Little attention has been paid to the unique uses of reference materials, such as the brevity of consultations, the need for multiple complementary consultations, greater or lesser need for professional intervention, impact of physical locations on use or level of use, and the impact of available staff on use.

INSTRUMENTS

Instruments included cover comparison of patron use to librarian use (Arrigona and Mathews), depth or intensity of collection use (Arrigona and Mathews; Van House, Weil, and McClure), general recording of use (Fussler and Simon; McClure and Heron; Murfin and Harrick; Van House, Weil, and McClure), and use and awareness of reference sources (Strother).

Arrigona and Mathews—Reference Collection Use Study
Fussler and Simon—Library Use Study Questionnaire
Lawrence and Oja—University of California Questionnaire
McClure and Hernon—Academic Library User Ticket; Public Library
    User Ticket; Count of In-House Users
Murfin and Harrick—Murfin-Harrick Reference Survey
Strother—Strother's Questionnaire A and B
Van House, Weil, and McClure—In-Library Materials Use

Chapter 7

Electronic Databases and Reference Assistance

Ralph Lowenthal and **Marjorie E. Murfin**

SCOPE

This chapter concerns the evaluation of electronic databases as reference sources. As with printed reference sources, databases are used not only by librarians in the process of finding answers to questions for users, but independently by patrons who occasionally request assistance. Thus, this chapter covers evaluation of ready reference electronic searching by librarians and direct user searching of electronic databases—electronic databases mounted locally and at remote sites, and CD-ROMs—where reference assistance is provided on request. Evaluation instruments and methods from the online searching literature are included when adaptation appears possible for evaluation of ready reference and direct user database searching. Mediated searches by appointment are not included.

IMPORTANCE OF RESEARCH

Although electronic databases have had a tremendous impact upon reference service practice, understanding of the effectiveness of databases as reference sources is limited. Assessment of the outcomes of ready reference and direct user searching is important, both for improvement of reference practice and for accountability purposes—to explain to the public, government, and other funding sources how well reference service is performing. Accessing an electronic database for information is not always successful; greater understanding of reasons for success and failure is required to design more effective searching systems. Comparison of effectiveness, efficiency, and cost of accessing different systems and databases is essential, particularly given the costs of electronic database access and increasingly limited library budgets. Research findings that provide answers to these issues will ensure that, in reference service, print and electronic approaches can be integrated with maximum effectiveness.

Important questions in these areas are the following: How successful are the various types of unaided users in performing their own database searches with and without assistance? Are some groups of users more successful than others? What databases and subjects are most and least successfully searched? What are the reasons for failure of unaided direct user searches? What types of reference assistance are most needed and most effective? What are the factors that make for effective ready reference searches? What types of questions are best searched manually and what types are best searched by computer? How does the success of unaided direct users compare with that of those who have reference assistance during their searches? On the same type of questions, how successful are direct users of expert systems as compared to users of traditional desk reference service?

STATE OF THE FIELD

Overview

Evaluation of the success of ready reference and direct user searching in electronic databases is similar to evaluation of traditional reference service in that the same methods may be used (for discussion of these methods, see Chapter 15, "Reference Effectiveness"). However, in the case of electronic searching, additional methods may also be used, such as analysis of transaction logs. Generally, methodology is fairly well developed in this area; a number of methods and instruments are available.

Patron Judgment of Outcome

User survey is a method frequently used to evaluate success of outcome. However, many user surveys, judged on the basis of results, are not sufficiently discriminating to be useful as a genuine tool for self-improvement. Particularly susceptible to inflated ratings, according to Cuadra, are "yes-no" 2-category scales. (Cuadra, Katter, Holmes, and Wallace, 1967). Instruments have been included when there are indications that positive bias has been controlled or minimized (Ankeny, 1991). Potentially useful instruments with some 2-category scales have been included, but it is suggested that these 2-category scales be modified to more discriminating scales. Three-category scales—fully satisfied, partly satisfied, and not satisfied—have been shown to work well without apparent inflation in academic and public libraries and also for results of mediated online searches (Sandore, 1990).

As well as judging success in finding what was wanted, direct users sometimes judge the relevance or usefulness of retrieved references. Other measures useful in evaluating the effectiveness of ready reference and direct user searching in electronic databases are quality of communication, level of intermediary's understanding, time saved, ease of use, currency and searching skill, and giving enough help. Information is also obtained on the user's purpose, number of citations retrieved, and so on (Auster and Lawton, 1984; Saracevic, Kantor, Chamis, and Trivison, 1988).

Patron and Librarian or Expert Judgment of Outcome

By use of this method, direct users perform their own actual searches in the natural setting. A librarian then performs a search for the *same* information and the patron judges the outcome of *both* searches. In this way, the margin of error and the shortcomings of direct user searches can be discovered. Kirby and Miller (1985) have used this method to explore the relative effectiveness of mediated and nonmediated searches.

In another related method, the user's search is not redone. Instead, each direct user's search is evaluated both by the direct user and by the intermediary providing assistance (University of Texas at Austin, 1984). This method could also be used to evaluate the success of the ready reference search in electronic databases.

Expert Judgment of Outcome

Unobtrusive observation has been used in evaluating online searching in public libraries (McCue, 1988) and could also be used in evaluating electronic ready reference searching. Direct users might also be observed unobtrusively; however, it may be difficult to gain sufficient understanding of the search being done without making users aware that they were being observed. If transaction logs are available, this will provide useful information on search strategy and errors (Peters, 1989; Hunter, 1991).

Direct users might be given a set of test searches in a particular database and their success evaluated. This method has already been used in judging success of online ready reference searching (Havener, 1988). In both the unobtrusive and test-by-agreement methods, the success of the search may be judged by one expert or a panel of experts (McCue, 1988; Saracevic, Kantor, Chamis, and Trivison, 1988; Sandore, 1990). Observation of actual searchers by agreement has also been used effectively by Puttapithakporn (1990). This method has the advantage that users are highly motivated to obtain information required for their classes.

RESEARCH NEEDS

Research has proceeded swiftly in this area, compared to other areas of reference evaluation, but patron reports as measures of utility or success need to be refined and standardized. Extensive research needs to be done comparing success of ready reference and direct user searches across libraries; through this research, factors can be identified that are associated with high and low levels of effectiveness in particular situations. The effectiveness of electronic databases as reference sources should be evaluated in experimental settings and also in actual situations where users search for their own information needs. Studying transaction logs appears promising in terms of monitoring users' success.

INSTRUMENTS

Instruments included cover success of direct user searches (Ankeny; University of Texas at Austin), success of mediated searches (Auster and Lawton; Saracevic, Kantor, Chamis, and Trivison; Tagliacozzo; University of Kentucky; University of Texas at Austin; Van House, Weil, and McClure), comparison of success of mediated and direct user searches (Kirby and Miller), reference question answering effectiveness (Murfin, Bunge, and Gugelchuk), and comparison of success of ready-reference searches using print and electronic sources (Havener).

Ankeny—Database Questionnaire
Auster and Lawton—User Responses to Online Search Requests
Havener—The Use of Print Versus Online Sources
Kirby and Miller—Questionnaires I and II
McCue—Online Searching in Public Libraries
Murfin, Bunge, and Gugelchuk—Reference Transaction Assessment
    Instrument
Saracevic, Kantor, Chamis, and Trivison—Utility Measures
Tagliacozzo—Follow-Up Questionnaire
University of Kentucky—Literature Search Evaluation
University of Texas at Austin—Questionnaires for End Users and
    Intermediaries
Van House, Weil, and McClure—Online Search Evaluation

Chapter 8

Worklife and Morale

Ralph Lowenthal and Marjorie E. Murfin

SCOPE

Covered in this chapter is assessment of psychological and social factors that may relate to the well-being of individual reference librarians and, in turn, to effective performance of reference work. As such, this chapter is closely related to Chapter 5, "The Reference Environment." Factors that affect the well-being of individual librarians most often include job stress, burnout, and anxiety. For psychosocial factors involved in the process of communication with patrons, the reader should consult Chapter 11, "Communication and the Reference Interface."

Research on this topic may be focused on the well-being of particular groups, but does not identify individual staff members. Often, it has as its goal the improvement of the profession by learning more about the effects of job stress, burnout, and anxiety on reference librarians and on the performance of reference work.

Instruments chosen for inclusion in this chapter include a survey of reference morale and climate that is made up of adaptations of several well-known tests from outside the library field, and two tests that can be used without modification to assess job stress. A wide selection of other instruments of this type can be found in *Experience of Work* (Cook, Hepworth, Wall, and Warr, 1981).

IMPORTANCE OF RESEARCH

A problem of concern to administrators and reference staff alike in any reference department is the well-being, both physical and mental, of those individuals who provide reference service to the public. The following questions arise in regard to well-being: How do staff perceive the organizational climate of their immediate work environment and of the library as a whole? How do they perceive their supervisors and their co-workers? Do they experience feelings of stress, frustration, hostility, anxiety, and exhaustion in performing reference service? If so, what are the probable reasons and how can this situation be improved? What is the general state of staff well-being and morale? What is their overall degree of satisfaction with their worklife and their level of commitment to reference work?

An advantage of assessing the above aspects of worklife is that problems in these areas can be discovered and needed improvements can be made. Perceived job stress has been shown to be significantly related to illness and absenteeism in other service-related fields. Recent research outside of the library field has also shown that the study of cybernetics, or control theory, can be used as a framework in which to understand the relationship between job stress, productivity, and quality of job performance (Edwards, 1992). The discrepancies between environmental characteristics and psychological factors can be minimized and reduced, and then attempts can be made to improve the quality of life and work in a department.

A corresponding disadvantage of assessing librarian morale and librarian perception of work climate is that it requires great care and sensitivity. A poorly conceived and administered attempt can result in a worsened situation. Where problems exist, staff may resent completing forms because they are seen as an intrusion into their personal lives, one more unnecessary burden, or a way for those in charge to identify and "retrain" workers with negative attitudes. Staff may feel that the study will serve no useful purpose because no action will be taken to improve existing conditions. When such feelings exist, assessment, if not done with great care, may result in a poor return rate with forms consigned to the wastebasket, untruthful answers, and randomly marked meaningless forms.

Surveys that study factors like morale, anxiety, stress, and working relations succeed only when individuals are assured of complete anonymity. Reference departments that are planning to carry out such surveys are encouraged to work in partnership with experts in the fields of psychology, education, business, or other appropriate fields who are experienced in test confidentiality. Reasons may vary why a department undertakes a survey. Some libraries may seek to reassure themselves that they do not have problems in relation to organizational climate, employee job satisfaction, quality of worklife, or morale. Others may have a genuine desire to determine employees' perceptions of the quality of their worklife and an equally sincere desire to work, from the top down, toward reducing stressors in the workplace and improving morale and well-being. A library or reference department may decide to work with an expert to carry out such a survey because there is a perception that problems exist. In all cases, effort should be made to protect all members of the tested unit from disclosure. The goal of all involved should be to seek changes in the unit's climate and environment without attaching blame or guilt to any individual, and the genuine desire should be to enhance unit cohesion and esprit de corps.

If such a survey is done for strictly research purposes, researchers should go to extremes to ensure test anonymity by having completed surveys sent directly to them, and published results should be void of information that could identity individual libraries or employees. A well-designed survey is one that avoids intruding into employees' personal lives and is only undertaken to improve staff worklife or to examine why certain factors affect individuals or organizations differently.

Despite difficulties, such assessment can lead to positive outcomes. Staff distress may not always be apparent; observations and impressions of staff well-being and morale may be considerably off the mark. Well-being and morale should be the primary concerns, both for humanitarian reasons and for reasons of providing good service to patrons.

STATE OF THE FIELD

Overview

Currently little has been done in the field of librarianship to study worklife and morale. In those studies that have been done the basic methodology has been the survey. Participants fill out questionnaires that ask them how they feel about particular issues, people, resources, and events that affect them daily. Most often the questionnaires are based on a scale ranging from feeling strongly positive about an item to feeling strongly negative. The scales can also be numerically constructed, for example from 1 (the worst case) to 5 (the best case). More important to the state of the research at this time, though, is *how* basic terms are defined when studying worklife and morale.

Job Stress

Stress is defined as the response or reaction of an individual to a perceived stressor in the environment, or in the individual. This response comes in the form of arousal of strong, demanding emotional states. Stressors may originate in the workplace or the home; their effect in stress reactions has been found to be cumulative. Both environmental and personal stress add together to produce life stress for a particular individual. Certain events and conditions are widely regarded as stressors. However, positive events such as holidays or the birth of a child also act as stressors and may add to the life stress level. Stressors can also be perceived differently among a group of people—for example, change may be perceived positively by one person but negatively by another.

While not yet studied in librarianship, literature outside of the field has shown that the severity of job stress reactions can be affected by the nature and characteristics of the work, by the level of stress outside of work, and by personal characteristics. When studying stress in the library profession all of these factors must be considered to predict the level of stress in an individual. Extensive research has been done and instruments are available in almost all areas related to worklife and well-being of workers, as can be found in Cook, Hepworth, Wall, and Warr (1981). In contrast, research on stress and librarians, particularly reference librarians, is in a beginning stage.

Job stressors and stress reactions in librarianship have been much discussed and debated; a number of articles recommend methods of reducing stressors and coping with stress in librarianship. Another area of considerable concern has been technostress (Bichteler, 1986; Westbrook, 1988; Bunge, 1991; Giesbrecht, 1991; Whitlatch, 1991; Kupersmith, 1992). Generally, studies have focused on identifying stressors in reference librarianship (Bunge, 1989), on technostress as it relates to librarianship and reference work (Bichteler, 1986; Westbrook, 1988), and on the stress reaction syndrome of burnout. By far the greatest number of studies have been done in this latter area and literature reviews are available (Blevins, 1988; Fisher, 1990; Blazek, 1992).

Responses to perceived work stressors in terms of emotional and physical well-being and performance have been less often studied. One study is available of reference librarian morale and performance (Lowenthal, 1990). However, response to stress in terms of well-being and performance has been of continuing concern in the psychological literature.

One important element in job stress reactions, as related in research outside of the library field, has been identified as the nature of the task itself. For example, elements of tasks that have frequently been related to stress reactions are volume of workload, frequency or number of stressful occurrences, and interruptions (Bube, 1986). As noted in one literature review, the performance of highly complex tasks under time pressure and the constant demand for accuracy and minute detail can be an important source of stress. The author also notes that stress affects performance by reducing the working memory capacity and that task results are adversely affected as task difficulty increases. Also, increased reaction time and more frequent errors on behavioral tasks are observed under stress (Bube, 1986). One reference expert notes, in regard to the reference task, that "reference librarians are among the few researchers of this world who are expected to perform with an audience in the midst of other demands and distractions (Roose, 1989).

The Burnout Syndrome

When perceived job stress becomes chronic, burnout may occur. One study illustrates this relationship (Whitehead and Lindquist, 1985). Burnout is defined by Maslach as a syndrome including feelings of low personal accomplishment, emotional exhaustion, hostility, and depersonalization (Maslach and Jackson, 1981). It is said to progress in stages from enthusiasm, through stagnation, hostility, and anger, to apathy. Maslach indicates that burnout is extremely serious in terms of the individual's life and work performance. Once burnout has progressed, it is not easily reversed. One study of libraries shows a relationship between burnout and reference performance. This study indicates that losses in performance occurred on all four Maslach dimensions. However, the sharpest downward loss in performance occurred on the depersonalization scale (Lowenthal, 1990).

The phenomenon of burnout, as explored by Maslach, has been written about extensively in regard to librarianship. The literature consists of analyses and recommendations, based on personal knowledge and experiences, and of studies of burnout in various fields of librarianship. This literature has grown to the extent that a number of literature reviews have appeared (Blevins, 1988; Fisher, 1990; Blazek and Parrish, 1992). The Maslach Burnout Inventory (MBI) has been used in a variety of cases to assess burnout in librarians of all types. Results in regard to reference librarians appear to indicate that some degree of burnout is certainly present, varying with circumstances and individuals. Greatest levels of burnout appear to be found in public reference librarians. One study, using the Maslach Burnout Inventory, reported 30% of staff at moderate or greater levels of burnout (Birch, Marchant, and Smith, 1986), while another, using the Staff Burnout Survey (SBS), reported 42% of staff at moderate or greater levels of burnout (Haack, Jones, and Roose, 1984). These results are generally in line with those found for teachers.

Results are less clear on burnout levels in academic reference librarians. One study found a low level of burnout, but the instrument used had not been validated (Smith and Nelson, 1983). Other studies of academic reference librarians have considered subject specialists and BI librarians (Blevins, 1988; Fisher, 1990; Blazek and Parrish, 1992). The existence of burnout in library work is supported by one interesting study of library directors, which found that 65% of directors responding to a survey were aware of burnout in their libraries and saw it as a serious problem (Taler, 1984).

Anxiety

Another important factor that has seldom been studied in relation to librarianship is anxiety. The effects of anxiety on health are of concern. In addition, a large body of psychological literature which indicates that anxiety and performance are linked: anxiety is described as interfering with attentiveness, leading to irrelevant thoughts, and making it necessary to expend more effort to accomplish a task (Bube, 1986). This literature shows, as previously discussed in regard to stress, that level of anxiety and performance follow a U-shaped curve, with both low and high levels of anxiety associated with decreased performance. Moderate anxiety, on the other hand, is associated with the best performance. One study assessing anxiety and reference performance shows a similar U-shaped curve, however, with lower anxiety having a considerably better performance than very high anxiety (Lowenthal, 1990).

Job Satisfaction, Commitment, and Morale

Studies of job satisfaction have focused on comparing the job satisfaction of different groups of librarians; these studies have found job satisfaction with reference work to be consistently higher than for other library work (Lynch and Verdin, 1987). Job satisfaction, commitment, and morale have been studied more extensively in the psychological, educational, and business literature. The broad concept of morale may be defined as including job satisfaction, commitment to the organization and to the profession, and, particularly, pride in work. Commitment is sometimes confused with job satisfaction because the two are closely related. It appears that satisfaction with a comfortable job may be present without commitment to the organization or to the profession. However, it appears less likely that commitment to an organization will exist under conditions of job dissatisfaction. Nevertheless, it might still exist on another level—that is, to the profession as a whole. The data from one study of public library reference librarians show both level of job satisfaction and level of commitment related to performance (Lowenthal, 1990).

RESEARCH NEEDS

Job stress research in regard to reference librarians needs to progress past the point of simply assessing the level of burnout and comparing it to that in other professions. More attention should be paid to moderate levels of burnout, and more research should be done on interventions which may reverse this trend before it progresses to the final stage. The profession needs to know more about what factors precede burnout and how they relate to individual personal characteristics, the nature of reference work, and the organizational and supervisory climate.

More sophisticated research should be conducted on the impact of stress reactions on the individual, on reference performance, and on library services as a whole. In particular, research needs to focus on those particular aspects of the job that have been found, in other human service work, to be associated with stress reactions and lowered performance. Questions of particular interest are how workloads, in terms of desk hours per day or week and volume of reference questions per hour, are related to perceived stress reactions, health, absenteeism, turnover, and reference performance. Work speed-up research, such as that done on computer operators, needs to be done (LeMay, Layton, and Townsend, 1990). Also needing study are the effects of interruptions and number or frequency of stressful occurrences across a number of reference departments. Stress reactions, anxiety, anger and hostility, and the burnout syndrome should be studied in relation to the types of interventions that can lead to lowered levels of job stress and improved coping in other human services work.

INSTRUMENTS

Instruments included cover stress (House and Rizzo; Nowack), morale (Lowenthal), and burnout (Maslach and Jackson).

House and Rizzo—Anxiety-Stress Questionnaire
Lowenthal—Morale Inventory
Maslach and Jackson—Maslach Burnout Inventory (MBI)
Nowack—Stress Assessment Profile (SAP)

Chapter 9

Reference Duties and Responsibilities

Ralph Lowenthal and Marjorie E. Murfin

SCOPE

This chapter focuses on the duties and responsibilities inherent to the performance of reference work. Much of this manual concerns how a reference department interfaces with patrons or maintains reference collections. In addition, topics such as reference librarian morale and training are covered. But before training needs or staffing levels can be determined, what reference librarians do—the nature of their duties and responsibilities—must be studied. This chapter shows in general how to determine and measure activities common to all reference departments.

IMPORTANCE OF RESEARCH

Analysis of reference duties and responsibilities can bring benefits in improved reference operations. Such questions as the following can be addressed: How much time are staff spending on various tasks? Which are considered most complex and most routine? Which tasks do staff have the most confidence in their ability to perform? What level of staff should perform various tasks? In which tasks are staff most interested? Only after answers to these questions have been obtained can the first step of training take place and action taken to systematically improve services and workloads.

STATE OF THE FIELD

Overview

Poorly conceived, planned, and executed studies where staff must keep a record of activities can result in ill-advised actions, less effective operations, and staff resentment. Staff may view task analysis as an activity that increases their workload but results in little benefit. They may also feel that the study is being done because supervisors suspect that staff are inefficient and misuse their time. Full staff cooperation must be secured before attempting task analysis; expected benefits and use of results should be discussed.

Task lists and methodologies are available to provide valuable assistance for those interested in analysis of reference tasks. Instruments listed at the end of this chapter represent the various types of task analysis. For information on measuring and assessing costs of reference service, see Chapter 14, "Costs and Outcomes."

Task Frequency, Time, and Costs

Methods that have been employed to study the frequency with which the task is performed and time required to accomplish the task include diaries, random alarm mechanisms, and estimates. Staff diaries require that staff record their activities over a sample period of time. Usually a prepared coded activity list is used. In some cases, the duration of the activity is recorded in minutes; in others, an activity code is recorded for every 15-minute period (Herner and Herner, 1967; Murphy, 1978; Lange, 1986). In contrast to the diary method, when random alarm mechanisms are employed, activities are recorded *only* at the times the alarm sounds (Spencer, 1980). Finally, staff may *estimate*, rather than actually *measure*, the amount of time spent per week in different activities. Murphy (1978) found that staff had fairly accurate perceptions of the *percentage* of time spent on different activities, but not *how often* they performed the activity or *how long* it took. Percentages of staff time and/or numbers of staff allocated to different reference activities have been reported on the national level and are useful for purposes of comparison (Watson, 1986).

Staff Perceptions

Another type of task analysis concerns staff perceptions about their tasks and activities in terms in intrinsic interest, importance, value, complexity, and level of skill required (Duncan, 1974; Reeves, Howell, and Van Willigen, 1977). Performing analysis of staff perceptions and observations of task frequency, time, and costs might obtain the best perspective on the frequency and value of tasks as well as other aspects of reference tasks and activities.

RESEARCH NEEDS

Existing studies of reference tasks, duties, and responsibilities badly need updating. Rapid changes in library technology, increasing emphasis on user education, and widespread decreases in funding have resulted in substantial changes in reference services. As a result, the type and nature of reference tasks and activities has undoubtedly changed; new studies are needed, using the proven methodologies provided above.

Updated studies are needed on the national level of staff time allocations to different reference functions (Watson, 1986). Reference tasks, duties, and responsibilities need to be reexamined in light of modern configurations of reference services. The profession needs to understand how staff perceive certain tasks and how these perceptions are related to stress, morale, job satisfaction, productivity, and quality of reference service outcomes. Investigation is needed to determine how successfully different types of personnel perform various tasks.

Finally, reference tasks, duties, and responsibilities need to be related to costs (Cochrane and Warmann, 1989) and to the quality of reference service outcomes. For example, do certain tasks and responsibilities tend to improve the reference skills of those who perform these tasks?

INSTRUMENTS

Instruments included cover duration of staff activities (Lange; Murphy) and staff perceptions about the nature of their activities (Duncan; Reeves, Howell, and Van Willigen).

Duncan—Survey of Actual and Potential Task Participation of Academic Library Reference Personnel

Lange—San Diego County Library Staff Workload and Reference Training Needs Survey

Murphy—Costing of All Reference Operations

Reeves, Howell, and Van Willigen—Activities Performed in the Reference Department

Chapter 10

Reference Training

Beth S. Woodard

SCOPE

This chapter concerns the evaluation of reference training. Training involves the acquisition of specialized skills judged essential to competent performance of reference services. In other words, reference training develops staff job-related skills and knowledge. A great deal has been written about the education of reference librarians, their continuing education needs, and the training programs for paraprofessionals who provide reference service. However, the evaluation of these training and in-service programs has been studied relatively infrequently in reference librarianship. Much of the library literature on training is descriptive in nature rather than evaluative. It is difficult to evaluate training when librarianship as a profession cannot articulate what constitutes competent performance and there is no consensus on what should be taught. In part, this is due to the complexity of the reference process itself, the difference from one reference collection and environment to another, and the difficulty in accounting for all the facets of training. Competent performance relies heavily on individual professional judgment and is an issue of internal process.

Professional trainers often divide training evaluation into several levels based on Kirkpatrick's model (1979): reactions, learning, job behavior, and results or organizational values and ultimate value. Librarians will find that much of the industry training literature is transferrable.

IMPORTANCE OF RESEARCH

While many in the profession appear to believe that library schools have the sole responsibility for training individuals to become reference librarians, the reality is that a great many people still require on-the-job training to perform well in their jobs. Library schools can effectively address the theory, strategy, and basic sources necessary to do reference work, but they do not train librarians to do reference work in specific locations. Each institution needs to orient individuals to the type of reference work done there, the kind of materials available in the collection, and the policies and procedures specific to that department. Many libraries recognize the need to help individuals learn about their institutions and conduct orientation programs or induction training; however, little actual training is done (Stabler, 1987).

An additional concern is the proliferation of technological advances, which changes the reference environment, necessitating continual adaptation to new sources, new searching techniques, and alternative search strategies. This continuing need for education, re-education, training, and retooling raises the serious question of how well we as a profession are accomplishing this task.

STATE OF THE FIELD

Overview

Jonathan S. Monat (1981, 48) describes evaluation as "a process of set activities comparing results against goals and established criteria." The evaluation of any training program assumes an established criteria such as written standards of competency for reference service. Unfortunately, there seems to be little agreement in this area. Until the profession comes to some consensus on items and levels of competencies, it will be difficult to evaluate reference training in a comparative way. Such competency descriptions should include areas of basic knowledge, deep understanding, skills, values, attitudes, and interest. In recognition of the lack of agreement on the behaviors a librarian ought to exhibit and follow when meeting an individual's information need, Jim Rettig (1992), former RASD president, established an ad hoc Committee on Behavioral Guidelines for Reference and Information Services, with David Tyckoson as chair. Several individuals, such as Tyckoson (1992), Gers and Seward (1985), Schwartz and Eakin (1986), Isenstein (1991), and Layman and Vandercook (1990), have reported initial attempts to identify behaviors that contribute to reference success (Griffiths, 1984). These efforts focus on behavioral outputs. In a notable exception, the Suburban Library System in Illinois (1986) has established a list of standards describing the kind and amount of training necessary for individuals who provide reference desk service.

Because there is no agreement on required proficiencies for beginning or experienced librarians or for paraprofessionals working at reference desks, individual libraries must establish their own internal lists of competencies. It is important for those concerned to agree with these competencies rather than have them imposed from the outside. Once agreement on the desired or required levels of proficiency has been achieved, the gap between existing or actual levels should be identified.

Needs Assessment

It can be assumed that a newly hired employee has no knowledge of local practice and will require at minimum orientation to the facilities, policies, and procedures of the organization (Stabler, 1987). Assumption of competency levels for new paraprofessionals or recent library school graduates, however, should be avoided. Questions sets or other tools to test knowledge and skill levels might be appropriate. An alternative would be to analyze tasks staff perform and design training around activities new employees are expected to complete. Task analysis is discussed in Chapter 9, "Reference Duties and Responsibilities." Another method is to survey and allow staff to choose areas for training. Lange (1986) describes one kind of needs assessment survey and points out that staff do not always recognize when they need training. Tacoma Public Library and the University of Michigan Library have also used extensive needs-assessment questionnaires (LAMA PAS Staff Development Committee, 1992).

Gaps between established performance expectations or standards and an individual's performance cannot always be resolved through training. Creth (1986) notes that a number of factors may contribute to poor performance; the first step should be to analyze the cause of the performance gap, not to rush into a retraining program. She provides a series of questions useful in determining if training is the appropriate action. Training that occurs without establishing relevancy risks redundancy and the fostering of poor participant attitudes. Hernon and McClure's (1987b) study involving training staff in the use of government documents indicated that the workshop covered material familiar to the participants; thus it is not surprising that the study found no significant changes in performance after training.

An effective assessment program to identify training needs should address the following questions: What behaviors constitute competent performance? What tasks do reference librarians perform? What tasks require training for competent performance of reference responsibilities? What is the discrepancy between desired or required levels of proficiency and actual or starting levels of proficiencies?

Staff Reactions

According to Kirkpatrick (1979) and Newstrom (1978), evaluation data must be gathered on several different levels to be useful. Trainee reactions, learning, on-the-job behavior, and the end results or organizational value are the main categories that should be considered.

Learner reactions to the training program must be gathered to determine if the training is relevant and if it addresses tasks or behaviors relevant to the job. Trainees may feel that the content was not appropriate for their levels or positions, or that its design might not be appropriate. Their reactions and attitudes may be measured before, during, and/or after the training sessions. The perceived relevance of the content, the amount of energy needed to learn or ease of learning, and the lack of threat or distraction may need to be measured.

Questions to be answered might include the following: How satisfied with the training were the participants? What were their reactions to program content or curriculum? What are their reactions to methods of training? How valuable was the information conveyed? Was the training relevant to job demands? Did participants perceive that concepts presented were relevant? Was the material well presented, using appropriate teaching methods? Was enough time allowed for training and practice?

How might one go about finding answers to these questions? There are a number of ways this data can be gathered. The typical, most common training evaluation is a questionnaire, which generally consists of a "happy scale" in which trainees indicate whether or not they "enjoyed" the workshop. These rating forms are prevalent in library reference workshops. They are low cost and quickly constructed and administered, but they tend to be based on opinion and need to be validated by other less subjective measures. Participant satisfaction can most easily be gathered using reaction sheets with Likert scales or rating scales. Kenneth Shearer and Duncan Smith (1992) include a number of rating forms as samples. Harold Fisher and Ronald Weinberg (1988) developed a 5-point Likert scale to gather not only information on participant's experience, but also trainer behavior, and answers to open-ended questions. Hittner (1981) includes a four-page workshop evaluation for each of seven modules including rating scales for instructor, methods used, outcomes, and content specific to each module.

Thomas Slavens (1979) developed a 7-step scale to assess attitudinal changes as a result of training. Other techniques that can provide a broader or more in-depth range of reactions can also be utilized. Visual observations—in which trainers monitor facial expressions, eye contact, and level of participation, comments between trainees and to instructors, questions about exercises, and attentiveness—can provide information about trainee attitudes and approaches to exercises. Interviews can gather information about reactions in greater depth than possible in simple reaction sheets. Trainee interviewing should be conducted with a sample of at least ten percent of the class (Tracey, 1992) Focus group interviews are particularly useful in difficult-to-measure areas. Interviews are time consuming but usually develop information and insights not revealed by other methods. Diaries kept by trainees may provide valuable and detailed information about reactions to training.

Although participant reaction is the most common and easiest method of evaluating training, Tracey (1992) observes that positive reaction is not strongly associated with job performance or the amount and kind of resulting organizational change. Consequently, trainee judgments need to be used in combination with other valuative techniques to ensure reliability and validity of judgments expressed.

Participants' Learning

The next level of evaluation identified in the training literature concerns whether or not individuals actually learn from participation in or attendance at a training program. Individuals may have positive reactions to sessions that are entertaining but not informative, or may not be engaged in the process enough to actually learn anything.

The key question to be answered here is whether training produces appropriate learning. More specifically, the following questions need to be answered: What facts, techniques, skills, or attitudes were understood and absorbed by the participants? If participants have learned something, was it from training or from a change in the environment or through passage of time? Was there enough feedback given to participants during the training session? Was there opportunity to practice or model behaviors during the training session? Was the amount of time allotted sufficient for the task? Do the materials developed teach the desired concept? If not, why not?

In order to determine if learning is related to the training program, it is important to learn what knowledge and skills participants have before training. The use of the classic pretest and posttest model is really the only way of determining if participants already had these skills and knowledge or if training is responsible for learning. Further, to ensure that outside factors are kept to a minimum, the use of a control group that has not been given training but has a similar work situation is encouraged. The causality of training is a particularly thorny design issue.

Performance should be measured within the training setting if possible. Hittner (1981) designed workshops to gather data during participatory activities. Obtrusive methods ordinarily are quick, inexpensive, and easy to administer. Paper-and-pencil tests, questionnaires, knowledge tests, job sample tests, simulations, visual observations, oral questioning, group discussion interviews, and rating forms are just a few examples of the techniques that can be used to evaluate the extent of learning accountable to training. While the use of sample sets to answer during sessions aimed at teaching types of sources is fairly common within training sessions, they are rarely "gathered" and analyzed for accuracy and completeness after a training session. Similarly, in sessions where online catalog skills are taught, performance could easily be measured through examination of transaction logs. Just how much knowledge was gained or the extent of skill mastery is rarely measured in reference training sessions, in part because of the complex nature of the reference interview and communication interactions.

On-the-Job Behavior

Even if trainees learn desired knowledge, behavior, and attitudes through training, they will not necessarily use them on the job. Questions that on-the-job behavior training evaluation can address include the following: How well can trainees apply techniques they have learned on the job? Of the concepts that are taught, which are being used? After a period of time, are these skills still being used? Which feedback mechanisms work best in supporting transfer of training? Do peer or mentor counseling systems improve effectiveness? When reference providers do not perform adequately, what are the causes? Are they due to inadequate tools or training, lack of specialized subject knowledge, or to a nonsupportive environment?

The best designs for evaluating on-the-job behavior use pretest, posttest, and control groups (Phillips, 1983; Kirkpatrick, 1979; Tracey, 1992; and Smith, 1980). Stephens (1988) and Gers and Seward (1988) report on the Maryland study conducted in 1983 and 1986, which indicates significant performance improvement through training. This study used pretest, posttest, and control groups to make sure that the changes in behavior were indeed due to training. An even better design would include time-series data, which would retest after a period of time to make sure skill levels are maintained.

Any newly learned skill feels awkward at first; if not reinforced, these behaviors will eventually disappear. The training literature deals extensively with this problem. Deborah Carver (1988) reviews and summarizes this literature for librarians, pointing out that, in addition to sequencing and making sure trainees have mastered one skill before proceeding to the next, action plans, follow-up sessions, and feedback are important techniques to consider after the training workshop is held. Support and commitment by management are important at this stage. Arthur (1990) and Isenstein (1991) describe peer coaching programs to facilitate this transfer. Isenstein notes that management has seen this as important enough to include observation of the behaviors learned in these programs as part of performance evaluation. Environmental factors (see

Chapter 5, "Reference Environment") may also influence the ability to transfer skills to the job setting.

When performance problems exist, an analysis needs to be taken to fully understand if inappropriate training has taken place. Allan and Reynolds (1983) and Salenger and Deming (1982) give models which help determine if training is needed or faulty; if the lack of job aids, feedback, and coaching affects the transfer of training; or if something in the environment interferes with its application.

Kirkpatrick (1979) suggests that on-the-job behavior be measured by as many different groups as possible: the individual receiving training, the supervisor, peers, and subordinates. In the reference situation, library users are also a potential source of information concerning on-the-job-behavior. Questionnaires, diaries, and interviews are obtrusive means to gain information on job behavior from the trainee. Brinkerhoff (1983) suggests that in-depth interviews can give valuable qualitative information about training programs not possible through more quantitative means. Because self-evaluations are difficult to validate, it is suggested that other measures be used as well.

Supervisor evaluation is the most commonly used performance evaluation technique (Association of Research Libraries, 1988; King, 1988; Jenkins and Smalls, 1990) and is potentially the most subjective. Techniques available to the supervisor can also be used by peer groups. Because other librarians or reference staff members are most familiar with an individual's performance, the use of peer evaluation techniques is often suggested in library literature (Schwartz and Eakin 1986). Visual observations using performance-based rating scales (also called "behaviorally anchored rating scales," or BARS) are common.

Subordinates, the last group suggested by Kirkpatrick (1979), do not work well in the reference context, unless one is examining mentoring or supervisory skills. An alternate evaluative group that might be utilized is the patron. Satisfaction measures of library users are covered extensively in Chapter 15, "Reference Effectiveness."

Techniques discussed to this point are all obtrusive. It is common knowledge that the very act of observing or testing someone can change behaviors; thus unobtrusive techniques have become more frequently used and are described in Chapter 15, "Reference Effectiveness." While there are distinct advantages to unobtrusive techniques, they are more difficult to administer, expensive, and time consuming.

Organizational Benefits

The ultimate benefit of training should be improvement of the performance of the organization or increased effectiveness in reference service and patron satisfaction. Questions answered at the organizational level include the following: Of what value was the training to the library? What is the cost of training to the organization? Does the value of improved performance meet or exceed the cost of training?

RESEARCH NEEDS

Reference training is still in its infancy; many areas are in need of research. Competent performance itself has yet to be satisfactorily defined. Many libraries do not conduct training programs (Stabler, 1987) let alone evaluate on any level except reactions. Libraries must collect data on training methods that work best for varied aspects of reference: communication skills, interview techniques, dealing with frustrated individuals, learning new sources in a variety of formats, and devising alternative search strategies. These data should be shared so that librarians can improve training programs.

More research needs to be conducted on the transfer to the job setting of skills and knowledge learned in training programs and in the educational programs of library schools. Coaching has been shown to be a promising technique for learning certain reference behaviors (Gers and Seward, 1988), but this research needs to be replicated in other locations and across longer periods of time to determine the long-term effects and cost-benefits. Little has been written about the impact of practicums and internships in reference education in library schools or on the impact that job swapping may have on appropriate referrals.

The ultimate result of training—such as increased effectiveness in answering reference questions—needs to be measured and analyzed in ways that give comparable data across libraries. Determining the relevancy of training, the appropriateness of techniques used, and the effect that training has on an individual's knowledge, attitudes, skills, and on-the-job behavior are areas for which there remains insufficient knowledge and great need for further research.

INSTRUMENTS

Instruments included cover assessment of training needs and workload (Lange), evaluation of skills (Hittner; Schwartz and Eakin), evaluation of training (Fisher and Weinberg; Hittner) and changes in attitudes as a result of training (Slavens).

Fisher and Weinberg—Training Feedback Questionnaire
Hittner—Individual Rating Scale for Communication Skills
Hittner—In-Service Training Program for Library Paraprofessionals Workshop Evaluation and Pre-Test or Post-Test
Lange—San Diego County Library Staff Workload and Reference Training Needs Survey
Schwartz and Eakin—Checklist of Reference Skills
Slavens—Semantic Differential Scale

Chapter 11

Communication and the Reference Interface

Helen M. Gothberg

SCOPE

Prior to 1968 when the first research about reference as communication appeared by Taylor, the belief was that good reference librarians were born not made. Today the profession recognizes that good reference skills can be learned. It is not enough for librarians to know library resources; they must be effective communicators. Human communication takes place on two levels: the cognitive or content of the message and the affective level or feeling conveyed by the message. Both are important in the reference interview. This chapter will deal only with emotional or interpersonal communications between reference librarians and library users.

IMPORTANCE OF RESEARCH

Much of the early literature on the subject of reference as communication was theoretical. Specific variables that could be tested had to be identified before research could commence. Subjective decisions about niceness or politeness are not researchable or sufficient as indicators of effective communications. At the same time, issues were raised by various writers suggesting that reference librarians were not approachable.

As the discussion broadened, there emerged two approaches to the research. One dealt with the verbal expression of emotion. In this sense, a number of psychological models that had been previously tested in other helping professions were identified. The other area was the nonverbal communication, or body language, used by librarians. Nonverbal communication is a broad area, which includes not only body language but physical appearance and environment. In some of these latter studies both verbal and nonverbal communication were considered.

Some questions posed by research asked if librarians could be trained to improve their communication skills and thereby reference accuracy; whether librarian nonverbal behavior affected the feeling state of the patron; and what environmental factors impacted on meeting the information needs of patrons. Lastly, the need to improve library public relations and the librarian image were explored.

Studying a librarian's interpersonal communication is an important part of reference evaluation. Each of the five reasons Murfin and Ruland (1980) provide to evaluate reference services generally can be applied specifically to interpersonal communications: 1) an increased ability to identify problem areas; 2) a greater base of objective documentation for problem resolution; 3) the provision of comparative bases for assessing the effects of change; 4) the development of standards and guidelines; and 5) the support for needed improvements in inadequate services and/or continued maintenance of good services.

STATE OF THE FIELD

Overview

Two reviews of the literature on the assessment of the effectiveness of interpersonal communication in reference appeared in 1984. Bunge covers both theoretical and experimental literature. Powell's review is limited to a critical appraisal of research in the area of reference effectiveness. Both provide a more extensive look at reference evaluation than can be covered in this chapter.

Nonverbal Communication

Immediacy (Mehrabian, 1971) and kinesics, or body language, are constructs that involve either a combination of verbal and nonverbal communication skills or nonverbal alone. Two early studies in this area were published in 1976. One used both verbal and nonverbal aspects of immediacy to determine whether a patron was more satisfied with the reference interview and the information received (Gothberg). The other study was limited to observed nonverbal behaviors (Kazlauskas). The Gothberg study was empirical and the Kazlauskas study made use of a case study approach. In both studies, nonverbal communication was found to be important in the reference interview. Gothberg found that patrons who received positive or immediate nonverbal communication were significantly more satisfied with the reference interview and with their own participation in negotiating the reference question. No significance was found, however, for satisfaction with the information received.

Some aspects of nonverbal immediacy were used in the Maryland Public Library study (Gers and Seward, 1985). This study attempted to associate a model of reference behaviors with correctly answered questions using unobtrusive testing of specific reference questions. Although there are weaknesses in the methodology of this study, verbal negotiation appeared to carry the most weight, but nonverbal cues were contributing factors. There was an indication that nonverbal cues, such as eye contact, relaxed body posture, attention, and mobility, were factors in the successful outcome of answering patron questions. A later study (Dyson, 1992) replicated the first study to a large extent, although some questions were different. This time a control group was used as well as the pretest group. Another significant and positive change in the methodology of this study was that no one surrogate specialized in one or two questions but covered a mix of questions.

One interesting study involved librarians and touching behavior (Fisher, Rytting, and Heslin, 1976). In this study it was found that a light touch of the patron's hand as they checked out books was perceived positively. Women tended to find this behavior more pleasing than men who were somewhat ambivalent in their responses. Both male and female library clerks were involved in the study, and there were no differences in responses between them. The subjects in this study were students in a university library. The same results might not occur within a public library. Literature suggests that touching is an important but frequently missing behavior in our society. Any library thinking about touching behavior at the circulation desk should replicate this study before deciding whether it is appropriate behavior.

Durrance (1989) made use of unobtrusive testing to make judgments about environmental factors. Durrance found that specific physical arrangements of desks and seating arrangements were less important than the communication about the purpose of that desk and the identity of people available to provide assistance. Signage systems and identification tags for reference staff were important. Some findings of this study should concern the profession. Less than four in ten librarians exhibited friendliness or self-confidence, and only a small percentage made the questioner feel comfortable or demonstrated interest in the patron. Durrance concluded that although accuracy is one measure of success it does not tell the whole story. Other factors need to be measured as well.

Other writers have been concerned with the reference desk, its signage systems, and its height. Larason and Robinson (1984) determined that one reference desk with better identification of its function had many more patrons than a second desk, which did not clearly define its function. Linda Morgan (1980) found that 72% or more of the patrons preferred a counter height desk. It may be that higher desks not only put librarians at eye level with patrons, but also make librarians appear to be more service oriented than those at office type desks.

Interpersonal Models

Counseling skills (Peck, 1975) was one of the first interpersonal models suggested as useful in developing improved relationships between librarians and users. The construct that emerged from this literature, largely dominated in its early stages by Carl Rogers (1957), who first suggested the term, was that of "empathy." The definition of "empathy" is to feel with another person, to be able to put yourself in his or her place. Attentive behavior reflected in good listening skills is also part of the counseling package. A consulting type of listening is sometimes called "content listening" or "active listening." Smith and Fitt (1982) suggested ways of applying active listening skills at the reference desk but did not test the efficiency of this practice in an experimental situation.

A dissertation study done at the University of Toronto (Crouch, 1981) used unobtrusive observation of librarian interpersonal behavior during the reference interview. This study made use of the FIRO-B (Fundamental Interpersonal Relations Orientation—Behavior) scale as a predictor of communication ability. Librarians took the FIRO-B test and then were evaluated for their communication effectiveness using another scale. The communication scale made use for the most part of a series of paired adjectives such as sensitive and insensitive on a 7-point scale. The outcome of this study suggested that the common factor contributing to open communication in the reference interview had to do with control scores. Librarians who wanted control were perceived negatively by patrons.

Another concept that comes from the field of psychology is that of self-disclosure. Thompson, Smith, and Woods (1980) first proposed this construct as a model for reference librarians. Self-disclosure is essentially sharing with another person feelings about something that has been said. Through self-disclosure, the librarian would let himself or herself be known to the patron as a person. Later Markham, Stirling, and Smith (1983) investigated whether self-disclosure would promote patron satisfaction with the reference interview and a willingness to return for reference assistance. They did not find significance between patron satisfaction and self-disclosure, although self-disclosure did seem to be effective in improving some aspects of the interview, especially items related to the librarian's communication.

Social and Psychological Factors

Social and psychological factors play a part in negotiation of the reference question. These are factors that cannot easily be changed. One study (Harris and Michell, 1986) dealt with the effects of gender on observers' judgments of librarian competence. This study had an interesting methodology in that it used videotapes of librarians and asked observers to rate the librarians. One variable in the study, inclusion or the degree to which the librarian instructed the patron in the use of reference resources, evoked differing responses between males and females. Harris and Michell found that female observers perceived librarians who displayed low inclusion to be warmer and more professional than did male observers. The reference interviews taped were described as competent in this study.

Australian researchers (Hatchard and Toy, 1986) looked into psychological barriers in the reference interview. This study asked librarians to identify barriers between the librarian and academic library users. The most important barriers identified included some that could not be easily changed such as language barriers for those students who do not speak English as a first language, students with physical disabilities, and students having to wait for books to be checked out. Other barriers could be changed, such as librarians being completely engrossed in their work, staff use of technical jargon, collections that are poorly organized, and staff inflexibility where rules are concerned. One other factor that supports the findings of Crouch (1981) was that of "Some librarians [being] on a power or control trip tend to 'show off' their knowledge" being ranked as a barrier by other librarians (204).

RESEARCH NEEDS

There has been a considerable amount of research into the nonverbal and psychological aspects of the reference interview. One problem with many of these studies is that the variables have not been tightly controlled. This is difficult to do in this type of study, but the one area that has not been explored sufficiently is the impact of training in these and other communication areas. The profession now has a fairly good idea of how a model reference interview should be conducted. Gers and Seward (1985, 34) have provided us with an excellent checklist of model behaviors that involve both verbal and nonverbal communication skills. Murfin, Bunge, and Gugelchuk have provided the profession with an excellent and reliable evaluation instrument (Murfin and Gugelchuk, 1987). More research needs to be carried out on the impact of training models on reference performance.

INSTRUMENTS

Instruments included cover a measure of user attitudes toward the librarian (Haase) and peer reviews (University of Arizona).

Haase—Counselor Effectiveness Scale
University of Arizona—CRD Reference Desk Performance Standards/
  Peer Review Form

Chapter 12

Reference Librarian Knowledge and Search Strategy

Jo Bell Whitlatch

SCOPE

Knowledge is defined as understanding acquired through experience or study. For a reference librarian the needed knowledge includes understanding of the subject matter of a question and familiarity with reference sources useful in answering a question. Specific expertise or skills in interpersonal communication and the reference interview are covered in Chapter 11, "Communication and the Reference Interface."

Searching is a skill that involves devising strategies appropriate to answering the question. Search strategy includes the study of theory, principles, and practice of making and using search strategies and tactics (Bates, 1979). Strategy deals with overall planning for the whole search as opposed to a tactic that deals with short-term goals and maneuvers. Bates notes that simpler "ready reference" questions are usually answered by mentally retrieving in a second or two the name of a suitable source, going to the source, and getting the answer. Thus, this type of question does not require a conscious search strategy. In contrast to Bates, Ingwersen (1982) avoids the term "search strategy" because it implies prior consideration of the entire process. Ingwersen prefers the term "search procedure" because he regards information search as a problem-solving task, involving trial and error; the search procedures used develop as various alternatives are attempted and result in varying degrees of success and failure. For purposes of this chapter, search strategy is defined as any search process involving plans, procedures, or tactics.

IMPORTANCE OF RESEARCH

Current research studies indicate that reference librarian knowledge and search strategy skills are influential in determining the quality of reference service provided. By studying knowledge and search strategy, librarians hope to identify more precisely types of knowledge and search strategy related to successful reference service. Such information also would be invaluable in designing education for reference librarians.

Research might identify those undergraduate majors that offer the best preparation for reference librarians. Librarians seek to answer the following questions when studying knowledge and search strategy: What knowledge should librarians acquire to ensure high success rates in reference? What search strategies would ensure high reference success rates for particular types of questions? and What alternate search strategies and sources can be used to answer the same inquiry successfully?

STATE OF THE FIELD

Reference librarian knowledge has been measured using a variety of instruments and methodologies. Unobtrusive studies use lists of test questions accompanied by previously identified answers in reference sources. Results from unobtrusive studies indicate that librarians often lack knowledge of sources that have the answers and are available in their libraries. Unobtrusive studies with an emphasis on librarian knowledge are works by Halldorsson and Murfin (1977), Hernon and McClure (1986a), and Woodard (1989). Prepared questions may not be representative enough of questions actually received at a particular reference site. However, Weech and Goldhor (1982) have found that unobtrusive studies may provide slightly more accurate assessments of actual success rates.

Test questions have also been administered obtrusively (Powell, 1978; Benham, 1987). Standard tests—the Graduate Record Examination (Benham, 1987) and the Remote Associates and Symbolic Reasoning Tests (Saracevic, Kantor, Chamis, and Trivison, 1988)—have been used to measure knowledge. Librarian self-assessments of knowledge have also been employed by Kantor (1981b) and Whitlatch (1990a). Murfin and Bunge (1988a) used matching user or librarian questionnaires for each transaction and collected assessments of reference librarian knowledge from both librarians and users.

Controlled experiments conducted by Havener have also improved the profession's understanding of the role format of sources can play in search strategy. Using a controlled experiment, Havener (1988) found that selection of the right format greatly increases chances of effectiveness and efficiency. While online ready reference searches were faster and more successful for bibliographic citation searches, print sources were more successful for source and directory questions. Using graduate students, Havener (1993) has also found significant differences in the influence of format (print, online, ondisc) upon search outcomes.

Studying search strategy is difficult and relatively little has been done. This may be because evaluating search strategy ideally requires personal observation to be able to see and record the entire transaction by a reference expert. Reference work is often fast-paced and much of the search strategy cannot be directly observed because development of the strategy takes place in the mind of the librarian. It is difficult to record the entire question, the context of the question, the availability of key sources, and the verbal information exchanged. This research methodology is labor intensive and requires using highly paid personnel. Another difficulty observed by Bates (1979) is that many reference questions appear to involve a simple matching process and not a search strategy. Given the complexities of the search strategy process, several methods have the potential to enhance our understanding. Unobtrusive reference testing can be used to test the effectiveness of various search strategies; a single question can be administered at many sites with data collected on the order and sources consulted (House, 1974; Hernon and McClure, 1986a). Because much of the strategy takes place in the mind of the librarian and cannot be directly observed, obtrusive methods are also important; librarians answering complex queries could keep records of search strategies employed, including the order and sources consulted, and could collect information on librarian and patron judgments of success.

RESEARCH NEEDS

Study of reference librarian knowledge and search strategy has been limited. Research should be replicated using the aforementioned instruments and methodologies. Research studies should be designed to incorporate several of the different methodologies for measuring knowledge and be administered across several sites. Connell (1991) has used a variety of methodologies to study knowledge acquisition of librarians; her study should be replicated at other sites. Other studies are needed to explore the influence of individual differences on reference success. Studying how the ideal search strategy works when all books were always on the shelf and computer databases were always available and how it works in reality would provide additional understanding of successful search strategies.

A goal of studies involving search strategy should be to design instruments and methodologies that are successful in determining the most effective and efficient search sequences when reference inquiries can be answered with more than one type of tool. Results of such studies could be used to develop procedures and guidelines for selecting the best search strategies.

The profession also needs to carefully consider if present expectations for reference librarian knowledge are realistic in a society experiencing an information explosion. As the amount of information available increases, expecting the human mind to keep track of the contents of all resources is unrealistic (Trautman and Gothberg, 1982). Librarians should conduct experiments with expert systems which are reference databases serving as guides to information within reference sources. Expert systems should provide in-depth approaches to reference tools superior to the catalog.

INSTRUMENTS

Instruments included cover reference librarian knowledge (Hernon and McClure; Kantor; Van House and Childers; Whitlatch), and search strategy (Hernon and McClure; Jahoda).

Hernon and McClure—Reference Question Tabulation Sheet
Jahoda—Instrument for Search Strategy and Development
Kantor—Analysis of Availability, Causes, and Behavior for the Reference Process
Van House and Childers—California Reference Evaluation Form
Whitlatch—Librarian and User Perceptions of Reference Service Quality

Chapter 13

Reference Volume, Staffing, and Accessibility

Marjorie E. Murfin

SCOPE

This chapter reviews a variety of useful methods and instruments for assessing reference desk activities related to volume, staffing, and accessibility. Volume of reference desk activity can be viewed generally in three different ways: as demand, as workload, and as contribution of the reference department to the library in terms of patrons benefited. Staffing involves hours of reference desk services as well as available numbers and types of personnel: librarians, library assistants, and student assistants. Accessibility concerns the ease with which users are able to access reference service.

IMPORTANCE OF RESEARCH

The study of reference desk activity can help to answer questions such as the following: What is the potential demand for reference service? How can reference question workload be assessed? How many users are being reached by reference service? Are hours of opening and desk staffing adequate? Is reference service sufficiently accessible? Are patrons experiencing delays?

No single instrument or method can supply answers to all these questions, but considerable progress has been made in these areas and a number of different methods and some comparative data are now available. Much can be learned from comparing volume and staffing statistics with available norms. A library should use a number of methods and results should be compared to obtain the clearest interpretation. For example, a library might look at the adequacy of its desk staffing by using as many as four different methods.

It is important to gain a full understanding of how demand, workload, capacity, and accessibility are related to each other in any particular library and to be able to document this relationship. This understanding, along with documentation, should help reference heads, reference staff, and library administrators to make sound decisions about hours and staffing as well as other aspects of reference desk activity.

Reference Transaction Counts

Information can be gained on volume, adequacy of desk staffing, and accessibility when the following conditions are observed: 1) using a standard definition; 2) collecting the right supporting data; and 3) properly interpreting statistics in the light of comparable data. Because the definition of a reference question developed by the Reference and Adult Services Division (RASD) was incorporated into a NISO Standard (American National Standards Institute, 1983) and used by the National Center for Education Statistics (NCES) in systems for collecting statistics from academic and public libraries, it is possible to collect consistent reference desk volume statistics.

Measuring and interpreting volume of reference desk activity has presented a number of difficulties. Many libraries seem to be unaware of the potential benefits of observing standard definitions and collecting supporting data on person hours, hours open, and turnstile count. Accurate turnstile counts are sometimes difficult to obtain. Generally statistics collected without adhering to standards are used without supporting or comparative data, for local purposes to determine busy versus less busy times, to study directional versus reference, and to examine walk-in versus telephone questions.

Using local definitions that mix reference and directional questions or that count some reference transactions twice, with the result of inflating the reference transaction count, prevents reference statistics from being meaningfully interpreted and applied (Kesselman and Watstein, 1987). Time and effort are required to collect any statistics on reference desk activity; although adhering to data collection standards may require some additional effort, utilizing such standards is attractive, given the difficulties of interpretation and limited usefulness of locally devised reference statistics.

Finally, libraries may not be aware of or able to obtain comparative data. National reference volume data for academic libraries are collected as part of the Integrated Postsecondary Education Data System (IPEDS) and for public libraries, by the Federal State Cooperative System for Public Library Data (FSCS). These data should be used with care as the reporting unit may represent either main library reference or all library locations. Some comparative figures for both public and academic libraries are also available in several sources (Heintze, 1986; Murfin, 1983; Sager, 1982; Watson, 1986; Goldhor, 1987; *Statistical Report*, 1988-; Rinderknecht, 1992). Other collections and analyses of reference statistics may also be consulted (Fairfax County Public Library, 1987;

Great Britain, Department of Education and Science, 1976; Green, 1976; Houston Academy of Medicine, 1987; International City Management Association, 1979; Kaske, 1980).

Measurement manuals developed by the American Library Association describe and give forms for reference volume data collection by patron report for academic libraries (Van House, Weil, and McClure, 1990), and by librarian report for public libraries (Van House, Lynch, McClure, Zweizig, and Rodger, 1987).

The majority of reference volume data are worthy of analysis. In regard to evidence for the reliability of reference desk volume statistics, Brooks (1982) found that public and academic library reference statistics did exhibit consistent characteristics, were not cyclical in nature, and did not replicate other statistics, such as circulation. He concluded that they were worthy of serious academic pursuit.

Ratio Measurements

Another useful method for assessing reference desk activity is based on ratios derived from already existing data. These measures require only three items of data for a sample week: person hours at desk, number of reference questions recorded, and turnstile count or enrollment. Data are then combined into three measures—termed potential demand or workload, percent of users reached by reference service, and capacity—which then can be compared to national norms. These measures have been sponsored by the ALA-LAMA National Data Collection and Use Committee, Task Force on the Comparability of Reference Statistics, and were introduced at a program presented by that committee in 1988 at the American Library Association Annual Conference in New Orleans. They have been used in several studies (Murfin, 1983; Rinderknecht, 1992) and are included in the Summaries of Instruments section (LAMA-NCDU). Also, the measure of ratio of staff to users has been used or recommended in several studies (Slater, 1981; Strayner, 1980).

Workload and Quality

Reference desk workload can be assessed in terms of total reference and directional transactions (that is, total patron contacts per hour), or in terms of reference questions only. Workload, in either of these terms, can also be assessed in relation to quality. Woodard (1989) has examined quality in relation to single or double staffing. Studies using the Reference Transaction Assessment Instrument (RTAI) examine quality in relation to the librarian's report of being busy (Bunge, 1985). For more information on this, see Chapter 15, "Reference Effectiveness."

Reference Transaction Counts Plus Other Data

There has been a strong desire on the part of reference managers to capture a maximum of useful data *in addition* to simple volume statistics. Some librarians have advocated transaction logs counting each reference and directional transaction during sample periods (Strong, 1980a; Joseph, 1984), while others have used a transaction slip method (Hallman, 1981; King, 1982). The Summaries of Instruments section includes forms by Joseph, King, Murfin and Harrick, and Strong. Both transaction logs and transaction slip forms are useful, particularly in determining whether management goals are being met (King, 1982; Joseph, 1984) and when monitoring increases and decreases in workload. The transaction log or slip method assists in interpreting the data because information on time taken, subject of questions, patron status, sources consulted, and outcome can be collected and then linked to the success of the outcome of each transaction. Demographic data on patrons can come from forms completed by each patron (Bunge, 1985) or be obtained from the patron by the librarian and recorded in the log (Joseph, 1984). Researchers have experimented with a variety of categories for classifying answering sources (Cole, 1946; Jahoda, 1977; Strong, 1980a; Hallman, 1981; Brown, 1985; Bunge, 1985; and Jahoda and Braunagel, 1980).

Validity and reliability of these forms have rarely been tested. Issues of concern include the accuracy with which information is recorded daily or periodically and validity and reliability of categories utilized on the forms, particularly for the recording of two kinds of data: types of questions (Kesselman and Watstein, 1987) and reference outcomes.

Other concerns are related to the difficulty of using the data on types of questions, sources used, and time taken to judge the librarian's performance on a question without some measure of outcome; knowing whether the outcome of a transaction was successful tells librarians a great deal about the appropriateness of sources used and time taken. However, outcome measures may also lack validity and/or reliability. Several studies have noted problems with the validity and reliability of librarian-reported reference fill-rate data (Van House, 1986; Murfin and Bunge, 1988b).

The particular nature of the patron's need, constraints, abilities, and level of familiarity with the subject or library system are usually not fully known or easily recorded by the librarian, and often have a strong influence on the appropriateness of sources used and time taken. These factors make it difficult to use transaction log data on types of questions, sources used, and time taken to determine whether questions were handled appropriately.

The reference environment may also affect the number and type of sources used, for example, when books are off the shelf or in use. For this reason, in addition to outcome data, data on problems in the reference environment are needed if appropriateness of the librarian response is to be judged. For more information on the reference environment, see Chapter 5, "The Reference Environment." For an in-depth discussion of issues involved in classifying reference questions, the reader should consult Chapter 4, "Question Classification." The reader should consult Chapter 15, "Reference Effectiveness," for a detailed discussion of measures of reference outcomes.

Accessibility

Lack of accessibility can be related to an excessive volume of reference questions and insufficient hours of service, as well as other factors such as location of the reference desk, efficiency of operations, and reference policy which may not encourage accessibility. In one instrument, a measure of accessibility has been combined with a measure of quality (Murfin and Bunge, 1989). A number of specific questions arise in regard to problems of accessibility.

Are sufficient hours of service maintained? How many patrons who need reference help would receive it if hours were extended? One method that might be used is that of comparison with other academic libraries (Murfin, 1983; Watson, 1986; Rinderknecht, 1992) and public libraries (*Statistical Report*, 1988-). Also, the ratio measurements described above may be used with the measure of capacity (reference questions per hour reference is open). Norms are given for this measurement (Murfin, 1983; Rinderknecht, 1992). Another method is the experimental extension of staffing. However, unless there is an over-whelming reservoir of demand, it may take some time for potential patrons to become aware that hours have been extended. A further method is to ask users in a general library survey whether the hours of reference service are sufficient (Chwe, 1978), or to judge from the number of reference questions asked of persons other than reference librarians (Carnegie Mellon, 1978).

How many patrons must wait at the reference desk and how long must they wait? How many leave without being helped? These questions have been investigated by observation of the reference desk (Kantor, 1980), queuing studies (Regazzi and Hersberger, 1978), and user surveys. (University of British Columbia, 1981).

How many patrons are discouraged from approaching the reference desk because librarians appear busy? This is a difficult problem to investigate, but it has been dealt with in general user surveys where all those in the library were asked if they asked for help. If they *had* a need for help but did *not* approach reference, they were asked why not and given a choice of reasons. One reason was because the librarian appeared too busy. An experimental study demonstrated that many users will decide not to approach the reference desk when the librarian appears busy (McMurdo, 1982). For more detailed information on this, see Chapter 1, "Assessing Library Services: The Reference Component."

Patrons who *are* able to obtain service may still not be able to obtain adequate time with the librarian. This has been assessed by asking patrons if they got enough time and by comparing this to librarians' reports of time spent per question (Bunge, 1985), or by studying time given each patron at peak and non-peak times (Regazzi and Hersberger, 1978).

Methods of assessment include reference desk observation and more formal queuing studies. These studies provide percentage figures for accessibility and estimates of patron delay time. An excessive volume of reference questions may result in lack of accessibility, as well as inadequate time being given to those patrons *able* to obtain service (Regazzi and Hersberger 1978). This queuing study showed that during busy times, in addition to queues forming, patrons obtaining service received 28% less time per question.

In a general library survey by the University of British Columbia, patrons were asked questions regarding whether they were able to obtain reference service without waiting and whether they left without obtaining service (University of British Columbia, 1984). One general library survey (Chwe, 1978) and one survey of reference users (Bunge, 1985) asked recipients whether they received enough time. In other user surveys, patrons were asked whether they were discouraged from approaching the reference desk because librarians were too busy. For additional information, see Chapter 1, "Assessing Library Services: The Reference Component."

RESEARCH NEEDS

Now that the definition of the reference question (as opposed to the directional question) has been established and accepted, there is a need to build on this foundation and develop a further standard breakdown of reference questions into mutually exclusive categories for use in daily recording. This method should be able to distinguish in a reliable fashion, types, subjects, and complexity level of reference questions. For more information on problems, issues, and developments in categorization of reference questions, see Chapter 4, "Question Classification." Along with this, a standard and meaningful method of recording librarian responses is also needed. Finally, this overall recording method should be simple enough that it could be used for regular daily recording in less busy libraries and for sample surveys in busier libraries. Such a standard method would be valuable for purposes of comparing the nature of reference demand or workload between libraries and between units in a single library, and for determining staffing and training needs. In addition, work on Rothstein's (1984) Reference Activity Measure should be continued, if possible. Some method of representing total reference activity, that is, the total contribution of reference to the library, should be developed.

A start has been made on accessibility research; further research on the national level should build on this foundation, using and improving these methods and developing new ones. An individual reference department needs to be able to compare its accessibility to that of other reference departments in similar libraries across the country. A method of determining comparative accessibility measures across libraries should take into account 1) those who wanted reference service but could not obtain it due to extremely busy staff, staff not visible, no staff on duty (limited hours), or other reasons; and 2) those who obtained reference service but got insufficient time. Finally, research should be done relating accessibility to quality. Research needs to attempt to answer questions such as the following: How can accessibility be increased without decreasing quality? How can quality be increased without decreasing accessibility?

INSTRUMENTS

Instruments included cover accessibility (Kantor; Regazzi and Hersberger; University of British Columbia; University of Colorado; University of California at Riverside; University of Massachusetts), staffing adequacy (LAMA-NDCU Committee), and volume of use (House, Weil, and McClure).

Kantor—Frustration Factor and Nuisance Factor
LAMA-NDCU Committee—LAMA-NDCU Experimental Staffing
    Adequacy Measures
Regazzi and Hersberger—Queuing Study
University of British Columbia; University of Colorado; University of
    California at Riverside; University of Massachusetts—Selected User
    Survey Items
Van House, Weil, and McClure—Building Use

Chapter 14

Costs and Outcomes

Marjorie E. Murfin

SCOPE

Four types of cost analysis methods are of particular interest to reference service: simple costing, cost preference, cost effectiveness, and cost benefit analysis. Simple costing is used to determine how much operations or parts of operations cost; no measure of value received is used. In the other three types of cost analysis studies, a measure of value is used to balance costs. Cost preference, cost effectiveness, and cost benefit analysis can all be used to compare alternative courses of action.

In the cost preference study, a service is judged in terms of where it ranks in regard to *other* activities. The user's overall ranking of (or preference for) a service is taken as the measure of value. For more on this type of study, see Chapter 2, "What Reference Services Should Be Offered?"

In the cost effectiveness study, the measure of value is the overall success of the outcome of a group of reference transactions, as judged by whatever method is deemed appropriate. For more on judgment of effectiveness, see Chapter 15, "Reference Effectiveness."

Simple costing, cost preference, and cost effectiveness studies should never be used to judge the worth or value of an activity. Instead, such studies should be accompanied by a benefit (Wilson, Starr-Schneidkraut, and Cooper, 1989) or cost benefit study to identify the value and worth of that activity before making decisions on its future. In actual fact, recommendations are often made on the basis of costing of operations alone (Robinson, 1986).

In the cost benefit study, the outcome of a group of reference transactions is again judged, but in terms of benefits derived by users as a result of reference service. This method attempts to look past whether the information was found or not found, to benefits to users of having that information, changes made in their lives, and societal benefits in general.

IMPORTANCE OF RESEARCH

The following questions arise in this area: How can the full cost of a reference transaction be determined? How can costs of each operation be obtained? What are the advantages of using program budgeting as opposed to line item budgeting in costing operations? How can overhead costs be determined? Is enough quality delivered to justify costs? Does level of reference librarian performance justify costs? Is reference service worth enough to patrons to justify its costs?

STATE OF THE FIELD

Simple Costing

Substantial progress has been made in costing reference operations. One study costed all reference operations using time spent plus overhead and found unit costs for a reference transaction and 104 other reference tasks (Murphy, 1978). A provocative cost analysis compares the cost of a reference transaction with that of a user education lecture and an online search (Cochrane and Warmann, 1989). In another study focusing on the reference collection in particular, a public library looked at cost per use to determine whether print or online format cost more per use for each of 40 serial reference sources (Anderson, 1987).

Unit costs for a reference transaction have also been figured in terms of costs for different types of reference questions (Spencer, 1980). In all of these cases, cost was figured on the basis of staffing time by minutes or hours spent, plus overhead in some cases. This first method is relatively simple because such cost figures are not difficult to obtain. However, objections are often made that this method does take into account the many costs additional to staffing for reference service, such as costs of the reference collection and continuing education (Lopez, 1973). A second method has been used where the entire cost of reference department operations is divided by the number of reference transactions in one year to arrive at the full cost of the reference transaction (Weech, 1974). This method has also been criticized because the reference department makes many other contributions to the library, and thus all costs of its operations should not be charged to the reference transaction alone (Rothstein, 1984).

A third method is to charge to the unit cost of the reference transaction *only* the portion of costs that go to support that particular activity. For example, the reference collection is frequently used by those who do not ask for reference assistance. The reference collection is maintained for all, not just those who ask reference questions. The disadvantage of this method is that it requires that many items of data be obtained, and some time and effort to calculate is needed (Murfin and Bunge, 1989). This method was used in a study of reference referral systems in California, and costs of $31 per question received were found. These questions were complex and difficult ones, which were referred from other libraries (Robinson, 1986).

Cost Effectiveness

Cost effectiveness measures should be used with care for reference service because they have potential for harm if inappropriately applied. Success may represent value when judged alone, but when *cost* is added to the model, the temptation is great to reduce the costliest parts of the operation, even though these may have the greatest societal benefits. The primary difficulty with cost effectiveness measures is an ethical one. As in the case of hospitals, the persons most in need of help often require the most time and effort and have the poorest prognosis, and thus are the least cost effective to serve. Cost effectiveness measures should *not* be used to judge the worth or value of parts of an activity, but instead to make a worthwhile activity as effective as possible for the least cost. This may mean that when quality is lower than desired, and finances are strained, an exploration of whether quality can be increased without at the same time increasing costs will be necessary. It may also require, in times of budget cuts, an exploration of how to preserve as much quality as possible in the face of less money.

A special library performed a cost effectiveness study in order to improve its effectiveness at the least increase in cost. The reference process was separated into steps and the step at which failure occurred in each transaction was identified. When the major areas of failure had been identified, new procedures were adopted and after a period of time cost effectiveness was checked again. The increase in quality resulting from the changed procedures was found to be proportionately greater than the increase in cost (Wessel and Moore, 1969).

Another method of estimating cost effectiveness suggested by McClure (1984) is cost per successful question. This has been used in several studies; in one study, cost in staff time per successful reference question was found to be $1.83, varying from $.84 to $4.08 for different libraries (Murfin and Bunge, 1989). Another study of retrospective online searches in an academic library found cost per relevant reference to be $.79 but cost per patron's question to be $19 (Standera, 1973).

Cost-effectiveness analysis may also be used to help determine which of a number of alternative methods is the most cost effective in accomplishing a goal. For example, one library compared the cost effectiveness of library tours and computer-assisted instruction (Lawson,

1990). Another study gave reference librarians test questions and compared quality of answers and time taken (which could have been translated into cost) for equivalent print and online sources (Havener, 1988).

Cost Benefit Analysis

Much cost benefit and benefit research has been done in regard to special libraries and information centers and reviewed (Griffiths, 1982). In cost benefit research, it is usual to make an assessment of benefits and then to translate those benefits into dollars to compare them to costs.

A major difficulty in a benefit cost comparison is determining not simply that benefits exist but how great they are and what they are worth. One study illustrates how the benefits of time saved should be estimated; an experimental study determined the exact amount of time saved using the online over the card catalog per search. This time was then valued according to the wages that faculty, graduates, and undergraduates could have earned, and an average was taken (Getz, 1987). This method of valuation is also recommended by Van House (1983).

Benefits may be measured in terms of the value the user gives to the search or assistance, and subsequent benefits from information obtained as a result of the search are then assumed, although they are unknown (Standera, 1973). They may be measured in terms of desirable personal outcomes such as increases in happiness, knowledge, and avoidance of unpleasant outcomes (Flood, 1973; Stuart, 1977; Dervin and Fraser, 1985). Or they may be measured in terms of external benefits, such as time saved, increases in wealth, productivity, creativity and innovation (Kramer, 1971; Jensen, Asbury, and King, 1980; Pitlack, 1980; Getz, 1987).

Benefits may also be measured in terms of the actual, rather than perceived, usefulness of the information, that is, whether or not it was actually acted upon or used in decision making. One study found that 91% of public library patrons used the information obtained as the result of asking reference questions (Goldhor, 1979). Another study found that 46% of clinicians made decisions based on the information obtained from a MEDLINE search (Haynes, McKibbon, Walker, Ryan, Fitzgerald, and Ramsden, 1990). In another study, 45% of users felt their searches had contributed substantially to the resolution of their problem (Saracevic and Kantor, 1988). Finally, impact may be measured by looking not just at whether or how the information was used but at the actual outcome of that use. In a study of clinicians, 92% of those who did searches in regard to a particular problem in patient care reported *some* improvement in patient care as a result of the search (Haynes, et al., 1990). Another study reported that seven lives were saved as a result of MEDLINE searches (Wilson, Starr-Schneidkraut, and Cooper, 1989; Haynes, et al., 1990).

Of the benefit studies done, most concentrate on assessment of benefits and do not continue on to figure costs and make comparisons. Several studies, however, do consider both benefits and costs. In a special library study users were asked how much time they had saved by literature searches, citation, and reference assistance. The resulting estimate of time saved was compared to costs of staff time in answering these questions. It was estimated that, for every staff hour spent on a literature search, engineering staff were saved about nine hours of effort, thus making a benefit cost ratio of 1 to 9 (Kramer, 1971). Murfin and Bunge (1989) assigned benefits in time saved as being seven times cost. Cost per successful transaction was found to be $1.83, leading to an estimate of benefits of about $13 per question. Twelve dollars was subtracted for each unsuccessful transaction, on the grounds that this represented frustration for the patron.

Cost benefit studies have been done more frequently in regard to online searching. An academic library study used patrons' willingness to pay as a measure of benefits they ascribed to the service. On this basis, retrospective searches cost $19 per question and had benefits of $7.50 per question (Standera, 1973). In another cost benefit study in a special library, 53% of clients reported dollar benefits in terms of increased earnings and time saved. A ratio of benefit to cost of about 3 to 1 was obtained (Jensen, Asbury, and King, 1980).

RESEARCH NEEDS

Methods have been developed for costing the reference transaction. These methods need to be refined, and standardized elements of costing data need to be developed with corrections for cost levels in various parts of the country. This might make the process easier for libraries to calculate unit costs of their operations. Cost norms might be made available for types and sizes of libraries in various parts of the country.

Before cost effectiveness analysis can proceed, more needs to be known about factors that affect the quality of reference service and about the relationship between quality, quantity, and cost. Finally, and most importantly, any type of cost analysis should be based on a firm foundation of benefit research. The benefits of reference service should be known and documented. The benefits of time saved, failures avoided, and life goals and satisfactions achieved as a result of reference service urgently need to be explored.

INSTRUMENTS

Instruments included cover simple costing (Anderson; Cochrane and Warmann; Murfin and Bunge; Murphy; Spencer), cost effectiveness analysis (Lawson; McClure; Murfin and Bunge; Standera; Wessel and Moore), cost benefit analysis (Jensen, Asbury, and King; Kramer; Murfin and Bunge), and benefit analysis (Wilson, Starr-Schneidkraut, and Cooper).

Anderson—Cost Per Use of Reference Sources
Cochrane and Warmann—Cost Analysis of Library Service
Jensen, Asbury, and King—Costs and Benefits
Kramer—Cost Benefit Formula
Lawson—Cost Effectiveness Comparison of Two Alternatives
McClure—Cost Effectiveness Measures
Murfin and Bunge—Cost Benefit Formula
Murfin and Bunge—Cost in Staffing Time Per Successful Question
Murfin and Bunge—Determining the Full Cost of the Reference Question
Murphy—Costing of All Reference Operations
Spencer—Cost Analysis for Types of Reference Questions
Standera—Cost-Effectiveness Account
Wessel and Moore—SCORE Cost Effectiveness Analysis
Wilson, Starr-Schneidkraut, and Cooper—Critical Incident Technique

Chapter 15

Reference Effectiveness

Frances Benham

SCOPE

This chapter covers the measurement and evaluation of reference service outcomes. In other words, how effective is reference service that is provided to users? Excellent reviews of the literature of reference evaluation are available (Rothstein, 1964; Weech, 1974; Lancaster, 1977; DuMont and DuMont, 1979; Cronin, 1982; Lynch, 1983; Powell, 1984). Murfin and Wynar (1984) have provided an extensive annotated bibliography of reference service, including evaluation, with coverage through 1982. Consideration here is focused on research efforts since the appearance of studies by Crowley (1971) and Childers (1971) introducing unobtrusive evaluation to library research. Unobtrusive studies and their impact are presented. The public library movement to improve performance through planning, goal setting, and measurement of service activities, or outputs, is reviewed. Obtrusive studies, mixed unobtrusive or obtrusive, and satisfaction studies are reviewed and recommendations for the future are made.

IMPORTANCE OF RESEARCH

In his 1974 *Library Trends* review of reference service evaluation of the previous decade, Weech concluded, as had Rothstein (1964) ten years earlier, with the still unfilled need for standards and guidelines as a foundation upon which reference research might more fully develop. He noted the potential of a relatively new research methodology, unobtrusive testing, as a possible means for gathering data on which national reference service standards might be based. He observed that it had effectively cast doubts on library claims of better than 90% reference accuracy and suggested that a program of nationwide unobtrusive testing to determine appropriate expectations might lead to performance standards. He noted that for this to occur the library profession would have to accept the technique as legitimate and appropriate.

Almost two decades after Weech's review, few of the problems he identified have been resolved. Indeed, the picture has become perhaps more confusing in some respects because of the volume of reported studies, many of them of limited value due to methodological weaknesses, and because of the lack of systematic development of the body of research reported to date. Little replication, common to other fields of research, has occurred in reference studies, with the exception of the unobtrusive testing of reference question response accuracy. In each such study, various input measures (collection size, budget, hours of service) have been correlated with response accuracy. The result has been the clear identification of the troubling problem of response accuracy with as yet no satisfying answers as to why reference librarians do not perform effectively in this area. Comparison of the existing body of research to blind men attempting to define an elephant (Murfin and Gugelchuk, 1987) seems appropriate. Concerns about the need for reference measurement data (Runyon, 1974; Zweizig, 1984) and relative roles and merits of measurement versus evaluation continue to surface with substantial recent attention focused on outcomes measurement and its place in the planning and management of library services (McClure, Zweizig, Van House, and Lynch, 1986; Hernon and McClure, 1987b; Van House, Lynch, McClure, Zweizig, and Rodger, 1987; Childers and Van House, 1989; Van House, Weil, and McClure, 1990). Survey research regarding satisfaction and success of outcomes has opened new lines of inquiry through the examination of reference encounters as viewed by both patron and librarian (Murfin and Gugelchuk, 1987; Whitlatch, 1990a). Overall, the literature reveals encouraging examples of increasing expertise, imagination, and willingness to submit research products for critical peer examination.

STATE OF THE FIELD

Unobtrusive Studies

Many research efforts were fueled by the excitement generated through the initial uses of unobtrusive evaluation. As applied to date in reference accuracy studies, unobtrusive research has only partly fulfilled its early promise. From initial reports by Crowley (1971) and Childers (1971) unobtrusive studies have used correctness on predetermined reference questions as measures of quality and effectiveness. More limited examination has been made of referrals, negotiation skills, search strategy, communications, and response consistency. Generally, unobtrusive studies have attempted, with varying results, to determine the impact of library inputs such as budget or collection data, or type of governance, on the level of output (i.e., accuracy of answers, referrals).

Crowley (1971) in the first recognized unobtrusive library research studied the impact of budget, absolute and per capita, on reference accuracy using unobtrusive telephone testing. Budget data did not predict reference accuracy, and test results were surprisingly low, at an average of 54%. Childers (1971) replicated Crowley's methodology and improved it with a larger sample of subject libraries, more questions, and more sophisticated data analysis. His results were surprisingly similar with 55% response accuracy, though he found some relationships between accuracy levels and strength of resources as measured by total expenditures.

The largest recorded unobtrusive study took place in 60 libraries of Maryland's 22 public library systems (Gers and Seward, 1985). Forty questions were applied in each library for a total of 2,400. Only 55% of the questions were answered accurately. The study sought to answer two questions: 1) To what degree is a hypothetical user of reference or information services likely to receive a correct answer to his or her question? and 2) What levels of resources and kinds of activities are most likely to lead to desired levels of performance? Though this study suffered from serious methodological problems, it did suggest the degree to which librarian reference transaction behavior affects the outcome of the interaction. Subsequent studies have verified this finding and the resulting Model Reference Behaviors Checklist (see Summaries of Instruments: Gers and Seward) has been cited widely. Dyson (1992) revisited the study in an effort to overcome some of the criticisms of the original work.

Childers assisted the libraries of Fairfax County (Virginia), Maryland County (Maryland), and Arlington County (Virginia) in an unobtrusive test of their telephone reference services. Eleanor Jo Rodger (1984a) reported an analysis of the Fairfax County Public Library data (See Summaries of Instruments: Rodger and D'Elia—Reference Accuracy Study). Accuracy results were in line with other unobtrusive telephone information services tests.

Christensen, Benson, Butler, Hall, and Howard (1989) examined the quality of reference services provided by reference student assistants and paraprofessionals using a 5-part management study that included an unobtrusive question test covering fact questions, bibliographic information, and negotiation skills (See Summaries of Instruments: Christensen, Benson, Butler, Hall, and Howard—Evaluation of Reference Desk Service). The authors concluded that extensive investments in training student assistants may not be cost effective given the accuracy level reported. Woodard (1989) also suggests it is questionable whether training needed to bring such staff to a higher level is justifiable.

Myers (1983) brought unobtrusive telephone testing to academic libraries. Responses to 12 predetermined fact questions obtained an accuracy level of 49%. There was evidence that staff did not always make effective use of answering sources available in the library. The Myers study is notable for its careful application and explanations of statistical methods used in the analysis of collected data. Jirjees (1983) applied a simulated test of reference accuracy and case study to a sample of academic libraries, which resulted in an accuracy score of 56.6%. Again, reasons for failure included ineffective use of answering sources owned by the library.

Hernon and McClure (1983, 1987b) broadened the use and potential of unobtrusive testing by examining data gathered by the method for the improvement of reference service. They reported in 1987 their use of combined unobtrusive testing and experimental design as a potentially practical means for self-diagnosing correct fill rate and to explore methods by which libraries might improve their correct answer fill rate, the percentage of test questions correctly answered. Based on four years of unobtrusive testing, Hernon and McClure suggest that correct fill rate is but the tip of a larger iceberg in which quality measures of other information services would shock the profession. They suggest that other areas in need of formal study are interpersonal skills of staff members, accuracy and appropriateness of referrals, costs of various services, use and nonuse of information technologies in the provision of service, and the quality of information services beyond "basic" activities such as the answering of factual or bibliographic questions. Their findings suggested that the most important factors affecting the quality of reference services are individually based (i.e., the attitude and competencies of individual staff members; Hernon and McClure, 1987b).

Hernon and McClure's *Unobtrusive testing and library reference services* (1987b) provides not only the report of two studies, but also a thorough examination of unobtrusive testing, its strengths, its weaknesses, and its potential as viewed by two scholar advocates who view unobtrusive testing as but one approach to reference evaluation, albeit an essential component (McClure, 1984). Their Reference Question Tabulation Sheet (see Summaries of Instruments) is accompanied by detailed instructions for implementation and the exacting requirements of the use of proxies to assure anonymity in the unobtrusive questioning process.

Childers (1978), quoting Webb, Campbell, Schwartz, and Sechrest (1966), viewed the foremost advantage of unobtrusive testing to be, if managed properly, that "the thing being observed will not behave in an unnatural way while it is being observed; and thus one would expect to get a picture of reality." Childers also listed its weaknesses: 1) it is a complicated type of study to manage; 2) it creates uneasiness in many who are hired as proxies; 3) not all kinds of inquiries lend themselves to uniform and simple judgment of responses; 4) the proxies can be exposed; 5) training proxies, developing questions and the criteria for judging them is time consuming; and 6) it is expensive. Hernon and McClure (1987b) added that it may not consider local unique situations, it provides data at one point in time, questions asked may not be representative of those typically handled, not all the reference staff are tested, and testing may not be done on those intended.

Finally, and of major importance, it has not enjoyed widespread acceptance by librarians or library managers. Ethical concerns regarding the testing of people without their knowledge and fears regarding the use of data derived from such testing help to explain the limited use of unobtrusive library tests (Hernon and McClure, 1986b). Concern has been expressed about its limited application to reference response accuracy generally on factual questions and bibliographic citation requests and its failure to examine other reference services commonly provided by libraries (Whitlatch, 1989). Childers (1987) estimated that unobtrusive testing has examined but a small fraction of the range of questions asked and points out that there is no empirical literature linking performance on one kind of reference service to performance on another kind. Tessier, Crouch, and Atherton (1977) and Murfin and Gugelchuk (1987) suggest that the use of only right or wrong answers does not allow for other possible outcomes, such as finding answers within an acceptable range or not finding what was sought but instead finding other useful information.

Despite its limitations, unobtrusive evaluation has provided information previously unavailable. Overall, findings from unobtrusive studies suggest the following about library staff performance: 1) they answer correctly about 55% of factual questions posed; 2) they often fail to refer questions when appropriate; 3) they often exhibit interpersonal communications problems and weak question negotiation skills; 4) they spend fewer than five minutes to answer a question; 5) they often fail to exhibit effective search strategies; 6) they seem not to know the local reference collection well; and 7) they appear often to work under the pressure of a heavy workload and limited staffing (Crowley, 1985; Hernon and McClure, 1987b).

Obtrusive Studies

Obtrusive studies, in which participants agreed to be tested, by Bunge (1967), Powell (1978), and Benham (1987) were not unlike reported unobtrusive tests in that they looked at input measures to understand accuracy on a reference test. Though participants elected to take part, reported accuracy scores fell within the range of unobtrusive test reports. The ability to gather information about individuals tested was believed by Powell and Benham to be an advantage over unobtrusive testing. Each study examined education variables but with somewhat mixed results. That respondents were aware they were being tested was viewed as a weakness of these studies, though they appeared to be easier and cheaper to conduct than unobtrusive testing, and they did suggest that variables related to individual competencies might prove of value in understanding response accuracy.

Bunge's study (1967) compared nine pairs of reference personnel on a number of factors, which he related to effectiveness in answering reference questions. Ronald R. Powell (1978) found that reference test performance was strongly related to reference librarian knowledge. Benham (1987) also found reference librarian scores on a performance test to be related to librarian knowledge.

Mixed Obtrusive or Unobtrusive

Weech and Goldhor (1982) evaluated reference accuracy unobtrusively in five public libraries by using test questions administered by proxies and obtrusively by requesting staff to answer a list of 15 questions. The cost of unobtrusive evaluation was higher than for obtrusive testing. The authors concluded that the method utilized does appear to make a difference, and they urged further examination of this question.

Output Measures

Reference evaluation reviews by Powell (1984) and Crowley (1985) indicated that Weech's hoped for impact through widespread unobtrusive testing had not occurred, and that while unobtrusive research continued to be viewed as significant, if not widely utilized, other trends were being developed. Library managers needed to set objectives and to obtain baseline data for planning and perhaps for evaluation. Generally they had neither the time nor the experience to undertake complex evaluations that might lead to desired library service improvements (Van House, 1986).

Public Library Association efforts to assist public library administrators in planning, goal setting, and collecting measurement data over time to assess possible library services improvement have enjoyed great acceptance by the public library community. *Output measures for public libraries* (Zweizig and Rodger, 1982) has been widely used, praised, questioned, explained, and criticized (McClure, 1984; D'Elia, 1985; Van House, 1985, 1986; McClure, Zweizig, Van House, and Lynch, 1986). With over 10,000 copies bought, the impact of the output manual has been significant because it built on public library management awareness of the need and value of such measures, and it provided simple procedures for computing them. The measures were easily understood, did not require great amounts of time or expertise to gather, compute, or analyze, and could be used in management decisions (McClure, Zweizig, Van House, and Lynch, 1986). The tradeoffs between the quality of the measures, the data produced by them, and the ease with which results were accessible to nonresearch-oriented users was misunderstood by some researchers, who criticized their lack of precision rather than their practical usefulness for library management (Van House, 1986). Though intended for internal use by libraries, it became apparent that the measures also were used for questionable comparisons among libraries with varied characteristics and use patterns within and across library systems. After three years of experience the public library community wanted more information about the measures and their interpretation. In addition, Public Library Association leaders recognized the need and opportunity to improve the measures, to provide more of them, and to provide more information about their appropriate use.

A second edition of *Output measures* (Van House, Lynch, McClure, Zweizig, and Rodger, 1987), also a bestseller, addressed the issues of role choices by libraries and comparative data. Although it encouraged internal comparison over time, recognition was given to the desire to compare performance with other libraries in similar situations. It announced the Public Library Data Service (PLDS) as a means for sharing measurement data from public libraries across the nation. Johnson (1993) revealed the acceptance of this service by reporting that most public libraries serving over 100,000 residents have supplied data to PLDS. A minority of libraries have chosen to report fill rates and document delivery, with most choosing to report circulation per capita, collection turnover, and reference transactions per capita. As a measure of service quality, Reference Completion Rate (see Summaries of Instruments: Van House, et al.), a librarian evaluation measure of successfully completed reference transactions, was among the least reported measures (Johnson, 1993).

In 1990 the Association of College and Research Libraries released *Measuring academic library performance: A practical approach* (Van House, Weil, and McClure, 1990), which was designed to assist academic libraries in the development of measurement data similar to that provided for public libraries through *Output measures*. Also a strong seller, its actual use has yet to be documented in the literature. Among its measures, Reference Satisfaction Survey (see Summaries of Instruments: Van House, Weil, and McClure) was included to provide data indicating the patron's level of satisfaction with relevance of information provided, amount of information provided, completeness of the answer received, helpfulness of the staff, and overall satisfaction. The measure was not intended to suggest causes of failure and readers are referred to Murfin and Gugelchuk (1987), Hernon and McClure (1987b), and Kantor (1981b) for assistance in this area.

Satisfaction or Success Measures

Patron satisfaction surveying had suffered disrepute with the initial findings of unobtrusive studies. Nonetheless, questions of librarian or patron relationships, especially related to whether patrons obtained satisfactory service, continued to be raised, casual surveys continued to be made in libraries, and researchers continued to seek information about the reference process.

Kantor (1981b) analyzed reference questions and identified four success measures: librarian's judgment of success, patron satisfaction, use of proper reference procedures, and accurate information. Five behavioral categories were developed to manage response: 1) librarian decided to try again or to renegotiate question, 2) librarian gave up, 3) librarian referred question, 4) patron quit, and 5) patron was satisfied. Kantor attempted to identify factors that could explain outcomes.

D'Elia and Walsh (1983) reported a public library study which demonstrated that user satisfaction is potentially useful for evaluating service performance within a library; because user satisfaction is affected by demographic characteristics of the users, it should not be used to compare performance for libraries serving different communities.

Gothberg (1976) demonstrated in a public library study that patrons were able to separate satisfaction with question negotiation from satisfaction with information found. Tagliacozzo (1977), in a study of MEDLINE users, found them able to distinguish between search helpfulness, usefulness, and resulting relevant references. The author suggests that surveys of user satisfaction should not be limited to an overall judgment, but should tap various aspects of the user's response to his or her information request. Auster (1983) and Tessier, Crouch, and Atherton (1977) indicate that user satisfaction is multidimensional and the user is a rich source of data to be tapped if all dimensions are to be identified. Auster suggests a set of questions, rather than one question, in surveys of user satisfaction.

Outcome studies of patron satisfaction, generally collected through surveys, are vulnerable to criticisms regarding questions of validity and reliability. D'Elia and Walsh (1983) indicate three areas of concern: 1) face validity (assumed when an instrument measures the variables it purports to measure, and when the instrument and the situation in which it is used are accepted by the subjects as reasonable); 2) content validity (assumed when the researcher can demonstrate that the content of the instrument samples adequately the subject matter about which conclusions are to be drawn); and 3) construct validity (assumed when the researcher can demonstrate through empirical corroboration that the instrument is measuring the psychological construct it claims to measure). Corroborating evidence can be demonstrated by showing systematic differences among groups responding to key questions in the survey. Questions of reliability (assumed when data elements are collected and measured in the same way over time and by all involved) become important with the repeated use of instruments (Van House, Lynch, McClure, Zweizig, and Rodger, 1987).

A major question of reference librarianship has been the poor performance reported by unobtrusive testing and the high levels of patron satisfaction also widely reported. Researchers suggest that patron evaluation is not valid because patrons, for example, positively biased toward the librarian, reflect their bias on patron surveys (Kantor, 1982; McClure, 1984; Weech, 1984; Zweizig, 1984).

Murfin and Gugelchuk (1987) observed that the literature of reference librarianship from 1976 through 1982 suggested that problems in reference services may be solved through focus on the individual librarian. During that period studies of reference personnel increased tenfold and covered such aspects as personality characteristics, concepts and attitudes, cognitive styles, and the role of the reference librarian in the communication process. Murfin and Gugelchuk further observed the trend since 1975 of focus on outcome studies, with 29 appearing in the literature. Of these 55% utilized unobtrusive observation, 21% utilized librarian judgment only, and 24% utilized judgment by the librarian and the patron. Among studies of the outcome of online searching, 81% utilized patron judgment, 5% utilized patron or librarian judgment, and 14% examined precision and recall.

Research available on user satisfaction suggested to Murfin, Bunge, and Gugelchuk the need for a potentially more adequate satisfaction survey instrument (Murfin and Gugelchuk, 1987). Their Reference Transaction Assessment Instrument (RTAI) (see Summaries of Instruments) was designed to 1) control possible bias in favor of the reference librarian; 2) prevent rater uncertainty in judging success by using precise and specific language in survey items; 3) prevent rater uncertainty in judging success of a scale with six anchored points; and 4) prevent blurring of the rating of success with other outcomes by providing separate ratings for a) success in finding what was wanted, b) satisfaction with the information or materials found or not found, c) satisfaction with service (helpfulness), d) amount learned, and e) communication difficulty. Instrument development was based on the work of Cronbach (1950) and Cuadra and Katter (1967).

The scoring system for RTAI was designed to add controls for positive bias. The criterion for complete success required three conditions: 1) that the patron mark "found just what was wanted" on the success scale; 2) that the patron mark yes on the satisfaction scale; and 3) that there be no marks for any of the nine listed reasons for dissatisfaction. With regard to the six service items (understood what was wanted, enough help, time, courtesy, clear explanations, knowledge), a partly negative mark by the patron was grouped with fully negative marks as "less than completely satisfactory" on that item (Murfin and Gugelchuk, 1987). The authors made no effort to address the question of whether patron judgment of success is sufficient, in and of itself, as the criterion for success. They accepted the view that, given the current state of knowledge about human behavior, the patron is in the best position to know his or her own needs, motivations, abilities, and constraints, factors the librarian cannot grasp. Lancaster (1984) identified 55 possible influencing factors and added the potential for chance to intervene. For the RTAI to have content validity it would need to reflect that complexity (D'Elia and Walsh, 1983). Also, it is assumed that the purpose of a survey of user satisfaction is potential service improvement. In designing the RTAI, the authors sought to include variables that might help in understanding possible failures. These included input, surrounding conditions, process, and outcome (Murfin and Gugelchuk, 1987). A librarian form was developed based on input and process variables suggested by previous studies, by reference librarians, and by experts, and judged by the authors to affect the outcome of the reference transaction. The librarian's form is longer than the user's survey, but it was believed necessary to achieve the best interpretation of results.

Murfin, Bunge, and Gugelchuk (Murfin and Gugelchuk, 1987) thus sought to manage the multiple dimensions of a reference transaction by separating ratings of service from those of success in finding what was wanted by including in a questionnaire ratings for success in finding what was wanted, satisfaction with the information or materials found or not found, and satisfaction with service (helpfulness, for instance), amount learned, and communication difficulty (Cronbach, 1950; Cuadra and Katter, 1967; Gothberg, 1976; Tagliacozzo, 1977). To attempt to overcome criticisms of self-reporting (Hernon and McClure, 1987b), they developed stringent requirements for determining success. Bunge and Murfin (1987) developed a quick turnaround automated scanning service for RTAI data for public and academic libraries. Forms are made available on request for library use; when returned to the authors the library receives its profile with data for each item in the profile all libraries of the same size and type, the top-scoring library in that size group, and all libraries in the sample.

Whitlatch (1990a), drawing on research efforts from business, psychology, sociology, and other disciplines, utilized a systems view including librarian and patron perceptions of reference transactions focusing on user satisfaction to determine whether information received was relevant, useful, complete, and sufficient, and the overall satisfaction and overall value of the reference service transaction (see Summaries of Instruments: Whitlatch—Librarian and User Perceptions of Reference

Service Quality). Whitlatch's book, *The role of the academic reference librarian* (1990b), is particularly rich in its consideration of relevant research literature on the reference environment, reference service effectiveness, service orientation of reference librarians, expertise of reference librarians, and reference librarians as communicators.

Whitlatch observed that as our society moves from a manufacturing-oriented to a more service-oriented economy, service organizations take on more importance in daily life. Researchers in business, psychology, and sociology have begun to examine the results of service organizations in light of previously developed knowledge about the products of manufacturing. The similarities and, particularly, the differences in manufactured and service products offer insights useful to service-oriented organizations like libraries (Whitlatch, 1989, 1990b). She notes that service products, unlike manufactured goods, are produced through client and service provider interaction.

Findings from business, psychology, and sociology suggested to Whitlatch (1989, 1990b) the study of reference effectiveness with the service encounter as the unit of analysis and assessing the service outcome as a joint product of the client and service provider. The results of this pilot study suggested possible improvements in service effectiveness through 1) a system that matches user information need to librarian subject expertise and 2) more staff training in eliciting user feedback and appropriate interpersonal skills (courtesy, interest, helpfulness). The selection and retention of staff who demonstrate such service orientations are vital. Finally, systems problems that interfere with user ability to obtain needed information should be addressed (Whitlatch, 1990b). Whitlatch's work provides an example of an effort to build on previously reported research to gain insight on reference effectiveness through exploration of a number of its dimensions.

RESEARCH NEEDS

The field of reference evaluation is confounded by simultaneous efforts to develop standard management measurement methods and procedures and to develop research that might explain and ultimately help the profession overcome problems such as those uncovered by unobtrusive testing. Hernon and McClure (1987b) have urged the profession to bear in mind that measurement may lead to evaluation and evaluation usually requires measurement, but the two processes are not the same. D'Elia (1985) demonstrated how measurement data can be interpreted incorrectly with the potential for poor management decisions.

Efforts to encourage effective measurement within libraries have gained wide acceptance (Van House, Lynch, McClure, Zweizig, and

Rodger, 1987; Van House, Weil, and McClure, 1990) and these should be continued. A recurring criticism of output measures has been that they were developed without a systematic foundation for selecting measures chosen, nor was there a systematic foundation for choosing included measures over other possible measures (Childers and Van House, 1989; Van House and Childers, 1993). Knowledge developed in management science defines effectiveness as multidimensional with no one definition appropriate for all organizations. This evidence suggests that no single definition of or approach to organizational effectiveness is inherently valid. Four models of organizational effectiveness are posited: a goal model, a process model, an open systems model, and a multiple constituencies model. Each model represents different aspects of an organization's effectiveness, but the aspects may overlap. Using these models, Childers and Van House (1989) conducted a national study to define effectiveness for public libraries. Of the top six service-oriented measures, none is matched in practice by a clear and widely shared performance measure. This work suggests how research can help the profession develop valid measures to describe library effectiveness, to set service objectives, and to begin to measure them. It is hoped that such efforts will be extended to other types of libraries.

The teaming of library practitioners and researchers is an encouraging sign for the future. Such teams as Murfin, Bunge, and Gugelchuk (Murfin and Gugelchuk, 1987), Murfin and Bunge (1988a), Van House, Lynch, McClure, Zweizig, and Rodger (1987), and Van House, Weil, and McClure (1990) indicate opportunities to assure that practitioner concerns are understood and considered along with the potential for greater use of rigorous research methods in evaluation efforts.

Another area of research that has received attention recently and which should be encouraged is the reference process, as well as outcomes of that process as viewed by those most intimately involved, the reference librarian and the library user. In studying user success, factors that have been found to be influential are expertise of individual staff (Halldorsson and Murfin, 1977; Benham, 1987), staff judgments of the importance of users' requests and of the status of users (Naegele and Stolar, 1960), feedback or knowledge of results (Gers and Seward, 1985; Whitlatch, 1990b), and interpersonal skills of individual librarians (Vathis, 1983; Michell and Harris, 1987; Durrance, 1989). These factors and their relationship to user judgements of satisfaction and success should be part of future research studies. The research literature cautions that self-reported data by any group of individuals should be immediately suspect, the limitations of such data recognized, and proper safeguards employed (Hernon and McClure, 1987b). Murfin, Bunge, and Gugelchuk (Murfin and Gugelchuk, 1987) and Whitlatch (1990b) have chosen to work in this difficult arena paying careful attention to such admonitions while attempting to build new understanding of complex human behavior. Murfin and Gugelchuk's RTAI norms-based questionnaire has been used in 178 libraries around the country. Whitlatch has brought to the attention of the library profession information on research-based findings from business, psychology, and sociology and applied them to reference evaluation. These thoughtful efforts to seek knowledge by building on existing research findings are encouraging and similar efforts are needed.

Unobtrusive testing continues to be regarded among researchers as one of the significant contributions to library research and evaluation. To date it has not been well accepted by the profession, perhaps because of its focus on reference accuracy. If unobtrusive research is to meet its early hopeful promise, it may need to seek new areas of success focusing on reference service factors that do not include reference accuracy. Successful application in another area may help to create the acceptance this methodology needs to help the profession overcome concerns it originally brought to light.

Future researchers should attend to the use of research terminology, carefully defining terms used to describe their work, and to the degree that it may be possible, it is hoped that definitions used will become standardized. Finally, the need for additional research is evident. Research should be reported in enough detail and with the clarity needed for replication, a significant need in reference research. It is hoped that evaluation of reference service outcomes will continue apace, and that at least some of the questions that continue to concern the profession may be put to rest, with improvements in the provision of reference services a result.

INSTRUMENTS

Instruments included cover unobtrusive measures (Christensen, Benson, Butler, Hall, and Howard; Fairfax County Public Library; Gers and Seward; Hernon and McClure), reference fill rate (Van House, Lynch, McClure, Zweizig, and Rodger), and satisfaction or success measures (Murfin, Bunge, and Gugelchuk; VanHouse, Weil, and McClure; Whitlatch).

Christensen, Benson, Butler, Hall, and Howard—Evaluation of Reference
    Desk Service
Fairfax County Public Library—Reference Accuracy Study
Gers and Seward—Model Reference Behaviors Checklist
Hernon and McClure—Reference Question Tabulation Sheet

Murfin, Bunge, and Gugelchuk—Reference Transaction Assessment
   Instrument
Van House, Weil, and McClure—Reference Satisfaction Survey
Van House, Lynch, McClure, Zweizig, and Rodger—Reference
   Completion Rate
Whitlatch—Librarian and User Perceptions of Reference Service Quality

Annotated Bibliography

Agada, John. (1984). Studies of the personality of librarians. *Drexel Library Quarterly* 20, 25-45.

The librarian personality has been a subject of interest since 1948 when the Public Library Inquiry suggested that there is a relationship between personality and the choice of librarianship as a profession. This article reviewed personality studies and observed changes in theories and methods of measurement that have taken place over the last 35 years. The author also presents a brief overview of the different approaches to understanding personality and a summary of the theories of vocational choice as related to personal traits and characteristics of personality.

Allan, Ann, and Reynolds, Kathy J. (1983). Performance problems: A model for analysis and resolution. *The Journal of Academic Librarianship* 9, 83-88. Also published in Lindsey, Jonathan A. (Ed.) (1986). *Performance evaluations: A management basic for librarians* (p.198-208). Phoenix, AZ: Oryx Press.

After the performance evaluation is conducted and problems have been identified, this model can be used to analyze why the problem exists. When used in conjunction with job standards, it can determine if more training is needed, if job aids need to be created, or if lack of feedback or practice contributes to ineffectiveness or decrease in performance. Nonsupportive supervisors or environments can also be identified.

Altman, Ellen. (1982). Assessment of reference services. In Gail Schlachter (Ed.). *The service imperative for libraries*. Englewood, CO: Libraries Unlimited.

Contains an excellent overview of the classification of reference questions. Altman notes that the process of analyzing reference questions by categories (i.e., time required to answer, source used, purpose of question, type of questioner, and type of question) have been in use in libraries since the 1920s. She questions the usefulness of the collected data in determining how to improve reference service.

American National Standards Institute. (1983). *American National Standard for Library and Information Sciences and related publishing practices: Library statistics*. New York: American National Standards Institute (now National Information Standards Organization). (NISO Z39.7-1983).

Defines the reference transaction as "an information contact that involves the use, recommendation, interpretation, or instruction in the use of one or more information sources, or knowledge of such sources, by a member of the reference or information staff." Information sources include 1) print and nonprint materials; 2) machine-readable databases; 3) the library's own bibliographic records, excluding circulation records; 4) other libraries and institutions; and 5) persons both inside and outside the library.

Anderson, Charles R. (1987). Budgeting for reference service in an on-line age. *The Reference Librarian* 19, 179-201.

A study was conducted in a public library of the cost per use of 40 serial reference books over a three-week period. In regard to printed sources, it was found that 27% of the sources accounted for 80% of the uses. The annual estimated use of these sources was 692 uses per year or an average cost (based on subscription price only) per item use of $9.10. Individual costs per use ranged from $1.81 to $58.50. A further study was then done comparing the cost of print sources to costs for online searches. Six hundred online searches were analyzed and costs were compared. **See Summaries of Instruments: Anderson—Cost Per Use of Reference Sources.**

Anderson, Margaret. (1988). Unobtrusive testing and library reference services. *Information Processing and Management* 24, 606-607.

One would be justified in criticizing the exclusive use of unobtrusive testing for evaluation of reference services, but the findings of Hernon and McClure, carefully documented and set out here, go a long way to encourage its use as one of our evaluation tools.

Anderson, Paul M. (1983). *A study of collection use at the University of Cincinnati Central Library*. (ERIC Document Reproduction Service No. ED 241 069).

This 1982 study measured in-house and circulation use by LC classification to select titles for retrospective conversion and remote storage housing. It found less use of serials and more use of older materials in humanities.

Ankeny, Melvon L. (1991). Evaluating end-user services: Success or satisfaction? *Journal of Academic Librarianship* 16, 352-356.

This study of 600 end-users of Business Connection and Dow-Jones News Retrieval asked users to rate success in finding exactly what was wanted on a six-point anchored success scale and satisfaction with what was found on a three-point scale. It was found that exactly what was wanted was found 43% of the time and 59% were satisfied, similar to findings of the relationship of success and satisfaction in other studies. They were also asked to rate these online services on a five-point continuum scale anchored only with "high" and "low." In regard to this scale, the *highest* category corresponded very closely with success in finding exactly what was wanted as measured by the more discriminating scale mentioned above (45% compared to 43%). However, the *next-to highest* category, with 37 percent, was very prone to inflation; a total of 82% rated the services high or next-to-high, much higher than either success (43%) or satisfaction (59%) measured on the more discriminating scale would warrant. This second category was clearly inflated in regard to representing success, since 75% of those who marked it also reported that they were unsuccessful. On a two-category "yes-no" success scale, used in a preliminary study, 78% reported that they had found what was wanted. On the final study, using the six-point anchored scale, only 43% reported finding exactly what was wanted. **See Summaries of Instruments: Ankeny—Database Questionnaire.**

Arrigona, Daniel, and Mathews, Eleanor. (1988). A use study of an academic library reference collection. *RQ* 28, 71-81.

Determines use of reference by subject. Findings showed librarians consulted different classifications than did unassisted patrons, while both patrons and librarians followed similar patterns within subject areas. **See Summaries of Instruments: Arrigona and Mathews—Reference Collection Use Study.**

Arthur, Gwen. (1990). Peer coaching in a university reference department. *College & Research Libraries* 51, 367-373.

In 1989, Temple University's reference department implemented a peer coaching program to reinforce training in positive reference behaviors, using the premise that exhibiting these behaviors would improve the accuracy of their reference service. Arthur reports positive attitudes, increased recognition of positive communication behaviors, increased self-awareness, and increased reinforcement of positive desk behaviors. Insights are shared regarding the development and coordination of such a program.

Association of Research Libraries. (1988). *Performance appraisal in research libraries*. (SPEC Kit 140). Washington, DC: ARL.

Contains documents on performance appraisal concerning criteria, peer review, and merit increase review.

Auster, Ethel. (1983). User satisfaction with the online negotiation interview: Contemporary concern in traditional perspective. *RQ* 23, 47-59.

Tighter budgets and increased need for accountability have forced library managers to examine the efficiency and effectiveness of their services. In the areas of online reference services, this means, among other things, ensuring that user needs are satisfied. This article reviews the online negotiation process and the interview in the reference process before zeroing in on specific aspects of the online negotiation interview and user satisfaction. The theoretical and methodological framework for user satisfaction studies stemmed from the social and behavioral sciences, especially those dealing with communication theory, group interaction, and verbal and nonverbal behavior. Future studies should focus on areas that have been recognized as important by concentrating on specific behaviors exhibited by the search analyst and their relationship with the satisfaction of the user employing techniques of the social and behavioral sciences that have been shown to be effective.

Auster, Ethel, and Lawton, Stephen. (1984). Search interview technique and information gain as antecedents of user satisfaction with online bibliographic retrieval. *Journal of the American Society for Information Science* 35, 90-103.

An experiment was conducted to determine the effect on user satisfaction of different interview techniques, such as open and closed questions. For assessing user characteristics and responses, a 33-item questionnaire was used covering the user's extent of knowledge before and after the search, new citations found, plans to read citations, additional information needed, value placed on new knowledge, consequences of missed information, and effects on the user's associates of failure or success. It was found that user satisfaction was higher when the search analyst used methods such as empathy, nonverbal expressions, and open and closed questions, and loosely structured the interview into five stages. Important user variables were stock of knowledge, ability to express content, and type of information needed and value placed on information. **See Summaries of Instruments: Auster and Lawton—User Responses to Online Search Requests.**

Bailey, Bill. (1988). Unobtrusive testing and library services. *Journal of Academic Librarianship* 14, 37-38.

The authors expand on what they have already learned about reference staff performance through the use of unobtrusive testing. Now the reader is in possession of all the facts concerning unobtrusive testing and can better assess its importance.

Baker, Sharon L., and Lancaster, F.W. (1991). *The measurement and evaluation of library services* (2d ed.). Arlington, VA: Information Resources Press. Revision of Lancaster (1977).

Chapter 5, "Evaluation of in-house use," is of particular value for reference collections.

Balay, Robert, and Andrew, Christine. (1975). Use of the reference service in a large academic library. *College & Research Libraries* 36, 9-26.

Balay and Andrew designed a form based on type of inquiry classified by source. Major categories used were general information, library directions, card catalog, bibliographic, book order files, data, Yale dissertations, referrals, interlibrary loans, stacks, library instruction, and other. They noted that considerable judgment was required in completing the form and that librarians were instructed to exercise their best professional judgment in choosing inquiry type. Interesting results related to type of inquiry were that very few (6.3%) inquiries were for data. Also, 10.7% of all questions in the general information and library directions categories required three or more minutes to answer. Therefore, it cannot be assumed that an information/direction question always permits a rapid answer.

Ballard, Thomas H. (1989). Planning and output measures. *Public Libraries* 28, 11-13.

Ballard calls attention to the existing body of user studies results which indicate that community characteristics determine use levels of libraries. He states that *Output measures for public libraries* ignores these findings which have been consistent over time. He notes that Illinois and New Jersey plan to tie library support to results of these measures without consideration of the adverse impacts for libraries serving poor and/or minority communities.

Barlow, S.H. (1938). A suggestion for estimating use of the reference library. *Library World* 41, 29-31.

An older study which suggests recording questions asked and classifying them as to type and decimal classification to show areas most used and staffing needed.

Bates, Marcia J. (1971). *User studies: A review for librarians and information scientists.* Washington, DC: Educational Documents Information Service, 1971. (ERIC Document Reproduction Service No. ED 047 738).
Reviews library users studies covering catalogs, reference services, circulation, browsing, use of library facilities, and information-gathering habits of scientists and the general public.

Bates, Marcia J. (1977). Factors affecting subject catalog search success. *Journal of the American Society for Information Science* 28, 161-169.
Reports results of a study of subject catalog use in an academic library catalog. In a laboratory setting reproducing a real search situation, 20 students searched for subjects in economics, psychology, and librarianship. The match between their terms and those used by the Library of Congress subject headings was studied. Catalog familiarity had a positive effect on success, while subject familiarity had a negative effect. The author reports that, on the whole, success was low.

Bates, Marcia J. (1979). Information search tactics. *Journal of the American Society for Information Science* 30, 205-214.
Briefly reviews the literature of human information search strategy. Defines four models of information search strategy and discusses 29 search tactics.

Bates, Marcia J. (1981). Search techniques. *Annual Review of Information Science and Technology* 16, 139-169.
Jahoda's conclusion that it is difficult, if not impossible, to automate the processes involved in question analysis and search strategy development still holds.

Bauner, Ruth E. (1978). Library use and the perceptions of student library users at Southern Illinois University-Carbondale. Doctoral dissertation, Southern Illinois University at Carbondale. *Dissertation Abstracts International* 39, 6379A.
Concluded that library use increases each year a student is in a college or university. Despite lack of consensus on relationship between library use and grade point average, greater academic achievement is linked to increased library use.

Bawden, David. (1990). *User-oriented evaluation of information systems and services.* Brookfield, VT: Gower Publishing Company.
Reviews types and philosophy of evaluation in general.

Beeler, M.G. Fancher, Grim, Jerry, Herling, John P., James, Stephen, Martin, Miles W., and Naylor, Alice. (1974). *Measuring the quality of library service: A handbook*. Metuchen, NJ: Scarecrow Press.

Directed toward practicing librarians; noted that no standard measurements had been developed for libraries to date. Reviews general data collection methods and measuring techniques for libraries, including failure at the shelf. Section on "How to conduct a use survey" (p. 101-105) helpful for reference adaptation. Forms included.

Benham, Frances. (1987). A prediction study of reference accuracy among recently graduated working reference librarians (1975-1979). In *Success in answering reference questions: Two studies*. Metuchen, NJ: Scarecrow Press.

Benham found reference librarian scores on a reference performance test to be related to librarian knowledge as measured by total correct sources named, Graduate Record Examination Quantitative score, hours on reference desk per week, and number of years in reference work since earning the MLS; 244 librarians answered 12 test questions. The mean average of correctly answered test questions was 52.7%. Benham's research suggests that expertise is an important factor in obtaining accurate reference answers.

Benham, Frances. (1988). Book Review: Unobtrusive testing and library reference services. *Government Publications Review* 15, 177-179.

In her review, Benham observes that Hernon and McClure have provided a lucid text that makes the intricacies of performance evaluation available to a wide audience.

Berelson, Bernard. (1949). *The library's public*. New York: Columbia University Press.

Summary of public library use studies done between 1930 and 1947. Of historical interest.

Bichteler, Julie. (1986). Human aspects of higher technology in special libraries. *Special Libraries* 77, 121-28.

Bichteler investigated special library employees who spend considerable time in computer interaction. She discusses effects and proposes solutions to technostress.

Binkley, Dave, and Eadie, Tom. (1988) *Evaluation of reference service at the University of Waterloo; 1985*. (CACUL Occasional Paper Series No. 1). [Ottawa]: Canadian Association of College and University Libraries.

The University of Waterloo conducted a survey of the effectiveness of reference service in 1985 with 246 forms being returned, for a return rate of 87%. During selected survey periods every user of reference was given a questionnaire. Among other questions, students were asked what they expected the person at the information desk would do for them, with alternatives of being given their information or receiving explanations of how to conduct their search. The library's philosophy was strongly geared to the latter. Students were then classified as self-servers or dependents. Ninety-two percent of students reported themselves as being self-servers. However, in the same survey only an average number strongly agreed that the service "lived up to their expectations," and a less than average number strongly agreed that the assistance was exactly what was needed.

Binkley, Dave, and Eadie, Tom. (1989). *Wisconsin-Ohio reference evaluation at the University of Waterloo.* (CACUL Occasional Paper Series, No. 3). [Ottawa]: Canadian Association of College and University Libraries.

Describes use of the Reference Transaction Assessment Instrument at the University of Waterloo. The success of users in finding exactly what was wanted was evaluated again by this library, using a six-point anchored scale. Success was found to be 56%, suggesting possible substantial inflation in the second category of the five-point scale used by this library in 1985. On this previous scale, the success item stated, "The information and/or assistance provided by the librarian was exactly what I needed"; 47.6% marked "strongly agree" and 34.4% "slightly agree" for a total of 82%.

Birch, Nancy, Marchant, Maurice, and Smith, Nathan. (1986). Perceived role conflict, role ambiguity, and reference librarian burnout in public libraries. *Library and Information Science Research* 8, 53-65.

A randomly selected sample of public libraries with budgets over $500,000 and more than ten professional librarians on their staffs were called. A total of 153 heads of reference agreed to participate and enough questionnaires were sent to them for all reference librarians on their staffs. Sixty-six percent of the questionnaires were returned. Results indicated that 35% of reference librarians were experiencing high levels of burnout. These scores were compared to those for teachers. Other findings were that older persons were at less risk than younger. Married persons were as less risk than single and full-time workers were more likely to burn out than part-time. Librarians with an M.L.S were more likely to burn out than those without an M.L.S. In cases of burnout, as years went on, lack of personal accomplishment became less intense and depersonalization more intense.

Blazek, Ron, and Parrish, Darlene Ann. (1992). Burnout and public services: The periodical literature of librarianship in the eighties. *RQ* 32, 48-59.

Library Literature and Library and Information Science Abstracts were searched for articles on burnout; 49 articles were found and studied using content analysis techniques. The authors found that stress appears to be more prevalent in reference than technical services librarians, is related to workplace factors, and occurs in all types of libraries.

Blevins, Beth. (1988). *Burnout: A history of the concept and an analysis of its presentation in library literature.* Unpublished master's paper for the M.S. in L.S. degree, University of North Carolina at Chapel Hill.

Reviews and analyzes how the concept of burnout has been presented in the library literature. Notes that, of 33 articles since 1979, only seven have incorporated survey research. Explores major themes and discusses recommendations for prevention and resolution of burnout.

Bloch, U., and Bloch, T. (1981). Occupational perceptions of librarians by high school students. *Library Quarterly* 51, 292-300.

Reports results of a study in Israel, where 700 high school girls were surveyed in regard to their perceptions of librarians. The Occupational Concept Test was used to measure values in regard to occupations.

Bloomfield, Masse. (1974). Testing for library-use competence. In John Lubans, Jr. (Ed.). *Educating the library user* (p. 221-230). New York: Bowker.

Sixteen library-use tests are analyzed here. A bibliography of available tests is also included.

Boll, John J. (1985). *Shelf browsing, open access and storage capacity in research libraries.* (Occasional Papers Number 169). Urbana: University of Illinois, Graduate School of Library and Information Science.

States that the greater proportion of academic library resources are nonbrowsable. Browsing is useful in casual searches but unreliable for research purposes. Includes a historical review of shelf arrangements. Also available as ERIC document (ED 260 721).

Bonn, George S. (1974). Evaluation of the collection. *Library Trends* 22, 165-304.

Notes statistical compilations do not in themselves measure quality. Defines optimum size as that needed to satisfy X% of patron requests.

Bostick, Sharon. (1993). The development and validation of the Library Anxiety Scale. In Marjorie Murfin and Jo Bell Whitlatch (Eds.). *First Preconference on Research in Reference Effectiveness*. (RASD Occasional Paper 16). Chicago: American Library Association, Reference and Adult Services Division.

The purpose of this study was to develop a valid and reliable instrument to measure library anxiety as defined by Constance Mellon (see Mellon, Constance A. (1986). Library anxiety: A grounded theory and its development. *College & Research Libraries* 47, 160-165). Methodology for developing the instrument is carefully outlined. The instrument was pilot tested on college freshmen and graduates from Ohio and Michigan, with 281 completed forms. Returns were analyzed and used in refining the instrument, followed by a second pilot test. A test-retest was done with three classes, including undergraduate classes in a community college and a private college, and a graduate class at an urban university, with 69 forms completed. The test was given twice at two- to three-week intervals with no formal library instruction given in the intervals. The total test-retest coefficient was .74, indicating an adequate level of stability. The final instrument clustered into five factors, which explained 51.8% of variation in library anxiety: 1) barriers with staff—25.4%; 2) affective barriers—8%; 3) comfort with library—7.4%; 4) knowledge of the library—6.1%; and 5) mechanical barriers—4.9%. All factors except knowledge of the library showed test-retest reliability. A Cronbach alpha of .80 indicated adequate internal consistency. Students over 50 were significantly more anxious; however, student sex and class level were not significantly associated with library anxiety.

Brancolini, Kristin B. (1992). Use and user studies for collection evaluation. In Joseph J. Branin (Ed.). *Collection management for the 1990's: Proceedings of the Midwest Collection Management and Development Institute, University of Illinois at Chicago, August 17-20, 1989* (p. 63-94). Chicago: American Library Association.

This overview points out that use-centered evaluation focuses on availability and accessibility of materials. Contains two questionnaires for academic users.

Brehm, Jack W., and Self, Elizabeth A. (1989). The intensity of motivation. *Annual Review of Psychology* 40, 109-131.

Reviews theories of motivation and related research literature.

Brinkerhoff, Robert O. (1983). The success case: A low-cost high-yield evaluation. *Training and Development Journal* 37, 58-61.

Brinkerhoff suggests that an effective alternative to evaluating training programs which have hard-to-measure benefits is the success case. Trainees for whom training seemed to work are selected. They are interviewed or studied through work-sample analysis, records analysis, and observations. This method seeks qualitative information about a few subjects rather than quantifiable data about many subjects. It attempts to answer the question: When training works, how well does it work?

Broadus, Robert N. (1980). Use studies of library collections. *Library Resources & Technical Services* 24, 317-324.

Reviews use studies done and draws five conclusions: Many books are never used over a period of many years; in-library use appears to parallel circulation; immediate past use may predict future use; recent materials are used most; and Americans generally make little use of foreign-language materials.

Brooks, Terence. (1982). The systematic nature of library output statistics. *Library Research* 4, 341-353.

Reports results of a study done on output statistics, including reference and in-library-use counts from 54 public, 15 academic, and seven other types of libraries to determine whether these statistics exhibited consistent characteristics. The Relative Fidelity of Measurement Model indicated that these output measures did not cycle and were not redundant. Concludes that these are variables worthy of serious academic pursuit.

Brown, Diane M. (1985). Telephone reference questions. *RQ* 24, 290-303.

Brown observes that some of Hieber's categories appear to overlap and that they give no indication of complexity of questions or depth of search. Brown modified Hieber's answer-format categories by combining the last two, "information-about" and "list-of-references," into one category, "gather information." She also monitored the level of complexity through the sources used to conduct the search. Sources used from least to most complex search were personal knowledge, card catalog, ready reference, general reference, and circulating collection. She found that answer format rather than subject was the factor determining the complexity of the question.

Brown, Maryann Devin. (1980). Library data, statistics, and information. *Special Libraries* 71, 478.

Describes a method by which to catalog impressions of library behavior. Develops a common framework about libraries. Defines data rules that should be followed.

Bube, Judy Lynn. (1986). Stress in the library environment. In *Alternative Library Literature* (p. 27-30). Jefferson, NC: McFarland and Co.

Presents an overview of stress, including information on stress and productivity and performance. References major stress research monographs.

Buckland, Michael K. (1979). On types of search and the allocation of library resources. *Journal of the American Society for Information Science* 30, 143-147.

Concludes that the traditional dichotomy of "known item" and "subject search" is inadequate. A more satisfactory method would be to regard every search as simultaneously and in varying degrees both information specific and document specific. Any combination of high and low degrees of these two types of specificity appears possible. Although librarians classify information desired as "factual" or "subject," in reality only some inquiries may be easily classified as factual or broad subject with many queries falling in between and containing a mix of both elements. People may also have queries that can be answered by only one specific document or any number of documents. Buckland observes that specificity should be regarded as a continuous variable and one that is not easy to measure.

Budd, John, and Coutant, Patricia. (1981). *Faculty perceptions of librarians: A survey*. Washington, DC: Educational Resources Information Center. (ERIC Document Reproduction Service No ED 215 697).

Reports on a survey of 137 faculty at Southeastern Louisiana University in regard to their perceptions of the status and professional contributions of librarians. It was found that the majority of faculty viewed librarians as professionals.

Budd, John, and DiCarlo, Mike. (1982). Measures of user evaluation at two academic libraries: Prolegomena. *Library Research* 4, 71-84.

A study was done in two academic libraries where the instrument developed by Steven Chwe was modified slightly and mailed to 1,000 students and 453 faculty with a return rate of 38% for faculty and 29% for students. The negative measure that was used, need deficiency, represented the case where performance fell short of the perceived importance of the item. Using this measure, it was found that questions regarding reference service received poor performance ratings relative to importance. Ratings for performance were significantly below ratings for importance in regard to librarians taking enough time to answer patrons' questions. It was noted that "students are apparently of the opinion that librarians are not willing enough to help them, or to take enough time with their questions. They are also dissatisfied with the answers provided by the librarians. **See Summaries of Instruments: Chwe—A Model Instrument for User Rating of Library Service and Selected User Survey Items.**

Bundy, Mary Lee. (1968). *Metropolitan library users; a report of a survey of adult library users in the Maryland Baltimore-Washington metropolitan libraries.* College Park, MD: University of Maryland, School of Library and Information Services.

A study was done in 1966 for six days over a six-week period on succeeding days of the week. Every fifth adult patron in the region's 99 library units was asked to mark the form before leaving. Return rate was 79 percent, resulting in a sample of 21,385 users. It was found that students constituted 47% of users with high school students predominating. In regard to purpose for library use, 33% came to obtain information or materials on a subject and 22% for a specific title. The most frequent subject was social sciences (32%) and applied sciences (21%). Bundy's sample of library users may be compared with the Wisconsin-Ohio sample of reference users in public libraries (Bunge and Murfin, 1983). Men and women appeared to ask reference questions in proportion to their numbers in the library (40% to 60%). As age increased, the tendency to ask reference questions appeared to increase. Housewives tended to ask fewer questions in proportion to their numbers. Those in the library for job-related purposes asked more questions in proportion to their numbers and those in the library for personal projects asked fewer. High school students asked fewer questions and college students asked more questions in proportion to their numbers in the library. In regard to subject for which users came to the library, those seeking social sciences and humanities materials and materials in certain applied sciences (having to do with medicine, home economics, animals, and plants) asked more reference questions than would have been expected, on the basis of their numbers in the library. Those in the library seeking materials in the pure sciences and agriculture and engineering asked fewer questions than would have been expected on the basis of their numbers in the library. Those seeking materials on business, education, law, travel, architecture, and art were twice as likely to ask reference questions as would have been expected on the basis of their numbers in the library. The satisfaction scales used in Bundy's and the Wisconsin-Ohio (Bunge and Murfin, 1983) studies were comparable and suggest that reference service is more successful than library service overall. While Bundy found 57% of library users were fully satisfied with their library visit, Bunge and Murfin found that 71% of public library reference users were fully satisfied and 60% found exactly what was wanted. Also, Bundy found that 12% of library staff in general were reported to be less than completely friendly while Bunge and Murfin found that only 1.5% of reference staff were reported to be less than courteous. **See Summaries of Instruments: Bundy—Public Library Use Study.**

Bunge, Charles. (1967). *Professional education and reference efficiency*. Springfield, IL: Illinois State Library.

A study was conducted to gather and examine data on the relationship between certain variables, particularly formal library education, and effectiveness in answering reference questions. Nine matched pairs, each consisting of one professional and one nonprofessional reference librarian, were selected from 12 medium-sized public libraries, both partners of a pair being from the same library. One member of each pair had little or no formal library education; the other had a fifth-year library degree. Each member of the pair was given a number of factual questions to answer. Participants were observed as they attempted to answer prepared questions. Search strategy, time taken to answer, and accuracy of answer were studied. Accuracy of answers and time spent per question were combined to produce an efficiency score. Findings included no significant difference in accuracy between trained and untrained staff, although trained staff took significantly less time per question. Trained participants were found to have performed significantly more efficiently than the untrained, although the differences were small. Among other results it was found that specific title responses occurred 33% of the time.

Bunge, Charles. (1984). Interpersonal dimensions of the reference interview: A historical review of the literature. *Drexel Library Quarterly* 20, 4-23.

A thorough but not exhaustive review of the literature on the reference interview. The author describes the changes in librarians' views of interpersonal interaction at the reference desk. Initially, good communication skills were considered innate; later they were considered skills that could be acquired. Recently, human relations have been considered as important as intellectual ability.

Bunge, Charles. (1984). Potential and reality at the reference desk. *Journal of Academic Librarianship* 10, 128-132.
The "gap between the ideals of reference librarianship...and the realities of reference service" cause frustration leading to burnout. Ideally, the patron is the center of reference service; however, as librarians are frequently evaluated according to nonclient-centered criteria, this leads to ambiguity of goals. Bunge discussed methods librarians can focus on to re-evaluate what they do and why.

Bunge, Charles. (1985). Factors related to reference question answering success: The development of a data-gathering form. *RQ* 24, 482-486.
Success of reference service was studied in 15 academic libraries in terms of patrons' reports of finding exactly what was wanted and being satisfied. Bunge notes that answering success fell off significantly when librarians reported being busy.

Bunge, Charles A. (1987). Book review: Unobtrusive testing and library reference services. *Library & Information Science Research* 9, 343-344.
In his review, Bunge notes that the book by Hernon and McClure does make some useful additions to the literature, including the report of a study using unobtrusive testing as a pretest and posttest strategy. The study was carefully done and is valuable as an example of how unobtrusive testing might be used beyond simply describing how bad things are.

Bunge, Charles A. (1989). Stress in the library workplace. *Library Trends* 38, 92-102.
Bibliographical survey of the literature on stress in general and stress in the library.

Bunge, Charles A. (1991). CD-ROM stress. *Library Journal* 116, 63-64.
Focuses on stress caused by CD-ROM reference tools. Discusses work overload, nonreference duties, patron attitudes and behaviors, and staff attitude. The need for training and the need for support from library administration is also discussed.

Bunge, Charles, and Murfin, Marjorie (1983). *The Wisconsin-Ohio Reference Evaluation Project*. Unpublished findings.
Over a nine-year period, 7,508 public and academic library reference patrons were surveyed in 121 public and academic libraries. Among findings of interest were the following. Eighty-eight percent of academic and 81% of public library reference patrons considered their questions important or very important. In public libraries, work- and school-related questions were considered more important than personal projects. Those who rated questions most important were students, persons in

sales/marketing, women, and unemployed. Nonfactual questions were considered more important than factual questions. Importance of questions rose with size of library in both public and academic samples. Patrons who rated their questions as more important were also more successful in finding what was wanted. Patrons in academic and public libraries reported that 7% to 9% of the time the reference staff were only partly or not knowledgeable. The catalog was used less often on factual questions than on other types of questions. In regard to types of questions asked, the simple "anything on a subject" with no qualifications or restrictions occurred on 14% of academic library questions and 23% of public library questions. Specific title questions represented 19% of public library questions and 14% of academic library questions.

Bunge, Charles, and Murfin, Marjorie. (1987). Reference questions—Data from the field. *RQ* 27, 15-18.
Data from the Wisconsin-Ohio Reference Evaluation Program for 31 academic libraries gave a success rate on reference transactions of 55.81% and a satisfaction rate of 67.94%.

Burns, Robert W. (1978). Library use as a performance measure: Its background and rationale. *The Journal of Academic Librarianship* 4, 4-11.
Although not addressing reference use specifically, this article details the centrality of use as the most valid measure of worth. Includes suggestions on design of such studies.

Burton, P.F. (1990). Accuracy of information provision—the need for client-centered service. *Journal of Librarianship* 22, 201-215.
Reviews a number of unobtrusive tests pointing to the 55% reference accuracy rate; cites Durrance (1989). Notes the need for interpersonal and communication skills to be fostered by library schools and advocates focused in-house training for librarians.

Cameron, Dee Birch. (1976). Public and academic library reference questions. *RQ* 16, 130-132.
Cameron classified questions using several different schemes. She found schemes easiest to use were one by William G. Jones (Categories are orientation, directory—requires data for answer, topical, citation, and holdings) and one by Billy R. Wilkinson (Categories are information, reference, search, and problem). She noted unexpected difficulties in the process of categorizing reference questions. What does one do with a single question when all categories in a scheme are not mutually exclusive and the question might fit into more than one category? She suggests that reference research could best be done by isolating one

particular characteristic at a time and testing each question in the sample to see whether or not the characteristic applies.

Campbell, David E., and Schlechter, Theodore M. (1979). Library design influences on user behavior and satisfaction. *Library Quarterly* 49, 26-41.

A holistic approach was taken in using three overlapping methods: interviews of students on their use and feelings toward the library, use diaries kept by students on their trips to the library, and observations which produced detailed behavioral maps of library use. Methods could be focused on use of reference areas.

Caputo, Janette S. (1984). *The assertive librarian*. Phoenix: Oryx Press.

Based on the idea that communication skills can be learned, Caputo's book defines assertiveness in a library context. She compares assertiveness to aggression in a series of practical examples and suggests alternative methods for dealing with problem behavior in the workplace. While not primarily directed at reference communication, interaction between librarians and library users is frequently discussed.

Carnegie Mellon University Libraries. (1978). *Academic library development program: Self study*. Pittsburgh, PA: University Libraries. (ERIC Document Reproduction Service No. ED 191 492).

In 1977, an in-library survey was done during selected times over a period of one week with 2,000 users being given forms. Return rate was 80%; 29% of users reported needing help, but only 21% reported asking for help (14% from "reference librarians" and 7% from "circulation librarians"). In the main library building, 17% reported asking for help from reference librarians, but reference department records and turnstile records for that period indicated that only 2% of users actually asked reference questions at the reference desk. In 1977, the library had no evening reference hours and supplied a total of 48 reference person hours in a typical week. The percentages of those needing help with various types of materials were as follows: books, 24%; periodicals, 37%; government documents, 100%; microfilms, 82%; newspapers, 16%. In regard to search strategy, 54% used the catalog, 21% browsed in the stacks, 17% consulted indexes, 14.7% consulted reference, and 7% consulted circulation. A three-point success scale of "mostly successful," "partly successful," and "unsuccessful" was used. Success rates reported were books 58.9%, periodicals 50%, and government documents 38.5%. Success rates for patrons in different subject disciplines varied from 42% to 65%. See **Summaries of Instruments: Carnegie Mellon University Libraries—Student Users Survey.**

Carver, Deborah A. (1988) Transfer of training: A bibliographic essay. *Library Administration and Management* 2, 151-153.

Carver reviews the training literature and summarizes research in helping trainees transfer skills learned to improved job performance.

Chen, Ching-Chih. (1976). *Applications of operations research models to libraries; a case study of the use of monographs in the Francis A. Countway Library of Medicine, Harvard University.* Cambridge, MA: MIT Press.

Applies Morse probabilistic models of book use in analyzing collective use of library books.

Chen, Ching-Chih, and Hernon, Peter. (1980). Library effectiveness in meeting consumer's information needs. In *Library effectiveness: A state of the art: Preconference on library effectiveness.* Chicago: American Library Association.

A study was done to examine everyday information needs of the population 16 years and older in six New England states. Interviewers called 2,400 randomly selected households and asked persons about a recent information need. In this process, 3,530 information needs were identified and 44% were work related. Most frequent needs were for technical job-related information followed by consumer issues, getting and changing jobs, and housing and household maintenance. Respondents reported information sources used or being used. The library was ninth behind own experience; friend, etc.; newspaper or book; someone in a store, company, or business; co-worker, professor, doctor, lawyer, or government official; television; and then libraries. Most helpful types of sources were interpersonal 52%, institutional 35%, and mass media 12%. Situations where the library was the most helpful source were job-related technology, consumer, and education. Occupations most frequently reporting library use were professional, technical and managerial, and students. **See Summaries of Instruments: Chen and Hernon—Information Needs.**

Chen, Ching-Chih, Hernon, Peter, Neenan, Peter A., and Stueart, Robert D. (1979). Citizen information seeking patterns: A New England study. *Executive Summary Report for the White House Conference on Library and Information Services.* Boston, MA: School of Library Science, Simmons College.

Among other results, the authors found that professional, technical, and managerial workers and students accounted for 56% of the situations in which libraries were used. **See Summaries of Instruments: Chen and Hernon—Information Needs.**

Childers, Thomas A. (1971). Telephone information service in public libraries: A comparison of performance and the descriptive statistics collected by the state of New Jersey. In *Information service in public libraries: Two studies*. Metuchen, NJ: Scarecrow Press.

A stratified sample of 25 libraries was drawn from a population of public libraries to study accuracy on an unobtrusive test of predetermined questions as it related to descriptive statistics collected by the state. Findings included the usefulness of the simulated patron telephone inquiry for gathering data quickly and inexpensively, and for presenting a more realistic picture of levels of information service than the obtrusive measures used heretofore. When all questions posed were considered, the percentage of accurate answers obtained was 55. The data lent substance to the hypothesis that the quality of a library's reference service is related to a combination of the number of professional personnel and the size of the book collection. It was further noted that the number of professionals bore a stronger relationship to the response variable than did the size of the book collection.

Childers, Thomas A. (1978). *The effectiveness of information service in public libraries: Suffolk County. Final report*. Philadelphia: Drexel University. School of Library and Information Science.

The study reports an unobtrusive reference accuracy evaluation of 56 Suffolk County public libraries. Most test libraries received 20 questions for a total of 1,110 question encounters. Thirteen questions were requests for factual material, one was a request for a book, three were requests for document citations, and three were "information escalators," to elicit question negotiation. Correctness of answers was judged: Correct (all correctness criteria were present), Mostly Correct (most correctness criteria were present; or all correctness criteria were present, but the response was couched in a doubtful or hesitant manner), Mostly Wrong (most of the criteria for judging the response were absent; or none of the criteria were present, yet the response was couched in a doubtful or hesitant manner), or Wrong (virtually all the correctness criteria were absent). Results demonstrated no pattern of performance that was very predictable on the basis of factors chosen for the study. It was posited that factors not studied may have a major influence on performance, such as group or individual personalities, size of reference collections, numbers of reference questions regularly handled, experience of the staff, or others.

Childers, Thomas. (1980). The test of reference. *Library Journal* 105, 924-928.

A report of the first large-scale unobtrusive reference evaluation, which was conducted in 56 Suffolk County, New York, public libraries.

Each library was asked 20 questions over a six-month period, most of them seeking simple factual information. A few asked for bibliographic information, several sought information about local social services, one requested a book, and three, called "escalators," sought to determine willingness and ability of reference staff to negotiate a question. Data were collected regarding referrals to other libraries or agencies to obtain requested information. In all, 1,110 questions were asked. In 56% of the encounters an actual answer was given, that is, a document, a fact, or a citation was provided in response to the question. About one-third of the time no response was given. Of these, about half included a referral out of the library, while about 17% provided no information at all. Two-thirds of referrals were to nonlibrary agencies. When an actual answer was given, 84% of the time it was correct or mostly correct. The escalator questions elicited no effort to negotiate in 67% of the cases with only 20% negotiating the query fully. It was concluded that clients would have difficulty predicting the quality of responses they might receive from a given library on a given question, nor could they expect their queries to be negotiated or referred. The author urged that reference service policies be developed and posed questions for reference librarians, library managers, and the field to consider.

Childers, Thomas. (1983). Review of output measures for public libraries. *Library and Information Science Research* 5, 233-235.
    The author summarizes 15 years of work leading to output measures which seem to have touched a felt need. The measures in the service domain emphasize the provision of materials, while information giving is covered by only two measures, programs by one, and auxiliary services (such as copying or meeting rooms) by none. No differentiation is provided for such reference activities as providing answers or bibliographic citations, reader's advisory work, referral, and bibliographic instruction. In spite of such concerns, the measures cover many concerns of managers and funders of library services and are viewed by the author as a landmark contribution for library management.

Childers, Thomas. (1987). The quality of reference: Still moot after 20 years. *Journal of Academic Librarianship* 13, 73-74.
    Childers, who along with Crowley (Crowley and Childers, 1971) introduced the unobtrusive research method to librarianship, observes that 20 years later studies using the method continue to conceive the reference process and to utilize the unobtrusive method in roughly the same way it was in the first two studies reported. This, he indicates, limits the idea of reference unrealistically given the range and variety of reference services commonly offered. Without systematic investigation, it cannot be asserted that correctness of responses to factual questions is

a key indicator of the overall quality of a library's reference service. No reported empirical data link performance on one kind of reference service with performance on another kind of service.

Childers, Thomas. (1989). Evaluative research in the library and information field. *Library Trends* 38, 250-267.

An example of true experimental design in evaluative research is found in Hernon and McClure's study.

Childers, Thomas, and Van House, Nancy A. (1989). The grail of goodness: The effective public library. *Library Journal* 16, 44-49. Also in Hannigan, Jane Anne. (1990). *Library lit. 20—the best of 1989.* Metuchen, NJ: Scarecrow Press.

The most substantial effort to address effectiveness has been by public libraries. Within 15 years the Public Library Association abandoned national standards and replaced them, in effect, with guidance encouraging the development of local objectives built around output measures. Development of the output measures was done without an empirical base. There was no systematic foundation for selecting recommended measures, nor was there a systematic foundation for choosing included measures over other possible measures. Local libraries have set objectives based on the output measures and are evaluating local performance based on them using measures and procedures developed under Public Library Association leadership. New knowledge developed in management science defines effectiveness as multidimensional with no one definition appropriate for all organizations. This evidence suggests that no single definition of or approach to organizational effectiveness is inherently valid. Four models of organizational effectiveness are posited: a goal model, a process model, an open systems model, and a multiple constituencies model. Each model represents different aspects of the organization's effectiveness, and the aspects may overlap. The authors used these models to perform a national study to define effectiveness for public libraries. Using input from seven significant constituent groups (library managers, library service staff, trustees, library users, friends of the library group members, local officials, and community leaders), eight dimensions of effectiveness, including 61 indicators, were identified. Six indicators that were selected in the top nine of every constituent group were interpreted as client-centered or service-centered. None of them is matched in practice by a clear and widely shared performance measure. Clearly these results pose challenges for the future of public library goal setting and evaluation. The dimensions need to be validated and ranked for importance and measures must be developed for them. Similar research should be conducted for other types of libraries.

Christensen, John O., Benson, Larry D., Butler, H. Julene, Hall, Blaine H., and Howard, Don H. (1989). An evaluation of reference desk service. *College & Research Libraries* 50, 468-483.

A five-part management study was used to assess reference quality by student assistants and paraprofessionals who took on the provision of all reference desk service except for questions referred to appropriate subject specialists. Extensive investments in training student assistants may not be cost effective given the accuracy level achieved on an unobtrusive test. Woodard (1989) suggests it is questionable whether such training can be justified. Murfin and Bunge (1988) suggest that paraprofessionals who handle less complex questions and consult other staff more frequently are more effective. Even if the investment in short-term student employees were not a factor, there are no clear data regarding the content of training needed for reference effectiveness. Considerable time is required to gather and administer data resulting from implementation of the five sections.

Christiansen, Dorothy E., Davis, C. Roger, and Reed-Scott, Jutta. (1983). Guide to collection evaluation through use and user studies. *Library Resources and Technical Services* 27, 432-440.

Provides librarians with a summary of types of methods available to determine extent to which books, journals, and so on are being used. Covers circulation studies, availability studies, in-house use studies, and citation studies.

Chwe, Steven. (1978). A model instrument for user-rating of library service. *California Librarian* 39, 46-55.

This model instrument for overall library evaluation rates responses in terms of "present condition" and "how important?" Three questions relate to reference accessibility. This instrument was used at two universities in Louisiana (Budd and DiCarlo, 1982). In regard to one reported measure—librarians taking enough time to understand and help with problems"—it was found in regard to this item that the present condition of this service was rated significantly below its importance. **See Summaries of Instruments: Chwe—A Model Instrument for User-Rating of Library Service.**

Ciliberti, Anne C. (1985). The development and methodological study of an instrument for measuring material availability in libraries. Doctoral dissertation, Rutgers University. *Dissertation Abstracts International*, 47, 7A.

An instrument was developed, adapted from previous research (Saracevic, Shaw, and Kantor, 1977), to assess availability of library material as measured by outcomes of both known-item and subject searches. Also, the validity of patron self-report data was investigated by comparing two groups of patrons, those who agreed to be observed and those who were not observed. Those patrons not observed were given forms and asked to return them at the completion of their searches. On both known-item and subject searches, patrons who *knew* they were *not* being observed reported being successful more often than could be substantiated by examination of their search forms. This result, however, was not supported by a later study (Ciliberti, Casserly, Hegg, and Mitchell, 1987). Follow-up was done when patrons who, as a result of their searches had found books and checked them out, were given postcards. They were asked to examine materials later, complete postcards, and return them. The most frequent reasons for seeking books were to find factual information and for general reading.

Ciliberti, Anne C., Casserly, Mary F., Hegg, Judith L., and Mitchell, Eugene S. (1987). Material availability: A study of academic library performance. *College & Research Libraries* 48, 513-527.
 This availability study differs from others because it assesses availability in regard to subject searches as well as specific title searches. A review of previous availability studies is given. The rate of availability, including both specific title and subject searches for this library, was 54%. The failure diagram developed for specific title searches was 1) bad citation for own item; 2) item not owned; 3) catalog use error on patron's part—couldn't find item, or wrong/incomplete call number; 4) item in circulation, on hold, or out of library; and 5) should be on shelf but can't be found, missing, sorting shelf, misshelved, waiting to be shelved, recataloging, reprocessing, or repair. A slightly different diagram is given for subject searching. Since it had previously been found by Ciliberti that self-reported success on materials availability surveys was higher than observed success, both methods were used. Six-hundred randomly selected users of the card catalog were given survey forms on which they reported searching success. In addition, 40 randomly selected users were observed by staff during consultation of the catalog and subsequent search of the book stacks. Return rate of forms was 72%. Results indicated 53% known-item searches and 47% subject searches. Undergraduates carried out an equal number of known-item and subject searches while graduates conducted slightly more specific title searches. When self-reported and observed searches were compared, success was not significantly different. In regard to known items, some 5% of error was due to bad citations, 8% to failure to find correctly shelved books, 14% to failure to use the catalog correctly, 14% to items charged out or on hold, 20% to the library not owning the item, and 38% to items missing from the shelves. In subject searches, 13% of failure was due to failure to use the catalog correctly to find subject

136 / *Annotated Bibliography*

headings, 15% of users were seeking subjects not represented in the catalog, 15% of items were in circulation, 15% of users failed to find correctly shelved books, 17% rejected the book after finding it on the shelf, and 26% of failures were due to library malfunction (missing and off-shelf books). Overall 63% of failure was due to library malfunction and 37% to patron error. Of library malfunction, 56% was due to off-shelf books, 25% to circulating items, and 19% to items not owned. Of patron error, 60% was due to failure to use the catalog correctly, 32% to shelf searching, and 8% to bad citations. Patron errors in catalog and shelf searching are described and discussed in detail. A 1989 availability study done in the same library updates the results of this study (Mitchell, Radford, and Hegg, 1994).

Ciucki, Marcella. (1977). Recording of reference/information service activities: A study of forms currently used. *RQ* 16, 273-283.
     Reported that academic libraries most frequently keep records of questions by type of reference transaction (most common are reference, ready reference, card catalog, bibliography, and instruction) and employ the use of a single tally for each question. On the other hand, the public library most frequently keeps a brief written statement of the reference question and infrequently uses the breakdown by type of reference transaction.

Clark, Philip M., and Benson, James. (1985). Linkages between library uses through the study of individual patron behavior. *RQ* 24, 417-426.
     A survey was given done in the main library and two branch libraries in a public library system. A questionnaire was given to all those entering the library, with 556 returns. Question-asking and borrowing behavior was studied. For each patron, *staff* filled in time of arrival and departure, number of items borrowed, and number of questions asked of anyone anywhere in the library. These data are unusual in that records of a reference question almost never indicate how many patrons are represented by the questions. Obviously some patrons must ask more than one question so that the number of patrons should be less than the number of questions. On the basis of total number of *questions* recorded here, it would appear that 32% of users surveyed asked questions but since some users asked more than one question, actually only 24% of *individuals* surveyed asked questions. The authors recommend that overall surveys are more effective than the present public library performance measures because they link individual and group patterns of use.

Cochrane, Lynn Scott, and Warmann, Carolyn. (1989). Cost analysis of library services at Virginia Polytechnic Institute and State University. In Janice Fennell (Ed.). *Building on the first century: Proceedings of the fifth conference of the Association of Academic and Research Libraries* (p. 55-62). Chicago: American Library Association.

A method was developed by which the full unit cost for basic library services, including reference services, could be determined and those that were appropriate for fee-based services identified. The formula arrived at takes into account departmental variable and fixed costs, library and university overhead, and fringe benefits. To determine unit costs for reference service, the cost of one reference transaction is calculated. For this, only the portion of the reference librarian's time spent at the reference desk is charged to the cost of a reference transaction. The costs for maintaining *all* library collections are in a separate budget. It was estimated that the full cost of one reference transaction was $9.22; a directional transaction was estimated at $3.53; an interlibrary loan requested at $5.23 and one filled at $9.23; one online search at $84.90 (including database costs); and one user education lecture at $15.27 per individual patron and $359.36 per group. Reference transaction costs *before* overhead were $6.24 per question; with library overhead they were $8.33 per transaction. **See Summaries of Instruments: Cochrane and Warmann—Cost Analysis of Library Service.**

Cole, Dorothy. (1946). Some characteristics of reference work. *College & Research Libraries* 7, 45-51.

A study was done in 13 public, academic, and special libraries, in which reference questions were recorded for a month in 1941. Records for 1,026 questions were obtained. Thirteen different question types were used. The most frequent types of questions reported were 55% factual, 20% "anything about a subject," 10% how-to-do-it, and 8% supporting evidence. Reference books constituted half of sources used on factual questions while they represented only 26% of sources used on "anything on a subject." In academic libraries, 21% of patrons asked indirect or confused questions.

Colorado State University. (1981). Questionnaire for library users. In *User surveys and evaluation of library services*. (SPEC Kit 71, p.71-72). Washington, DC: Association of Research Libraries, Office of Management Studies.

Elicits user response to physical facilities and collections access. Patrons were asked if at any time in the past they had encountered certain problems. Of patrons who expressed an opinion on each item, 35% had difficulty in locating a reference librarian, 40% found the reference shelves crowded, 41% found the noise level unacceptable, 56%

found the table space inadequate, 22% found the lighting inadequate, and 72% reported uncertainty as to the arrangement of materials. This instrument does not provide use data. It has, however, an item that asks the user to "please mark the areas where you asked for information from library staff members" and locations are listed. **See Summaries of Instruments: Colorado State University—Questionnaire for Library Users.**

Connell, Tschera Harkness. (1991). Librarian subject searching in online catalogs: An exploratory study of knowledge used. Doctoral dissertation, University of Illinois at Urbana-Champaign. *Dissertation Abstracts International 52*, 2307A.

Designed to identify the knowledge used by experienced librarians while searching for subject information in online catalogs. Data were collected through use of think-aloud protocols, transaction logs, and structured interviews. These multiple methods were used to study knowledge acquisition—what experts know and how they organize what they know. Techniques of knowledge acquisition are used by knowledge engineers in building expert systems. Knowledge was defined as knowledge of objects (facts), events (experience), performance (process), and metaknowledge (knowledge about the structure of knowledge). She found that most participants seemed to follow the same search steps each time they began a search. Metaknowledge rules, a basic set of concepts, are identified in the study and should undergo further testing.

Cook, John D., Hepworth, Susan J., Wall, Toby D., and Warr, Peter B. (1981). *Experience of work: A compendium and review of 249 measures and their use.* New York: Academic Press.

Covers commitment, occupational mental health and ill-health, job involvement and job motivation, work values, beliefs and needs, perceptions of the job, work role, job context, organizational climate, leadership style, and perceptions of others.

Cornell University. Albert R. Mann Library. (1984). Information resources in agricultural research. In *User studies in ARL libraries.* (SPEC Kit 101, p. 107-114). Washington, DC: Association of Research Libraries, Office of Management Studies.

A summary was done in 1983 of faculty in the College of Agriculture. Results are not presented but the questionnaire used is given. It includes a section where faculty were asked to rate (from unimportant to essential) a list of 26 information needs such as locating citations, reading annual literature reviews, scanning current journals, consulting known experts, attending conferences, and accessing census data. A second list of current and proposed services is given to be rated the same way, including quick reference service, longer reference consultation, immediate photocopying, and no-restrictions interlibrary loan. **See Summaries of Instruments: Cornell University—Information Sources in Agricultural Research.**

Courtois, Martin P., and Goetsch, Lori A. (1984). Use of nonprofessionals at reference desks. *College & Research Libraries* 45, 385-391.
 This survey indicates that support staff, including student assistants, staff reference desks, especially during evenings, weekends, non-peak hours, and when librarians are not available. Often a support staff member must attempt to answer the question or refer the patron to make an appointment when a librarian is available. The authors provide suggestions for the training of support staff to relieve some of the problems related to the use of such staff.

Creth, Shelia D. (1986). *Effective on-the-job training: Developing library human resources.* Chicago, IL: American Library Association.
 The author believes that improved job training is an unrealized source for library effectiveness. Provides an overview of the training process and chapters on specific training needs, planning training, implementation, and evaluation of training. Includes a brief discussion of the role of other librarians (who are not supervisors) in evaluating training of reference librarians. The appendix contains job training plans, including one for reference librarians.

Crews, Kenneth D. (1988). The accuracy of reference service: Variables for research and implementation. *Library & Information Science Research* 10, 331-355.
 Recommends Hernon and McClure's study as one offering details that future researchers might want to follow.

Cronbach, Lee J. (1950). Further evidence on response sets and test design. *Educational and Psychological Measurement* 10, 3-31.
 The author notes that continuum scales (e.g., least-greatest; agree-disagree) are prone to response sets. He noted that response sets "dilute the test and lower its value." The term, *response set*, refers to the tendency of a rater to mark all or most responses in a particular direction. This frequently takes the form of strong positive bias in library surveys. For example, instead of giving serious and thoughtful consideration to his or her own perceptions in relation to each of the questions, the rater simply finishes the rating task quickly by marking all boxes in the two most favored categories. This tendency appears to be triggered by unanchored scales, that is, scales where the meaning of the five points between the top and bottom are not clearly defined. Under conditions of

uncertainty as to which of two ratings to give, the rater will tend to assign the higher rating. Cuadra terms this the "fail-safe" reaction (Cuadra and Katter, 1967; Cuadra, Katter, Holmes, and Wallace, 1967). As a consequence, most ratings on library surveys with unanchored continuum scales are likely to be inflated to a greater or lesser degree. Cronbach recommends "best choice" answers be used instead. Possible answer choices are given in descriptive phrases, as in a multiple-choice test. He notes in regard to unanchored items that "any form of measurement where the subject is allowed to define the situation for himself in any way is to be avoided."

Cronin, Blaise. (1982). Performance measurement and information management. *Aslib Proceedings* 34, 227-236.
This literature review on performance measurement considers methods that have been used: unobtrusive testing, failure analysis, and cost-benefit analysis. Common sense evaluation, librarian attitudes, user input, and potential areas for evaluation are considered.

Crouch, Richard Keith Chamberlain. (1981). Interpersonal communication in the reference interview. Doctoral dissertation, University of Toronto, Canada.
This is the original library study to make use of Haase's *Counselor Effectiveness Scale*. It was used by observers to collect data in the natural setting in rating communication style of 25 randomly chosen reference librarians. Using measures of the FIRO psychological scale, communication effectiveness of reference librarians was measured in terms of inclusion, control, and affection needs. The FIRO-B is well known, reliable, and available in the *Seventh Mental Measurement Yearbook*. It is based on the work of William Schultz (1960) and explains behavior as being derived from three dimensions: inclusion needs, control needs, and affection needs. The results indicated that high communication scores were significantly associated with librarians' low mid-range Wanted Control scores. **See Summaries of Instruments: Haase—Counselor Effectiveness Scale.**

Crowley, Terence. (1971). The effectiveness of information service in medium size public libraries. In *Information service in public libraries: Two studies*. Metuchen, NJ: Scarecrow Press.
A study was conducted to develop a methodology for comparing information services available to adult patrons of public libraries. Predetermined questions were posed by anonymous proxies in 12 libraries based on absolute and per capita expenditures. Questions generally were fact type with half requiring some knowledge of current affairs. Findings indicated a response accuracy rate of 54%. Anonymous

inquiry as an unobtrusive measure was shown to be a uniquely valuable method for obtaining performance data on library information service, allowing the investigator to sample responses as they would actually be given. This report was quickly followed by numerous unobtrusive studies and the development of a number of widely varied measures and techniques for evaluation of library services.

Crowley, Terence. (1985). Half-right reference: Is it true? *RQ* 25, 59-68.

A serious survey, and in some ways a reminiscence by the researcher who introduced unobtrusive testing to reference evaluation 18 years earlier, of subsequent unobtrusive research and its impact on reference practice. The author concluded that the method had become fairly well established, though the results seemed to be ignored, noting that until librarians deal with the issue of accuracy in reference work, they will remain passive observers of popular culture.

Crowley, Terence. (1988). Unobtrusive testing and library reference services. *Government Information Quarterly* 5, 187-189.

The most innovative part of the study involved testing whether reference accuracy could be improved by concentrated one-shot training of reference staff. Librarians in the field who object to certain questions as being unrepresentative cannot be as easily dismissed as Hernon and McClure do. Inconsistency in scoring is also noted—sometimes the title and page number is judged correct and in another the exact number must be supplied. These criticisms should not be taken as reason to dismiss or lessen the significance of the research reported here.

Cuadra, Carlos, and Katter, Robert V. (1967). Opening the black box of relevance. *Journal of Documentation* 28, 291, 293.

It was found that if a respondent was uncertain about how to represent a rating on a particular scale, the tendency was to assign a higher rating.

Cuadra, Carlos, Katter, Robert V., Holmes, Emory H., and Wallace, Everett M. (1967). *Experimental studies of relevance judgments: Final report, volume II. Description of individual studies*. Santa Monica, CA. System Development Corp.

Presents very significant evidence concerning the design of rating scales. Six- to eight-category scales were shown here to have superior information preserving qualities over two- and four-category scales. Anchored scales were also shown to be more effective than unanchored scales.

Daiute, R.J., and Gorman, K.A. (1974). *Library operations research.* Dobbs Ferry, NY: Oceana Publications.

Tries to fill a gap in data on in-library book use through interviews. Develops an empirical method for measuring book readership within the library. Correlates types of users with the nature of material in use.

Davis, Richard A., and Bailey, Catherine A. (1964). *Bibliography of use studies.* Philadelphia, PA: Drexel Institute of Technology, School of Library Science.

Reviews periodical, science, and other use studies.

Davis, Roger, and Reed-Scott, Jutta. (1983). Guide to collection evaluation through use and user studies. (ALA/RTSD Guidelines). *Library Resources and Technical Services* 27, 432-440.

These guidelines have been revised in the 1989 *Guide to the evaluation of library collections*, q.v.

D'Elia, George. (1980). Development and testing of a conceptual model of public library user behavior. *Library Quarterly* 50, 410-430.

Users were asked to give their best estimate of the number of times they had visited and had telephoned the library in the past year. Intensity of library use was measured by the duration of visits. Data were also obtained from each user on number of different services generally used during each visit and the importance to them of library use.

D'Elia, George. (1980a). User satisfaction as a measure of public library performance. In *Library effectiveness: A state of the art* (p. 64-73). Chicago: American Library Association.

A user satisfaction scale (very dissatisfied, dissatisfied, slightly satisfied, satisfied, very satisfied, extremely satisfied) was compared to a grading scale of 13 response categories from A to F. It was found that user grade was a more cognitive and discriminating measure than user satisfaction.

D'Elia, George. (1985). Materials availability fill rates—useful measures of library performance? *Public Libraries* 24, 106-111.

The author demonstrated that title fill rate, subject and author fill rate, and browsers' fill rate do not measure library performance or output per se but rather do measure patron success within the library, where such success is a function of both library performance and patron behavior. When search results are cumulated to calculate the fill rates, the potential variation due to patron behavior differences is included but not controlled. Thus, the reported differences among fill rates from a set of libraries could be due to differences among the performances of the libraries, or to differences among the behaviors of the samples of patrons drawn from within the libraries, or both. It was concluded, therefore, that the fill rates are confounded and unacceptable measures of library performance.

D'Elia, George, and Rodger, Eleanor Jo. (1987). Comparative assessment of patrons' uses and evaluations across public libraries within a system: A replication. *Library and Information Science Research* 9, 5-20.

In-house surveys of patrons were conducted in 20 libraries of Fairfax County Public Libraries. While the libraries differed in the amount of resources available, study findings indicated no meaningful differences among samples for reasons given for selecting the library to visit; no meaningful differences among samples in uses of the library; and no meaningful relationships between uses of the library and reasons for selecting the library or evaluations of library facilities. However, there were meaningful differences among samples in evaluations of library facilities visited. Study results corroborate findings by D'Elia and Walsh (1983).

D'Elia, George, and Walsh, Sandra. (1983). User satisfaction with library service—a measure of public library performance? *Library Quarterly* 53, 109-133.

This paper reports the results of a public library study which demonstrates that user satisfaction is potentially useful for evaluating the performance of services within a library and that, because user satisfaction is affected by the demographic characteristics of the users, it should not be used to compare presumed levels of performance for libraries serving different communities. User satisfaction was found to be unrelated to the user's degree of library use. It was suggested that, given the complexity of user behavior and our limited understanding of it, user satisfaction should be used cautiously as a measure.

Dervin, Brenda. (1976). The everyday information needs of the average citizen: A taxonomy for analysis. In Manfred Kochen and Joseph C. Donohue (Eds.). *Information for the community*. Chicago: American Library Association.

Dervin has developed a scheme that taps the universe of average citizen information needs and attempts to provide a set of mutually exclusive and exhaustive categories into which all citizen information needs can be classified. Nineteen major categories were developed and interjudge reliability was 93% for coding within these major categories. Although these categories may not be completely mutually exclusive, the high reliability provides a consistent classification scheme. Major categories are neighborhood, consumer, housing, housekeeping and household maintenance, employment, education and schooling, health, transportation, recreation and culture, financial matters and assistance, public assistance and social security, discrimination and race relations, child care and family relationships, family planning and birth control, legal, crime and safety, immigration, migration and mobility, veterans and military, public affairs, political, and miscellaneous. Information typologies will help practitioners classify and analyze the type of information required for successful information delivery service. For example, television tends to incorporate only "ends" information (information about goals) without presenting "means" information (on how to obtain goals), and thus is not a useful source for decision making. At least three different types of "means" information are needed to satisfy everyday needs: 1) information about alternative means to achieving a goal; 2) information about criteria with which to evaluate "means" information; and 3) measurement information useful for applying the criteria to evaluate the "means."

Dervin, Brenda. (1983). *An overview of sense-making research: Concepts, methods and results to date.* Paper presented at the meeting of the International Communications Association, Dallas, Texas.

Discusses the purpose, roots, and premises of sense-making research, presents models, and describes methods of data collection. Gives definitions of S-M variables and discusses each variable in detail. Describes work to date, including theoretical, critical, and empirical studies. Each empirical study is annotated and discussed. Reviews some special analytic approaches and describes how results of S-M research fit in with theory and common sense. Describes how S-M research results can be used by practitioners and presents techniques. Outlines research agenda. Appendixes include 15 verbatim interviews, overview of definitions of S-M variables, and statements of respondents and interviewers of what they have learned from S-M research. Concludes with notes and bibliography.

Dervin, Brenda (1992). From the mind's eye of the user: The sense-making qualitative-quantitative methodology. In Jack D. Glazier and Ronald D. Powell (Eds.). *Qualitative research in information management* (p. 61-84). Englewood, CO: Libraries Unlimited.

Sense-making research, pioneered by the author, is used to study needs, images, and satisfaction of information users. The rationale and theoretical foundations of the approach are discussed. Dervin notes that we must study the information-seeking process from the viewpoint of the user, not the observer. "We ask users questions which start from our worlds, not theirs." Sense-making methodology is described with diagrams. Also described are other methods derived from sense-making research focused on real experiences. One is where respondents focus on a step of the information-seeking process. Other derived approaches include impact research and study of how users perceive messages (for example, messages conveyed in instruction manuals). The interview is central to these methodologies. Descriptions of six sense-making studies are given with a specific illustrative example of participants' responses. In the conclusion, the author notes that sense-making research has many characteristics of qualitative research and yet is also systematic in its approach, and amenable to the systematic power of quantitative analysis.

Dervin, Brenda, and Fraser, Benson. (1985). *How libraries help.* Sacramento, CA: California State Library.

A random sample of California residents was interviewed by telephone as to the benefits derived from their last library uses. Eighty-one percent, or 814 persons, recalled their last library visits and were interviewed in regard to benefits obtained. Eighty-nine percent reported they found directions, and got skills, ideas, and understanding. Emotional support goals were very high with 90% reporting emotional support goals such as getting happiness, pleasure, rest, and relaxation. Benefits in order of frequency were as follows: got ideas/understanding; accomplished or finished something; got happiness, pleasure; felt good about self; got confirmation of doing right thing; got skills needed to do something; got started or motivated; felt rested, relaxed; took mind off things; was reassured or hopeful; planned, made decisions; kept going when it seemed hard; felt not alone, made contact with people; and got out of or avoided a bad situation. Among other results, the most important factor in predicting how a person will be helped by the library was the user's purpose and specific information need. The authors conclude that approaches which describe the user's actual purpose and situation will be more powerful in predicting information-seeking behavior and library use than demographic and other variables. **See Summaries of Instruments: Dervin and Fraser—Helps Users Obtain from Their Library Visits.**

Dervin, Brenda, and Nilan, Michael. (1986). Information needs and uses. *Annual Review of Information Science and Technology* 21, 13-33.

Authors theorize that changing paradigms favor cognitive user-centered approaches rather than systems-centered ones. Reviews the literature of information needs and uses for the period 1979 through 1986. Includes a comprehensive bibliography.

Devore-Chew, Marynelle, Roberts, Brian, and Smith, Nathan. (1988). The effects of reference librarians' nonverbal communications on the patrons' perceptions of the library, librarians and themselves. *Library and Information Science Research* 10, 389-400.

A nonverbal study at a university library which investigated the effect of a reference librarian's touch, forward lean, and smile combined with gender in the reference setting. No significant correlations among various factors were found using Haase's *Counselor Effectiveness Scale*. The authors suggest that the testing instrument could be one among other possible problems. **See Summaries of Instruments: Haase—Counselor Effectiveness Scale.**

Donnelly, Anna M. (1993). Reference Environment Problems Checklist: A suggestion towards analyzing dysfunctional reference. In Marjorie Murfin and Jo Bell Whitlatch (Eds.). *First preconference on research in reference effectiveness.* (RASD Occasional Paper 16). Chicago: American Library Association, Reference and Adult Services Division.

Reviews the development and application of the Reference Environment Problems Checklist in light of the few existing studies on multiple environmental factors that impact on reference service. **See Summaries of Instruments: Donnelly—Reference Environment Problems Checklist.**

Dougherty, Richard M., and Blomquist, Laura L. (1974). *Improving access to library resources: The influence of organization of library collections and of user attitudes toward innovative services.* Metuchen, NJ: Scarecrow Press.

Study focused on two academic libraries and faculty attitudes toward library effectiveness, and the effects of physical dispersion of resources on those attitudes. After interviews and checking class reading lists, a list of LC classes was drawn up to produce a "document dispersion pattern" for each faculty member involved. Physical distances of resources were measured. Humanities showed less dispersion than the sciences and social sciences. The study found that many relevant documents were not used due to distance of location.

Dubester, Henry. (1961). Stack use of a research library. *American Library Association Bulletin* 55, 891-893.

Patrons were interviewed in Library of Congress stacks to determine if subject or "size" shelving was better. Results showed in some areas that subject shelving wasn't necessary for efficient use. Distinguishes between users seeking information and item-specific publications.

DuMont, Rosemary Ruhig, and DuMont, Paul F. (1979). Measuring library effectiveness: A review and an assessment. *Advances in Librarianship* 9, 103-141.

This literature review of library effectiveness considers ways effectiveness can be measured: goal achievement, cost and time efficiency, user satisfaction, performance optimization, use of human resources, and ability to survive. Environmental, behavioral, and structural criteria are considered. Evaluation problems are analyzed for workload indicators, physical standards, cost-benefit analysis, and user studies. Theories of effectiveness are presented along with an input/output model for the near and distant future.

Duncan, Cynthia B. (1974). Analysis of tasks performed by reference personnel in college and university libraries in Indiana University. Doctoral dissertation, Indiana University. *Dissertation Abstracts International* 35, 489A.

A survey was done in college and university libraries in Indiana in 1973 to determine the performance of professional and nonprofessional tasks by reference librarians. Thirty-six reference librarians completed questionnaires with descriptive information about themselves and a task inventory of 118 items checked with "does" and "should" and an importance of tasks index. Each participant was then interviewed. The author found that 70% to 80% of time was spent in reference-related tasks. **See Summaries of Instruments: Duncan—Survey of Actual and Potential Task Participation of Academic Library Reference Personnel.**

Durrance, Joan C. (1989). Reference success: Does the 55% rule tell the whole story?" *Library Journal* 114, 31-36.

This study was based on an unobtrusive investigation of the reference interview and the environment in which it occurred. Durrance observes that the primary contributors in recent years to the study of reference effectiveness using unobtrusive measures have been Hernon and McClure. The study focused not on measures of accuracy as most unobtrusive studies but the willingness of the inquirer to return to the same staff member at a later time. Observers are more willing to return to a librarian who has weak interviewing skills or gives inaccurate answers than they are to a librarian who makes them feel uncomfortable, shows no interest in their question, or appears judgmental about the inquiry. The author concluded that, while accuracy was an important measure of reference success, the environment also can either interfere or facilitate the reference interview. Library school students asked reference questions of their own choosing in 142 different libraries; 266 reference interviews were conducted over one year in 142 libraries (58% public, 37% academic, 5% government or special libraries). Success was rated in terms of strategy, accuracy, satisfaction with answer, and willingness to return to that reference staff member. By this last measure, 63% of interviews were successful. Durrance believes that patrons' willingness to return is related to being able to identify the persons who helped them. In this regard there was much uncertainty. It was found that only 35% of the students were *sure* that they had been helped by a *librarian*. The observers found some lack of clarity in identifying the reference desk, poor signage, and confusing environmental clues. Durrance found that "The environment seems as much to interfere with as to facilitate an effective reference interview" (p. 36); and that the profession continues to perpetuate its 100-year-old characteristics. She suggests stronger efforts be made to improve interviewing skills. **See Summaries of Instruments: Durrance—Reference Interview and the Environment.**

Dyson, Lillie Seward. (1992). Improving reference services: A Maryland teaching program brings positive results. *Public Libraries* 31, 284-289.
In this follow-up study of reference performance in Maryland public libraries, it was concluded that communication behaviors which could be learned were the determining factors in good performance. A number of factors were identified as being important behaviors, with verifying the reference question being the primary one.

Eagan, Ann. (1991). Noise in the library: Effects and control. *Wilson Library Bulletin* 65, 44-47.
Offers observations on physiological and psychological effects of library noise, especially in the technological environment.

Eaton, Gale. (1991). Wayfinding in the library: Book searches and route uncertainty. *RQ* 30, 519-527.
Reviews how library buildings affect users' feelings and the effects on information wayfinding. Discusses speed and directness as measures of success. Refers to the literature of environmental psychology.

Edwards, Jeffrey R. (1988). Research in stress, coping, and health: Theoretical and methodological issues. *Psychological Medicine* 18, 15-20.
Considers problems in stress research and suggests possible solutions. Covers areas such as confounding factors in stress research; different ways in which individuals perceive stressors; sources of stress aside from life events; stress produced by individuals themselves; coping and health; coping at different stages in the stress process; the stress of coping; how outcomes are determined; and health outcomes.

Edwards, Jeffrey R. (1992). A cybernetic theory of stress, coping, and well-being in organizations. *Academy of Management Review* 17, 238-274.

Presents a theory in which employee stress is defined as the difference between an employee's perceived state of well being and the desired state of well being, provided that the difference is of concern to the employee. Stress impacts negatively on the physical and psychological well being and results in coping behavior. The author explains his theory in detail and implications are considered.

Elcheson, Dennis R. (1982). Management of reference information services: A dynamic resource allocation and simulation model. Doctoral dissertation, University of California, Berkeley. *Dissertation Abstracts International* 43, 2481A.

A complex computer-based model, REFSIM, was developed to aid in long-range planning for information services in the Lawrence Livermore Library in Oak Ridge, Tennessee. One purpose of the model was to predict the long-term effects of changes to the reference environment and to project the behavior of a reference services organization under varying conditions of resource availability and customer demand. Its short-term goal was to help a reference service provide regular service, stay within budget, maintain staff levels, and satisfy present users. Its long-term goals were to attract new users, upgrade physical facilities, and obtain continuing funding. It was also designed to help determine the optimal configuration of services and resources. To this end, it made tradeoffs and balanced costs, performance, and benefits. This model is based on ten aspects of reference department operations: 1) costs and allocations, 2) staff, 3) collections and information sources, 4) equipment, 5) facilities, 6) value of department to upper management, 7) customers, 8) volume of requests, 9) performance, and 10) customer satisfaction. A large number of variables are involved in this model, as, for example, 57 variables in the costs and allocations system alone. A library must first furnish a large amount of data about its reference operations. These data must then be converted into numbers from 0 to 1 and inserted into the model. For example, for one variable, quality of online searches, a past survey was used where quality had been rated on a scale from highly relevant to not relevant. Highly relevant becomes 1 and not relevant becomes 0 and the *overall* quality of all the searches can then be assigned a number somewhere in between according to the results of the past survey. Types of reference service used in this model for the special library were lookup, retrospective, and SDI. As presented here, this method is promising for special libraries, but unfortunately the computer language in which it was written is not easily transferrable. Also, it would be difficult for most libraries to obtain the large amount of data required and to execute the model without special help from someone experienced in its use. If the program were transferred to a widely used computer language and adapted for other types of libraries, it might prove useful.

Eliot, Charles William. (1902). The division of a library into books in use, and books not in use, with different methods for the two classes of books. *Library Journal* 27, 51-56.

An early use study by the president of Harvard University. Discusses storage, and merits of browsing.

Elliott, Jannean L, and Smith, Nathan. (1984). Burnout. *School Library Media Quarterly* 12, 136, 141-45.

Discusses job stress faced by school librarians and factors that intensify burnout. Presents a personal case study of a burnout victim—a junior high school librarian.

Emerson, Katherine. (1977). National reporting on reference transactions, 1976-1978. *RQ* 16, 199-207.

Reviews the history of the development of definitions for reference and directional transactions. Definitions are 1) Reference Transaction—an information contact that involves the use, recommendation, interpretation, or instruction in the use of one or more information sources, or knowledge of such sources, by a member of the reference/information staff. Information sources include print and nonprint materials; machine-readable databases (including computer-assisted instruction); library bibliographic records, excluding circulation records; other libraries and institutions; and persons both inside and outside the library. A question answered through utilization of information gained from previous consultation of such sources is considered a reference transaction even if the source is not consulted again; and 2) Directional Transaction—an information contact that facilitates the use of the library in which the contact occurs and its environs, and that may involve the use of sources describing that library, such as schedules, floor plans, handbooks, and policy statements. Examples of directional transactions are directions for locating facilities such as restrooms, carrels, and telephones; directions for locating library staff and users; directions for locating materials for which the user has a call number; supplying materials such as paper and pencils; and assisting users with the operation of machines.

Evans, G. Edward. (1970). Book selection and book collection usage in academic libraries. *Library Quarterly* 40, 273-308.
Examines more than two dozen factors that influence use. Concludes that a limited amount of contact with a large number of patrons has more influence on selecting titles that will be used than does frequent contact with a limited number of patrons.

Fairfax County Public Library. (1987). *Information services profile, Fairfax County Public Library*. Chicago: Public Library Association.
Presents detailed reference volume statistics for the Fairfax County Public Library System. Analyzes reference and directional transactions and telephone and walk-in questions by times of day.

Fine, Sara. (1984). Research and the psychology of information use. *Library Trends* 32, 441-460.
The author discusses the use of psychological research in relation to the study of the reference interview. She notes that some studies make use of the library as a laboratory and includes the Crouch (1981) study as one of those making use of the natural setting for research. This article supports the notion of using psychological models to study the relationship between patron and librarian in the reference interview.

Fisher, David P. (1990). Are librarians burning out? *Journal of Librarianship* 22, 216-235.
A critical analysis of stress and burnout studies published in the last ten years.

Fisher, Harold E., and Weinberg, Ronald. (1988). Make training accountable: Assess its impact. *Personnel Journal* 67, 73-77.
Fisher and Weinberg describe an attempt to develop a reliable assessment instrument to evaluate the efficiency of a training program at Bellcore. Based on a literature and a phone survey, the authors conclude that most evaluative instruments were simple, open-ended reaction sheets. They developed a questionnaire of 18 items, which evaluated the capability of trainers to get their messages across and select materials that could be applied on the job. **See Summaries of Instruments: Fisher and Weinberg—Training Feedback Questionnaire.**

Fisher, Jeffrey D., Rytting, Marvin, and Heslin, Richard. (1976). Hands touching hands: Affective and evaluative effects of an interpersonal touch. *Sociometry* 4, 416-421.
In this library study conducted to investigate the effect of touching on library patrons, touch recipients who were not consciously aware of

being touched did not differ from those who were aware, and the results of being touched on the hand by the librarian was positive.

Fisher, Kenneth, and Alexander, Carlos. (1976). Survey of Olin Library users. In *User Surveys*. (SPEC Kit 24). Washington, DC: Association of Research Libraries, Office of Management Studies.

Response rates from this study provide the basis for using exit surveys. In a pretest the authors gave out 50 forms to library users as they *entered* the library and 50 to those *leaving* the library. Those given out to users upon entrance had a return rate of 52 percent; those given out on leaving had a return rate of 80 percent. Using the latter method, the final study achieved a return rate of 97 percent.

Flood, Barbara. (1973). Aggravation quotient: Search time/user time. In Helen Waldron and F. Raymond Long (Eds.). *Innovative developments in information systems: Their benefits and costs, proceedings of the 36th annual meeting of the American Society for Information Science* (p. 65-66). Westport, CT: Greenwood Press.

Proposes a new measure of library effectiveness called the Aggravation Quotient. The time spent trying to locate an item is divided by the time spent actually using the item. Maintains that the AQ affects user behavior in that users will tend toward the least aggravating or frustrating sources. Suggests that this factor should receive more serious consideration.

Ford, Geoffrey. (1973). Research in user behavior in university libraries. *Progress in Documentation* 29, 85-106.

Reviews the literature on user behavior covering 1) factors affecting demand for library service, including information channels, uses of information, the individual user, and systems and organizations; 2) interaction between libraries and users, including measures of effectiveness, catalogs, and instruction in library use; and 3) utilization of library materials. Overall conclusions are presented, as well as a bibliography of 111 items. Notes that findings on library skills tests are contradictory and questions their validity. Some other investigators believe these tests measure common sense and general academic ability and correlate with the Terman Concept Mastery Test. Suggests that they measure scholastic aptitude rather than library knowledge as such.

Ford, Geoffrey. (1990). *Review of methods employed in determining the use of library stock*. London: British National Bibliography Research Fund Report.

Excellent overview of methods that examine the use of library collections. Includes a literature review summarizing findings. Sample survey forms are reproduced.

Fraley, Ruth A., and Anderson, Carol Lee. (1990). *Library space planning: A how-to-do-it manual for assessing, allocating and reorganization collections, resources, and facilities* (2d ed.). New York: Neil-Schuman Publishers.
Good overview of fundamentals.

Frank, Donald G. (1984). Management of student assistants in a public services setting of an academic library. *RQ* 24, 51-57.
The author presents information about the activities and procedures associated with student assistant management in a public services setting of an academic library. He provides criteria for selection, explains the importance of orientation/training, and emphasizes the need for student assistants to gain a basic understanding of library operations. The values of open communications and support for student assistants are discussed.

Franklin, Hugh, Knittel, Marjorie, and Maughan, Laurel. (1991). *Arranging materials and services in a university library reference area for effective use.* Corvallis, OR: Oregon State University. (ERIC Document Reproduction Service No. ED 339 381).
Reports on assessments of new configuration of reference service areas. **See Summaries of Instruments: Franklin, et al.—Reference Arrangement Survey.**

Frantz, Paul. (1991). Expanding the repertoire of reference. *Reference Services Review* 19:4, 85-96.
Favors using regular browsing as a method for librarians to learn their reference collections.

Fussler, Herman H., and Simon, Julian L. (1961). *Patterns in the use of books in large research libraries.* Chicago: University of Chicago Library.
Probably the most cited and influential work in the literature of book use. The study is a statistical survey of the use of the University of Chicago libraries by analysis of circulation records, by expert advice, and by sampling browsing use. Detailed methodology and sample techniques and results are included. The purpose was to find the age at which monographic and serial works could be retired to storage. Results suggested that nonrecorded use is roughly proportional to recorded use, which has implications for storage policies that will minimize the amount of lost nonrecorded use on materials stored. Results indicated that there

might be three to nine times as much browsing as recorded use. Less browsing occurred on the lowest shelves; 56% of book use occurred by persons who didn't have a call number or title. In effect, over half of all users found books at the shelf by browsing rather than with call numbers or titles. See Summaries of Instruments: Fussler and Simon—Library Use Study Questionnaire.

Gal, Cynthia A., Benedict, James., and Supinski, Deborah M. (1986). Territoriality and the use of library study tables. *Perceptual and Motor Skills* 63, 567-574.

Preference shown among college students for carrels that define territories with high boundaries. Suggests more carrel seating should be provided in high density population working areas.

Garvey, William D., Lin, Nan, Nelson, Carnot, and Tomita, Kazuo. (1972). Research in patterns of scientific communication: I. General description of research. *Progress in Information Storage and Retrieval* 8, 111-122.

This study of 200 research efforts in psychology found that less than 1 in 7, or 14%, of ideas originated from formal media. After the idea had been generated, the process of developing it makes heavy demands on the formal information systems, such as libraries.

Giesbrecht, Walter. (1991). Staff resistance to library CD-ROM services. *CD-ROM Professional* 4, 34-38.

Studied responses to CD-ROMs in academic libraries by monitoring electronic bulletin boards. Presents list of problems, including increased stress.

Gers, Ralph, and Seward, Lillie J. (1985). Improving reference performance: Results of a statewide study. *Library Journal* 110, 32-35.

This statewide study of the reference interview was conducted by the Maryland State Department of Education. They developed and tested a model of reference behaviors that included approachability, comfort, interest, negotiation (inquiry), and follow-up (evaluation). When librarians solicited feedback from users by asking them if their questions were answered, correct answers were reported 76% of the time. Librarians who did not solicit feedback supplied correct answers 52% of the time. Training librarians in these skills increased accuracy in answering reference questions using unobtrusive methods. While the model they used is a reasonable one based on prior research, the lack of a control group in the study means there can be less confidence in the results.

Gers, Ralph, and Seward, Lillie J. (1988). "I heard you say"...peer coaching for more effective reference service. *The Reference Librarian* 22, 245-260.

Gers' and Seward's (1985) study of public libraries in Maryland led them to conclude that better communication skills equaled better job performance in reference. The next obvious question is how to train and maintain these skills. The authors feel the answer lies in careful peer coaching combined with a reward system. Based on the 1983 Maryland Survey data (Gers and Seward, 1985), the authors assert that patrons can expect to receive correct answers 80% of the time if reference librarians exhibit identified model reference behaviors 90% of the time. Gers and Seward describe appropriate feedback and other strategies to facilitate the transfer of training. In the 1983 survey, two libraries correctly answered 42.5% and 70% of 40 questions. After retesting, the second statewide survey indicated that the same libraries scored 97.5% and 92.5 percent, respectively.

Getz, Malcolm. (1987) Some benefits of the online catalog. *College & Research Libraries* 48, 224-240.

Reports results of a cost-benefit study of the online catalog in an academic library. An availability study of success in known-item searching was done before the implementation of the online catalog in 1985. It was done again soon after the online catalog was implemented. An overall survey form was given to patrons entering the library for an entire day. Response rate was 60% with 1,690 usable forms. An increase in library use was not found in the first year after introduction of the online catalog. In order to measure the benefit of the online catalog as opposed to the card catalog, two measures were used: time saved and items found that would not otherwise have been found. A simulation study was done where groups of experienced and inexperienced users were given six author/title citations chosen at random. Each student timed four steps of the process: at the catalog, in the stacks, return to circulation, and check-out. Citations were different for the before and after studies. Inexperienced students found items eight seconds faster in the online catalog. Experienced students found them 19 seconds faster. The number of author/title searches done per year was estimated and time saved was figured for each group. Users' time was valued by wage rates of $25 per hour for faculty, $7.50 for graduate students, and $5 for undergraduates. The value of user time saved per year was estimated as being $8,000 to $18,000 per year. Another measure of benefit was the increased probability of success. Availability studies of user success in finding specific titles were done before (637 users) and after (325 users) implementation of the online catalog. Before implementation of the online catalog, success in finding and obtaining specific titles was

57.6%. After implementation of the online catalog, success in finding and obtaining specific titles was 64%. The author concluded that the bringing together of all campus holdings in a union online catalog accounted for five percentage points of improvement in the second study. The value of increased success in locating specific titles was estimated to be 12,344 additional successful author/title searches per year. One dollar was given as the value of each of these additional searches, for a total of $10,000 to $20,000.

Gitler, Robert L. (1939). *A study of the use of reference materials and the reference functions in certain special libraries in the fine arts with attention to implications for library training agencies.* Unpublished master's thesis, Columbia University, New York.

Questionnaires were completed by New York fine arts librarians indicating what reference materials they used and what reference functions they performed. Approximately two-thirds of their time was spent in administrative and direct informational reference service.

Glogoff, Stuart. (1983). Communication theory's role in the reference interview. *Drexel Library Quarterly* 19, 56-72.

The author examines a number of verbal and nonverbal models of communication. Verbal models include those by Shannon-Weaver, Vavrek, and Rettig. Environmental aspects of communication are also considered important to the success of the reference transaction.

Goldhor, Herbert. (1979). The patrons' side of public library reference questions. *Public Library Quarterly* 1, 35-49.

Reference staff of the Urbana Free Library, Urbana, Illinois, recorded certain information for 100 telephone reference requests over a six-month period. Patrons who agreed to participate in the study gave their names. They were called back by a research assistant and asked about their information needs. In regard to origin of their questions, 43% arose from personal interests, 31% were job-related, 18% were school-related, and 8% arose from curiosity; 91% reported having made some use of the answer. Out of all questions, in one case the person acted on what the author had determined to be wrong information. Perspectives of librarian and patron do not always agree on whether the question was answered. The author concludes that the questions were clearly meaningful reflections on the currents of patrons' daily lives.

Goldhor, Herbert. (1987). An analysis of available data on the number of public library reference questions. *RQ* 27, 195-201.

Presents a collection of reference volume statistics for public libraries in different population size groups for years between 1970 and 1983.

Statistics collected from individual library annual reports and annual compilations of library statistics for certain states represent some 900 different libraries. Data are grouped by year and size of population served and include volume of reference questions and circulation. The author notes an apparent increase in reference questions over the years covered.

Gothberg, Helen. (1976). Immediacy: A study of communication effect on the reference process. *Journal of Academic Librarianship* 2, 126-129.
    Presents the results of a study done to examine the communication process during the negotiation of a reference question. Two reference librarians in a public library were trained to display both positive and negative responses. Sixty patrons approaching the desk were observed and given questionnaires later. Patrons who had been exposed to positive behaviors were more satisfied with the negotiation of the question and with their own participation. However, in regard to their satisfaction with the information found, positive or negative behaviors did not appear to make a difference.

Gothberg, Helen M. (1986). The beginnings. *The Reference Librarian* 16, 17-18.
    The author discusses how communication came to be recognized as a significant part of reference services and describes briefly relevant studies on the topic.

Gothberg, Helen M. (1987). Managing difficult people: Patrons (and others). *The Reference Librarian* 19, 269-283.
    This article focuses on six types of difficult people. The different personality types are partially based on Robert Bramson's *Coping with difficult people*.

Great Britain. Department of Education and Science. (1976). *Staffing of public libraries*. London: HMSO.
    This 1973 survey of 39 public libraries includes reference statistics. One unusual statistic reported is number of questions handled in one year per staff member. This figure is reported to be 3,089 reference questions per reference department staff member.

Green, Joseph. (1976). Urban and suburban public library statistics. In *The Bowker annual of library and book trade information 1976* (p. 248-249). New York: R.R. Bowker Co.
    Includes reference statistics for 17 public libraries from 1975 through 1978.

Griffiths, Jose-Marie. (1982) The value of information and related systems, products and services. In Martha Williams (Ed.). *Annual Review of Information Science and Technology*. White Plains, NY: Knowledge Industries Publications.

Reviews the published literature on value assessment and on application of measures of value to information products and services. The final section of the review discusses reported problems encountered in value assessment of information.

Griffiths, Jose-Marie. (1984). Our competencies defined: A progress report and sampling. *American Libraries* 15, 43-45.

A noteworthy attempt to articulate competencies of experienced reference librarians through literature reviews and extensive interviews with reference professionals.

Guide to review of library collections: Preservation, storage, and withdrawal. (1991). Subcommittee on Review of Collections, Collection Management and Development Committee, Resources Section, Association for Library Collections and Technical Services. Chicago: American Library Association.

Outlines methods for determining actual use. Urges ongoing and systematic review. Edited by Lenore Clark.

Guide to the evaluation of library collections. (1989). Subcommittee on Guidelines for Collection Development, Collection Management and Development Committee, Resources Section, Resources and Technical Services Division, American Library Association. Chicago: American Library Association.

Outlines collection-centered techniques, and use-centered techniques of evaluation. Edited by Barbara Lockett.

Gunning, Kathleen, and Spyers-Duran, Kimberly. (1993). Evaluation of Reference Expert: An expert system of selecting reference sources. In Marjorie Murfin and Jo Bell Whitlatch (Eds.). *First preconference on research in reference effectiveness*. (RASD Occasional Paper 16). Chicago: American Library Association, Reference and Adult Services Division.

An expert system was designed at the University of Houston for aiding users in selecting print and CD-ROM indexes and reference sources. One month after the system was made available a survey was conducted and 85 completed questionnaires were received and analyzed. Findings are presented in detail. Among other results, the authors found that 36.5% were very familiar with their research topics; 18.8% were not familiar with their research topics; and 64.4% intended to use CD-

ROM databases. Of those respondents who indicated that Reference Expert had recommended a CD-ROM database, 48.9% said they had been unaware that this database would be useful for their topic.

Haack, Mary, Jones, John W., and Roose, Tina. (1984). Occupational burnout among librarians. *Drexel Library Quarterly* 20, 46-72.

Ninety-two librarians who attended a conference program took the Staff Burnout Survey (SBS). Many of the librarians were also reference librarians. Results indicated that 28% reported ongoing psychological tension and 14% reported severe chronic psychological manifestations. Thus a total of 42% librarians in the survey reported moderate to high burnout. Burnout drawings are presented and interpreted.

Hall, Blaine H. (1985). *Collection assessment manual for college and university libraries*. Phoenix: Oryx Press.

See p. 64-68, "Measuring in-library use," to determine the ratio between-in library use and outside circulation, and to obtain in-library use counts by subjects and/or types of materials. Intended for periodical use study but may be adapted for reference.

Halldorsson, Egill A., and Murfin, Marjorie E. (1977). The performance of professionals and nonprofessionals in the reference interview. *College & Research Libraries* 38, 385-395.

Twenty-five sets of "indirect" and "faulty information" questions were asked at two university library reference centers, one staffed by librarians and the other by support staff. "Indirect questions" are those where patrons with specific information needs ask for materials on general subjects or for sources they think may contain the information they seek. On indirect questions, librarians were more successful than support staff—90% compared to 62%. "Faulty information" questions contain incorrect information. For faulty information questions, librarians were significantly more successful than support staff—52% compared to 20%. Librarians were more successful than support staff because of both greater personal knowledge of subject matter and greater knowledge of reference sources.

Hallman, Clark N. (1981). Designing optical mark forms for reference statistics. *RQ* 20, 257-264.

Describes a study done at the University of Nebraska at Omaha, where six types of data were collected daily for two years. Data included day, time, directional or reference, in-person or by telephone, subject areas of question, and sources used. The study utilized computer-scannable forms where data could be read automatically into the computer. Sophisticated analysis could then be done without the time and effort required for keypunching. Descriptions and details of this method are given with sample forms.

Halperin, Michael, and Strazdon, Maureen. (1980). Measuring students' preferences for reference services: A conjoint analysis. *Library Quarterly* 50, 208-224.

Describes a study done to measure students' preferences for different combinations of services and different levels of service quality in a university library. As a pretest, 15 students ranked 20 aspects of reference service in order of preference. Halperin found that those aspects of reference service considered most important were (in priority order) completeness or quality of answer, amount of time spent waiting for service, knowledge, helpfulness, and attitude of librarian. Following this pretest, a conjoint analysis was carried out with 100 students. Each student was given 16 cards and asked to rank the eight items on each card in order of preference. The factors ranking highest were completeness of answer, free database service, attitude of staff, hours of service, interlibrary loan, knowledge of librarian, time needed to answer, and wait for service. Instruction in the use of the library and availability of printed guides ranked 11 and 12. Lowest rankings were given to translation of foreign documents, vertical files, and sex of the librarian. The first three factors were ranked the same by graduates and undergraduates, but there were differences in regard to other factors in strength of feeling. **See Summaries of Instruments: Halperin and Strazdon—Patron Preference for Different Aspects of Reference Service; and Halperin and Strazdon—Reference Service Preferences.**

Handley, John C. (1991). Sampling by length. *Journal of the American Society for Information Science* 42, 229-232.

Gives formulas for arriving at unbiased estimates of use. Cites Fussler and Simon as early model for use sampling.

Hardesty, Larry, Lovrich, Nicholas Jr., and Mannon, James. (1979). Evaluating library-use instruction. *College & Research Libraries* 40, 309-317.

An instrument was developed and pretested. The instrument consists of 10 attitudinal items and 26 skills items. The instrument was administered to 133 freshmen, who were then given library instruction. Twenty-nine students taught by the same instructors in a separate class were used as a control group. Eight weeks later all were given the original test and pretest and posttest scores were compared. The control group dropped while the library instruction group gained 2.7 items (a significant difference). The measure of 14.9 correct of 20 skills questions was equal to that of a class of graduating seniors who also took the test. Positive gains were shown for all levels of student aptitude (as measured by SAT). Attitude changes are also discussed. **See Summaries of Instruments: Hardesty, Lovrich and Mannon—Library-Use Instruction Evaluation.**

Harris, C. (1977). A comparison of issues and in-library use of books. *ASLIB Proceedings* 29, 118-126.

Study conducted 1973-74 at Newcastle upon Tyne Polytechnic found that up to 20 times as many more books are consulted than as indicated by in-library use recording (table counts). Tracking was done by a book slip method (user asked to throw away slip in book if book was consulted), and date stamp method (reshelved books date-stamped with ink of a different color from charge date).

Harris, Roma M., and Michell, B. Gillian. (1986). The social context of reference work: Assessing the effects of gender and communication skill on observers' judgments of competence. *Library and Information Science Research* 8, 85-101.

A public library study, which examined observers' judgments about reference librarians' behavior making use of video tape, found differences in male and female responses to the amount of instruction received.

Hatchard, Desmond B., and Toy, Phyllis. (1986). The psychological barriers between library users and library staff—an exploratory investigation. *Australian Academic and Research Libraries* 17, 63-69.

This article reports on an exploratory study which sought to identify psychological barriers between college students and library staff. The data suggested that student personality traits were involved in how students felt about asking for help.

Havener, W. Michael. (1988). The use of print versus online sources to answer ready reference questions in the social sciences. Doctoral dissertation, University of North Carolina. *Dissertation Abstracts International* 50, 565A.

A sample of test questions was prepared by the author using previously asked reference questions for which successful online ready reference searches had been done. In 1987, 61 librarians in randomly selected libraries were mailed a list of 12 test questions. One group was asked to conduct online ready reference searches and the other to use print sources to find answers. Participants were also asked to keep records of time taken for each question. Answers were returned along with other information about the searchers and the searches themselves. The investigator then compared the results of the online searches to results of the searches for the same answers in printed sources. Four types of reference questions were studied: requests for facts (verification type facts and directory type facts) and requests for ten bibliographic references on a subject. (one-concept and two-concept). References on a subject were found faster and more successfully online (particularly two-concept subjects). Facts were found faster and more successfully in print. This indicates that selection of formats greatly increases chances of effectiveness and efficiency. Online ready reference searches were faster and more successful for bibliographic citation searches. Print sources were more successful for source questions and directory questions. Success rates for verification type facts, 95%; directory type facts, 88%; ten references on a single subject, 60%; ten references on a multiple subject, 52%. Environmental problems were reported on 11% of print searches (books off shelf, or in another location), and 17% of online searches (hardware/software problems). In regard to total number of reported problems, environmental problems were reported twice as often for online searches. **See Summaries of Instruments: Havener—The Use of Print Versus Online Sources.**

Havener, W. Michael. (1990). Answering ready reference questions: Print versus online. *Online* 14, 22-28.

The author designed a controlled experiment. Using only print sources, 31 experienced reference librarians answered a set of 12 questions provided by the author. Using only online sources, 30 different experienced reference librarians answered the same set of questions. Six questions were requests for citations to documents on a subject and were labeled conceptual questions. Six questions were requests for specific facts and were labeled factual questions. The use of online sources in answering requests for citations on a conceptual topic was faster, yielded higher recall, and more completely satisfied the request than the use of print sources. For factual questions, print sources were twice as fast as online and equally successful.

Havener, W. Michael. (1993). Print, online, or ondisc: The influence of format on the outcome of searches by graduate students. In Marjorie Murfin and Jo Bell Whitlatch (Eds.). *First preconference on research in reference effectiveness*. (RASD Occasional Paper 16). Chicago: American Library Association, Reference and Adult Services Division.

A study was done where 41 graduate students each researched the same set of 18 social science ready reference questions. One-third of the searches were done using print sources, one-third using online sources, and one-third using ondisc sources. The efficiency (time required to complete a transaction), success (retrieval of correct and relevant information), and effectiveness (a ratio of efficiency to success) of the three treatments were compared. Differences between question types were also analyzed as were interactions between treatments and question type. Results indicated the existence of statistically significant differences among outcomes.

Haynes, R. Brian, McKibbon, Ann, Walker, Cynthia J., Ryan, Nancy, Fitzgerald, Dorothy, and Ramsden, Michael F. (1990). Online access to MEDLINE in clinical settings. *Annals of Internal Medicine* 112, 78-84.

A study was done of physicians performing their own searches on MEDLINE using GRATEFUL MED software. The authors then followed the outcomes of the searches in terms of those where patient care was affected. The part of each record used in decision making was identified. In 47% of these searches, clinical decisions were affected. For 92% of searches originating from patient care problems, participants reported at least *some* improvement in patient care.

Heibing, Dottie. (1990). Current trends in the continuing education and training of reference staff. *The Reference Librarian* 30, 5-15.

Cites Durrance (1989) as offering a different measure of reference success: the willingness of the inquirer to return to the same staff member at a later time. Urges librarians to do a better job of determining what the patron really wants.

Heintze, Robert A. (Ed.). (1986). *Library statistics of colleges and universities 1982.* (U.S. Department of Education, National Center for Education Statistics). Washington, DC: U.S. Government Printing Office.

Gives summary of reference volume statistics for a typical week from 3,052 academic libraries for public and private institutions: doctoral, comprehensive, general baccalaureate, two-year, and specialized. It should be noted that statistics for large doctoral institutions may be flawed in that some libraries may have reported data only for the main library reference area while others may have reported totals that included multiple service points.

Henson, Jim. (1987). *Summary/analysis: Field responses to the reference referral study report.* Sacramento, CA.: California State Library.

Reports results of a study of the California reference referral system, done by a consultant during five months in 1986 and including 17 system reference centers and the Bay Area Reference Center (BARC) and the Southern California Answering Network (SCAN). The study was initiated by the state librarian because severe funding problems were anticipated and it was estimated that BARC and SCAN, even with reduced staffing, would require close to one million dollars in 1987. Functions studied included question answering, statewide education and training, development of specialized resources, and quality control, all of which were funded by the California Library Services Act. Among other aspects, the study examined direct costs for question handling, defined as including staff time and benefits, database costs, telephone costs, material purchased for center or host library, and supplies and equipment used in direct reference service. Not included were any staff training costs or costs for statewide educational functions. Direct costs per reference question received averaged $31, varying from $17 to $115. BARC and SCAN, the super reference providers, averaged $76 and $83 per question received during this period. BARC and SCAN also provided an informal estimate of $150 per question *answered*, which compared almost precisely with an estimate supplied by an information broker. General benefits were listed as reported by various groups or persons, but a benefit study using techniques such as the critical incident technique (Wilson, Starr-Schneidkraut, and Cooper, 1989) was not done. Recommendations were made by the Select Committee on Super Reference and the consultant that BARC and SCAN be phased out over a period of years and that the 17 regional system reference centers be combined into fewer strong regional centers. Other cost saving recommendations were flexible guidelines (not regulations) to limit the amount of time put into an answer, use of less skilled personnel for routine searching, and increasing question-handling productivity. Some of those who responded to the study, although they wanted to retain third-level reference, felt that more emphasis should be put on second-level reference and less on super reference. Other responses noted that these third-level questions were costly to answer because they were complex and required very experienced staff and sophisticated resources.

Herner, Saul. (1954). Information-gathering habits of workers in pure and applied science. *Industrial and Engineering Chemistry* 46, 228-236.
    This study of information-gathering habits found that heavy users of the literature do not generally delegate their documentation tasks, while those who are less dependent on the literature are more likely to delegate. The authors report that, in general, pure scientists made considerably less use of reference assistance than the applied scientists. More experienced and sophisticated users of the literature used distinctly fewer tools and techniques than the less experienced and sophisticated.

Herner, Saul, and Herner, Mary. (1967). Information needs and uses in science and technology. *Annual Review of Information Science and Technology* 2, 1-34.
    Covers studies done in 1966. Sections are based on method and cover present state and problems of user studies, diaries and user-administered records, interviews, observation, questionnaires, indirect studies, and

combined techniques. In regard to the diary method, the Herners note that studies show that scientist users will not cooperate in keeping diaries except for relatively short periods of time. There is also the danger that small samples will not be representative. They also note that it has been known for more than 13 years that pure scientists are more dependent on the literature than industrial scientists and technologists. Pure scientists prefer a small heavily used core of information media and methods and use a narrower variety of tools and techniques than applied scientists. Also mentioned is the reluctance of pure scientists to delegate information needs, presumably because of the highly specialized, creative, and personal nature of their work. Several studies have found that heavy users of the literature such as scientists do not generally delegate their documentation tasks through use of reference service. Those who are less literature-dependent, such as applied technologists, are more prone to delegation.

Hernon, Peter, and McClure, Charles R. (1983). *Improving the quality of reference service for government publications*. Chicago: American Library Association.

Reports the results of an unobtrusive study of the accuracy of answers to reference questions asked at 17 academic depository libraries in the Northeast and Southwest. Only 37% of questions were correctly answered. Provides recommendations for improvement of documents reference service.

Hernon, Peter, and McClure, Charles R. (1986a). The quality of academic and public library reference service provided for NTIS products and services: Unobtrusive test results. *Government Information Quarterly* 3, 117-132.

Personnel from 12 academic and public libraries participating in the United States Government Printing Office Depository Program were asked five pretested questions. The correct answer fill rate for all 12 libraries was 41.7 percent. To identify factors contributing to success researchers monitored search strategies and comments made by library personnel. They concluded that many general reference and documents personnel have limited familiarity with NTIS. A typical search strategy that a number of personnel employed in response to test questions was to first consult the *Monthly Catalog*. If that source did not yield the answer, they might or might not explore the *Publications Reference File*, the *GPO Monthly Catalog Subscription Service*, and the *Government Reports and Announcements Index*. Includes a table summarizing the percentage of correct answers in previous unobtrusive evaluations of reference service. **See Summaries of Instruments: Hernon and McClure—Reference Question Tabulation Sheet.**

Hernon, Peter, and McClure, Charles R. (1986b). Unobtrusive testing: The 55% rule. *Library Journal* 111, 37-41.

The authors extended unobtrusive testing to government documents by testing general reference and government documents staffs with 15 questions with predetermined answers. Results corroborated findings of earlier unobtrusive studies. The authors suggest that the profession re-examine its priorities and degree of commitment to the provision of information services.

Hernon, Peter, and McClure, Charles R. (1987a). Quality of data issues in unobtrusive testing of library reference service: Recommendations and strategies. *Library and Information Science Research* 9, 77-93.

Discusses issues relating to the reliability, validity, utility, and value of unobtrusive testing and provides suggestions for improving the quality of unobtrusive testing. Includes a table summarizing the requirements for quality data in unobtrusive testing. Recommends combining unobtrusive testing with other methods of data collection. Additional data collection strategies that would enrich findings from unobtrusive studies are briefly described.

Hernon, Peter, and McClure, Charles R. (1987b). *Unobtrusive testing and library reference services.* Norwood, NJ: Ablex Publishing Company.

This book reports unobtrusive testing of public and academic library personnel assigned to a depository department/collection and to a general reference department/collection in 26 libraries located in four geographic regions of the United States. Also reported is an experimental study intended to provide libraries with a means of self-diagnosis and potential improvement in the quality of reference services. In 1985, Hernon and McClure pretested service providers of government documents and found 63.5% accuracy. Approximately one month later, staff members received training (either lecture or slides) and then were unobtrusively posttested. The correct answer fill rate for the posttest was 52.5 percent. There was no significant difference in learning outcomes for the two different methods used to present the information in the workshops. Participants expressed opinions that both interventions covered material they already knew. The authors' objectives are to place unobtrusive testing in the context of reference service evaluation, to assess the correct fill rate as a performance measure and to report study findings, to refine unobtrusive testing as an evaluation methodology, to explore new applications for unobtrusive testing, to assist library staff in implementing ongoing evaluation of services, to discuss the impact of selected findings on larger issues related to library management and library education, and to identify additional research areas involving the use of unobtrusive testing. Research reported in this book complements previous research reported in *Improving the quality of reference service for government publications* (1983). As well, it provides excellent guidance for the implementation and analysis of unobtrusive testing, and it broadens the scope of the method for evaluation purposes.

Hernon, Peter, and Pastine, Maureen (1977). Student perceptions of academic librarians. *College & Research Libraries* 38, 129-139.
    Reports results of a survey of 700 students at the University of Nebraska. Most students were unaware that librarians had special training or subject expertise. Eight-seven percent of students surveyed perceived verbal interaction with librarians as a learning experience "sometimes" to "frequently." They appreciated being encouraged to return for further assistance when needed. Politeness and friendliness were perceived to be the most appreciated qualities in librarians.

Hewins, Elizabeth T. (1990). Information need and use studies. *Annual Review of Information Science and Technology* 25, 145-172.
    Affirms the 1986 Dervin and Nilan premise (Dervin and Nilan, 1986). Five-year review of studies found them scattered in many disciplines. Concludes that user behavior and perception should drive systems research more than ever.

Hieber, Caroline E. (1966). *An analysis of questions and answers in libraries*. Unpublished master's thesis, Lehigh University. Bethlehem, PA.
    Hieber (1966) devised a question classification based on the format of answer that seemed to satisfy the user. The five groups were 1) exact reproduction (pictures, maps, diagrams, speeches, historical documents, laws, poems, musical scores); 2) fill-in-the-blank (short answers, lists, tables); 3) descriptive (short or long descriptions); 4) information-about (information on a subject examined by librarian and user); and 5) list-of-references (citations, abstracts only).

Hittner, Amy. (1981). Individual rating scale for communication skills...in-service training program for library paraprofessionals workshop evaluation and pre-test/post-test. In Donna R. Bafundo (Ed.). *In-service training program for library paraprofessionals: A report*. Fairfax, VA: Consortium for Continuing Higher Education in Northern Virginia. (ERIC Document Reproduction Service No. ED 207 536).
    This program was designed to develop competence in basic reference skills and to reinforce positive service attitudes. It used a pretest and posttest design to evaluate modules. A significant increase in participants' perceptions of their understanding of the technical library skills

was found. There was evidence that participation in one or more modules of the program resulted in measurable improvement in library technical skills. **See Summaries of Instruments: Hittner—In-Service Training Program for Library Paraprofessionals; and Hittner—Individual Rating Scale for Communications Skills.**

House, David E. (1974). Reference efficiency or reference deficiency. *Library Association Record* 76, 222-223.

House explored variations in answers to the same reference question among 19 libraries. Library school students studying reference service made 20 visits to 19 libraries and asked simply for all available information on David Shepherd, the artist known for his paintings of African wildlife. Twelve libraries were able to produce no information at all, six produced some information, and two were able to trace most or all of the information known and to add new items. The principal factor causing variation in answer seemed to be lack of any logical strategy for searching the collection.

House, R.J., and Rizzo, J.R. (1972). Toward the measurement of organizational practices: Scale development and validation. *Journal of Applied Psychology* 56, 388-396.

The authors set out to develop a scale to measure job-induced stress and its possible outcomes in feelings and physical symptoms. **See Summaries of Instruments: House and Rizzo—Anxiety Stress Questionnaire.**

Houston Academy of Medicine. Texas Medical Center Library. (1987). *Annual statistics of medical school libraries in the United States and Canada, 1985-1986* (9th ed.). Houston, TX: Houston Academy of Medicine. Texas Medical Center Library.

Gives reference statistics for 121 U.S. medical school libraries.

Hunter, Rhonda. (1991). Successes and failures of patrons searching the online catalog at a large academic library: A transaction log analysis. *RQ* 30, 395-402.

A study was done at North Carolina State University where transaction logs were used to gather data on failure rates, usage patterns, and causes of problems. Results show that 54% of searches failed. Subject searching was most often used, but was least successful. Problems experienced by patrons were often due to failure in interacting with the system, typographical errors, and the use of uncontrolled vocabulary. Transaction log analysis proved to be a practical and useful method for studying user searching behavior in an online catalog.

Ingwersen, Peter. (1982). Search procedures in the library—analyzed from the cognitive point of view. *Journal of Documentation* 38, 165-191.

Considers user behavior during shelf searches. Thirteen librarians and five users participated in an experimental design involving tape recording and analyses of verbal protocols. The tape recording was supplemented by observation of subjects' behavior and actions and by self comments of subjects viewing the tape immediately after recording. Ingwersen concluded that search procedures consisting of more than a couple of search possibilities are composed of both conscious assimilation and processing of information from materials, which are incorporated in the further search process, and more or less random associations and impulses from the environment. Also notes that Jahoda's test of the descriptive model is interesting with regard not only to investigating the reference process itself but also to the didactic implementation of the study results.

The International City Management Association. (1979). *Municipal yearbook, 1979*. Washington, DC: The International City Management Association.

A survey of 900 municipal libraries in 1977 found that the ratio of yearly reference questions to total library (not reference) staff was approximately 1,500 reference questions to one library staff member. Figures are given for different size groups in terms of population.

Isenstein, Laura J. (1991). On the road to STARdom: Improving reference accuracy. *Illinois Libraries* 73, 146-151.

In analyzing why Baltimore County Public Library used follow-up questions only 21% of the time in the 1986 Maryland survey, even after receiving training and coaching, Isenstein concluded that individuals needed help in learning to coach appropriately. In Spring 1988, intensive training sessions were held, followed by assignments, follow-up workshops, and consistent coaching. The trainers were successful in having these behaviors added to performance evaluations with observations occurring two times a month. The author describes in detail the training process employed by the Baltimore County Public Library to teach reference librarians effective peer coaching techniques utilizing Model Reference Behaviors. Emphasis is placed on technical feedback which is solicited, not imposed; descriptive, not evaluative or judgmental; specific, not general; directed at modifiable behavior; and given in a timely manner.

Ivey, Allen E., and Authier, Jerry. (1978). *Microcounseling: Innovations in interviewing, counseling, psychotherapy, and psychoeducation* (2d ed.). Springfield, IL: Charles C. Thomas.

Appendix IV contains Haase's Counseling Effectiveness Scale and data on its development. Information on item selection, reliability, and validity of the scale is included. **See Summaries of Instruments: Haase—Counselor Effectiveness Scale.**

Jahoda, Gerald. (1977). *The process of answering reference questions.* Washington, DC: Office of Education. (ERIC Document Reproduction Service No. ED 136 769).

A study was conducted to determine how librarians answer reference queries and to develop materials for teaching the answering process. As part of the study, Jahoda developed a list of types of expected answers: 1) dates (specific dates); 2) events (involving people); 3) illustrations; 4) numeric information (scientific properties or statistics); 5) organizations; 6) persons; 7) addresses and general locations; 8) publications (citations, including bibliographies, document locations, or verification/completion of bibliographic data); 9) terms or subjects (abbreviations, words, phrases, definitions, abstracts, annotations, recommendation of publications, or general or background information); and 10) unspecified or other (list particular wanted). Jahoda then combined the queries under the descriptors into four types: general background on a subject; factual information about people, organizations, or products; queries about specific publications; and queries about words and phrases. In collecting and analyzing 1,558 queries answered by 27 public libraries, he found almost half to be requests for background information and slightly over one-third to be for factual information. Jahoda also developed categories of answer-providing tools: atlases, maps; biographical sources; card catalogs, union lists; dictionaries; encyclopedias; guides to the literature; handbooks, manuals, and almanacs; indexes, bibliographies and abstracts; monographs, texts; nonbiographical directories; primary publications, including dissertations, reports, primary journals, and conference proceedings; and yearbooks. **See Summaries of Instruments: Jahoda—Instrument for Search Strategy and Development.**

Jahoda, Gerald. (1989). Rules for performing steps in the reference process. *Reference Librarian* 25/26, 557-567.

Summarizes rules for performing steps in reference process and discusses assumptions underlying rules and directions for future research. An assumption underlying the discussion is that reference librarians answer queries by matching them with their perceptions of relevant portions of information resources, both inside and outside the library. Each of the 13 steps is discussed in terms of objectives, facts, and rules. Step number eight is the search sequence of types of answer-providing tools—Jahoda notes that rules for selecting search sequence are not now available. A test on a representative sample of queries, such as queries

used in unobtrusive studies of reference, could be used to develop rules
for search sequence of types of answer-providing tools as well as some
of the other steps in the reference process.

Jahoda, Gerald, and Braunagel, Judith Schiek. (1980). *The librarian and
reference queries: A systematic approach.* New York: Academic Press.
    Presents a model of the reference process, which involves 1)
extracting essential information from the user's request; 2) negotiating
if query clarification is necessary; 3) selecting types of answer-providing
tools; 4) selecting specific titles to search; 6) translating query words into
the language of answer-providing tool; 7) selecting the correct answer;
and 8) communicating the answer to the user and soliciting feedback. In
searching for an answer, many reference librarians mentally select
categories of reference tools, such as dictionaries or encyclopedias that
will likely contain an answer. Selection of suitable categories of answer-
providing tools can be performed by becoming familiar with the types of
given and wanted information found in such tools. When asked a familiar
query, the librarian is able to go directly to a specific title with
confidence that it contains a satisfactory answer, In trying to answer
queries never answered before, however, some librarians think first in
terms of reference tools likely to contain answers. Individual titles within
each type have certain basic characteristics and similar types of
information content. In trying to satisfy requests, a method is needed to
choose a sequence for searching each tool category. The authors note
that there is undoubtedly an optimum search sequence, but present level
of knowledge has not yet provided any generalizations about the best
sequence for searching potentially useful reference tools. All things being
equal, the optimum search sequence should provide the most complete
answer in the least time.

Jahoda, G., Eyles, H.H., Lawson, V.L., Paskoff, B.M., and Pond, M.J.
(1987). *The process of answering reference queries: Toward an
analytical model.* Tallahassee, FL: School of Library and Information
Studies.
    Presents work on the development of rules for performing three of
the steps in the reference process. The three steps are message selection
(i.e., selecting essential information in the request of a library user),
selection of types of answer-providing tools, and selection of search
sequence of types of answering sources. Proposes that the sequence of
searching reference sources is based on two factors: 1) match of basic
information unit of the query (i.e., wanted descriptors) with basic
information unit of type of answer-providing tool; and 2) ease of access
to answer in type of answering source. Conducted a small-scale test of
12 queries. Concludes that more testing is needed before any conclusions

about the sequence of search of reference sources may be drawn. Rules for search sequence would help in training of reference librarians, in evaluation of reference work, and in determining which steps of the reference process can be done by computers.

Jain, A.K. (1969). Sampling and data collection methods for a book-use study. *Library Quarterly* 39, 245-252.
    Describes 1966 study at Purdue. Discusses sampling of in-library use as an independent sample. States little is known about book usage within the library. Jain's 1968 doctoral thesis (Purdue) was on a statistical study of book use.

Jain, A.K. (1972). Sampling in-library book use. *Journal of the American Society for Information Science* 23, 150-155.
    Noted that little study has been done on unrecorded use, whether reshelving was done by library staff or patrons. Presents a plan for sampling in-library use: the library is divided into areas and inspection rounds are made. Formulas provided.

Jenkins, Barbara Williams, and Smalls, Mary L. (1990). *Performance appraisal in academic libraries*. Chicago, IL: ACRL, College Libraries Section, College Library Information Packet Committee.
    Contains examples of instruments for evaluating librarians' performance.

Jennerich, Elaine Zaremba, and Jennerich, Edward J. (1987). *The reference interview as a creative art*. Littleton, CO: Libraries Unlimited, Inc.
    Comparing reference librarians to actors, reference training to learning a new role, the reference interview to a performance, and the reference desk to a stage, the authors put the topic into context for staff development. Suggestions on determining reference desk arrangements are offered in "Physical Setting," p. 48-53.

Jensen, Rebecca, Asbury, Herbert, and King, Radford. (1980). Costs and benefits to industry of online literature searches. *Special Libraries* 71, 291-297.
    Describes a client survey conducted by NASA Industrial Applications Center at UCLA. A total of 159 clients were interviewed over the telephone in regard to benefits from a computerized literature search. Over 53% identified dollar benefits in terms of savings or increased income. Of those who identified dollar benefits, 38% were increased earnings for current applications, 12% for new applications, and 50% for savings in time. The ration of benefits to cost was 3 to 1. Over a five-

year period, the ratio was 7 to 1. See **Summaries of Instruments: Jensen, et al.—Costs and Benefits.**

Jirjees, Jassim M. (1983). The accuracy of selected Northeastern college library reference/information telephone services in responding to factual inquiries. In *The accuracy of telephone reference/information services in academic libraries: Two studies*. Metuchen, NJ: Scarecrow Press.

Unobtrusive measurement and case study were applied to a sample of four-year colleges with graduate programs. The study included a simulated telephone test of reference accuracy using factual questions. The study revealed that the reference departments studied did not have written policies for providing reference/information services. There was a wide discrepancy between what the library directors and the reference department heads thought was being done, and the actual situation as revealed through the reference test which resulted in a mean accuracy level of 56.6%. Reasons for failure included the following: libraries did not use their own or other resources available; they did not make use of subject specialists; staff claimed no time to answer questions; staff did not know how to use or misinterpreted information in some sources; poor staff attitudes; and staff were working under stress.

Johnson, Debra Wilcox. (1993). Reflecting on the public library data service project: Public libraries over five years, 1987-91. *Public Libraries* 32, 259-261.

This report marks the sixth anniversary of the voluntary data collection project, Public Library Data Service. This article covers the five years from 1987-1991. More than 70% of public libraries serving more than 100,000 residents participated. Nearly 15% of public libraries serving populations from 50,000 to 99,999 are represented. The most frequently reported data are those related to demographic data. Public libraries increasingly are using the role-selection process to assist in planning. Enough libraries are reporting output measures to show ranges of responses for several of these measures.

Jordan, Thomas E. (1989). *Measurement and evaluation in higher education: issues and illustrations*. Philadelphia: The Falmer Press, Taylor and Francis Inc.

Helpful for broader assessments in academic institutions.

Joseph, Margaret A. (1984). Analyzing success in meeting reference department management objectives using a computerized statistical package. *The Reference Librarian* 11, 183-193. Also in Katz, Bill, and Fraley, Ruth A. (1984). *Evaluation of reference services*. New York: Haworth Press.

Reports on a study to evaluate reference management objectives. Analysis indicated reference department objectives: 1) Provided brief assistance to relatively large numbers of patrons rather than in-depth assistance to relatively few patrons; 2) Emphasized service to students, faculty, and staff with an established criterion of 80% of service to institutionally affiliated patrons and 20% to others; 3) Provided service to patrons who were not institutionally affiliated on a secondary basis; 4) Used reference staff optimally when possible by having support staff handle directional questions and librarians handle reference questions; 5) Provided egalitarian reference service, by basing decision as to level of staff assigned to provide service not on patron status but on patron need, staff skill, and staff availability; 6) Had librarians handle more complex, time-consuming questions and support staff handle relatively less complex, quick-answer questions; and (7) Handled directional questions as quickly as possible. **See Summaries of Instruments: Joseph—Library Survey Form.**

Kantor, Paul. (1980). Analyzing the availability of reference services. In Neal Kaske (Ed.). *Library effectiveness: A state of the art: Proceedings of the ALA preconference on library effectiveness* (p. 131-149). Chicago: American Library Association.

Describes a method where the reference desk is observed at random intervals over a period of time, with the following noted: number of staff free, assisting others or doing other work, and number of patrons waiting. The Frustration Factor measure is the percentage of time someone is free to help. The Nuisance Factor measure is the ratio of the time patrons spend waiting to the time they spend being helped. Availability in 13 libraries averaged approximately 72%, ranging from about 30% to 100%. **See Summaries of Instruments: Kantor—Frustration Factor and Nuisance Factor.**

Kantor, Paul. (1981a). Levels of outputs related to cost of operation of scientific and technical libraries. *Library Research* 3, 1-28.

The author performed an extensive cost analysis of library service using data on 45 libraries for 1978-1979. In regard to reference questions, a unit cost was obtained by dividing the volume of reference questions for a year by a portion of the operating budget. A figure of $10.80 per reference transaction was found.

Kantor, Paul B. (1981b). Quantitative evaluation of the reference process. *RQ* 2, 43-52.

Data from 2,062 queries, gathered in 16 libraries, were collected and analyzed in terms of causal factors that inhibit the delivery of service and behavioral outcomes of the reference process. The analysis identified a chain of essentially independent conditions that must be met in order for users to obtain the information they seek. Five causal factors and behavioral outcomes are identified. Results for all queries were that in 69% of queries patrons were satisfied. Librarian knowledge (librarian reports cannot think of an appropriate source) accounted for very few failures and collection (library does not have the source) accounted for most failures. A weakness in this method is that the librarian may indicate the library does not have a source that will answer the query when in fact the librarian is not aware of an appropriate source that the library owns. **See Summaries of Instruments: Kantor—Analysis of Availability.**

Kantor, Paul B. (1982). Evaluation of and feedback in information storage and retrieval systems. *Annual Review of Information Science and Technology* 17, 99-120.
 Kantor reviews the literature on evaluation and feedback and finds it surprisingly large, due in part to the meaning of feedback as it is used in management and in information storage and retrieval. He finds use of the term "evaluation" to be overworked; often it is more or less quantitative description of operating policies, demand levels, or user attitudes. He notes that demand, through users' judgment, is presented as a measure of system effectiveness when, in fact, it may be mandated and reflect simply the absence of effective competition. With respect to the value of retrieved items, he indicates the general agreement that end-users are the best judges, but that their judgment is clouded by many other factors that influence their understanding and actions. Kantor notes that his branching analysis technique relies upon the librarian's judgment of success or failure and does not have widespread acceptance.

Kantor, Paul. (1984). *Objective performance measures for academic and research libraries*. Washington, DC: Association of Research Libraries.
 Describes performance measures based on simulation, availability, and flow analysis. Includes bibliography of items related to these measures and particularly to availability analysis. **See Summaries of Instruments: Kantor—Measurement of Effort By Simulation.**

Kaske, Neal K., and Aluri, Rao. (1980). An analysis of reference statistics reported in the 1977 Library General Information Survey. (Paper presented at the Library Research Round Table, ALA Summer Convention, New York). (ERIC Document Reproduction Service No. ED 202 486).
 Reports on an analysis of reference and directional question totals from 3,000 academic libraries from the National Library General Information Survey. Fifty-five percent of transactions were directional

and the percent of directional transactions decreased as the size of the library rose.

Katz, Bill, and Fraley, Ruth A. (Eds). (1985). *Conflicts in reference services.* New York: Haworth Press.

A collection of articles that was originally published as the Spring/Summer 1985 *Reference Librarian* on various forms of conflict: personal, philosophical, and interpersonal. Articles on paraprofessionals at the reference desk suggest the importance of a strong self-image and possible strategies for dealing with the ordinary problems of everyday life at the reference desk.

Katz, Bill, and Fraley, Ruth A. (Eds). (1986). *Reference services today: From interview to burnout.* New York: Haworth Press.

Originally published as the Winter 1986 *Reference Librarian*, it contains a number of articles that reflect the subject matter of this chapter. Much of this issue concerns interpersonal skills and their effect on a librarian's credibility, job satisfaction, and library image.

Kazlauskas, Edward. (1976). An exploratory study: A kinesic analysis of academic library public service points. *Journal of Academic Librarianship* 2, 130-134.

Describes kinesic analysis as the study of body movements. Employs a case study approach. Reports results of a study of public services staff at four academic libraries. Observations numbered 148, and data were grouped into positive and negative behaviors and into patterns. Implications for public service management are noted.

Kent State University Libraries. (1976). *Survey of student opinion.* Kent, OH: Kent State University Libraries.

Survey forms were mailed to users with a return rate of 52%. Overall, 51% reported themselves as reference users. Those who reported almost never using reference were asked to mark their reasons (don't need help, librarians too busy, librarians can't help, librarians unwilling to help). Data were analyzed by class and it appeared that reports of librarian unwillingness were greatest at lower class level, while reports of librarians being too busy were greatest at high class levels. Overall, 73% of those who did not use reference reported that they knew how to find what they needed by themselves. Other reasons were librarians too busy (10%), librarians unwilling (8.1%), librarians not able to help (6.4%), and users did not know the service was available. The tendency to ask for help rose with class size with 45% of underclass, 53% of upperclass, and 52% of graduates being reference users. There appeared to be a greater tendency to ask for reference help among *infrequent* library users than among *frequent* library users. Around 21% of weekly library users reported themselves as reference users, while 45% of those who use the library infrequently (several times per quarter or less) reported themselves as reference users.

Kernaghan, John A., Kernaghan, Salvinija G., O'Keefe, Robert D., and Rubenstein, Albert H. (1979). The influence of traditional services on library use. *College & Research Libraries* 40, 214-225.

It was hypothesized here that the more library services, including reference, are provided, the more the library will be used. A sample was used of 653 medical students in five medical schools who were surveyed by a questionnaire asking about their approaches to finding information. Libraries were also asked to rank themselves on these services. Results, in regard to reference service, indicate that the more users perceive library staff members are willing to help them in their information seeking, the more frequently they will use the library.

Kesselman, Martin, and Watstein, Sarah Barbara. (1987). The measurement of reference and information services. *The Journal of Academic Librarianship* 13, 24-30.

The authors reviewed the collection and publication of statistics and data related to reference and resources use. They developed a framework for procedures and policies for data collection and analysis. This study tested for consistency in classifying reference queries. They found that different reference personnel were not consistent in categorizing the same questions as short reference, long reference, directional, or referral. Much of the variation of responses occurred due to differing perceptions of directional versus referral, short reference versus long reference, and directional versus reference transactions.

Kim, Choong Han, and Littel, Robert David. (1987). *Public library users and uses*. Metuchen, NJ: Scarecrow Press.

Analyzes the ways people use the public library and aims to offer library professionals a practical method of assessing and appraising local information needs. Covers in-house/reference uses. Sample questionnaire forms are included.

King, Geraldine. (1982). Try it—you'll like it: A comprehensive management information system for reference services. *Reference Librarian* 3, 71-78.

Describes a system of evaluation useful for training new staff, staff development, and evaluation of individual reference librarians by managers. King notes that "Reference librarians are highly intelligent, highly motivated professionals. Once they have set their objectives and priorities as a group, the role of the reference manager is to facilitate and co-ordinate their working together in the least obtrusive, least hierarchical way. The member of the group whose responsibility is communication and monitoring, the reference manager, needs a lot of information." **See Summaries of Instruments: King—Reference Transaction Slip.**

King, Geraldine. (1988). *Managing employee performance.* (T.I.P. Kit No. 11). Chicago: ALA Office of Library Personnel Resources.
Contains examples of instruments for evaluating librarians' performance.

King, Geraldine, and Mahmoodi, Suzanne H. (1991). Peer performance appraisal of reference librarians in a public library. In *Evaluation of public services and public service librarians.* (Allerton Park Institute no. 32). Urbana-Champaign, IL: University of Illinois Graduate School of Library and Information Science.
Describes an instrument designed specifically to evaluate the performance of reference librarians. The instrument, a competency-based self-evaluation, and the related forms for the peer appraisal process are included in the paper; there is also a lengthy discussion of the development, implementation, and evaluation of this instrument.

Kirby, Martha, and Miller, Naomi. (1985). Medline searching on BRS Colleague: Search success of untrained end users in a medical school and hospital. *National Online Meeting Proceedings* (p. 255-263). Medford, NJ: Learned Information.
End-users were given brief instructions, after which they performed searches of their own choice on BRS Colleague. Following each search, a trained searcher redid the user's search. In 60% of the cases, the user reported that the second search added important new items and was better. **See Summaries of Instruments: Kirby and Miller—Questionnaires I and II.**

Kirby, Martha, and Miller, Naomi. (1986). Medline searching on Colleague: Reasons for failure or success of untrained end users. *Medical Reference Services Quarterly* 5, 17-33.
A previous study by the authors (Kirby and Miller, 1985) showed that end-user searches often missed relevant references. This study did not, however, indicate why relevant references were missed. In the present study, the same 52 searches used in the original study were re-examined. "Incomplete" searches were studied and were defined as those where users indicated that the librarian's search found relevant references they had missed in their own searches. Problems with search strategy were the greatest cause of failure and occurred on 68% of searches, system

failures (errors in use of commands and/or connectors—and, or, not, same) on 22% of searches, and errors in database selection on 10% of searches. The most frequently used features were 1) "and," 77 percent; 2) truncation, 38 percent; 3) field qualifiers (ti, etc.), 29 percent; and 4) position operators (with, etc.), 15 percent. Success rates for the different approaches were 1) "and," 81 percent; 2) field qualifiers, 38 percent; 3) truncation, 29 percent; 4) position operators, 19 percent; and 5) "or," 10 percent. Conclusions were that "untrained users using simple strategies need to be warned against overconfidence in search results." Successful searches were those where the topic was suitable for a simple search. See **Summaries of Instruments: Kirby and Miller—Questionnaires I and II.**

Kirkpatrick, Donald L. (1979). Techniques for evaluating training programs. *Training and Development Journal* 33, 78-92. Originally published in a four-part series in *Journal of the American Society of Training Directors* 13, November 1959, 3-9 and December 1959, 21-26, and *Journal of the American Society of Training Directors* 14, January 1960, 13-16 and February 1960, 28-32.

A wide variety of evaluation techniques are suggested and described in the following four areas: reaction, learning, job behavior, and results.

Kobasa, Suzanne C. (1979). Stressful life events, personality, and health: An inquiry into hardiness. *Journal of Personality and Social Psychology* 37, 1-11 January.

Two groups of middle and upper executives from a large utility company were studied in relation to life stress and illness. A group was identified with high scores on stressful life events, as measured by the Holmes Rahe Schedule of Life Events. A subgroup was then identified who reported becoming sick after stressful life events. The two groups—100 high stress/high illness subjects and 100 high stress/low illness subjects—were given a questionnaire covering demographics, perceptions of stressful life events, and several personality tests. None of the demographic variables yielded significant approaches. The authors found that high stress/low illness or "hardy" groups 1) perceived less stress in their lives; 2) felt more in control of their lives, found life more meaningful, and had an internal locus of control; 3) were more committed to themselves and their lives, and showed less alienation from self, others, work, and so on; and 4) liked challenge and were more adventurous.

Kohl, David F. (1985). *Acquisitions, collection development, and collection use: A handbook for library management*. Santa Barbara, CA: ABC-Clio Information Services.

Summarizes main findings of numerous studies reported in library journal literature from 1960-1983. Significantly, few are related to reference use.

Kottenstette, J.P. (1969). Student reading characteristics: Comparing skill levels demonstrated on hard copy and microform presentation. In J.B. North (Ed.) *Proceedings of the American Society for Information Science* 6. Westport, CT: Greenwood Press.

A study was done where materials of differing degrees of difficulty were read by students in hard copy and microform. It was found that there was no difference in comprehension between the forms. However, easy materials took longer to read on microfilm.

Kramer, Joseph. (1971). How to survive in industry: Cost justifying library services. *Special Libraries* 62, 487-489.

Reports on a study done by the author in the Boeing Company Aerospace Group Library from 1967 through 1969 for 24 months. Questionnaires were mailed to 353 patrons who had received subject bibliographies; 153 were returned for a 43% return rate. Another group of 215 users were then called and given a previously asked citation-verification question and asked how much time it would probably take them to find the answer. For every staff hour spent on a literature search, engineers reported being saved about nine hours of labor. For every staff hour spent on verification questions, engineers reported being saved 27 hours. **See Summaries of Instruments: Kramer—Cost Benefit Formula.**

Krulee, G.K. and Nadler, E. (1960). Studies of education for science and engineering: Student values and curricular choice. *IRE Transactions in Engineering Management* 7, 146-158.

In a study of students in science and engineering, it was noted that science students placed higher value on independence and learning for its own sake than engineering students. Engineering students were more concerned with personal success and vocational training.

Kuhlthau, Carol Collier. (1984). The library research process: Case studies and interventions with high school seniors in advanced placement English classes using Kelly's Theory of Constructs. Doctoral dissertation, Rutgers University. *Dissertation Abstracts International* 44, 1961A.

This study examined process-oriented library instruction as opposed to source-oriented library instruction. Problem areas examined were student constructs of and experiences with the search process, and interventions that might assist students in the search process. Twenty-seven high school seniors in advanced English placement classes were studied. An intervention group of six had discussions of the search process and additional opportunities for discussion and writing. The intervention group made better use of time, sources, and the media specialist while in the library, and had more clearly focused papers. Constructs changed in regard to formulation of focus and sequence in use of sources, but the construct of the very limited role of the reference librarian in the search process did not change. The methods developed in this study for process-oriented library instruction may be adapted for library skills instruction.

Kuhlthau, Carol Collier. (1988a). Developing a model of the Library Search Process: Cognitive and affective aspects. *RQ* 28, 232-242.

Formulates a theory of the process of searching for information based on a study conducted in a large eastern suburban high school. Discusses various theories of the search process. An exploratory study was conducted using 26 high school seniors preparing research papers on a literary theme. Instruments and methods used were search logs, journals of feelings, thoughts, and actions, flow charts and time lines, observations, and short writings about topics. Six of the students agreed to be interviewed six times for 45-minute taped sessions. These data were used to develop a six-stage model of the search process, including task initiation, topic selection, prefocus exploration, focus formulation, information collection, and search closure. **See Summaries of Instruments: Kuhlthau, Turock, George, and Belvin—The Information Search Process.**

Kuhlthau, Carol Collier. (1988b). Longitudinal case studies of the information search process of users in libraries. *Library and Information Science Research* 10, 257-304.

In this longitudinal investigation into the information search process of library users, four students were studied as high school seniors in 1983 and again after completing four years of undergraduate education. The user's perspective is the focus of the study and students describe their thoughts and feelings in narrative form during seven stages of the search process. One student reported that she went to the catalog for broad subjects in humanities and social sciences and to abstracts for the sciences. Students reported translating their purposes into types of information in the "focus" stage. Some reported asking for help early in the process and some after encountering problems. Often needs were brought to friends and instructors in preference to the library. The greatest use of the library was in stage 5, collection of information. Librarians were reported to have played a minimal role in the process. Librarians were expected to answer location questions and little else, and they were not expected to have sufficient subject expertise to recommend sources. Instruction given was described as inadequate. Some comments were, "I would look like a jerk if I asked a librarian to help me," "Best to ask the professor," "Librarians don't know enough about science," "I don't think they ever heard of anyone asking how much a chemical costs," and "They would tell me ridiculous things like to go through all the *New York Times* from such and such a year." One student expected librarians to lack sufficient expertise to help on subject questions but that they should seek out students and ask them if they needed help. The author discusses the advantages of the interview method. See **Summaries of Instruments: Kuhlthau, Turock, George, and Belvin—The Information Search Process.**

Kuhlthau, Carol Collier. (1988c). Perceptions of the information search process in libraries: A study of changes from high school through college. *Information Processing & Management* 24, 419-427.
    A longitudinal study was done of how students perceive the information search process in libraries. Students were followed over a four-year period from high school through college. The model of the search process is provided and student perceptions are related to the model. The cognitive theory underlying the model is discussed. See **Summaries of Instruments: Kuhlthau, Turock, George, and Belvin—The Information Search Process.**

Kuhlthau, Carol, Turock, Betty, George, Mary, and Belvin, Robert. (1990). Validating a model of the search process: A comparison of academic, public and school library users. *Library and Information Science Research* 12, 5-31.
    This research project built on Kuhlthau's earlier study, but used a different methodology and expanded coverage to public, academic, and school libraries. The research process, as defined here, is that of the extended literature search rather than the search for a fact or isolated elements of information. Respondents were asked who they had talked to about their projects, with 39% reporting talking to subject experts, 25% to reference librarians, 20% to friends and family, and 13% to peers working on similar tasks. Consultation of others did not show significant differences across types of libraries, except for school libraries, or across stages of the process. Results indicated that public library adults were significantly more confident at initiation of the search process than in other libraries. Academic participants, however, were significantly more confident at the closure stage than those in school libraries. In regard to actions, school library participants had significantly lower means in browsing, asking questions of librarians, and in six other actions. In the majority of cases, a preference was indicated for finding everything first and then reading, rather than the process-oriented

approach of reading to learn along the way. It is suggested that reference librarians become sensitive to the stage of the process the user is in when a question is asked. **See Summaries of Instruments: Kuhlthau, et al.—The Information Search Process.**

Kupersmith, John. (1992). Technostress and the reference librarian. *Reference Services Review* 20:2, 7-14, 50.
Discusses the demands of the new information technology and recommends ways reference librarians can reduce the effects of technostress.

LAMA PAS Staff Development Committee. (1992). *Staff development: A practical guide*. 2d ed. Chicago: American Library Association. Ed. by Anne Grodzins Lipow and Deborah A. Carver.
Chapters 1 through 5 provide background on basic principles of staff development such as adult learning theory, transfer of training, and instructional design. The methods section includes planning, preparing, and implementing, as well as resources for staff development. Staff development policy statements from several institutions and needs assessment surveys from the Tacoma Public Library and The University of Michigan are reproduced.

Lamble, J. Hoskin. (1951). Statistical representation of reference library use. *Library Association Record* 18, 291-292.
This represents one of the earliest attempts to relate volume of reference transactions to number of users in the reference area.

Lancaster, F. Wilfred. (1977). *Measurement and evaluation of library services*. Washington, DC: Information Resources Press.
Measurement and evaluation are covered for such aspects as reference, collections, public catalogs, technical services, retrieval systems, and physical access. Libraries are guided to develop their own assessment programs. See also 2d edition under Baker and Lancaster (1991) above.

Lancaster, F. Wilfred. (1982). Evaluating collections by their use. *Collection Management* 4, 15-43.
Detailed treatment of methods of determining in-house use, but concentrates on circulating materials and journals.

Lancaster, F. Wilfred. (1984). Factors influencing the effectiveness of question-answering services in libraries. *Reference Librarian* 11, 95-108.
Lancaster identified 55 possible influencing factors under the following headings: will the library receive a question, will the library accept the question, can answer be found, policy factors, collection

factors, librarian factors, question-related factors, user factors, environmental factors, and referral factors. The range and diversity of factors indicate that the effectiveness of question-answering activities is governed by a complex set of variables, which can be further impacted by chance. The development and growth of electronic information sources will result in the decline in importance of some of the influencing factors.

Lancaster, F. Wilfred. (1988). *If you want to evaluate your library....* Champaign, IL: Graduate School of Library and Information Science, University of Illinois.

Useful chapters on collection use analysis, especially in-house use. Similar information in Baker and Lancaster (1991) above.

Lange, Janet M. (1986). *San Diego County Library Reference Service Project Final Report.* San Diego: County of San Diego.

In 1986 an extensive study was done of reference service in the San Diego County Libraries covering use, patron satisfaction, type of questions, staff workload, reference collection evaluation, staffing levels, and training needs. **See Summaries of Instruments: Lange—San Diego County Library Staff Workload and Reference Training Needs Survey.**

Langrish, J., McGibbons, M., Evans, E.G., and Jevons, F.R. (1972). *Wealth from knowledge.* London: Macmillan.

This study on innovation examined 158 important ideas associated with technology innovations in award winning firms. Fifty-six percent of ideas came from *outside* the company. Of those, only 9% came from published literature. However, 23% came from the innovator's common knowledge base acquired over the years, in which published literature may have played a part.

Larason, Larry. (1975). Behavioral response to the location of a reference service in an academic library environment. Doctoral dissertation, University of Oklahoma. *Dissertation Abstracts International* 36, 4824-5A.

Explores academic reference service location and consequence environmental impact on usage by patrons.

Larason, Larry, and DiCarlo, Rebecca. (1962). *Personal space and user preference for patterns of carrel arrangement in an academic library.* Paper presented at the Annual Convention of the American Library Association, Philadelphia, PA. (ERIC Document Reproduction Service No. ED 222 166).

Covers personal space requirements. Carrel pattern and position significantly affect use.

Larason, Larry, and Robinson, Judith Schiek. (1984). The reference desk: Service point or barrier? *RQ* 23, 332-338.
Theory and practice involved in reference area design. Using a marketing approach, Larason and Robinson made recommendations for placement and design for an approachable reference desk.

Lawrence, Gary S., and Oja, Anne R. (1980). *The use of general collections at the University of California; A study of unrecorded use, at-the-shelf discovery and immediacy of need for materials at the Davis and Santa Cruz Campus Libraries*. [Davis, CA?]: University of California.
Reports on the importance of shelf browsing in finding needed information (12% to 77%). Findings for unrecorded use include the following: There were about six unrecorded uses for every recorded use; unrecorded use/recorded use ratio is greater for bound periodicals than for books; 32% of uses were selected for browsing; and unrecorded use does not equate with at-the-shelf discovery and the two should be treated separately in studies. **See Summaries of Instruments: Lawrence and Oja—University of California Questionnaire.**

Lawson, V. Lonnie. (1990). A cost comparison between general library tours and computer-assisted instruction programs. *Research Strategies* 8, 66-73.
A study was done at Central Missouri State University to determine relative cost effectiveness of library tours versus CAI instruction. Freshmen enrolled in eight English classes were divided into three groups (tours, CAI instruction, and no instruction) and were given a pretest and posttest to measure amount learned. It was found that the majority of students using CAI learned as much as or more than those participating in the tour. Tour costs included librarian and classroom faculty time in terms of hourly rates. Computer costs included disks, software, hardware, programming, service, laboratory assistants, and maintenance. Costs were computed for a five-year period. If hardware had to be purchased, the CAI alternative was the most expensive, costing $9,707 the first year. Without hardware purchases for start-up and without laboratory assistants, costs were $907. Costs for the tour were $1,111. **See Summaries of Instruments: Lawson—Cost Effectiveness Comparison of Two Alternatives.**

Layman, Mary, and Vandercook, Sharon. (1990). Statewide reference improvement: Developing personnel and collections. *Wilson Library Bulletin* 64, 26-31.

Using Transform's model reference behaviors, the authors conducted training modules for paraprofessionals providing reference assistance in California public libraries. Their objective was to demonstrate 20% improvement in reference behavior, increase accuracy of information provided by 10%, and improve ability to understand and fill information needs of special populations by 5%. Contact Terence Crowley, currently at San Jose State University School of Library and Information Science, for the instrument.

Lederman, Linda Costigan. (1981). Fear of talking: Which students in an academic library ask librarians for help. *RQ* 20, 382-393.

Reports results of a study done to determine whether fear of talking influences a library user's decision to consult a reference librarian. Forty-eight students in all, testing high, medium, and low in communication anxiety, were sent to the library to locate answers to specific test questions. They were told that they might proceed with their searches in any way and that they might turn to materials, to librarian assistance, or to both, as desired. A search was considered to be concluded when the student consulted the librarian. Searches were observed and the number of steps taken *before* consulting the reference librarian were noted. Out of 48 students, 15% consulted the librarian as the first *step*. Sixty-four percent consulted the reference librarian after one or more attempts had been made to find the information. Twenty-three percent made three to four attempts before seeking help. A final 12% consulted the librarian only after five or more attempts had been made. No significant relationship was found by the author between communication difficulty and tendency to ask for help.

Leighton, Philip D., and Weber, David C. (1986). *Planning academic and research library buildings* (2d ed.). Chicago: American Library Association.

Revision of Keyes Metcalf's 1965 benchmark work.

LeMay, Moira, Layton, Frances, and Townsend, David. (1990). A model of human responses to workload stress. *Bulletin of the Psychonomic Society* 28, 547-550.

Observations took place on ten experienced computer operators who were under time stress, when baseline time for a job was cut by greater and greater amounts of time. The operators were only able to perform 20% faster, but no more. Errors remained constant over all conditions.

Lewis, David W. (1987). Research on the use of online catalogs and its implications for library practices. *Journal of Academic Librarianship* 13, 152-157.

Presents a review of research on users of online catalogs. Notes that patterns of behavior observed in the card catalog were adapted to card technology. Often behavior patterns are different in the online environment.

Long, Linda J. (1989). Questions negotiation in the archival setting: The use of interpersonal communication techniques in the reference interview. *American Archivist* 52, 40-50.

In addition to examining verbal and nonverbal communication skills involved in the archivist-patron relationship, this article also includes paralinguistic elements of communication, such as pitch, stress, and volume of voice as areas worthy of study. Long provides a good review of the literature.

Lopez, Manuel. (1973). Academic reference service: Measurement, cost and value. *RQ* 12, 234-242.

The author stresses the importance of measurement and evaluation of reference service so that library administrators can be assured that reference service is delivering full value for costs incurred. Emphasizes that cost analysis should consider *all* costs, including reference collection costs and overhead.

Lowenthal, Ralph A. (1990). Preliminary indications of the relationship between reference morale and performance. *RQ* 29, 380-393.

A study was conducted of 37 reference department staff members in seven public service units in four public libraries. A morale questionnaire consisting of a battery of recognized instruments was completed. After completing this questionnaire, the libraries participated in the Reference Transaction Assessment Program (Murfin and Gugelchuk, 1987) and performance scores for reference departments were obtained. The sample size was not large enough to permit drawing of substantive conclusions; however, it suggests strongly that the success rate of the units is related to staff morale and feelings of emotional well being as well as to environmental factors including rapport with the unit head, patron relations, group cohesion, and work environment.

Lushington, Nolan. (1987). Output measures and library space planning. *Library Trends* 36, 391-398.

Connects library performance measures and library space planning and collection management. Output measure surveys are suggested to establish hierarchies of use and design of environments which house library collections.

Lynch, Mary Jo. (1983). Research in library reference/information service. *Library Trends* 31, 401-420.

Lynch reviews reference research of last ten years, defining reference as the provision of information in response to questions. Covered are measurement; evaluation; innovation, including online searching and information and referral; information needs and uses; the process of asking and answering questions in the reference interview; and artificial intelligence. Lynch notes that Jahoda's work covered much more than question negotiation and included several modules for teaching how to search for information once it is determined what information is needed. This topic has received a great deal of attention in recent research.

Lynch, Beverly P., and Verdin, Jo Ann. (1987). Job satisfaction in libraries: A replication. *Library Quarterly* 57, 190-202.

Replicates a 1983 study by Lynch and Verdin on job satisfaction in three academic libraries (Job satisfaction in libraries. *Library Quarterly* 53, 434-447). Two of the same academic libraries, plus an additional library matched on size and other factors, participated in the second study. The following findings from the replication corroborate findings of the earlier study: Professional staff members reported higher job satisfaction than other staff. Reference librarians reported higher job satisfaction than librarians in other functional units. Reference librarians reported that their work provided greater autonomy and was less routine than librarians in other functional units who reported on their work. There was no difference in satisfaction by sex of librarians. Department heads were most satisfied, followed by unit managers, and then by first-level supervisors. Those with no supervisory responsibilities reported the lowest levels of satisfaction.

Mandel, Carol A., and Herschman, Judith. (1983). Online subject access: Enhancing the library catalog, *Journal of Academic Librarianship* 9, 148-155.

Reviews literature on subject searching by users in the online catalog. Based on a report prepared by the Council on Library Resources in 1981. Presents ten findings in regard to subject searching and discusses reasons for search failures. Also covers failure analysis, free-text versus controlled searching, and studies of user needs. Discusses research on search failures, enhancing subject access, and the user interface.

Marchant, Maurice. (1970). *Effects of the decision making process and related organizational factors on alternative measures of performance in university libraries.* Doctoral dissertation, University of Michigan. *Dissertation Abstracts International* 31, 6639A. (University Microfilms No. 71-15, 228).

The instrument used by the author asked faculty, administrator, and staff to judge the importance and quality of various library services. Reference was considered more important than circulation but less important than technical services. The quality of reference was perceived as highest, followed by that of circulation and technical services.

Markey, Karen. (1980). *Analytical review of catalog use studies.* Columbus, OH: OCLC, Inc. (Research Report OPR/RR-80/2).
Presented in five sections: I. Descriptive Review of Catalog Use Studies; II. Generalizations about Subject Searching Gleaned from Catalog Use Studies; III. Table of Catalog Use Studies; IV. Bibliography of Catalog Use Studies; V. Cited Author Index. Notes that studies show that users are likely to perform more known-item than subject searches at the card catalog as their years of formal schooling increase. Reviews studies on the catalog's controlled vocabulary. Discusses factors related to users' selection of subject terms to access the catalog. Considers how well these subject terms are selected by users and how successfully they match the catalog's controlled vocabulary. In the section on failure in the catalog, studies are analyzed in terms of factors that affect catalog success.

Markham, Marilyn, Stirling, Keith H., and Smith, Nathan M. (1983). Librarian self-disclosure and patron satisfaction in the reference interview. *RQ* 22, 369-374.
Using a construct known as self-disclosure, this study investigated if there was a relationship between self-disclosure and patron satisfaction. Overall there was no significant difference, but there was a positive effect for questions that were not purely factual and required more dialogue between the librarian and the patron.

Martyn, John. (1974). Information needs and uses. In Carlos A. Cuadra (Ed.). *Annual Review of Information Science and Technology* 9. New York: Knowledge Industry Publications.
Traces research on information needs and uses worldwide during 1972-1973. The majority of references originate from the United Kingdom. Covered are system-oriented studies, component-oriented studies, and background research.

Maslach, Christina, and Jackson, Susan E. (1981). *Maslach Burnout Inventory Manual* (2d ed.). Palo Alto, CA: Consulting Psychologist Press.
Provides in-depth assistance in setting up and interpreting the Maslach Burnout Inventory. Also serves as a reference and guide into the making of the inventory.

Mason, Ellsworth, and Mason, Joan. (1984). The whole shebang—comprehensive evaluation of reference operations. *Reference Librarian* 11, 25-44.

The authors suggest comprehensive practical arrangements in physical reference layout.

Matthews, Joseph R., Lawrence, Gary, and Ferguson, Douglas (Eds.) (1983). *Using online catalogs: A nationwide survey.* New York: Neal-Schuman.

Reviews findings in regard to online catalog use. In particular, notes that there appears to have been a radical change in the use of subject searching since the introduction of the online catalog.

McClure, Charles. (1984). Output measures, unobtrusive testing, and assessing the quality of reference services. *Reference Librarian* 11, 215-333.

Advocates unobtrusive observation as a method for determining reference effectiveness. Discusses four possible reference service output measures, three of them useful as cost-effectiveness measures: 1)% of correct answers; 2) correct answers per staff hour; 3) time taken divided by correct answers; and 4) cost per correct reference answer. In order to obtain the last answer, the total cost of reference services for a period of time is divided by the number of correct answers during the same period. For example, the average amount of time taken per successful question was 7.62 minutes at a cost of 24 cents per minute or $1.83. See **Summaries of Instruments: McClure—Cost Effectiveness Measures.**

McClure, Charles R., and Hernon, Peter. (1989). *Users of academic and public GPO depository libraries.* Washington, DC: U.S. Government Printing Office.

Contains an in-house materials user log. This study was the first national depository user survey of its kind. A large-scale study was conducted in the fall of 1988 with 80% of the 1,054 depository libraries participating. Average number of users per week ranged from 143 to 243 for academic library depositories, and from 68 to 127 for public library depositories. Demographic characteristics of users were established. See **Summaries of Instruments: McClure and Hernon—Academic Library User Ticket; Public Library User Ticket.**

McClure, Charles R., Zweizig, Douglas L., Van House, Nancy A., and Lynch, Mary Jo. (1986). Output measures: Myths, realities, and prospects. *Public Libraries* 25, 49-52.

The authors describe the wide acceptance of the 1982 edition of *Output measures for public libraries* (Zweizig and Rodger), respond to issues developed as a result of its use, including its measures in their management as opposed to research context, its purpose to measure services provided, problems in data collection, the joint role of both patron and library behaviors in determining library performance, sample sizes, interpretation of output measure scores, library self-diagnostic versus national comparability, and improving public library output measures. A new edition of *Output measures* was announced for January 1987 (Van House, Lynch, McClure, Zweizig, and Rodger).

McCue, Janice Helen. (1988). *Online searching in public libraries: A comparative study of performance.* Metuchen, NJ: Scarecrow Press.

An unobtrusive study of online searching in 21 public libraries was done in 1984. A single multifaceted question was presented to a searcher in each library. The question was designed to be searched in ABI/IN-FORM and National Newspaper Index. The same question was also searched in those databases by seven outside experts. Results of both sets of searches were evaluated by panelists on a seven-point system of scoring. Follow-up interviews were then conducted with the online searcher and supervisor to collect information on factors that might have affected quality of results. It was found that the more citations were retrieved, the higher the judges rated the quality of the search. Broad search strategies emphasizing recall resulted in greater quality. In libraries that did not charge for online searches, searches were of lesser quality. The author notes that the library with the highest quality score did user evaluations of its service. **See Summaries of Instruments: McCue—Online Searching in Public Libraries.**

McMurdo, George. (1982). *The effect of busy library staff on rate of approach by clients in an experimental psychology study.* Washington, DC: Educational Resources Information Center. (ERIC Document Reproduction Service No. ED 221 212).

Describes three studies indicating user reluctance to approach library staff. Results indicate that a librarian who does not appear busy will be approached 70% to 80% more often than one who appears to be busy. Recommends further research in librarian-client relations.

Mehrabian, Albert. (1971). *Silent messages.* Belmont, CA: Wadsworth.

Based on a series of studies, Mehrabian concluded that a therapist could make judgments about how patients were feeling about the dialogue between them based on a construct he termed immediacy. Immediacy is made up of both verbal and nonverbal cues. It was used in the dissertation study by Gothberg.

Mellon, Constance. (1986). Library anxiety: A grounded theory and its development. *College & Research Libraries* 47, 160-165.

This study explored the feelings of university students using the library for research. Personal writing, collected in composition courses for beginning students over a two-year period, was analyzed and it was found that 75% to 85% of students in these courses described their initial responses to library research in terms of fear. Students revealed strong feelings that their library skills were inadequate, and that this inadequacy was shameful and should be hidden. They felt that this inadequacy would be revealed by asking questions. Students were required to do in-class essays discussing how they felt about their ability to use the library, how their feelings changed, and their feelings at the present time.

Menzel, Herbert. (1958). Planned and unplanned scientific communication. In *Proceedings of the International Conference on Scientific Information*. Washington, DC: National Academy of Sciences, National Research Council (p. 199-243).

Notes the value of serendipitous unplanned discovery of information in scientific research. Some of this unplanned discovery of information comes from personal contacts and some from browsing.

Metz, Paul, and Litchfield, Charles A. (1988). Measuring collections use at Virginia Tech. *College & Research Libraries* 49, 501-513.

Reports that a study of circulation and in-house use (periodicals) shows similar subject distribution.

Michell, B. Gillian, and Harris, Roma M. (1984). Evaluating the competence of information providers. *Proceedings of the American Society for Information Science* 21, 63-67.

A study conducted with 320 public library users to determine the impact of gender on perceived competence of the reference librarians. One important result of this study was that the gender of the patron was a factor in making judgments as to the competence of the information provider—perhaps more so than the gender of the librarian. The Crouch (1981) study is briefly noted in this article.

Michell, B. Gillian, and Harris, Roma M. (1987). Evaluating the reference interview: Some factors influencing patrons and professionals. *RQ* 27, 95-105.

This study examines differences between public library patrons and librarians in their assessments of the competence of librarians whom they observed in videotaped reference interviews. These interviews varied in the level of nonverbal warmth shown by the librarian toward the patron and in the level of inclusion exhibited (inclusion is the process in which the librarian instructs the patron in the use of reference tools). Results revealed that librarians were harsher judges of competence than patrons; however, like users, librarians gave their highest competence ratings in response to videotapes in which the reference librarian showed warmth toward the patron. An unexpected finding was that female librarians gave lower competence ratings than either male colleagues or patrons of either sex. Several possible explanations for this result were presented.

Miller, Edward P. (1973). An effectiveness measure for information center operations. In Helen Waldon and F. Raymond Long (Eds.). *Innovative developments in information systems: Their benefits and costs, proceedings of the 36th annual meeting of the American Society for Information Science* (p. 151-152). Westport, CT: Greenwood Press.

Suggests a simple measure which combines both client preference and management view of feasibility. Users are given a ballot which lists, for example, three alternative actions, with advantages and disadvantages of each. Rather than ranking alternatives for *each* item, respondents vote *both* yes and no by assigning a percentage to each, according to the strength of feelings. For example, one might vote 80% yes and 20% no to alternative A; 50% yes and 50% no to alternative B; and 30% yes and 70% no to alternative C. Management then votes a percentage of feasibility or probability that the alternative will be instituted. Preference and feasibility percentages are then multiplied to obtain a ratio. The largest ratio will represent the best alternative. Other benefits of this method are that it discloses any divergence between the views of management and users. Study of the "yes" vote percentages should also help in setting priorities for change if it should later become possible. **See Summaries of Instruments: Miller—Preference and Feasibility Measure.**

Mitchell, Eugene, Radford, Marie, and Hegg, Judith. (1994). Book availability: Academic library assessment. *College & Research Libraries* 55, 47-55.

This study replicates an earlier availability study (Ciliberti, Casserly, Hegg, and Mitchell, 1987). In the earlier study on known-item searches, patrons found 54% of desired books, while in the replication, 64% were found. The percentage of error due to library performance (not owning book, book in circulation, library malfunction—book not on shelf for some reason) was substantially reduced. However, user error in retrieving correctly-shelved books from the stacks increased as a percentage of total errors. Subjects' search success declined from 50% to 44%, again with the percentage of errors increasing in the last step of the process, retrieval from the shelf. Overall, retrieval errors were the greatest source of patron errors.

Monat, Jonathan S. (1981). A perspective on the evaluation of training and development programs. *Personnel Administrator* 26, 47-52.

Monat advocates designing evaluation prior to conducting training, taking into consideration desired objectives and costs. Specification of a set of criterion measures, an examination of internal and external validity, as well as maturation, or the influence of the passage of time, should be considered. Specific evaluation designs are suggested which measure costs, productivity, quality, and people.

Moore, Carolyn M., and Mielke, Linda. (1986). Taking the measure: Applying reference outputs to collection development. *Public Libraries* 25, 108-110.

In-library use per capita (limited to reference materials) was measured in a one-week sample survey multiplied by 50, as described in Zweizig and Rodger's *Output measures for public libraries*.

Morgan, Linda. (1980). Patron preference in reference service points. *RQ* 19, 375-377.

Linda Morgan had the opportunity to observe two reference desks in the same area of a library. One was a low desk and the other was a high service counter. Based on her observations, she concluded that the higher service counter was preferred by patrons in interacting with librarians.

Morse, Philip McCord. (1970). *On browsing: The use of search theory in the search for information.* Cambridge, MA: M.I.T. Operations Research Center.

Users reported on tasks they performed while in the library. Concentrates on circulation; offers mathematical formulas.

Mosher, Paul H. (1984). Quality and library collections: New directions in research and practice in collection evaluation. *Advances in Librarianship* 13, 211-238.

Defines collection evaluation as assessment of utility and appropriateness of a library's collections to its users and programs. Discusses the methods of shelflist counts, collection characteristics, and citation studies. Notes gap between theory and research, and states that mathematical formulas in the literature may be of more interest to the deviser than useful to librarians.

Mount, Ellis, and Fasana, Paul. (1972). An approach to the measurement of use and a cost of a large academic research library system: A report of a study done at Columbia University Libraries. *College & Research Libraries* 33, 199-211.

Study was conducted 1968-1969.

Murfin, Marjorie. (1970). A study of the reference process in a university library. Kent State University, School of Library Science. Unpublished Master's thesis.

All reference transactions in an academic library during predetermined periods were observed by the investigator, who recorded questions and dialogue. Assistants followed patrons unobtrusively and after ten minutes asked patrons to note what they had wanted on a brief form and indicate satisfaction with what they had found (satisfied, partly satisfied, not satisfied). Among other results, it was found that 25% of questions were indirect or confused. In regard to source use, 29% of sources used by librarians were drawn from immediate specific title responses.

Murfin, Marjorie E. (1983). National reference measurement: What can it tell us about staffing? *College & Research Libraries* 44, 321-333.

This study of 71 U.S. academic libraries of different sizes showed that the best predictors of volume of reference transactions were enrollment, reference desk person hours, and turnstile count. These accounted for .71, .64, and .62 of variation, respectively. The ratio of reference questions to library building turnstile count in 71 U.S. academic libraries of different sizes showed that approximately 2.8% to 7.2% of users in the library were involved in reference transactions. See **Summaries of Instruments: LAMA-NDCU Committee—LAMA-NDCU Experimental Staffing Adequacy Measures.**

Murfin, Marjorie E. (1989). *Comparison of reference success in Canadian and American libraries participating in the Wisconsin-Ohio Reference Evaluation Program.* (CACUL Occasional Paper Series, No. 4). [Ottawa]: Canadian Association of College and University Libraries.

This paper provides a detailed comparison of reference transaction success among three Canadian libraries and American libraries holding at least one million volumes. Canadian results were compared to a database of results of American library participants in an effort to develop a body of normative data on reference activities in academic libraries. See **Summaries of Instruments: Murfin, Bunge and Gugelchuk—Reference Transaction Assessment Instrument.**

Murfin, Marjorie E., and Bunge, Charles A. (1988a). Paraprofessionals at the reference desk. *Journal of Academic Librarianship* 14, 10-14.

This study suggests that reference support staff who handle less complex questions and consult other staff members more frequently are more effective. These results were obtained through the use of the Reference Transaction Assessment Instrument (RTAI) for 1,607 transactions in 20 academic libraries. For all 20 libraries the average success score for reference support staff was 50.5% as opposed to 60.4%

for reference librarians. Patrons who gave reasons for dissatisfaction reported needing more in-depth information or wanting a different viewpoint than was provided significantly more often when they were assisted by reference support staff. Also, reference support staff received significantly lower patron ratings than reference librarians on the following: getting enough help and explanations, clear explanations, knowledgeable about questions, and providing enough time. The RTAI is a norm-referenced survey instrument designed to provide a profile for an individual library, with data for each item in the profile for 1) all libraries of the same size and type; 2) the top-scoring library in that size group; and 3) all libraries in the sample, based upon use of a standardized form and sampling strategy. Several questions in the form directly address librarian knowledge and search strategy. **See Summaries of Instruments: Murfin, Bunge and Gugelchuk—Reference Transaction Assessment Instrument.**

Murfin, Marjorie E., and Bunge, Charles A. (1988b). Responsible standards for reference service in Ohio public libraries. *Ohio Libraries* 1, 11-13.
Discusses formulation of reference standards for success of the reference outcome. Presents data collected through the Reference Transaction Assessment Instrument (Murfin and Gugelchuk, 1987) on self-rating of success by reference librarians as compared to ratings of success by patrons. Seven academic libraries had average patron ratings at the lowest level (between 0% and 50%); yet of these seven, librarians in one on the average rated success at the 70%+ level (excellent) and librarians in five others on the average rated the success as good (60% to 69%).

Murfin, Marjorie, and Bunge, Charles. (1989). *A cost effectiveness formula for reference service in academic libraries.* Washington, DC: Council on Library Resources.
Four measures are described. The first is an experimental method for determining the full cost of the reference transaction in an academic library. It is based on time spent per minute in actually working on reference questions, rather than desk hours completed. It also charges only a part of reference collection costs to the reference transaction. Findings were that the full cost of the reference question to the test library was $5.20 with library and university overhead added. Without library and university overhead, the full cost was $2.23. The difference between these figures and those of Cochrane may be partially due to the method of cost analysis and partially due to the considerably greater number of reference hours open and fewer questions on the part of the latter library. The second measure described is a cost-effectiveness

index, incorporating accessibility, quality of communication, success of outcome, and time taken. This is illustrated by data from 44 academic libraries who participated in the Wisconsin-Ohio Reference Evaluation Program. The third measure described is a cost-effectiveness formula, suggested by McClure (1984), of cost per *successful* transaction. It was found that it cost $1.43 to successfully answer a faculty question as opposed to $2.14 per successful question for a continuing education/non-degree student. Short answer facts were the most cost effective at $0.91 per successful transaction and requests for bibliographies the least cost-effective at $4.33 per successful question. Surprisingly, the "something, anything about a subject" question was one of the least cost-effective types of questions at $2.85. The most cost-effective subjects were etiquette and writing at $0.86 and $0.93, and the least cost-effective were housing at $6.67, pollution at $7.36, and transportation at $8.62. The fourth measure described is a cost benefit formula, with a benefit measure of $13 per successful transaction. This, in turn, is based on the benefit ratio of a user time saved as being at least 7 to 1 or 7 times cost. A disbenefit of $12 is subtracted for every failed transaction on the grounds of the frustration encountered by the patron. It was found that benefits earned per transaction by professionals and support staff were equal on simple questions but professional librarians earned substantial benefits in relation to cost on complex questions while support staff did not. **See Summaries of Instruments: Murfin and Bunge—Cost Benefit Formula; Murfin and Bunge—Cost in Staffing Time; and Murfin and Bunge—Determining the Full Cost of the Reference Question.**

Murfin, Marjorie, and Gugelchuk, Gary. (1987). Development and testing of a Reference Transaction Assessment Instrument. *College & Research Libraries* 48, 314-338.
    This survey of academic libraries analyzing both patron responses and librarian self-evaluation forms for the same reference transaction results in two reliable evaluation instruments. In 15 academic libraries reference survey forms were given out to patrons on arrival at the reference desk. Return rate was 88%. Notes that Jahoda has made important advances in identifying reference process factors and that the Reference Transaction Assessment Instrument form was designed based on Jahoda's work. **See Summaries of Instruments: Murfin, Bunge, and Gugelchuk—Reference Transaction Assessment Instrument.**

Murfin, Marjorie, and Ruland, Fred. (1980). Measurement of reference transactions: An in-depth statistical study of demand and capacity in twenty-two libraries over a two-year period. In Neal Kaske (Ed.). *Library effectiveness: A state of the art: Proceedings of the ALA*

Preconference on Library Effectiveness. (p. 194-218. Chicago: American Library Association.

Records of reference question volume, person hours, and library gate count were examined for 22 departmental libraries in a large university library system. It was found that the best predictors of volume of reference questions for a typical week in the fall quarter were a combination of reference staff desk person hours and primary users (enrollment in the discipline represented by that department library). This combination accounted for .73 of variation. Turnstile count alone (in the eight libraries for which it was available) accounted for .80 of variation. Among other results, it was found that fewer reference questions per library user were asked in science and technology libraries.

Murfin, Marjorie, and Wynar, Lubomyr. (1984). *Reference service: An annotated bibliographic guide: Supplement 1976-1982*. Littleton, CO: Libraries Unlimited.

This work and its predecessor, published in 1977, provide the most comprehensive annotated bibliography available on the literature of library reference service through 1982.

Murphy, Marcy. (1978). Criteria and methodology for evaluating the effectiveness of reference and information functions in academic libraries: A regional case study. Doctoral dissertation, University of Pittsburgh. *Dissertation Abstracts International* 39, 1173A.

A study was done in the Air Force University Library in 1973 to generate profiles of departmental functions and fix quick dollar estimates on costs of reference service functions. More than 100 reference tasks were costed in terms of staff time. Reference staff kept diaries for ten days on the number of minutes spent in each listed activity. These same data were obtained again through interviews where staff estimated the percentage of time allotted to major activities during that time period. It was found that the most time consuming tasks were, in order, answering reference questions, reference collection development, professional reading, attending professional meetings, interacting with other staff, reviewing new books, maintaining files, and processing mail and memos. **See Summaries of Instruments: Murphy—Costing of All Reference Operations.**

Myers, Marcia J. (1983). The effectiveness of telephone reference/information services in academic libraries in the Southeast. In *The accuracy of telephone reference/information services in academic libraries: Two studies*. Metuchen, NJ: Scarecrow Press.

Forty academic libraries participated in an unobtrusive telephone test of reference answering skill. Responses to 12 predetermined fact questions obtained an accuracy level of 49%. Performance was poorest on queries that could not be answered with the usual tools. There was evidence that even when the library owned the source, staff either did not consult, did not know how to use, or misinterpreted information from the source. The author's primary conclusion was that there are differences in effectiveness among classifications of academic libraries as measured by accuracy on a fact-type test conducted by telephone, with size of library a greater contributor to effectiveness than classification per se. The author recommended that quantitative standards be developed for reference/information services.

Naegele, Kaspar D. and Stolar, Elaine Culley. (1960). The librarian of the Northwest. In Morton Kroll (Ed.). *Library development project reports: Vol. 4—Libraries and librarians of the Pacific Northwest* (p. 51-137). Seattle: University of Washington Press.
   Notes that librarians do not consider all clients of equal interest. Librarians distinguish users in terms of the importance of their requests or, as is less likely to be admitted freely, by librarians' view of the clients themselves.

Nahl-Jakobovits, Diane, and Jakobovits, Leon. (1988). Problem solving, creative librarianship and search behavior. *College & Research Libraries* 49, 400-408.
   Discusses problem solving in relation to search behavior and gives a model of the search process as 1) clarify the question; 2) identify a source for finding the information; 3) translate the question into the words of the source; 4) conduct the search; and 5) locate the materials. Relates this to bibliographic instruction. Stresses the role of motivation in problem solving. Gives nine groupings of skills involved in information processing and eight skills involved in notetaking. Gives list of five common errors in copying call numbers, eight errors in using the catalog, and five errors in searching in general. Analyzes seven skills involved in solving research problems.

New York University. (1981). Elmer Holmes Bobst Library: A survey. In *User surveys and evaluation of library services*. (SPEC Kit 71, p. 13-24). Washington, DC: Association of Research Libraries, Office of Management Studies.
   A library survey was given to a selected sample of classes to some 1,748 students. In this survey library users were asked what subject they were seeking on their present library visits. Findings of interest were that infrequent library users appeared more likely to seek reference help than frequent library users. Forty-three percent reported being users of the reference collection. It was the fourth most popular collection after the

general stacks (61%), reserves (55%), and periodicals and newspapers (52%). Eight percent reported using government documents; 13% of all surveyed used the reference collection more frequently than any other library resource. In regard to success, a four-point anchored scale was used as follows: In most instances my success in finding the information and materials I need is Excellent—found everything (7%); Good—found most things (48%); Fair—found some things (31%), and Poor—found few things (14%). In regard to success combined with efficiency, 31% of respondents reported, "I am usually able to find what I am searching for without wasting time and effort." **See Summaries of Instruments: New York University, et al.—Selected User Survey Items.**

Newstrom, John W. (1978). Catch 22: The problem of incomplete evaluation of training. *Training and Development Journal* 32, 22-24.
    The author argues for more rigorous evaluation designs by summarizing the contrasting conclusions from the use of the four evaluation criteria: reaction, learning, behavior, and results. The value of information obtained increased through the levels as does the difficulty of assessment, making the frequency of use highest in reaction evaluation and lowest in results.

Nitecki, Danuta (1993). User criteria for evaluating the effectiveness of the online catalog. In Marjorie Murfin and Jo Bell Whitlatch (Eds.). *First preconference on research in reference effectiveness.* (RASD Occasional Paper 16). Chicago: American Library Association, Reference and Adult Services Division.
    Explores the use of qualitative research methods in soliciting user criteria of quality. Twenty-four users of the online catalog were interviewed with regard to importance of various factors in judging the quality of an online catalog. Effectiveness factors were ease of use, search strategy, selection information, location information, and coverage (i.e., content) of the online catalog. First-time and experienced users had different viewpoints; however, considering both groups, ease of use and location information were most often ranked first.

Nolan, Christopher W. (1991). The lean reference collection: Improving functionality through selection and weeding. *College & Research Libraries* 52, 80-91.
    Discusses reference collections in academic libraries and offers guidelines for selecting materials that focus on their suitability for true reference functions and expected frequency of use.

Novak, Gloria (Ed.). (1987). The forgiving building: A library building consultants' symposium on the design, construction and remodeling of libraries to support a high-tech future. With contributions by Anders C. Dahlgren, David Kapp, Jay K. Lucker, David Kaser, Margaret Beckman, and Donald G. Kelsey. *Library Hi Tech* 5, 77-99.

Future-oriented design suggestions deal with practical environmental issues, lighting, sound/noise control, adaptations to future needs, and more.

Nowack, Kenneth. (1990). Initial development of an inventory to assess stress and health risk. *Stress Management* 4, 173-180.

This study describes how the inventory of 123 items was developed. Criterion-related validity of this instrument was shown with respect to separate measures of psychological and physical health. Items are combined into 14 scales, which, in turn, compress into six scales: Stressors, Health Habits (Global Health Habits, Exercise, Rest/Relaxation, Nutrition, and Preventive Hygiene), Social Support Network, Type-A Behavior, Cognitive Hardiness, Coping Style (Positive Thoughts, Negative Thoughts, Cognitive Avoidance, Problem-Focused Coping, Psychological Well-Being). Scale 15 reflects the presence and degree of response bias.

Oldman, Christine, and Wills, Gordon. (1977). *The beneficial library, Cranfield Institute of Technology.* Bradford, England: MCB Books.

This extensive evaluation of the library includes a survey form, interviews, and an information diary of library use kept by students for one week. The diary covered purpose or educational task, how they heard about the desired information/materials, where they found the information, and the usefulness of what was found. A study was done at the Cranfield Institute and at Loughborough University with groups of management and mechanical engineering students, with the purpose of studying attitudes toward library usage. Individual and group interviews were conducted with a sample of users. An attitude survey was given to all faculty and students in the School of Management to relate user attitudes to library behavior. In another part of the study, all students in three courses were asked to record every input of information to their courses, regardless of whether or not their sources were in the library. Panel discussions were also held with all classes. Questions on expectations were given and results indicated that expectations were very modest and in line with reality. Panel members from Loughborough used the library more frequently and were also more critical. The Loughborough library education program caused users' expectations to rise because the library was doing more for them. Problems with the diary method were that some respondents might have been less likely to use the library because they had to report each use, or because it would reveal how little they did, or because they forgot to record. Some members left the panel due to annoyance with recording. By the fifth week, 50% had dropped out of the program. It was found that business students utilized a great deal more written information than engineering students, using 14 bits of information as opposed to the engineers' four bits. The percentage of failure in finding what was wanted was greater for engineers. Differences in information-seeking styles were also found among individuals from "information-beavers" to "don't want to know any more." Information-beavers could be systematic or unsystematic. They also found that library and information use was dependent on the stage of the information-seeking process, with greatest use at the beginning and end of the process.

Osgood, Charles E., Suci, George J., and Tannenbaum, Percy H. (1967). *The measurement of meaning*. Urbana, IL: University of Illinois Press.

The authors describe a systematic and analytical attempt to assign meaning to quantitative measures by means of a technique called semantic differential. Although limited in some cases by small samples and by lack of establishment of equality in scale intervals, most of their paired words are fairly reliable and their approach can be applied to use in survey scales in a number of different fields.

Palais, Elliot S. (1981). Availability analysis report. In *User surveys and evaluation of library services*. (SPEC Kit 71, p.73-82). Washington, DC: Association of Research Libraries, Office of Management Studies.

An analysis of availability of materials was done at the Arizona State University Library during test periods in spring and summer. Availability rates of 60% and 61% were found. A list of similar availability scores for six other libraries is given as follows: 52%, 53.8%, 56%, 60.4%, 62%, 63%, 64%. In regard to user error, it was found that 6.9% of users failed to find an item in the catalog even though it was listed there, and 13.1% failed to find an item on the shelf even though it was there, amounting to 20% total user error. User error was larger than any other factor since 5.5% of items were not owned, 7.8% were checked out, and 14.3% were not on the shelf where they should have been.

Parker, Treadway C. (1973). Evaluation: The forgotten finale of training. *Personnel* 50, 59-73.

The author organizes evaluation techniques, such as job sample tests, simulations, and interviews, into categories which approximate those used by Kirkpatrick (1979). Summarizes four areas of evaluation—job performance, group performance, participant satisfaction, and participant knowledge gain—and suggests appropriate evaluation techniques for each category.

Paskoff, Beth M., and Perrault, Anna H. (1990). A tool for comparative collection analysis: Conducting a shelf list sample to construct a collection profile. *Library Resources & Technical Services* 34, 199-215.
The approach described could be applied to reference materials, and results compared with use profiles.

Paterson, Ellen R. (1979). A survey of subject reference questions. *The Unabashed Librarian* 31, 25.
The survey used subjects assigned for book budget allocations and compared percentage of questions with percentage of total student credit hours. Subjects used were art, English, foreign language, music, philosophy, speech-theatre, economics, geography, history, political science, psychology, sociology/anthropology, biology, chemistry, geology, mathematics, physics, education, health education, physical education, and recreation.

Pearson, A.W. (1973). Fundamental problems of information transfer. *Aslib Proceedings* 25, 415-424.
The author argues that the value of information varies according to the time at which it is received. Information must be relevant to present activity; if that activity is progressing at an acceptable rate, receptivity to information is low. More receptivity to information in the less pressured phase at the beginning of a project is to be expected. Interest will also vary between, for example, those engaged in research of an exploratory nature and those in the development area.

Peck, Theodore P. (1975). Counseling skills applied to reference services. *RQ* 14, 233-235.
This is an older article and was one of the first suggesting that counseling techniques could be successfully applied to the reference interview. Peck recommends the use of empathy, attentive behavior, and content listening in the reference interview.

Perrine, Richard. (1968). Catalog use difficulties. *RQ* 7, 169-174.
Describes two studies conducted by the RASD Catalog Use Committee in university and public libraries across the country. The purpose of these studies was to attempt to diagnose the catalog use difficulties of patrons. Problems reported were those that came to the attention of reference librarians and were reported to them on forms. Filing arrangement, subject headings, cross references, call numbers, title added entries, and bibliographical information are ranked approximately in that order as causes of difficulty. Results are discussed in detail for each problem and causes of difficulties are analyzed.

Peters, Thomas. (1989). When smart people fail: An analysis of the transaction log of an online public access catalog. *The Journal of Academic Librarianship* 15, 267-73.

Reports on a transaction log study of the online catalog in an academic library. The failure rate of searches analyzed was 40% overall, and 30% for author searches, 44% for title searches, and 52% for subject searches. Fourteen categories of failure are discussed. More than 20% of errors were spelling and typographical; 30% were due to items actually held but not in the database due to incomplete reconversion and exclusion of some formats.

Phillips, Jack J. (1983). *Handbook of training evaluation and measurement methods*. Houston: Gulf Publishing Company.

Phillips reports results of a survey of 154 organizations to determine attempts to evaluate training. Of 110 responses, 77% measure reactions, 50% measure learning, and 54% attempt to measure behavior. In a second questionnaire and selected interviews, very few were found to be conducted in a systematic way. Phillips reviews several approaches to evaluation and gives guidelines for evaluation data.

Phipps, Shelley, and Dickstein, Ruth. (1979). The Library Skills Program at the University of Arizona: Testing, evaluation and critiques. *Journal of Academic Librarianship* 5, 205-214.

In fall of 1976 at the University of Arizona, an evaluation was carried out of the effectiveness of the Library Skills Program (LSP) based on use of the *Workbook on library skills* by Miriam Dudley. During the first week of school a pretest of 16 questions based on units in the *Workbook* was given to 280 LSP students in lower-level English classes and to 207 students in a control group, not receiving library instruction. Eight weeks later a posttest was given to both groups. Results indicated that the pretest showed no significant difference between groups. The posttest, however, showed a significant difference in success in favor of those in the Library Skills Program. **See Summaries of Instruments: Phipps and Dickstein—Library Knowledge Questionnaire.**

Piech, Carlo R., Newman, G. Charles, and Delmont, Mary K. (1986). Butler Library displays vital signs; Signage as a remedy for environmental problems. *College & Research Libraries News* 47, 379-381.

Stresses a signage system as an important step in creating clear patron guidance through the library.

Pierson, Robert. (1985). Appropriate settings for reference service. *Reference Services Review* 13, 13-29.

Focuses on 13 characteristics every reference service area should have. Specific design techniques are suggested. Floor plans are included.

Pings, Vern, and Anderson, Fanny. (1965). *Study of the use of Wayne State University Medical Library, Part 1.* Detroit, MI: Wayne State University School of Medicine Library.

This study of use was based only on observation and the purpose was to determine the flow pattern of the use of a medical library. Two-hundred persons were observed over a three-week period and 14 library areas were observed. Members of the library staff followed the movements of the randomly selected users, recording the locations used and time spent. Data were analyzed in terms of user categories, areas used, and time spent. However, inadequate sampling methods produced a nonrepresentative sample. Nevertheless, the method used was of interest and the author discuss advantages and disadvantages of unobtrusive observation in this situation.

Pitlack, Robert. (1980). *Online data searching as a tool for motivating innovation.* Arlington, VA: Educational Resources Information Center. (ERIC Document Reproduction Service No. ED 190 085).

Reports on a study done to determine whether access to new ideas, as found by online searching, would stimulate innovation and creativity. Twenty voluntary participants from a small high technology company were studied before and after being exposed to online searching. Tests indicated that a statistically significant increase in perceived level of innovation occurred after contact with online searching. Also observed was a relationship between frequency of online searching and level of new idea generation.

Potthoff, Joy K., and Montanelli, Dale S. (1990). Use of library facilities: Behavioral research as a tool for library space planning. *Journal of Library Administration* 12, 47-61.

Reviews library and behavioral literature to identify methods for analysis of library space planning. Includes questionnaires, interviews, behavior mapping, and time budgets.

Poulet, Roger, and Moult, Gerry. (1987). Putting values into evaluation. *Training and Development Journal* 41, 62-66.

Interviewed 70 individuals on the experience of taking a course, both objectively and more subtly as it impacted on the individual. Two scales were developed: 1) the action potential as willingness of the participants to implement what they have learned and 2) the external and internal blockages as a measurement of the resistance to change.

Powell, Ronald R. (1978). An investigation of the relationships between quantifiable reference service variables and reference performance in public libraries. *Library Quarterly* 48, 1-19.

Powell found the reference test performance scores to be strongly related to reference librarian knowledge as measured by experience in answering questions, the MLS degree, the number of reference and bibliography courses completed, the number of professional publications regularly read, and membership in professional associations. Fifty-one librarians completed the 25 test questions. The mean percentage of test reference questions answered correctly was 59%.

Powell, Ronald R. (1984). Reference effectiveness: A review of research. *Library and Information Science Research* 6, 3-19.

A review of a range of definitions of effectiveness from the field, the literature of the evaluation of reference services and effectiveness, particularly research-based reports on reference questions, reference users, reference staff performance, cost-benefit analysis, combination of output measures, and combined input/output measures. The author concludes that there are a variety of definitions of effectiveness and different techniques recommended for measuring it. Research studies that have been conducted tend not to adhere to any one definition and demonstrate a great variety of measurement and analysis techniques. They tend to be more applied than basic research and few actually are identified as research on reference effectiveness. Powell concludes that there needs to be an effort to promote more efficient and effective research.

Puttapithakporn, Somporn. (1990). Interface design and user problems and errors: A case study of novice searchers. *RQ* 30, 195-204.

Identifies and categorizes problems novice searchers encountered in a database-searching task with a CD-ROM product. Data were collected by observation, self-administered questionnaires, and selective interviewing. System-use errors and inefficiencies are defined, excluding typographical errors, as covering incomplete screens, menu selection problems, inability to interpret abbreviations, misunderstanding of system messages, inability to exploit full capability of system, and crowded help screens.

Qualitative collection analysis: The conspectus methodology. (1989). (SPEC Kit 151). Washington, DC: Association of Research Libraries, Office of Management Studies.

Conspectus approach attempts to understand collecting patterns and correlate these with actual use.

Raffel, Jeffrey, and Shishko, Robert. (1969). *Systematic analysis of university libraries: An application of cost-benefit analysis to the MIT libraries.* Cambridge, MA: MIT Press.

This survey was mailed to 700 MIT faculty and students to obtain information about how library resources should be allocated. Response rate was 40%. Users were given 20 alternatives to improve services or save money, along with the costs and benefits of each alternative. Users were asked to check those items they would choose to keep and those they would eliminate under three different budgetary conditions. In other words, users were asked to "balance the budget" under three different budgetary conditions. Results indicated that of five cost-cutting actions, cutting reference staff was the third choice, after centralizing reserve and putting books in storage. Of nine actions requiring additional cost, adding reference librarians ranked sixth. At the highest budget level, 36% of faculty, 51% of graduates, and 30% of undergraduates wished to add reference staff. At the $0 budget level, 25% of graduates, 24% of undergraduates, and only 7% of faculty wished to cut reference staff. **See Summaries of Instruments: Raffel and Shishko—Benefit Survey.**

Raisig, L. Miles, Smith, Meredith, Cuff, Renata, and Kilgour, Frederick. (1966). How biomedical investigators use library books. *Bulletin of the Medical Library Association* 54, 104-107.

This study dealt with use of monographic works borrowed by researchers from a medical library. A total of 430 interviews were held with 130 persons asking how they had learned about the books they borrowed. Results indicated that 21.5% had learned about their books by chance, 20% had citations from other publications, 16% from the card catalog, 15% from previous use, 12.4% from personal recommendations, 4.6% from a monthly accession list, 3% from the new book shelf, .6% from librarians, and 7% miscellaneous. In regard to purpose for using their books, 28% used them for general information, 12.6% for fact finding, 11% for lecture preparation, 9.4% for theory, 9% for bibliographical information, 6.1% for background research, 4.8% for results, 1.8% to substantiate personal views, and 4.2% miscellaneous. Seventy-five percent found that the books met their purposes.

Reeves, Edward B., Howell, Benita, and Van Willigen, John. (1977). Before the looking glass: A method to obtain self-evaluation of roles in a library reference service. *RQ* 17, 25-32.

Based on evaluation by a reference staff of their own duties over a three-month period. Staff were interviewed and 45 duties listed. Staff then rated these duties on a seven-point scale according to 1) number of staff needed to do task; 2) frequency; 3) difficulty level; and 4) confidence in ability to perform. Duties were grouped into 1) instruction maintenance; 2) skill; 3) patron service; 4) housekeeping; and 5) performed for other departments. Concerning staff perceptions of tasks, positive correlations were found between importance and interest, interest and complexity, and importance and complexity. **See Summaries of Instruments: Activities Performed in the Reference Department.**

Regazzi, John J., and Hersberger, Rodney M. (1976). *Library use and reference service: A regression analysis.* Paper presented at the American Library Association Annual Conference, 95th, Chicago, Illinois, 18-24 July 1976. (ERIC Document Reproduction Service No. ED 129 219).

Results from this study of an academic library suggest that the number of reference questions asked is strongly related to the number of persons using the reference area. Analysis of hourly counts of patrons using a reference room were used to predict peak and idle times. The study found that room use had more dramatic influence on reference questions than on directional questions. Hourly counts of persons using the reference area were correlated with number of reference and directional questions for that same period and a correlation of .74 was found.

Regazzi, John, and Hersberger, Rodney M. (1978). Queues and reference service: Some implications for staffing. *College & Research Libraries* 39, 293-298.

In response to a problem in regard to lines forming at the reference desk in an academic library, a queuing study was carried out. One finding of interest was that patrons were given 28% less time per question during busy hours of the day. **See Summaries of Instruments: Regazzi and Hersberger—Queuing Study.**

Rettig, James R. (1992). Behavioral guidelines for reference librarians. *RQ* 31, 5-7.

During his tenure as president of RASD, Rettig appointed an ad hoc Committee on Behavioral Guidelines for Reference and Information Services, with Dave Tyckoson as chair, and charged its members to draft a set of behavioral guidelines to follow when providing reference and information services.

Richards, James M., Jr. (1990). Units of analysis and the individual differences fallacy in environmental assessment. *Environment and Behavior* 22, 307-319. "Ecological fallacy" is the error of interpreting results based on ecological entities, such as environmental settings, as though the results apply to individuals, and vice versa. Asserts future research on environment assessment should use settings as the primary units of analysis. Relates to classroom environments, but theory could be applicable to libraries.

Rinderknecht, Deborah. (1992). New norms for reference desk staffing adequacy: A comparative study. *College & Research Libraries* 53, 429-436.

This study provides a ten-year follow-up to a previous study of reference staffing adequacy done in 1978 (Murfin, 1983). Survey data for a typical week in the fall were requested from 220 academic libraries at four-year institutions of all sizes. Over 100 libraries were able to provide all the requested data. These libraries were grouped by weekly gate count. Results indicate that, between 1982 and 1992, in four of five size groups, actual reference desk workload per hour per person had increased. Another measure, potential patron load, is based on figures for a typical week of patrons in the library compared to reference person hours available. Potential patron loads over 200 (patrons per available reference staff hours) have appeared to be related to lower question answering success. Nineteen libraries in the study had patron load ratios above 200.

Robertson, W. Davenport. (1980). A user-oriented approach to setting priorities for library services. *Special Libraries* 71, 345-353.

A user-oriented model was developed for setting priorities for services in the National Institute of Environmental Health Science Library in 1978. A total of 1,200 questionnaires were sent out to research staff of three organizations of similar sizes with a return rate of 35%. Respondents were asked to rank 11 aspects of library service from 1 to 11 in regard to the order they thought the library should follow in allocating personnel and fiscal resources. Results indicated that the highest priority group included journal purchases, computerized literature searching, interlibrary loan, and book and technical report purchases. The middle priority group included reference, circulation, cataloging, and copying. The lowest group included physical facilities, newsletter, audiovisual, and equipment. In summary, there was a great amount of agreement among the users overall and a close correspondence among rankings by users at the different organizations. Librarians also ranked aspects and their rankings are compared to those of users. It is suggested that, in order to use this model of priorities as an aid in planning, one should begin at the top of the list and provide those services in the top cluster and then work down the list. Library resources should not be devoted to services in the bottom cluster, unless the higher ones have been taken care of first. **See Summaries of Instruments: Robertson—Library/Technical Information Services.**

Robinson, Barbara M. (1986). *A study of reference referral and super reference in California, Vol. I: Main report.* Sacramento, CA.: California State Library.
See Henson (1987).

Rodger, Eleanor Jo. (1984a). *Fairfax County Public Library user study: Users, use and uses of the Fairfax County Public Library.* Chicago: American Library Association, Public Library Association.

Focused on demographics and perceptions of users and includes questionnaires. A user survey was done with forms given out to users in 20 libraries in the Fairfax County System. The return rate was 85%. The study investigated who used the library, how, and why and found that 29% used the reference collection; this number varied from 18% for the smallest library branches to 38% for the regionals. Thirty-eight percent browsed or read books in the library. Reference collection size varied from 2,500 to 11,000. It was found, in general, that the larger the library, the greater the use of the reference collection. Those who fitted the profile of "research users" were far more likely to use reference materials. Use of the reference collection appeared to relate primarily to the user's reasons for coming to the library. Users were asked to indicate the importance of their library visits to them in five categories, from unimportant to extremely important. Some findings of interest were as follows: 75% considered their library visits to be important, very important or extremely important. It was found that there were no demographic differences between reference users and nonusers. The author reports that in a previous study it was found that 67% of those who left the library *without* having found what they wanted did *not* ask for help. In this study, 36% reported that they needed help at some time during their library visit but only 28% reported asking for help. Reasons for *not* asking for help were, in order, wasn't that important (30%), figured out problem myself (22%), librarians were too busy (20%), feel awkward asking for help (8%), and didn't think librarians could help (7%), and didn't know whom to ask (7%). In regard to search strategy, the following was reported: went directly to stacks (38%), used reference collection (29%), asked a librarian for help (28%), and used microfiche catalog (27%). **See Summaries of Instruments: Rodger and D'Elia—User Study.**

Rodger, Eleanor Jo. (1984b). *Reference accuracy at the Fairfax County Public Library: A report of a co-operative telephone and information service study.* Springfield, VA: Fairfax County Library.

Answers to 12 questions regarding the reference transaction process were sought. Of 350 questions, 56% were answered completely and correctly and 35% were answered either incompletely or with no source cited for the information given. Patrons expressed satisfaction with staff telephone manners for 86% of the calls. The instrument is intended for use in determining accuracy of answers rather than for gathering patron satisfaction data.

Rodger, Eleanor Jo, and Goodwin, Jane. (1987). To see ourselves as others see us: A cooperative do-it-yourself reference accuracy study. *Reference Librarian* 18, 135-147.
   Reports on an unobtrusive evaluation of a multisystem telephone reference service. Reference librarians participated in planning, implementing the study, and analyzing results. This report includes only results of data gathered about the Fairfax County Public Library telephone reference service. The major conclusion is that reference staff will participate willingly in such a study and that data useful for improving the service can be developed.

Rogers, Carl. (1957). The necessary and sufficient conditions of therapeutic personality change. *Journal of Consulting Psychology* 21, 95-103.
   Rogers presents his concept of the three conditions for a successful interpersonal relationship through observation of the therapeutic process. These conditions are genuineness, unconditional positive regard, and empathy. All of these are described in some depth.

Roloff, Michael E. (1979). Communication at the user-system interface: A review of research. *Library Research* 1, 1-18.
   This is an older review of the literature, but it is of interest because the studies in this area are critiqued by a professor in the Department of Communication Studies at Northwestern University. The author felt that much of the research assumed a simplified view by using only one variable to test a given effect, when in fact there are probably multivariate relationships.

Roose, Tina. (1989). Stress at the reference desk. *Library Journal* 114, 166-7.
   Roose discusses the relationships between stress and performance and the reference environment. She notes that reference librarians are the only researchers of this world who are expected to perform with an audience in the midst of other demands and distractions. The results of an earlier study by Haack, Jones, and Roose (1984) are summarized as well as the stages of burnout, which are enthusiasm, stagnation, frustration, and apathy. Burnout progresses from humor to humorlessness, from concrete to abstract, and from human interaction to withdrawal. Pictures,

drawn by public service librarians and indicating the different stages of burnout, are shown.

Ross, Johanna. (1983). Observations of browsing behavior in an academic library. *College & Research Libraries* 44, 269-276.
   Describes a study at University of California-Davis in 1982, which used unobtrusive observation to determine browsing activity. Approach could be applied to reference materials use. Corresponds to the Fussler and Simon study.

Rothstein, Samuel. (1964). The measurement and evaluation of reference service. *Library Trends* 12, 456-472.
   A review of measurement and evaluation of reference services up to 1964, including the range of reference services typical of the time. Author notes the lack of standards and service objectives necessary to evaluation. Also noted is the lack of attention given to effectiveness despite consistently high levels of accuracy reported by libraries along with high levels of reported patron satisfaction with services. Rothstein concludes that measurement and evaluation of reference services have been more discussed than attempted, and he suggests needed research.

Rothstein, Samuel. (1984). The hidden agenda in the measurement and evaluation of reference service. *Reference Librarian* 11, 45-52.
   Suggests developing a "reference activity measure" to account for all of the activities occurring in the reference room, rather than limiting evaluation to reference questions answered. Weights may be assigned to each activity relative to its importance and time for completion. Counterbalances the prevailing self-service structure of reference areas. The author notes that "a count of reference questions dealt with represents only a small part of what reference librarians actually do and contribute...My experience suggests that the total reference uses of a library are probably many times as great as the number of reference questions answered...Reference librarians reporting only on questions answered have been guilty of selling their contributions short...Data should represent the full array of reference activity." Advocates development of an index measure which would represent the total contribution of reference to the library in terms of patrons benefited. One component of this index would be total volume of use of the reference collection including use by unaided patrons. Suggests other measures and notes that data should "represent the *full* array of reference activities: in surveys which indicate the 'drawing power' of the service; in tests which suggest the worth of the service in terms of time and money saved by the consumer; and above all user studies which demonstrate the degree of consumer satisfaction achieved by the service."

Rothstein, Samuel. (1989). An unfinished history: Developmental analysis of reference services in American academic libraries. *Reference Librarian* 25/26, 365-409.
Overview suggests areas for future investigation.

Rubin, Richard. (1986). *In-house use of materials in public libraries.* Champaign, IL: University of Illinois Graduate School of Library and Information Science.
Findings suggest need to supplement/replace table count method since it misses patron reshelving. Largest number of print items used in the library was reference books, followed by nonfiction circulating books. Between 47% and 63% of adult library patrons used materials only in the library; most spent under 30 minutes in the library, but in-house users spent half an hour or more. Summary appeared in *Public Libraries* 25, 137-138 (1986).

Runyon, Robert. (1974). The library administrator's need for measures of reference. *RQ* 14, 9-11.
Problems in library management statistics include definitions, validity, timeliness, and completeness. Reference statistics should provide a key to understanding patron past usage and future requirements. Department heads need data for scheduling, staffing, and performance overview, and library managers need data to assess outreach and user communication programs.

Sager, Donald J. (1982). *Research report on the American public library.* Columbus, OH: OCLC Inc., Office of Research.
Presents a detailed breakdown of reference volume statistics for a typical week from data obtained from the national LIBGIS III survey. Gives reference and directional transactions for a typical week in public libraries in six size groups (by population served). Also gives a section on attendance where turnstile counts for a typical week are reported for the same six size groups.

Salenger, Ruth D., and Deming, Basil S. (1982). Practical strategies for evaluating training. *Training and Development Journal* 36, 20-29.
A model is provided for performance analysis which helps determine whether training is an appropriate solution for a performance problem.

Sandore, Beth. (1990). Online searching: What measure satisfaction? *Library and Information Science Research* 12, 33-54.
A telephone survey was done of 200 users who had received searches done at the Chicago Public Library Computer-Assisted Reference Center. Each of 171 users was phoned two weeks after the search had been

performed. The survey focused on what the users had done with the information received, whether they were satisfied with it, how often the service was used, and how useful it was. Information was also supplemented by a data sheet completed by the staff member at the time of the search. Users were asked how many references had been relevant and how satisfied they were on a three-point scale: satisfied, somewhat satisfied, and not satisfied, overall for the whole search, and with the value of their search results. They were also asked to judge the number of references that were relevant. Satisfaction in general was 91.1% while satisfaction with search results was 60.4%. Of those present for the search, 53% were satisfied; of those not present, 73% were satisfied. The information was needed for immediate use by 73% of patrons. Results indicated that as users receive more information (beyond ten to 20 items) less of it seems to be judged relevant. Results also indicated that 41% of patrons attempted to locate and read only five to nine of the citations; the author concludes that many patrons use much less information than they actually receive.

Saracevic, T., Shaw, W.M., and Kantor, P.B. (1977). Causes and dynamics of user-frustration at an academic library. *College & Research Libraries* 38; 7-18.

Reports on a study of users seeking specific items in an academic library. Success in finding these items was 48% in 1972 and 56% in 1974. Percentage of failure to find items due to user error was 18% to 20%.

Saracevic, Tefko, Kantor, Paul, Chamis, Alice Y., and Trivison, Donna. (1988). A study of information seeking and retrieving. *Journal of the American Society for Information Science* 39, 161-216.

A study was conducted from 1985 to 1987. Forty users (48% academic faculty, 37% graduate students, and 15% from industry) posed one written question apiece related to their ongoing research or work and supplied one tape recording apiece on the underlying problem and intent of their research. Each user also marked on a four-point scale in regard to problem (well or poorly defined), intent (open to many avenues or well defined), probability that knowledge exists (highly improbable to definitely exists), and personal knowledge (little to considerable) on the subject. Thirty-nine paid searchers used various combinations of written and taped documentation, with and without use of a thesaurus. Each of the 40 questions was searched nine times for 360 searches and 8.956 retrieved references were sent to users. Seventy percent considered the results worth more, or somewhat more, than the time it took, and 45% considered the result worth more than $50. Users judged 59% of references as relevant or partially relevant. Forty-five percent of users scored contribution of the search to resolution of their problems in the upper two categories of a four-point scale. Sixty percent of users scored satisfaction with results of their searches in the upper two categories of a five-point scale. Written questions were scored on a five-point scale by 21 non-searcher judges in regard to five characteristics: subject domain clarity, specificity, complexity, presuppositions or implications. Each of the 40 questions was scored ten times. Interjudge agreement was significant for complexity or number of concepts and specificity of subject and presence of presuppositions. References were more likely to be judged relevant if the question was very complex. They were less likely to be relevant if the question was very specific. One objective of this study was related to cognitive traits and decision making of searchers. Searchers were given three tests: the Remote Associates Test (RAT), the Symbolic Reasoning Test (SRT), and the Learning Styles Inventory (LSI). The study concentrated on language ability as measured by the Remote Associates Test, logical ability as measured by the Symbolic Reasoning Test, preferred style of learning as measured by the Learning Style Inventory, and the amount and type of searching experience. The researchers found that searchers who achieved higher scores on language ability, particularly word association, were more successful in the retrieval of relevant items. Searchers indicating concrete experience as their preferred learning style had significantly lower odds for both precision and recall. This finding suggests that concreteness in learning diminishes both search precision and recall. In regard to information searchers had to work with, the searches with the highest precision (64%) and recall (63%) were those where the searchers had a taped description of the problem and the intent for use of the information. The lowest precision (57%) and recall (16%) were by searchers who worked only from the written question. This suggests that the problem at hand and the user's intent were the most powerful elements in the effectiveness of the result. Use of a thesaurus was most important, after the statement of intent, in giving high recall. The relationship of the scales to precision, as judged by experts, in terms of odds ratios was as follows: Problem Resolution 3.21; Satisfaction 2.49; Worth (in terms of time taken) 2.4; and Dollar Value 1.69. This indicates, for example, that if problem resolution was judged high, it was three times more likely that precision would also be judged high. The relationship of the measurement "number of relevant items received," as judged by users, to precision as judged by experts, was also close with an odds ratio of 2.95 and for "partially relevant" 2.43. Number of relevant items received per search as judged by patrons was considered by the author to be a more sensitive measure than the five other overall utility measures. Five attributes (subject, clarity, specificity, complexity, and presupposition) were developed to classify questions. Judges, who were not the librarian searchers, classified the questions. Consistency of their judgments was compared. They found that different question types produced different retrieval results. Saracevic and others also suggested that several variables influence information seeking, including 1) problems perceived by users; 2) intent for use of the information; 3) internal knowledge state of the user; and 4) public knowledge expectations of user. Their results suggest that problem definition and user estimate of how much information may be available contributes to the final evaluation. **See Summaries of Instruments: Saracevic, et al.—Utility Measures.**

Schneekloth, Lynda H., and Keable, Ellen Bruce. (1991). *Evaluation of library facilities: A tool for managing change.* (Occasional Paper No. 191). Champaign, IL: University of Illinois, Graduate School of Library and Information Science.

Presents two case studies on academic facility evaluation. Seven key issues are found to be involved: materials processing; behavior settings; resolution of public, private, and interface functions; design; interface with technology; environmental controls; and managing the processes of change.

Schultz, William C. (1960). *FIRO: A three-dimensional theory of interpersonal behavior, the interpersonal underworld.* New York: Holt, Rinehart and Winston.

FIRO-B is a concept that attempts to provide a framework for evaluating interpersonal behavior. Its original intent was to be used in counseling environments. Three kinds of relations are identified: inclusion, control, and affection. Scales to measure FIRO-B are included in the book.

Schwartz, Diane, and Eakin, Dottie. (1986). Reference service standards, performance criteria, and evaluation. *The Journal of Academic Librarianship* 12, 4-8.

Reference librarians at the Alfred Taubman Medical Library at the University of Michigan sought to establish a list of reference service standards, which led to the creation of a checklist of reference skills used in performance evaluations. **See Summaries of Instruments: Schwartz and Eakin—Checklist of Reference Skills.**

Selth, Jeff, Koller, Nancy, and Briscoe, Peter. (1992). The use of books within the library. *College & Research Libraries* 53, 197-205.

Refutes assertion that circulation reflects in-library use of books. Although primarily relating to circulating materials, the approaches and pitfalls to be avoided in analyzing in-library use can be of value in examining reference materials use as well.

Seng, Mary. (1978). Reference service upgraded: Using patrons' reference questions. *Special Libraries* 69, 21-28.

Classified 18,738 reference questions of University of Texas at Austin into three types: 1) direction (concerned with physical location); 2) information (answered from personal knowledge or consulting only card catalog); and 3) general reference (answered through use of information sources). General reference questions are further subdivided into public catalog assistance, use of indexes and specialized reference titles, bibliographic style, factual reference questions, and explanatory reference questions. Notes that reference librarians are able to improve the efficiency and effectiveness of their services by establishing their own databases of reference questions by noting each question asked for a six-month period and tabulating the results. Collection of data pinpoints areas in which users' questions identified obvious deficiencies in collections, facilities, and staff training. The data also serve to alert reference librarians to consider users' questions in terms of improving service, providing for new disciplines, providing a source of frequently asked questions for training new staff, and contributing to reference collection development policy.

Shearer, Kenneth D., and Smith, Duncan. (1992). *Workshop evaluation: Forms follow function.* Chicago, IL: Continuing Library Education Network/Round Table, American Library Association.

This publication provides an overview of the evaluation process and reproduces 15 sample evaluation forms. No descriptions are given of how these forms have been used, nor is reliability or validity data provided. Names and addresses of several individuals who are willing to respond to questions about workshop evaluations are included.

Slater, Margaret. (1963). Types of use and users in industrial libraries: Some impressions. *Journal of Documentation* 19, 12-19.

This article reports on the qualitative aspects of a questionnaire study of use made of special library/information units in science and technology. This was done to gain information that would make it possible to classify users and predict their needs with reasonable accuracy. Nontechnical executive types were found to be more likely to ask the librarian to look up information while technical executive types were more likely to look it up themselves. Working scientists, engineers, and researchers were slightly more likely to look up information themselves. Technicians (applied) were considerably more likely to ask for help and took longer to find the material if left to do it themselves. They appeared to be the least efficient group when it came to library searching. They had a greater need for facts and used handbooks more often and periodicals less often. Those executives, who were not themselves scientists or technologists, were the *most* likely of any group to ask for help. Nontechnical types, in general, were the most likely to ask for help. Executives, working scientists, and engineers depended heavily on periodical sources.

Slater, Margaret. (1981). *Ratio of staff to users. Implications for library-information work and the potential for automation.* (Aslib Occasional Publication no. 24). London: Aslib.

Reports results of a survey on staffing in special libraries in Great Britain and notes that only 14% of librarians were satisfied with current ways of assessing staffing levels. Supports a ratio of staff to users as a viable and useful method.

Slavens, Thomas P. (1979). The development and testing of materials for computer-assisted instruction in the education of reference librarians. *Information Reports and Bibliographies* 8, 5-13.

Results were analyzed for the six concepts identified as most relevant to the objectives of the program: computer, automation, technology, teaching machines, programmed instruction, and freedom. The noncomputer group attitudes toward the concepts changed significantly in a more positive direction for programmed instruction. When broken down into evaluative (the first 11 items) and potency scales (the next five items), significance was found on the evaluative scale with positive change occurring on the concepts of teaching machines and programmed instruction. The computer group demonstrated no significant changes in attitudes. This instrument was not sensitive to attitudinal changes on the part of the computer group as a result of their interactions with the computer. The author hypothesizes that the noncomputer group developed stronger positive attitudes through association with individuals in the computer group. **See Summaries of Instruments: Slavens—Semantic Differential Scale.**

Slote, Stanley J. (1989). *Weeding library collections* (3d ed.). Englewood, CO: Libraries Unlimited.

Reviews methods and techniques, including Fussler and Simon's approaches. Notes reference weeding may be very subjective.

Smith, Martin E. (1980). Evaluating training operations and programs. *Training and Development Journal* 34, 70-78.

Smith describes a matrix which looks at the questions we want to know, what might be measured, what to look at or the source of the data, and alternative data gathering methodologies. He discusses problems in designing evaluation and implications for action.

Smith, Nathan M., and Fitt, Stephen D. (1982). Active listening at the reference desk. *RQ* 21, 247-249.

Active listening is a communication skill used extensively in family counseling which the authors recommend as appropriate for the reference interview. A number of specific examples of dialogue between the reference librarian and the patron are given.

Smith, Nathan M., and Nelson, Veneese C. (1983). Burnout: A survey of academic reference librarians. *College & Research Libraries* 44, 245-249.

A survey was done to assess burnout in full-time academic reference librarians. Seventy-five United States universities with enrollments of 20,000 or more were selected; five questionnaires were sent to reference heads in each university library, with instructions to distribute them randomly to reference staff. Questionnaires consisted of four parts: 1) job and work characteristics; 2) personal life; 3) demographic information; and (4) the Forbes Burnout Survey. Return rate was 69%. Of those surveyed, there were no cases of high burnout and only 2% experienced mild or greater burnout. Significant correlations with higher levels of burnout were perception of lack of control over stress, gastrointestinal disturbances, headaches, sleeplessness, back problems, lack of success on the job, and not wanting to be in the same job a year from now. Also correlated with higher burnout was lack of money for the library and/or personal needs and lack of time to do all that had to be done. Study of the five highest burnout cases showed that all five felt they had little input into library policy and that they all were expected to publish. The low levels of burnout found in this study for academic reference librarians has been questioned because the Forbes Burnout Survey was used, rather than the Maslach Burnout Inventory, which not only has been tested and validated but also has a large body of data available for comparative study.

Smith, Nathan M., and Nielson, Laura F. (1984). Burnout: A survey of corporate librarians. *Special Libraries* 75, 221-227.

A mail survey was sent to a random sampling of corporate libraries requesting that the reference librarian fill it out and return it. Response rate was 41%. The Maslach Burnout Inventory was used. Scores overall were significantly lower than for other occupational groups. However, the greatest problem centered around lack of personal accomplishment.

Sommer, Robert. (1970). The ecology of study areas. *Environment and Behavior* 2, 271-280.

The author is a professor of psychology. Data from several thousand college students on 23 campuses were summarized. Study revealed that most students (up to nine-tenths) were in libraries to study with their own books and will not use the collections. Design and library outreach implications. Suggests that designers and social scientists work in teams. At time of writing, the author felt man-environment interface was still in the groundbreaking stage.

Spencer, Carol C. (1980). Random time sampling. *Bulletin of the Medical Library Association* 68, 53-57.

A work-sampling study was performed at the National Library of Medicine where staff were given a pocket-sized random alarm mechanism and were asked to record on a form categories of questions engaged in when the alarm sounded. About 40 observations per day were obtained for two months, covering a total of 1,566 working hours. The number of alarms for verification questions, for example, was divided by the *total* number of alarms to obtain the percentage of time staff worked on verification questions. This percentage was then multiplied by the total number of hours worked (1,566) to obtain the number of estimated hours spent working on verification. This method was used to determine costs per question for different types of questions. The authors found that in 1979, at a wage cost of $10 per hour (labor cost alone), it cost $2.52 for a reference question. Breakdowns by type of question were $1.40 quick fact, $4.06 biographical, $3.37 verification, $2.73 citation retrieval, $0.82 instructional, $1.69 referral, $4.57 subject research, and $9.09 consult. **See Summaries of Instruments: Spencer—Cost Analysis for Types of Reference Questions.**

St. Clair, Jeffrey W., and Aluri, Rao. (1977). Staffing the reference desk: Professionals or nonprofessionals. *The Journal of Academic Librarianship* 3, 149-153.

Presents an analysis of questions asked at the reference desk of a university library serving primarily undergraduate students. Attempts to ascertain how many reference questions could be answered by nonprofessional library employees at the reference desk. Questions were classified into four types: 1) directional; 2) instructional; 3) reference; and 4) extended reference (usually take more than five minutes). Through an examination of the skills required to answer each question in each category, the authors conclude that carefully trained nonprofessionals at the reference desk can competently answer 80% of all questions.

Stabler, Karen Y. (1987). Introductory training of academic reference librarians: A survey. *RQ* 26, 363-369.

Stabler designed a survey which solicited information about reference librarians and their departments, gathered information about components of their training programs, and collected new librarians' perceptions of training programs. Over 61% of new librarians characterized their orientation sessions as poorly organized. Only 22% indicated that there was a written training plan. There seemed to be high significance between the rating of the effectiveness of the program and the existence of a written plan. Of the 89 respondents, 78 were not asked to evaluate their training program.

Standera, Oldrich R. (1973). Costs and effectiveness in the evaluation of an information system: A case study. In Helen Waldron and F. Raymond Long (Eds.). *Innovative developments in information systems: Their benefits and costs. Proceedings of the 36th Annual Meeting of the American Society for Information Science* (p. 219-221). Westport, CT: Greenwood Press. A method was devised to obtain a monthly record with cost effectiveness and cost-benefit data for computerized literature searches. This method was demonstrated through a case study. For retrospective service, cost per relevant hit varied from $0.22 to $0.31; costs per question varied from $16.50 to $19. For SDI searches, cost varied from $0.32 to $0.79 per relevant hit and from $8.80 to $13.50 per question. Databases varied in percentage of relevant citations from 50% to 95%. **See Summaries of Instruments: Standera—Cost-Effectiveness Account.**

Statistical Report. (1988-). Chicago: Public Library Association, Public Library Data Service.

Gives a wide variety of public library statistics both in summary form and by name of individual library. Of particular interest for reference are annual figures by library name for volume of reference transactions, turnstile count, and in-library use. Statistical summaries are also given by size of population served. Output measures are provided for reference transactions per capita (reference transactions divided by the population served) and reference completion rate (as judged by the librarian). Among graphs of interest are reference transactions per capita by population group. It is interesting to note that as population served becomes *greater*, circulation and turnstile count per person *decreases*, but reference transaction per capita *increase*.

Steffenson, Martin B., and Larason, Larry D. (Eds.). (1978). *The user encounters the library: An interdisciplinary focus on the user/system interface.* Monroe, LA: Library Training Institute. (ERIC Document Reproduction Service No. ED 266 791).

Three papers are of environmental interest: (3) "Environmental psychology: factors in library environments." (Williams H. Ittelson) 18p.; (4) "Personal space and facilities usage." (Robert Sommer) 17p.;

(6) "Architectural approaches to design and behavior." (Nancy Mc-Adams) 9p.

Stephens, Sandy, Gers, Ralph, Seward, Lillie, Bolin, Nancy, and Partridge, Jim. (1988). Keep on learning: Reference breakthrough in Maryland. *Public Libraries* 27, 202-203.

Report on the findings of the 1983 unobtrusive study of the Maryland Department of Education which indicated that factors contributing to improved reference performance are basic communication behaviors that are within the control of the librarian. Most important among them are verifying the patron's request, using open probes to draw out the patron's specific question, and asking at the end of the transaction, "Does this completely answer your question?" A training program was developed to prepare librarians in these behaviors. A follow-up study revealed their effectiveness: The pretest of 60 public libraries in Maryland in 1983 showed that "library users had only a 55% chance of getting a complete and correct answer." It identified a set of model reference behaviors. After training, a second study conducted in 1986 showed that the same libraries gave correct answers 77% of the time. A control group of untrained libraries only had 60% correct answers.

Stenstrom, P.F. (1990). Our real business. *Journal of Academic Librarianship* 16, 78-79.

Notes Durrance (1989) indicated librarians need excellent interpersonal skills, as well as source expertise. Asserts bibliographic instruction is not a panacea, and may give patrons the impression that asking for help is wrong.

Stevens, Norman. (1987). Unobtrusive testing and library reference service. *Wilson Library Bulletin* 62, 75-76.

The most significant part of Hernon and McClure's study is their effort to establish the correct answer fill rate as a performance measure, to refine unobtrusive testing as an evaluation methodology and to explore new applications of that procedure, and, in particular, to assist library staff in using that performance measure and those techniques in implementing the ongoing evaluation of library service in local situations.

Stevens, Rolland. (1956). The study of the research use of libraries. *Library Quarterly* 26, 41-51.

Observes that materials used for research may not be library-classified in that field (examples: American history and sociology). Social sciences and humanities embrace a more diverse body of literature, which affects research use approaches. Research habits affect library use and have implications for library management. Mentions studying the design of digital computers and psychological factors as related to literature searching.

Strayner, Richard. (1980). The use of empirical standards in assessing public library effectiveness. In Neal Kaske (Ed.). *Library effectiveness: A state of the art: Proceedings of the ALA Preconference on Library Effectiveness.* (p. 351-369). Chicago: American Library Association.

This Australian study attempted to discover factors influencing public library use. It was found that "number of staff person hours in public areas" was the best predictor of volume of use of circulation.

Strong, Gary E. (1980a). Evaluating the reference product. *RQ* 19, 367-372.

Describes a survey given by the Washington State Library based on a user ticket which gathers a variety of data about library use and reference service in particular. Patron reports indicated that 70% had received the materials or information sought but 80% were satisfied with the service they received. Strong classified users into three major categories: 1) those who are seeking information or library materials for job-related purposes; 2) those seeking information or library materials for school, educational or learning purposes; and 3) those seeking information or library materials for leisure/personal purposes. He observed that one problem is that the categories are not mutually exclusive and another is that 19% of users did not respond to the question. See **Summaries of Instruments: Strong—Patterns of Information Requests Survey.**

Strong, Gary E. (1980b). *Patterns of information requests at the Washington State Library.* Olympia, WA: Washington State Library.

Strong used question categories: 1) Directional (location of materials or facilities within the library, hours, library policies, equipment operation); 2) Bibliographical Verification (used only if citation is verified or corrected); 3) Author/Title or Periodical Title/Article (request for known items); 4) Subject/Reference (involves use, interpretation, or instruction in use of one or more information sources); and 5) User's Advisory and Update (recommendation of specific titles requiring knowledge of the collection). See **Summaries of Instruments: Strong—Patterns of Information Requests Survey.**

Strother, Jeanne D. (1975). *An investigation of the relationship of faculty knowledge and use of current reference and para-reference books especially pertinent to their fields.* Master's thesis. Muncie, IN: Ball State University. (ERIC Document Reproduction Service No. ED 112 854).

Investigates reference habits of selected faculty members, how they learn of, and use how they use older/newer reference materials. Two thousand users were given forms on entering the library and a return rate of 80% was achieved. Success rates were highest for those seeking books, with lower success rates for periodicals and government documents. Found that in a given discipline, a large number of new reference materials escapes faculty attention; older, better-known sources tend to be used. Nonuse appeared to be predicated on lack of knowledge of sources' existence. Suggests need for librarians to publicize reference materials and that further study be done on disclosing concealed faculty reference needs. **See Summaries of Instruments: Strother—Strother's Questionnaire A and B.**

Stuart, M. (1977). Some effects on library users of the delays in supplying publications. *Aslib Proceedings* 29, 35-45.

The interlibrary loan and book recall operations at Lancaster University were studied. Two questionnaire samples of users were taken in 1974 and 1975 with forms put in requested materials when they arrived and were handed to the patron. "Disbenefit" was a measure of the degree of frustration and inconvenience users had encountered before the book arrived with four categories: no effect, a little inconvenient, inconvenient, and highly inconvenient. Users were asked how much they would have been willing to pay to have had the item available when they asked for it. Users were asked to complete forms `before` looking at the requested publication. Staff were the least affected while undergraduates suffered the greatest disbenefit. Demands for class work were most affected and research was least affected. Disbenefit or extent of frustration proved to be a useful measure. The average cost users would have been willing to pay to avoid the delay when they needed an item as soon as possible was about $1.50.

Suburban Library System Reference Service. (1986). *Reference evaluation manual for public libraries.* Oak Lawn, IL: Suburban Library System.

The Suburban Library System committed to quality reference services through the passage of the SLS Minimum Reference Standards for Public Libraries in 1986. A manual was developed which provided instruments for use in a variety of reference settings. Data collection and analysis information is included for patron satisfaction with answers, classification of questions asked by subject, reference completion rate, reference transaction per capita, and degree to which patrons obtain accurate and complete answers. At the time of this writing, the manual is being revised.

Swigger, Keith. (1985). Questions in library and information science. *Library & Information Science Research* 7, 369-383.

Librarianship has traditionally focused on intellectual content of works in collections and studied questions in relationship to possible sources. However, one way to view libraries is that they are storehouses of answers to questions, not storehouses of recorded knowledge. In this case, the focus of collection development is users' needs for information. Collection development would be a process of studying users' information needs so that materials will be available that contain answers to questions patrons are likely to ask. In this view, questions are seen as indications of information need. At the direct service level—reference service—librarians must be concerned with the expressed information needs of specific patrons.

Swope, Mary Jane, and Katzer, Jeffrey. (1972). Silent majority: Why don't they ask questions? *RQ* 12, 161-166.

Users of an academic library in the card catalog area, the index area, and the open stacks were interviewed to determine whether they had a need for help, and if so, whether they had asked or intended to ask for help. Forty-one percent of those interviewed said they had a question they would like to ask, but 65% of that total said they would *not* ask a librarian. However, 72% of the non-askers said they would ask the interviewer or another student or a friend. Of the total non-askers, reasons given were as follows: dissatisfied with previous service (42%), question is too simple for librarian (29%), don't want to bother the librarian (29%). Users did not give as reasons that librarians were too busy or that they already knew how to find what they wanted. They did give the impression that they were willing to ask directional questions but did not want to appear stupid by asking more substantive types of questions.

Tagliacozzo, Renata. (1977). Estimating the satisfaction of information users. *Bulletin of the Medical Library Association* 65, 243-249.

Data are analyzed here from a study where a follow-up questionnaire was sent to a sample of MEDLINE users who had requested searches at seven information centers within a two-month period. Ninety percent found the searches to have *some* degree of helpfulness, 80% found them generally to have some usefulness, while the percentage who found *some* relevant references was closer to 60%. Users who had the most knowledge of the subject (who found missed references) rated the service lower than those with the least knowledge (found no missed references) rated the service higher. Recommends that a single overall judgment of a service should be looked at suspiciously, in particular if the rating scale measures a global judgment of the service (such as "helpfulness," "success," "worthiness," and "value") rather than the appraisal of specific search results. A questionnaire therefore should not be limited to eliciting an overall judgment, but should tap several aspects of the user's reaction to the outcome of his or her request for information. See **Summaries of Instruments: Tagliacozzo—Follow-Up Questionnaire.**

Tagliacozzo, Renata, Rosenberg, Lawrence, and Kochen, Manfred. (1970). Access and recognition: From users' data to catalogue entries. *Journal of Documentation* 26, 230-249.

Reports results of a study based on surveys of catalog use at three university libraries and one public library. Both known-item and subject searches are analyzed along with reasons for failure. A bibliography is given. Further analysis is done in another article by the same three authors in (1970): Orthographic error patterns of author names in catalog searches. *Journal of Library Automation* 3, 93-101. (June 1967).

Taler, Izabella. (1984). *Burnout: A survey of library directors' views.* (ERIC Document Reproduction Service No. ED 283 524).

Surveys were sent to 90 academic library directors in large institutions in New York. Return rate was 40%. Of those returning questionnaires, 65% perceived that job burnout was a problem in their libraries.

Taylor, Robert S. (1967). *Question-negotiation and information-seeking in libraries.* (Studies in the Man-System Interface in Libraries, Report No. 3). Bethlehem, PA: Center for the Information Sciences, Lehigh University.

A class in information science chose reference questions for which they wanted answers in their own academic work. Students kept personal diaries of each step of the search process, recorded their thinking at each stage, and gave reasons for each step in their search process. Sources searched and final outcome were recorded. They were asked, following class discussion, to write descriptions of their searches for specific information on any topics of interest to them at that time. This was felt to be better than one based on artificially generated searches because they could draw on their own interests and experiences and they could determine when they had answers acceptable to themselves. They were allowed to use any sources they wished and to ask advice from anyone. They were instructed to conduct the searches in whatever way seemed easiest and most efficient. They were not restricted exclusively to the library although they were requested to use the library somewhere in their searches. Full data are given for four searchers. Of these four searchers, three found the information they were seeking. Some findings of note were as follows: In one of the four searches, the student, instead of doing the searching *himself,* posed the question to another student. This then created a situation where a student was searching for the answer to an artificially generated question that did not represent a real information need to him. In contrast to the other three searchers, he gave up without finding an answer after looking briefly in the catalog and examining two books on the shelf. One book actually had the answer but the searcher failed to select the correct chapter from the table of contents and did not use the index. Of all the sources located and examined by these four searchers, only 18.5% were already known to them. All of the questions were factual. None of the four searchers identified a *specific* answering source from the catalog alone. However, 75% identified the *correct shelf area* from the catalog. Some probable errors in searching were not trying a title approach in the catalog, not using the subject headings list, and not using book indexes. The percentage of titles used that were located by the following strategies were titles found in catalog, 41%; professor or other, 22%; own text or known item, 18.5 percent; shelf search in subject area, 11%; and reference librarian, 7%. The success of the various approaches in identifying a source with the desired fact were reference librarian, 100% (one case only); shelf search, 75%; consulting professors, etc., 25%. However, items given by professors, when combined with library items, resulted in success in one case. The numbers of potential answering sources examined by searchers varied from two to 17. Of the three searchers working on their own questions, all found the answers by combining information from two to seven different sources. One of the four searchers attempted to consult reference *before* beginning his search but, finding the desk unstaffed, consulted the catalog, went to the shelf, and examined 17 books in an unsuccessful search. Two of three searchers consulted professors or other students at some point in their searches.

Taylor, Robert. (1968). Question-negotiation and information seeking in libraries. *College & Research Libraries* 29, 178-194.
    A classic study into the process of question-negotiation between reference librarian and patron. This research formed the basis of many studies that were to follow.

Tessier, Judith A., Crouch, Wayne W., and Atherton, Pauline. (1977). New measures of user satisfaction with computer-based literature searches. *Special Libraries* 68, 383-389.

The authors posit three assumptions about the measurement of user satisfaction: 1) the user's satisfaction will be a function of how well the product fits his requirement; 2) the user's state of satisfaction is experienced within the frame of his experience; and 3) that people may seek solutions within an acceptable range instead of an ideal or perfect solution. It is suggested that there are additional focuses of user satisfaction and that observation of the user is a rich source of data that should be tapped.

Thompson, Mark J., Smith, Nathan M., and Woods, Bonnie L. (1980). A proposed model of self-disclosure. *RQ* 20, 160-164.

An outline for a proposed model of self-disclosure for reference work. This article provides the theoretical basis for the study on the same construct by Markham, Stirling, and Smith (1983).

Tibbo, Helen. (1993). An experimental study of the way in which search strategy influences retrieval success. In Marjorie Murfin and Jo Bell Whitlatch (Eds.). *First preconference on research in reference effectiveness*. (RASD Occasional Paper 16). Chicago: American Library Association, Reference and Adult Services Division.

The author compared the effectiveness of various Boolean search strategies in retrieving subject information in terms of recall and precision. A special database, the Cystic Fibrosis database, was used; in this database a series of reference questions had been formulated and experts had provided relevance ratings to all documents in relation to these particular questions. Thus, the retrieval success of each Boolean strategy executed in the Cystic Fibrosis database could be accurately judged. Nine search strategies were tested. Results indicated that there does not appear to be a way to achieve total recall of all highly relevant documents without paying a high cost in precision. The use of synonyms increased recall and use of descriptors improved precision.

Tobin, Jayne C. (1974). A study of library use studies. *Information Storage and Retrieval* 10, 101-113.

Brief history of use studies, and analysis of citations in *Library Literature* 1960-1973. Demonstrated little had been published in such areas as usage in non-U.S. libraries, minority group usage, nonusers, and usage in rural districts. Calls for large-scale use studies—regional, national, international.

Tracey, William R. (1992). *Designing training and development systems* (3d ed.) New York: AMACOM.

Although addressing human resource development managers and training and development practitioners, Tracey provides insights into the process of training that is useful for reference librarians. Two separate chapters address criterion measures and training evaluation. Provides a good overview of evaluation methodologies.

Trautman, Rodes, and Gothberg, Helen M. (1982). A reference tools database: A proposed application for a microcomputer at the reference desk. *The Reference Librarian* 5/6, 195-198.

Explains the type of information the authors attempted to include in a reference database which would be a guide to locating information within reference sources.

Trueswell, R.W. (1969). Some behavioral patterns of library users: The 80/20 rule. *Wilson Library Bulletin* 43, 458-461.

Points out that in business 80% of the number of warehouse transactions are from only 20% of the items stocked (sometimes expressed as the 75/25 rule). Suggests this principle of use be applied in developing core collections.

Tyckoson, David A. (1992). Wrong questions, wrong answers: Behavior vs. factual evaluation of reference service. *The Reference Librarian* 38, 151-173.

Tyckoson's article focuses on the behavioral evaluation of reference services. He agrees with the importance of fact-based reference testing through unobtrusive methods, but he notes that factual questions make up a very small part of the actual reference desk experience. He recommends obtrusive evaluation by a supervisor using a behavioral checklist made up of 25 items. Indicators are divided into four categories: availability, communication skills, search strategy skills, and individual attention to patrons. The scales are included in the article but have not had objective testing.

University of British Columbia. (1984). UBC library survey 1980. In *User studies in ARL Libraries*. (SPEC Kit 101, p.7-23). Washington, DC: Association of Research Libraries, Office of Management Studies.

During a sample week 12,000 questionnaires were passed out in the library with a return rate of 50%. Out of 5,341 persons who answered the question about their last use of reference service, 2,022, or 39%, reported having had to wait for service, 4% of the patrons had to wait over five minutes, and an additional 3.59% left without being helped. About 9% of those who had to wait (or 192 persons) considered the wait too long and left. Of those who waited for service but did *not* leave, 28% waited one to two minutes, 47% waited three to five minutes, and 25% waited over five minutes. Reference desk service was the most used and most preferred reference service. Respondents were given a list of nine items and asked which types of library instruction they had previously used and which was *most* helpful. Results were as follows in regard to *use*: reference assistance, 69%; library handouts, 54%; help from friend, 50%; class tour or lecture, 44%; tour joined on own time, 20%; lecture/tour from instructor, 15%; library workbook or exercise, 10%; term paper clinics, 7%; self-operated A/V presentation, 7%. results in regard to the *most helpful service* were reference, 44%; class tour/lecture, 18%; help from friend, 15%; library handout, 8%; tour joined on own, 5%; term paper clinic, 3%; lecture/tour from instructor, 3%; library workbook or assignment, 2%; and self-operated A/V presentation, 1%. In regard to reference collection use, 47% reported being users of the reference collection; 21% of all users were weekly users and 26% were occasional users. Users were asked to judge ease of use in three categories: fairly easy, fairly difficult, and very difficult; 94% said the card catalog was fairly easy to use, 80% said the micro-catalog was fairly easy to use, and 76% said the microlist of serials was fairly easy to use. In regard to asking for help, if an item was not on the shelf users were given choices of possible actions: 58% would ask for help, 63% would make a check of the circulation list, 23% would come back again and check, and 29% would give up. Reasons given by those who did not ask for help at the reference disk were didn't need help (67%), reluctant to ask (17%), not sure of kinds of help available (11%), and previous experience unsatisfactory (5.5%). See **Summaries of Instruments: University of California at Los Angeles, et al.—Selected Items from Overall Library Survey; and University of British Columbia, et al.—Selected User Survey Items.**

University of California at Los Angeles. (1981). Report of the Task Force on Library Service to Undergraduates, 1979. In *User surveys and evaluation of library services.* (SPEC Kit 71, p. 35-56). Washington, DC: Association of Research Libraries, Office of Management Studies.

   Survey forms were given to some 772 students in three large undergraduate classes. One item asked students to mark those services important to them. Importance ratings were as follows: study space (65%), research materials (53%), periodicals (41%), audiovisuals (34%), reference (32%), reserve (32%), conference rooms (28%), recreational reading (28%), recreational listening (22%), library instruction (21%), microforms (16%), recreational viewing (14%), interlibrary loan (12%), and online searching (9%). In regard to reference use, 66% had used reference (14% were regular users and 52% occasional users). A three-point scale of "good," "satisfactory," and "poor" was used to rank library services with a rating of 93% good or satisfactory. Another item in the questionnaire gave a list of six items and asked students what sources they had found helpful in assisting them to use the library.

Reference desk service was the most used and the most preferred service. Results were as follows: reference service, 30%; fellow students, 24%; library guides (printed), 16%; public library staff reference help, 8%; library skills program in English department, 5%; and library tours, 5%. A third question asked if they felt that further guidance in library use would help them. Results: Yes-52%, No-48%. Those who had answered "yes" were given a list of seven items and asked which of them would be helpful, with results as follows: More instructional and direction signs, 27%; term paper clinics, 21%; handbooks or pamphlets, 14%; organized course, 11%; library tours, 10%; self-paced library skills courses, 8%; and library lecture, 8%. **See Summaries of Instruments: University of California at Los Angeles, et al.—Selected Items from Overall Library Surveys.**

University of California at Riverside. (1981). Use of Library Services Questionnaire. In *User surveys and evaluation of library services*. (SPEC Kit 71, p. 1-12). Washington, DC: Association of Research Libraries, Office of Management Studies.

Questionnaires were distributed within the General Library according to a prearranged schedule, and those in branch libraries were placed in boxes for users to take; 1,584 were returned. On one question, users were asked if they had ever been misdirected from one library service point to another with 12% reporting that they had been. This survey used a number of two-category scales and three-category scales biased in a positive direction. (A later survey instrument has been placed in SPEC Kit 101). These scales serve as an illustration of the positive bias that can result from use of three-category biased scales and two-category yes-no scales. Overall opinion of the library's services: Excellent (55%), Satisfactory (44%), Unsatisfactory (1%). "Was your visit to the library today: Very successful (30%), Successful (64%), Unsuccessful (6%). "Did you find what you wanted?: Yes (79%), No (21%). **See Summaries of Instruments: New York University, et al.—Selected User Survey Items.**

University of California at Riverside. (1983). *Public services in research libraries: Report of the Service Performance and Service Needs Task Force*. Riverside, CA: University of California, The Library, (unpublished).
See Weingart (1983).

University of California at Riverside. (1984). UCR library services survey. In *User studies in ARL Libraries* (SPEC Kit 101, p. 32-42). Washington, DC: Association of Research Libraries, Office of Management Studies.

Includes questionnaire only. Full report with data available in Weingart (1983). **See Summaries of Instruments: University of California at Riverside—UCR Library Services Survey.**

University of California at Santa Barbara, University Library. (1986). *Report of the Task Force on Facilities, Space and Equipment*. Santa Barbara: University of California at Santa Barbara, University Library. (ERIC Document Reproduction Service No. ED 297 730).

Broad-based investigation on the best use of facilities, space, and equipment. May serve as a model for conducting similar investigations.

University of Cambridge Library Management Research Unit (LMRU). (1975). Factors affecting the use of seats in academic libraries. *Journal of Librarianship* 7, 262-287.

Library use was studied at 17 libraries and seating at 21 libraries to refine building norms for reader places in future university library buildings. Four measurements were employed: a library use questionnaire, a survey of study patterns questionnaire, observations of seating use, and exit interviews. Of 4,866 persons interviewed and using seats, 39% reported using reference material in their libraries.

University of Cincinnati. (1984). Survey of the effectiveness of record systems. In *User studies in ARL libraries*. (SPEC Kit 101, p. 62-80). Washington, DC: Association of Research Libraries, Office of Management Studies.

Survey data was obtained from two campuses of the University of Cincinnati with 900 returned forms. A question was asked regarding how easy it was to find periodicals or journals in the library and results were as follows: Very easy (37.7%), next highest category (43.6%). Another question asked about how well users were able to carry out certain functions in locating periodicals. Questions asked whether they were able to 1) Determine whether the library subscribes to a periodical: Always (55%), Often (34.9%); 2) Find out whether the library has received a current issue: Always (40.5%), Often (34%); 3) Determine what issues are bound: Always (36.1%), Often (37.3%).

University of Kentucky Library. (1981). Literature Search Evaluation. In *User surveys and evaluation of library services*. (SPEC Kit 71). Washington, DC: Association of Research Libraries, Office of Management Studies.

Presents a form used in the University of Kentucky Libraries to determine the quality of online searches from the patron viewpoint. A useful item concerns the user's reason for wanting the search. **See**

Summaries of Instruments: University of Kentucky Libraries—Literature Search Evaluation.

University of Massachusetts. (1976). User survey: University of Massachusetts Reference Department. In *User surveys*. (SPEC Kit 24). Washington, DC: Association of Research Libraries, Office of Management Studies.

A two-page instrument is provided to be used to survey users of reference services. The first part asks questions about reference use in general; the second part asks about the user's most recent experiences at the reference desk. One question asks whether or not there was a wait and, if so, about the nature of the delay. Following this a question is asked about what type of information/assistance was wanted with seven alternatives supplied. Another question asks whether the user could find the same information again if needed. Finally users check service on a scale from courteous to rude. An open-ended question asks for comments and suggestions. No information on results or experience with use is provided.

University of North Carolina, Charlotte. J. Murrey Atkins Library. (1976). *Academic library development program: A self study*. Charlotte, NC: The Library. (ERIC Document Reproduction Service No. ED 142227).

In 1976 a user survey was distributed to all faculty and students in dormitories and also given out at various distribution points on campus with 611 student forms and 109 faculty forms returned. The survey consisted of an image survey and importance and success sections, and a survey concerning new services. Of particular interest was the portion of the survey where users were asked what types of information needs were most important in their work and how successful the library was in providing for those needs. Students ranked "locating simple facts for course and research purposes" as maximal information needs. Simple facts were defined as addresses, spelling of names, and so on and simple summaries (e.g., biographical sketch prepared from multiple sources) They indicated the library provided for these needs with only average success. Faculty indicated little or no need in these areas. They did, however, have a significant requirement for citation services and for locating complex data for research purposes. No more detailed findings are presented.

University of Texas at Austin Library. (1984). Questionnaires for end users and intermediaries. In *User studies in ARL libraries*. (SPEC Kit 101). Washington, DC: Association of Research Libraries, Office of Management Studies.

The University of Texas at Austin did a study of the effectiveness of end-users searching Search Helper and BRS After Dark where the end-users had intermediaries available for help when needed. Both end-user and intermediary completed a form after each search. The patron form asks users to rate satisfaction on a scale from 1 to 5 and what percentage of references retrieved were relevant. The intermediary portion asks for judgments on staff time needed, type of help provided, user's familiarity with the terminal, ability to use the system, and enthusiasm for searching. **See Summaries of Instruments: University of Texas at Austin—Questionnaires for End Users and Intermediaries.**

User surveys. (1988). (SPEC Kit 148). Washington, DC: Association of Research Libraries, Office of Management Studies.

Contains two *use* studies done at the University of Michigan (1983-84) and Washington University (1986-87). Exit questionnaires are reproduced. Earlier SPEC Kit compilations are *User statistics and studies* (1976) (SPEC Kit 25)—contains a 1972 University of Pittsburgh analysis of hourly lending and reference use statistics by means of comparison line graphs; *User surveys and evaluation of library services* (1981) (SPEC Kit 71); and *User studies in ARL Libraries* (1984) (SPEC Kit 101).

Van Heck, Charles., III (1993). Use and user studies: An application to theological libraries. *Journal of Religious & Theological Information* 1, 97-111.

Surveys components of past use/user studies (techniques, models, theories) as applied in the theological environment.

Van House, Nancy. (1983). A time allocation theory of public library use. *Library and Information Science Research* 5, 365-384.

Develops a model of public library use where a consumer makes decisions about allocating time to various activities, based on costs of time and expected benefits. The cost of an individual's time is set at that individual's wage rate. Library use by different groups of users is studied and observed patterns are shown to be consistent with differences in costs of user time.

Van House, Nancy A. (1985). Output measures: Some lessons from Baltimore County Public Library. *Public Libraries* 24, 102-105.

The author records the experience of a large city library system in its use over several years of *Output measures for public libraries* with particular attention to problems of measurement within the system as a result of the varying libraries within BCPL: branches, cross branch comparisons, system performance, cross system comparisons, and the importance of consistency in following procedures in data collection. The author concludes with the purpose and limitations of the measures as well as their practical value.

Van House, Nancy A. (1986). Public library effectiveness: Theory, measures, and determinants. *Library and Information Science Research* 8, 261-283.

Public library effectiveness efforts are placed within the context of theoretical and empirical research on organizational effectiveness. The construct, measures, and determinants of public library effectiveness are investigated. *A planning process for public libraries* and *Output measures for public libraries* are shown to assume a goal-based definition of effectiveness. A possible model of the determinants of public library output measures is presented. Data from the Baltimore County Public Library System in Maryland were used to evaluate the validity, reliability, and sensitivity of output measures. All within library branch correlations were strong and statistically significant at the .01 level for four output measures. However, reference fill-rate did not demonstrate reliability: within branch correlation was not significantly different from zero. The author recommends larger sample sizes of 400 to 500 reference transactions.

Van House, Nancy A. (1989). Output measures in libraries. *Library Trends* 38, 268-279.

Kantor's measure of reference success relies on the judgment of the librarian. Not surprisingly users often judge the same transaction differently.

Van House, Nancy A., and Childers, Thomas. (1984). Unobtrusive evaluation of a reference referral network: The California experience. *Library & Information Science Research* 6, 305-319.

Reports on the evaluation of the California statewide reference referral network. Utilizes existing records of actual reference transactions evaluated by a panel of judges. The network components averaged 79% answered completely and correctly. **See Summaries of Instruments: Van House and Childers—California Reference Evaluation Form.**

Van House, Nancy A., and Childers, Thomas. (1993). *The public library effectiveness study: The complete report*. Chicago: American Library Association.

The purpose of the study was to define effectiveness for the public library institution. Explores a variety of models of effectiveness, including the goals model; the process or natural systems model; the open systems or systems resource model; and the multiple constituencies approach. A list of 61 indicators for describing public library effectiveness was developed and key external and internal constituencies were surveyed about the usefulness of the indicators. All respondents rated each of the 61 indicators on a five-point Likert scale (1 = *not important to know* to 5 = *essential to know*) or selected "no opinion." Several of the effectiveness indicators are related to reference assessment, for example: 1) percentage of reference questions answered; 2) user's evaluation of services; 3) amount of staff contact with users; 4) extent to which staff are helpful, courteous, and concerned; 5) how much information library has about other libraries' collections; 6) speed of service to user; 7) number of reference questions asked by users; 8) quality of staff (education, talent); 9) services to special groups, such as minorities, the aging, toddlers, and others; and 10) staff morale. Considering all respondents together, six indicators were scored within the top ten indicators by all constituent groups: convenience of hours, range of materials, range of services, staff helpfulness, services suited to community, and materials quality. The various constituencies agreed more than they disagreed about what constitutes effectiveness. Correlations of indicator choices were lower between library service staff or library managers and library users (.58 and .57) than correlations between library service staff or library managers and other groups, such as community leaders (.77 and .80), local officials (.79 and .82), and trustees (.91 and .90). Concludes other measures are needed to cover the full range of dimensions of effectiveness in addition to those employed in *Output measures for public libraries* (Van House, Lynch, McClure, Zweizig, and Rodger, 1987).

Van House, Nancy A., Lynch, Mary Jo, McClure, Charles R., Zweizig, Douglas L., and Rodger, Eleanor Jo. (1987). *Output measures for public libraries: A manual of standardized procedures* (2d ed.). Chicago: American Library Association.

Experience with the measures and procedures in the first edition of *Output measures* (Zweizig and Rodger, 1982) resulted in calls for improvements, which are reflected in the second edition. Although internal comparison over time is preferred, the need for information about libraries in similar communities and with similar resources was evident. It was decided that the availability of such data would enhance library planning efforts. As a result the Public Library Development Program was created and the decision was made to revise *Output measures* to make measurements methods easier or more appropriate, to expand explanations for ease in understanding, to provide more information on interpretation and the use of results, and to more closely integrate measurement and evaluation with the processes presented in *Planning and role setting for public libraries*. Measures are provided in the following areas: library use by the community, materials use, materials access, reference services, programming, further possibilities for analyzing data or constructing measures, and special client groups. Determines annual in-library materials use per capita by means of hourly counts of materials left on tables during a sample week period; this number is multiplied by 50 (weeks) and divided by the population served. Libraries are encouraged to begin with a few measures and add others as needed and feasible. Guidance is provided for selection of measures which may result in fulfilling specific objectives. Instruction is provided to obtain the most valid, reliable, and comparable results possible. The authors respond to criticisms regarding validity and reliability by noting that the measures provide for useful internal comparison of performance over time (including data developed from the use of the first edition) and through implementation of the Public Library Data Service comparison of similar libraries from across the country. **See Instruments with Annotations: Reference Completion Rate.**

Van House, Nancy A., Weil, Beth T., and McClure, Charles R. (1990). *Measuring academic library performance: A practical approach.* Chicago: American Library Association, Association of College and Research Libraries.

Offers a set of practical output measures for academic libraries. The Association of College and Research Libraries board of directors, based on the recommendation of the ACRL Task Force on Performance Measures, set goals to stimulate librarian interest in performance measures and to provide practical assistance for the conduct of measurements of effectiveness with minimum expense and difficulty. The result is this manual, which the authors state presents instruments or measures to measure the impact, efficiency, and effectiveness of library activities, to quantify or explain library output in meaningful ways to university administrators, to be used by unit heads to demonstrate performance and resource needs, and to provide data useful for planning. The measures are intended to be replicable in all types of academic and research libraries, to be decision-related, to be easy and inexpensive to use, to be user-oriented, and to be linked to library goals and objectives. They are designed primarily for internal use. Libraries are expected to select from measures provided those most useful for their needs. Encouragement is given for periodic replication. The authors state that only basic math is needed for implementation. The manual is divided into two sections: the first is about measurement in general, and the second is a procedural guide for each measure including definitions, steps for collecting and analyzing data, and information about each measure and its possible use. Each measure was tested and retested in academic and research libraries. Those named include eight libraries at the University of California at Berkeley and three other California academic libraries. A general user survey form has been developed that asks users about the frequency and success of various library activities. Pretest data are not given, but data from a "sample General Satisfaction Survey Report" are given. These data show that 24% of users asked a reference question during the test week and that 51% found it was very easy to use the library, with 23.9% marking the next highest category for a total of 74% in the two top categories. The percentage of reference questions reported "completely successful" was 45.7%, with 21.3% marking the second highest category, for a total of 67%. The work includes a form designed to evaluate mediated online searches. The outcome measures that might be adapted for end-users and ready reference searches are questions on relevance, amount, and currency of material retrieved. The last item asks for an overall satisfaction rating for that particular search. The interest and need of academic librarians for guidance of the type provided in this manual may be evidenced by the fact that it has sold almost 4,000 copies since its release, a high number if weighed against the number of colleges and universities across the country. Its impact on library performance has yet to be determined. **See Summaries of Instruments: Van House, et al.—Building Use; Van House, et al.—General Satisfaction Survey; Van House, et al.—In-Library Materials Use; Van House, et al.—Online Search Evaluation; and Van House, et al.—Reference Satisfaction.**

Van Pulis, Noelle, and Ludy, Lorene E. (1988). Subject searching in an online catalog with authority control. *College & Research Libraries* 49, 523-533.
　　A study was done of 203 users searching for subjects of their own choosing in an online catalog. Users approaching terminals at predetermined times were given brief questionnaires to complete. Users were asked to write down the actual terms used to search the catalog. Eighty percent were single-concept terms. Only 15% used subdivided headings. Only 13% of headings used by *first-time* subject searchers had correctly formulated headings. Overall, 53% of entered terms matched subject headings in the catalog. However, another 15% were found by alphabetical proximity in the screen display. Another 14% were found by use of cross references. Thus, these three combinations yielded a total of 81%

of desired subjects. Seventy-four percent reported that the computer catalog showed the topic for which they were searching. With the aid of an alphabetical display of subject plus cross references, 81% of user terms searched in the catalog matched similar catalog terms. User searches were compared to those of a previous study, done before cross references had been implemented in the catalog. Sixty-nine percent of users' subject searchers were reported as successful at that time. Addition of cross references should have raised that success to 75%.

Vathis, Alma Christine. (1983). Reference transaction and end product as viewed by the patron. *RQ* 23, 60-64.

This is an analysis of the literature as user studies, interpersonal information needs, and communication that seeks to identify parameters of value that the patron associates with the transaction and final product of an information search. The author concludes that patrons acquire information to make sense of their world, reduce uncertainty, and make value judgments, first on the subjective, interpersonal level and second, on the objective, intellectual level. The "completeness of answer," when judged by the patron, involves positive strokes from the librarian and progress toward need fulfillment rather than the criteria librarians often use to judge information services.

Veatch, Lamar. (1982). Output measures for public libraries. *Public Libraries* 21, 11-13.

The author, an editor of *Output measures for public libraries* (1982), provides the rationale and planning that resulted in the development of these measures. The measures and their use in local libraries is briefly described. Public libraries are encouraged to accept this relatively new concept of determining library effectiveness over time based on locally established objectives.

Von Seggern, Marilyn. (1989). Evaluating the interview. *RQ* 29, 260-265.

Points out the need for continuous improvement of interviewing skills supported by Durrance's (1989) study. Several methods were used to collect data including the audio cassette taping of interviews by five reference librarians, observation by a third party, and the Murfin, Bunge, and Gugelchuk assessment instrument. The author concluded that this data-gathering technique had a number of disadvantages because it was too intrusive and time consuming to be used with any frequency.

Wagers, Robert. (1978). American reference theory and information dogma. *Journal of Library History, Philosophy, and Comparative Librarianship* 13, 265-281.

Jahoda is one of the investigators who has carefully analyzed the components of the inquiry. The focus has been upon a limited range of inquiries which have specific information as their end product. This limitation has served to demote the place of instruction in the reference process. Such a narrowing of scope may be productive if it serves to isolate key factors but misleading if vital elements are not taken into account.

Wagers, Robert. (1980). Reference and information service—the inner game. *Wilson Library Bulletin* 54, 561-567.

Jahoda has constructed a reference course around the concept of query analysis, improving our understanding of the role of query terms in searching.

Wagner, Gulten. (1983). *Use of personal space in libraries: A review.* (ERIC Document Reproduction Service No. ED 267 806).

Relates use of personal space to communication process in libraries. Gives 20-year literature review by categories such as seating preferences, proxemics, and study carrel use.

Watson, Paula D. (1986). *Reference services in academic research libraries.* Chicago: American Library Association.

Presents results of a survey of 66 reference departments in medium-sized and large academic libraries for the years 1982/83. Data tables give figures by individual library names for reference transactions for a typical week (and yearly, if available), weekly desk person hours, average number of desk hours per week per librarian, and hours reference service is open per week. Many other reference department statistics are given which are useful for comparison purposes.

Webb, Eugene J., Campbell, Donald T., Schwartz, Richard D., and Sechrest, Lee. (1966). *Unobtrusive measures: nonreactive research in the social sciences.* Chicago: Rand McNally.

A basic introduction to the use of a research methodology which collects data based on observation and the use of physical records. Test subjects are not aware of their role with the intent that researchers will encounter unbiased behavior and attitudes during the investigation. It requires careful training of test administrators for uniform data collection on subjects. This seminal work, widely cited in social science literature, resulted in the introduction of unobtrusive testing of reference accuracy to library research.

Weech, Terry. (1974). Evaluation of adult reference service. *Library Trends* 22, 315-335.

This comprehensive review covers areas such as enumeration and classification of questions, characteristics of reference clientele, personnel and organization, standards, test questions, and unobtrusive observation. Updates the 1964 *Library Trends* review by Rothstein, noting that the earlier work influenced recent trends in reference evaluation. Weech found that the literature continued to concentrate on measurement rather than evaluation, with indications of the need to establish goals and objectives against which measures might be judged and evaluations made. To facilitate comparisons with the earlier review, Weech followed Rothstein's general categories: enumeration and classification of reference questions, analysis of reference clientele, study of reference collections, reference personnel and organization, cost analysis, standards of reference services, and test questions and unobtrusive measures. Weech reported the results of a 1972 survey by Bunge to determine the degree to which reference evaluation was conducted in American libraries. Findings suggested little activity. The review concluded that there remained a lack of standards and guidelines against which reference evaluation might be made, and that the primary trend seemed to be in the area of unobtrusive testing of reference performance. A section on cost analysis evaluation notes that prior to 1972, the Los Angeles Public Library divided the reference budget by the number of questions handled in one year and arrived at a figure of $0.82 per question. Weech notes that Palmour and Gray looked at staffing costs by type of question in the reference and research libraries of Illinois and found $0.32 for simple fact questions, $0.45 for bibliographical citations, $1.04 for multiple facts, and $2.77 for complex facts.

Weech, Terry. (1984). Who's giving all those wrong answers? Direct service and reference personnel evaluation. *The Reference Librarian* 11, 109-122.

The author argues that if we are to determine the extent to which the performance of individual reference staff may affect the overall performance of a library's reference service and if we are to improve the level of service provided, the next step in reference service evaluation would seem to demand the evaluation of individual staff performance. A review of the literature regarding evaluation of the provision of direct reference service produced limited results but suggested the need to go beyond education and experience credentials and the subjective assessments of personality to properly predict and evaluate the performance of individual reference staff. The online literature offers promise in that it seems to emphasize staff accountability and evaluation of individual performance. Some element of the process should include peer evaluation used successfully in other fields and which could enhance the standing of reference librarianship by indicating a concern for quality.

Weech, Terry L., and Goldhor, Herbert. (1982). Obtrusive versus unobtrusive evaluation of reference service in five Illinois public libraries: A pilot study. *Library Quarterly* 52, 305-324.

Reference service in five public libraries was evaluated unobtrusively by using test questions administered by proxies and obtrusively by requesting reference staff to provide answers to a list of 15 questions. Researchers found slight but statistically significant relationships between method of evaluation (unobtrusive or obtrusive) and results of evaluation (70% versus 85% complete and correct answers). Contains tables summarizing results of unobtrusive and obtrusive evaluations in public libraries.

Weech, Terry L., and Goldhor, Herbert. (1984). Reference clientele and the reference transaction in five Illinois public libraries. *Library and Information Science Research* 6, 21-42.

In 1982, five libraries participated in a study where each library surveyed 125 reference patrons over a period from one week to three months. Patron names were obtained and each library then sent brief questionnaires to these patrons several days after the question had been asked. Seventy-five percent of questionnaires were returned. Library staff also completed a questionnaire for each patron's question and data were combined and analyzed. Among other results, it was found that there was a significant association between specific librarians and number of sources used. Some librarians consistently used multiple sources, while others used only one source to answer the reference questions they received. They also found that women asked a higher percentage of questions arising from school assignments and personal need, and men asked a higher percentage of questions related to work. Weech and Goldhor also classified questions from five public libraries into school assignments, job related, personal need, curiosity, and other. They found that neither user satisfaction nor librarian disposition (answered; referred; not answered or referred) was significantly associated with how the question arose.

Weingart, Doris; Montanary, Barbara; Brown, Velia; Halman, Ruth; Hiebert, Ruth; Ill, Diane; Kooiman, Sue; and Malloy, Lois. (1983). *Public services in research libraries: A self study: Report of the Service Performance and Service Needs Task Force.* Riverside, CA: University of California (Unpublished).

This survey was mailed out to all faculty and staff and a sample of 500 graduate and 1,000 undergraduate students with return rates for these groups, in order, 56%, 45%, and 38%. The survey covered 48 items, including one section where 21 different services/departments were listed with brief descriptions of their functions and locations. Columns were given for patrons to check 1) awareness, 2) use (in terms of times per year used), and 3) satisfaction in terms of satisfied or dissatisfied. More respondents reported having used reference desk service (UG-77%, G-81%) than any other reference service: brochures, UG-47%, G-43%; computerized search, UG-13%, G-42%; government documents, UG-22%, G-37%; library instruction, UG-18%, G-21%; IL UG-13%, G-63%). Reference desk service was also used most *intensely* (used at least six times per year), reference desk, UG-35%, G-55%; IL, UG-10%, G-42%; government document, UG-18%, G-37%; brochures, UG-14%, G-18%; and library instruction, UG-2%, G-4%. Reference was also the most widely used *library* service except for circulation. Another item: If a library problem was encountered I would *first* ask for help rather than trying to solve problem myself, UG-80%, G-66%, F-97%. Other findings of interest were that graduate students appeared to be less likely to be embarrassed about asking for help and that the tendency to ask reference questions rose with class level. Overall, graduates tended to use service such as reference, computer searches, brochures, interlibrary loan, documents, and library instruction considerably more frequently than undergraduates. Embarrassment and hesitation about asking questions seems characteristic of undergraduates (11%), since graduates refused to answer this question. Undergraduates' reasons for not approaching the desk were: Embarrassed to ask, 11%; Staff looked too busy, 15%; Didn't know it was O.K., 1%; Didn't think anyone could help me, 1%. Useful data are given in regard to library instruction from both faculty and student viewpoints. Satisfaction data are given. Among other results were those where users were given a list of five library services and asked which ones would help increase their knowledge of the library's resources and services. Responses were as follows: written guides, UG-35%, G-39%; individual help by a librarian-UG-29%, G-22%; brief lecture and tour of library, UG-16%, G-20%; lecture in class, UG-10%, G-8%; Library exercise, UG-10%, G-9%. See **Summaries of Instruments: University of California at Los Angeles, et al.—Selected Items from Overall Library Surveys; and University of California at Riverside—UCR Library Services Survey.**

Wender, Ruth W., Fruehauf, Esther L., Vent, Marilyn S., and Wilson, Constant D. (1977). Determination of continuing medical education needs of clinicians from a literature search study: Part I-The study. *Bulletin of the Medical Library Association* 65, 330-337.

This paper is based on an award-winning entry in the 1976 Library Research Roundtable Competition. Reports results of a study of searches requested by physicians and medical students, looking for differences in nature and complexity between the two groups. Requests were examined in terms of MESH subjects and subcategories for value in determining continuing education needs. To verify this approach, questionnaires were sent to Oklahoma physicians to determine whether they would request continuing education in the same areas as those of their previous search questions. Correlations indicate that study of literature requests is a good way to determine areas where continuing education is needed.

Werking, Richard Hume. (1980). Evaluating bibliographic education: A review and critique. *Library Trends* 29, 153-172.

Presents a review of the literature concerned with evaluation of bibliographic education. Analyzes problems in test construction.

Wessel, C.J., and Moore, K.L. (1969). Criteria for evaluating the effectiveness of library operations and services: Phase III. Recommended criteria and methods for their utilization. (ATLIS Report No. 21). Washington, DC: John Thompson and Co.

Describes a cost-effectiveness method that permits a library to check the cost effectiveness of its reference service at intervals over a period of time. **See Summaries of Instruments: Wessel and Moore—SCORE Cost Effectiveness Analysis.**

Westbrook, Lynn (1984). Catalog failure and reference service. *RQ* 24, 82-90.

A study was done in an academic library to determine what barriers existed between catalog users and reference librarians. Questionnaires were distributed to users of the catalog during preselected hours. Return rate was 60% with 1,100 completed forms. The questionnaire consisted of 20 items, which asked users about knowledge of the catalog, experiences over time in regard to asking for help, and attitudes toward reference librarians. It was found that 59% did not know that virtually all books were listed in the catalog. Only 15% to 23% of catalog users reported that they asked for help on difficult or unproductive searches. 37% of freshmen felt they usually succeeded in their catalog searches. Busyness had the strongest impact on discouraging users from asking for help with 40% feeling the librarian was too busy to help. Twenty-seven percent felt awkward about asking for help and 3.7% felt librarians were rude. Sixteen percent did not know where to locate reference staff and 40% were not sure of the librarian's ability and skill in using the catalog and/or did not perceive it as greater than their own.

Westbrook, Lynn. (1987). Reference evaluation. In *Performance evaluation in reference service in ARL libraries*. (SPEC Kit 139, p. 40). Washington DC: Association of Research Libraries, Office of Management Studies.

Consists of a one-page questionnaire with three open-ended questions, asking patrons about past experience with reference service in the main library.

Westbrook, Lynn. (1988). Getting in gear: A short-term program to revitalize your BI staff. *Research Strategies* 6, 177-84.

Discusses causes and symptoms of technostress as it relates to school librarians. Includes several actual case studies of victims of technostress.

White, Marilyn Domas. (1987). *The reference interview: Impact of environmental constraints*. Crystal City, IA: District of Columbia Library Association and Virginia Library Association. (ERIC Document Reproduction Service No. ED 309 784).

Two models of the reference interview are related to environmental factors in reference service, including physical organization and staffing.

White, Marilyn Domas. (1990). *The Arizona Clinical Interview Rating Scale: Its applicability and adaptability for the evaluation of pre-search reference interviews*. Washington, DC: Office of Education. (ERIC Document Reproduction Service No. ED 320 574).

This paper discusses the applicability and adaptability of the Arizona Clinical Interview Rating Scale (ACIRS) for use in a reference environment. This scale was developed in 1976 at the University of Arizona College of Medicine to evaluate the interview performance of medical students. It was used in this study as a guide to evaluating the pre-search interview in online searching. The scale emphasizes process-related criteria, not content. White contended that in spite of some problems the scale was useful.

White, Ruth (Ed.). (1971). *A study of reference services and reference users in the metropolitan Atlanta area*. Athens, GA: Georgia University. (ERIC Document Reproduction Service No. ED 058 912).

One part of this extensive study of reference service in all types of libraries consisted of a user questionnaire. Library science students asked the questions of patrons in academic, public, school, and special libraries in the Atlanta area. During busy hours of the day, all patrons leaving the reference areas of these libraries were interviewed. (Several libraries refused to allow the patrons to be interviewed). Responses obtained were 128 from academic libraries and 94 from public libraries. Results for the following search strategies are given first for academic and then for public libraries: catalog 61%, 48%; going directly to shelves 16%, 28%; asking a librarian for help 17%, 20%. Those reporting having ever used reference in that library 86%, 70%. Those who would try to solve a reference problem *themselves* first 74%, 74%. Those who use reference in-person rather than by phone 93%, 70%. Those who reported that the reference department needed improvement 58%, 31%. Type of improvement needed; environment/atmosphere 35%, 12%, materials 61%, 82%, personnel 4%, 6%.

Whitehead, John, and Lindquist, Charles. (1985). Job stress and burnout among probation/parole officers: Perceptions and causal factors. *International Journal of Offender Therapy and Comparative Criminology* 29, 109-119.

This study of 108 Alabama probation/parole officers used mail questionnaires. Analysis of results indicated that job stress factors such as case overload, inadequate resources, and problems related to client control had a significant impact on presence and level of burnout.

Whitlatch, Jo Bell (1978). Service at San Jose State University: Survey of document availability. *Journal of Academic Librarianship* 4, 196-199.

Reports on a study to determine to what extent users were finding desired materials in the library. The typical user found 58.9% of items originally sought. Only 34% of those who had partial or no success at the catalog asked for help.

Whitlatch, Jo Bell. (1980). *San Jose State University Library services: A summary of the results of the spring 1980 faculty and student user survey*. Washington, DC: Educational Resources Information Services. (ERIC Document Reproduction Service No. 206 279).

A survey was given to a random sample of classes where it was completed during the period by 1,470 students. A survey was mailed to 1,753 faculty with a response rate of 25%. Results were analyzed by cross tabulation of variables. The student study is of interest for its high return rate and sample of library users and nonusers. Of all students surveyed, 36% used this library less than once a month, and 12% never used it. Nonusers were significantly more likely to be part time, female, white, and freshmen. Also of interest is the finding that a higher proportion of students with GPAs below 2.00 seldom use the library, as compared to those with GPAs of 3.6-4.00. Faculty and students expressed strong preferences for reference service over library instruction. The preferred methods of instruction were, in order; asking a librarian, 83%; audiovisual, 72%; research lecture, 70%; tour, 57%; computer, 55%. In regard to the most frequent source of consultation, students reported books, 25%; professors, 21.5%; other students, 14%;

this library, 31%; other libraries, 15%. Course requirements were shown to be an important determinant in frequency of library use. In regard to library use, 66% of those in courses requiring frequent library use were frequent library users. Fifteen percent of those in courses requiring infrequent library use were frequent library users. Only 13% of all users surveyed had never used reference service. It was found in regard to majors that those in the social sciences reported library resources being required 29% of the time, and those in sciences and technology reported library resources being required only 13% of the time. Social science majors, when compared to science and technology majors, more often used books (69%; 58%) and bound periodicals (68%; 61%). Thirty percent of users reported sometimes needing help with the catalog. Satisfaction was measured by a two-category yes-no scale. Ratings for different reference services were: directional desk, 86.2%; reference desk, 84.4%; computer searches, 83.1%; and government documents, 76.8%. satisfaction ratings for other library services were: circulation, 80.2%; ILL, 74%, reserves, 83.8%; microforms, 90%.

Whitlatch, Jo Bell. (1987). Client/service provider perceptions of reference service outcomes in academic libraries: Effects of feedback and uncertainty. Doctoral dissertation, University of California, Berkeley. *Dissertation Abstracts International* 49, 986A.

As part of a more extensive study, Whitlatch collected data on purpose of question from five academic libraries. Categories were school course work; research or publication; other job related; and personal, leisure, or recreational interests. However, purpose was not significantly related to any of the reference service outcomes. Most of the questions also fell in the school course work category, leaving insufficient numbers in the remaining categories. **See Summaries of Instruments: Whitlatch—Librarian and User Perceptions of Reference Service Quality.**

Whitlatch, Jo Bell. (1989). Unobtrusive studies and the quality of academic reference services. *College & Research Libraries* 50, 181-194.

Notes that Hernon and McClure and others employing unobtrusive testing use factual queries. Suggests that factual queries are a minority of queries in academic libraries and thus do not adequately represent the main body of questions in academic libraries. A study was done of 397 reference transactions in five academic libraries in northern California. Of the total, 11.3% were for specific facts, 18% were for location of specific citations, and 70.7% were subject or source related. Sixty-six percent of users reported finding what was wanted and 75% reported being satisfied. Whitlatch also collected data on questions asked and answers supplied and then classified questions into three categories:

factual, bibliographic (i.e., specific title); and subject/instructional. She found that users reported significantly different success rates for each question category. Also reports that librarians tend to judge factual questions to be more difficult because answering factual questions involves use of less familiar, less frequently used sources.

Whitlatch, Jo Bell. (1990a). Reference service effectiveness. *RQ* 30, 205-220.

Summarizes results of test of a model of the reference process. Information on study results also is included in Whitlatch (1990b). **See Summaries of Instruments: Whitlatch—Librarian and User Perceptions of Reference Service Quality.**

Whitlatch, Jo Bell. (1990b). *The role of the academic reference librarian.* New York: Greenwood Press.

Examines key factors related to successful reference practice in academic libraries. Whitlatch collected data on user and librarian perceptions of reference service for 257 transactions from five academic libraries. Reference librarians who provided reference desk services from five academic libraries participated. These 62 librarians asked users at random to complete a questionnaire regarding services received. The librarian completed a form on the same transaction, which then was matched with the correct user questionnaire by means of a code. Data were collected on 1) librarian perceptions of service value, user perception of service value, and user self-report of success or failure in locating needed information; and 2) client socialization, task-related knowledge, service orientation, librarian job satisfaction and motivation, time constraints, feedback, and type of assistance. Results of the study indicate that variables that influence service outcomes can be divided into three broad categories: 1) those concerned with technical knowledge of the job (task uncertainty or task-related knowledge); 2) those concerned with social skills and abilities (service orientation, feedback); and 3) those involved with system constraints (time constraints, collection and circulation management, bibliographic access systems). The study suggests that feedback, service orientation, task-related knowledge of providers, and time constraints are important variables to study in service settings. User reports of informing the librarian if the questions have been answered are the only variable that significantly explained variation in all three service outcomes. The importance of feedback was supported by an analysis of failures. Analysis of failure indicated that in 35.3% of the cases failure appeared to be related to study variables, but the rest (64.7%) were due to system failure (book checked out, not on shelf, and so on). The study confirmed the importance of evaluating service encounters from both provider and client perspectives. Interpersonal skills appear very important in determining service effectiveness. Results related to service orientation suggest that patron and staff perspectives are very different. Negative relationships between librarian attitudes toward the importance of advising users of all feasible alternative solutions and user service value and user success indicate that librarians with this philosophy do not produce service of most value to users, nor does this philosophy appear to facilitate user success in locating needed information. Whitlatch found that task-related knowledge is important because it is positively associated with all three service outcomes. She found significant relationships between librarian self-reports of subject knowledge, librarian judgments of routineness of questions, and all three service outcomes: librarian judgments of service value, user judgments of service value, and user success in locating material. Librarians report good subject expertise (1 or 2 on a scale of 7) for only 51.8% of all transactions. Task-related knowledge may be less significant for library clients when an intermediary is involved in service provision. Study results suggest that patrons expect to receive quick, concise information. Generally, shorter time lengths were associated with more valued service outcomes. Implications for reference practice are suggested. **See Summaries of Instruments: Whitlatch—Librarian and User Perceptions of Reference Service Quality.**

Whitlatch, Jo Bell. (1991). Automation and job satisfaction among reference librarians. *Computers in Libraries* 11, 32-34.
    Discusses the effects of automation on job satisfaction and relates this to performance. Presents a job strain model and suggests ways in which a job can be designed to reduce technostress.

Wiberley, Stephen E., Jr. (1989). Patterns of information seeking in the humanities. *College & Research Libraries* 50, 638-645.
    Found humanists spend most of their time alone, reading; seldom consult reference librarians; use a limited number of bibliographical sources, but use is intensive with new topics.

Willett, Holly G. (1992). Designing an evaluation instrument: The Environment Rating Scale "in process." *Journal of Youth Services in Libraries* 5, 165-173.
    Describes the Environment Rating Scale for Public Library Children's Services. Covers physical facilities and staff behavior and attitudes.

Wilson, S.R., Starr-Schneidkraut, N., and Cooper, M.D. (1989). *Use of the critical incident technique to evaluate the impact of MEDLINE* (Final Report). Palo Alto, CA: American Institute for Research in the Behavioral Sciences. (Sponsored by the National Library of Medicine, Office of Planning and Evaluation. Bethesda, MD. NTIS order #PB90-142533/XAB).

Three aspects of MEDLINE searches were studied including the motivation for seeking a search, the impact of the information on the user's decision-making process, and the ultimate impact of the information on the outcome of the situation that prompted the search. The study reveals eight incidents in which the life of a patient was saved due to the information which the physician had obtained from the MEDLINE search. Results indicated that, in regard to impact, about 60% of all respondents using the search for patient care were able to identify at least one search having a high impact within the past year. The figure for searches done for research purposes was 50%, and for teaching 27%. In regard to the impact of not finding needed information, 23% of ineffective searches were for patient care and, of those, there were probably some negative effects on patient care in some cases. Ineffective searches were sometimes overcome by other options such as having someone else perform the search, or by doing a manual search, or by coming across the information by accident in another source. Several ineffective searches had negative impacts on research papers planned by participants. **See Summaries of Instruments: Wilson, et al.—Critical Incident Technique.**

Wood, Fiona. (1982). *Use and perception of an academic library. A survey at the Australian National University.* (ERIC Document Reproduction Service No. 226 739).

Results of a 1981 survey of 1,000 patrons. Copies of three questionnaires are included (for undergraduates, postgraduates, and academic staff) to ascertain use and satisfaction with library services, including reference.

Woodard, Beth S. (1989). The effectiveness of an information desk staffed by graduate students and nonprofessionals. *College & Research Libraries* 50, 455-467.

Woodard designed an unobtrusive test of information desk service, which included questions from five categories: 1) bibliographic (whether the library owned a particular book or journal with a known title or author); 2) research guidance (how to find information on a particular subject); 3) procedural or instructional (request for information on how to use a library source); 4) ready reference (requests for brief factual information); and 5) directional (locations of library facilities, collections, or staff). Questions used in testing were actual questions recorded in 1986 at the University of Illinois, Urbana-Champaign. By question type, of those questions capable of being answered at the information desk, the highest success levels were for directional and procedural types of questions. Woodard notes that Murfin and Bunge (1988a) found that paraprofessionals who handle less complex questions and consult other staff members more frequently are more effective. The findings of Murfin and Bunge are supported by Woodard's study, which indicates that more accurate answers and referrals are provided when staff members are available for consultation. Accuracy was 67% and correctness of referrals was 77% with *single* staffing as compared to 82% and 88% when double-staffed. Notes that Hernon and McClure's studies use in-person rather than telephone questions. While Hernon and McClure's proxies were instructed to seek out professionals, nonprofessionals may also have been included but are not identified separately.

Yocum, James C., and Stocker, Frederick D. (1980). *The Development of Franklin County Public Libraries, 1980*. Columbus, OH: Center for Business and Economic Research, College of Administrative Science, The Ohio State University.

A study was done of public library users in 27 Franklin County, Ohio, libraries. Ninety specially trained attendants handed out questionnaires to users entering the library at predetermined times and took attendance counts at each library. Return rate was 70% amounting to 10,496 completed forms. Users were asked about their library visits over a period of time. For use of services over a period of time, results indicated that 56% used "help from the librarian about where to find it," 46% used "special assistance by the reference librarian," and 23% used "help from the librarian about what to read." In regard to search strategy the following was found: use catalog (77%), browse shelves (75%), use reference collection (67%), use reference librarian to help find materials (56%), and special assistance from reference librarian (46%). One item on the questionnaire gave a list of 14 standard services and 12 "newer" services and asked respondents to indicate how often they were used (never or hardly ever; moderately-about half the time; always or nearly always). A measure used that could be construed as quality and/or importance was "What should the library do about this service in the future?" The highest degree of satisfaction (as measured by the desire to keep the service the same) was for special assistance by the reference librarian; help from the librarian about where to find it; and help from the librarian about what to read. The following results are given in terms of percentages for 1) reduce, eliminate, or avoid, 2) keep about the same, 3) enlarge or improve: reference collection, 2%, 48%, 44%; special assistance by reference librarian, 2.5%, 73.9%, 15.5%; card catalog, 1.5%, 64%, 26.6%; help from librarian about where to find it, 2.5%, 72.5%, 14%; browsing book shelves, 2.5%, 56.7%, 28.9%; and help from librarian about what to read, 6.5%, 71%, 11.3%. Library users were also asked to give their top three reasons for going to the particular library where they received the questionnaire. Twelve possible reasons were given. Composites of the most frequently given reason for library use in order were closeness to home (31%), good books and periodicals (15.2%), helpful library staff (10.7%), good reference collection (7.9%). Composite ratings were also given for each of the 27 libraries. For helpful library staff these ratings varied from 4.5% for one library to 26% for another. For good reference collection, they varied from 2.6% for one branch to 20.6% for the main library. Among other results, it was found that "helpful library staff" were most important to women, nonwhites, older ages, and lower income patrons. Includes a form for a field study of nonusers. **See Summaries of Instruments: Yocum and Stocker—Survey of Public Library Users.**

Zweizig, Douglas. (1984). Tailoring measures to fit your service: A guide for the managers of reference services. *The Reference Librarian* 11, 53-61.

The author states the need to reduce time spent looking at meaningless data and to use data efficiently to improve performance. If data are to be useful to the manager, they must relate to the planning of the reference unit. Because planning is done in a repeating series, measurement needs to be done periodically to inform the process. Because organizational goals change over time, measures must be adapted or replaced to remain relevant to the decision process. Guidance is provided regarding what should be measured and how the measure will work. Managers are urged to determine the degree of precision needed for each decision process and to sample for that level, and no more, as the purpose is to improve service, not bog down in statistics.

Zweizig, Douglas, and Dervin, Brenda. (1977). Public library use, users, uses: Advances in knowledge of the characteristics and needs of the adult clientele of American public libraries. *Advances in Librarianship* 7, 231-255.

Advocates investigation of library uses, rather than library users, as "utilities" around which libraries may plan programs and measure effectiveness.

Zweizig, Douglas, and Rodger, Eleanor Jo. (1982). *Output measures for public libraries: A manual of standardized procedures* (1st ed.). Chicago: American Library Association.

One of a number of products developed by the Public Library Association, the 1982 edition of output measures identified a set of measures related to common public library service activities and included a set of standardized procedures for those measures. Experience with the measures and procedures resulted in calls for improvements, including optional service profiles, or roles, from which each library could choose a few upon which to focus. In 1987, a new edition was published (Van House, Lynch, McClure, Zweizig, and Rodger).

Summaries of Instruments

AUTHOR: Anderson, Charles R.
TITLE/NAME OF INSTRUMENT: Cost Per Use of Reference Sources
PURPOSE: To analyze the relative cost of using online and print sources for ready reference searching. Developed for a public library.
DESCRIPTION AND EXPERIENCE WITH USE: The author conducted a study of the cost per use of 40 serial reference books over a three-week period. Shelvers tallied individual uses by both staff and patrons for each book for three weeks and then estimated annual usage on the basis of 50 weeks. They obtained annual costs of standing orders for these 40 sources and divided the annual cost of each source by the number of uses in one year to obtain cost per use. A further study was then done comparing the cost of print sources to costs for online searches. Six hundred online searches were analyzed and costs compared.
USE: This study was performed in the Northbrook Public Library in Northbrook, Illinois in 1986-1987.
REVIEW OF THE INSTRUMENT: This method of estimating the use of print serial sources seems to work well. Sources under study are marked with a label, "Please do not reshelve this book." Annual standing order costs are readily available. This method could be useful in cases where solid evidence of how often a source is used is lacking. If staff use could be separated from patron use, the data would then have maximum usefulness.
VALIDITY AND RELIABILITY: No data available.
BIBLIOGRAPHIC REFERENCE: Anderson (1987).
AVAILABILITY: Those wishing to use this method should consult the article by Anderson (1987).

AUTHOR: Ankeny, Melvon
TITLE/NAME OF INSTRUMENT: Database Questionnaire
PURPOSE: To determine the success of end-users in searching Business Connection and Dow Jones News Retrieval. Might be used in any type library with other databases.
DESCRIPTION AND EXPERIENCE WITH USE: Consists of a one-page questionnaire of 12 items. This instrument is based on the patron form used in the Reference Transaction Assessment Instrument developed by Bunge, Murfin, and Gugelchuk (Murfin and Gugelchuk, 1987). It

uses the same six-point scale used to measure success in traditional reference service. For a search to be considered successful, the end-user must mark 1) that he or she found exactly what was wanted, 2) that he or she was fully satisfied, and 3) none of the ten listed reasons for dissatisfaction.

USE: This instrument was used by the author in a study of 600 unaided end-user users in the Business Library at Ohio State University in 1987/88.

REVIEW OF THE INSTRUMENT: One advantage of this instrument is that reliability and validity data are available. Another is that end-user success can be compared with patron success in traditional mediated desk reference service by use of the same scale. Also, this instrument can be used for the purpose of determining which groups of users are experiencing the most failures and what databases and types of searches are least successful. Disadvantages of this method are that the specific errors made by users can't be detected and the specific reasons for failure will need further investigation by other methods. Also, not all aspects of the computerized search are investigated and more information on the users' exact purpose, number of citations desired, and so on would be helpful.

VALIDITY AND RELIABILITY: This measurement of success in traditional reference service has been found to have a reliability coefficient of .90. It also had indications of construct validity in that results obtained by use of this method correspond to those obtained by unobtrusive observation in traditional mediated reference desk service.

BIBLIOGRAPHICAL REFERENCE: Ankeny (1991).

AVAILABILITY: This instrument is available on an accompanying disk under the file name Ankeny.

AUTHORS: Arrigona, Daniel, and Mathews, Eleanor
TITLE/NAME OF INSTRUMENT: Reference Collection Use Study
PURPOSE: To ascertain which subject areas in reference were most used, and to determine if the subject areas of the reference collection used by reference librarians to answer questions correspond to the subject areas used by patrons to answer questions on their own.

DESCRIPTION AND EXPERIENCE WITH USE: Table count data were collected for four weeks using a scoring sheet consisting of 105 boxes, with two vertical boxes per LC class group. Table counts tend to underrepresent real use. "Prior research systematically describing reference service creates the context for discussing this study's rationale and methodology. The hypotheses were that librarians and patrons use the reference collection differently and that collection use varies across subject classifications and material types" (Arrigona and Mathews, 1988, p. 71). A "use was defined as a referral to, or reshelving of, a particular reference item" (p. 73). Reference collection use was examined by "analyzing requests used by librarians responding to the reference requests and by patrons seeking information on their own. Types of materials consulted and their Library of Congress call letter classifications were examined and then interpreted by use indexes, measures that relate amount of use to relative size of reference subject areas" (p. 71). "An index of use is a ratio found by dividing the number of uses by the number of volumes in each call letter area" (p. 76).

USE: Conducted 10 February to 7 March 1986 in Iowa State University's Parks Library open stack reference collections. Comparisons of reference collection use by librarians and patrons were ranked by call letter groups, and the ten most used call letter groups of both reference works and abstracts/indexes.

REVIEW OF THE INSTRUMENT: Results can be used to show patterns and intensity of use, collection strengths and weaknesses, and to inform management decisions on reference access and organization.

VALIDITY AND RELIABILITY: No information available.

BIBLIOGRAPHIC REFERENCES: Arrigona and Mathews (1988).

AVAILABILITY: This instrument is available on an accompanying disk under the file name Arrigona.

AUTHORS: Auster, Ethel, and Lawton, Stephen

TITLE/NAME OF INSTRUMENT: User Responses to Online Search Requests

PURPOSE: To undertake a systematic investigation of searcher techniques, amount of new information gained by users, and their ultimate satisfaction with the quality of items retrieved. Used in academic libraries but could be adapted for other types of libraries.

DESCRIPTION AND EXPERIENCE WITH USE: An experiment was conducted to determine the effect on user satisfaction of different interview techniques such as open and closed questions. For assessing user characteristics and responses, a 33-item questionnaire was used covering the user's extent of knowledge before and after the search, new citations found, plans to read citations, additional information needed, value placed on new knowledge, consequences of missed information, and effects of failure and success on the client's work group. Satisfaction was measured with 1) helpfulness of searchers; 2) length of bibliography; 3) time taken; 4) value of bibliography; 5) values of materials *examined*; 6) currency; 7) value in meeting purpose; and 8) price. This scale has five anchored points; very low, low, moderate, high, and very high.

USE: A study was done using two search analysts known to the authors and employed in education libraries of Canadian universities. Each analyst conducted 60 interviews with clients: 15 with open questions, 15 with closed questions, 15 with no pauses, and 15 with moderate pauses. A total of 120 interviews were completed. Two to four weeks after a search had been completed, the user was telephoned and an evaluation interview conducted.

REVIEW OF THE INSTRUMENT: The method of having search analysts conduct actual interviews using different styles of communication could be a useful technique. Another study of computerized searching used variations of experimental techniques where conditions were varied systematically and the impact of each condition was assessed (Saracevic, Kantor, Chamis, and Trivison, 1988). This work should also be consulted by those interested in applying this type of method. Scales are well designed and anchored at each point. The user response form has particularly good coverage of extent of knowledge before and after the search. Another merit is the thoroughness and comprehensive coverage in two pages of almost all important factors in a computerized search. With regard to quality or value, the most useful measures appear to be percent of references that were relevant, value of bibliography, value of materials located by the bibliography, and, *most importantly*, utility of the search result for your intended purpose.

VALIDITY AND RELIABILITY: The authors report Hoyt estimates of reliability for each of six scales varying from .65 to .86. They note, "We view the reliability of the scales to be adequate for statistical analysis since in all cases the coefficients are well above zero. At the same time, we would note that only the satisfaction scale has a coefficient near 0.90, the value generally required when scores are to be used in assessing individuals."

BIBLIOGRAPHICAL REFERENCE: Auster and Lawton (1984).

AVAILABILITY: This instrument is available on an accompanying disk under the file name Auster.

AUTHOR: Bostick, Sharon L.

TITLE/NAME OF INSTRUMENT: The Library Anxiety Scale

PURPOSE: To measure the construct of library anxiety in college students of all levels.

DESCRIPTION AND EXPERIENCE WITH USE: Consists of 43 statements describing college students' feelings about the library. Responses are to be marked on computer-scannable answer sheets with five choices: strongly disagree, disagree, undecided, agree, and strongly agree. Students are also asked to code in age, sex, and academic status. The author notes that this portion may be expanded or altered if additional data about patrons and their library experience are desired. This additional data could be correlated with library anxiety.

USE: The instrument was pilot tested on college freshmen and graduates from Ohio and Michigan, with 281 completed forms. Returns were analyzed and used in refining the instrument followed by a second pilot test. A test-retest was done with three classes, including undergraduate classes in a community college and a private college and a graduate class at an urban university, with 69 forms completed. The test was given twice at two- to three-week intervals with no formal library instruction given in the intervals.

REVIEW OF THE INSTRUMENT: This well-designed and thoroughly tested instrument provides an answer to the problem of investigating the way in which library anxiety impacts library users. In addition to its obvious value for library instruction programs, the instrument could have great usefulness to reference if used to investigate the questions of how library anxiety affects user information-seeking patterns and user success and satisfaction. The design and development of this instrument has the potential to serve as a model for developing other instruments for the study of patron information seeking behavior.

VALIDITY AND RELIABILITY: Cronbach's alpha for the instrument is .80, indicating internal consistency. The Pearson product correlation for test-retest stability is .74.

BIBLIOGRAPHIC REFERENCES: Bostick (1993).

AVAILABILITY: This instrument is available on an accompanying disk under the file name Bostick.

AUTHOR: Bundy, Mary Lee

TITLE/NAME OF INSTRUMENT: Public Library Use Study

PURPOSE: To obtain a full picture of the use of public libraries in the Maryland Baltimore-Washington metropolitan areas. Developed for public libraries.

DESCRIPTION AND EXPERIENCE WITH USE: This instrument explores information-seeking behavior and satisfaction based on present-visit-only experiences. It consists of a one-page, 22-item questionnaire. Questions are included on reason for coming to the library including alternatives for those seeking information or materials on a subject and those seeking specific titles, purpose for which the information is needed, types of use made of the library including asking a librarian for help, degree of satisfaction (completely, partially, not) and reasons for not being completely satisfied, and any further plans to obtain the information/materials not found. Other items concern any difficulties encountered in using the library and transportation and frequency of library use. Demographic data obtained were age, sex, occupation and schooling.

USE: A study was done in 1966 for six days over a six-week period on succeeding days of the week. Every fifth adult patron in 99 library units was asked to mark the form before leaving. Return rate was 79%, resulting in a sample of 21,385 users.

REVIEW OF THE INSTRUMENT: Despite its age, this is an extremely well-designed overall survey. With the aid of computer cross-tabulations a wealth of useful data could have been obtained for the libraries concerned. The reference component includes only the alternative "help from a librarian," and could be expanded and improved. It also includes, under difficulties in using the library, "staff not friendly." If the reference component were expanded and improved this survey would have high potential in terms of knowledge gained. The discriminating measure of satisfaction is useful. However, if it were changed to a measure of success, such as how many users found what they seeking, it should be possible to explore whether those who seek reference help are more successful than those who do not. A success scale of "completely successful," "partially successful," and "not successful" could be used. Other good points are further definition of need by providing a category for those seeking specific books and its list of activities, reasons not satisfied and further plans, and the writing in of subject area being sought. Also good is the list of difficulties that might have been encountered. If many of these measures were cross-tabulated with satisfaction by library, much useful information could be obtained. This survey form is highly recommended for its basic elements.

VALIDITY AND RELIABILITY: No information available.

BIBLIOGRAPHIC REFERENCE: Bundy (1968).

AVAILABILITY: This instrument is available on an accompanying disk under the file name Bundy.

AUTHOR: Carnegie Mellon University Libraries

TITLE/NAME OF INSTRUMENT: Student Users Survey

PURPOSE: To obtain data for a self study.

DESCRIPTION AND EXPERIENCE WITH USE: To explore the information-gathering habits of library users. Designed for an academic library. Responses are, except for one item, based on present-visit-only. The four-page questionnaire asks for purpose in coming to the library, and type of materials being sought (i.e., books, periodicals, government documents). The next question asks, "How did you conduct your search for the materials you wanted?" (Choices are card catalog, periodical indexes, browsing through stacks, reserve room, asked reference librarians for information, asked circulation desk librarian, and some other way). Users were next asked whether they needed help and, if so, with what materials they needed help. Following this, they were asked whether they needed help from a librarian in locating the materials they wanted. If so, they were asked with which materials they needed help and given the same previous list of materials to check. The last questions asked how successful they were in locating each type of material on a three-category scale (mostly successful, partly successful, and unsuccessful). The authors recommend against using items 12 and 18.

USE: A survey of in-library users was done for one week in November 1977 by Carnegie Mellon University Libraries.

REVIEW OF THE INSTRUMENT: A strong point of this instrument is the success scale that appears, based on results of this survey, to be free of positive bias and to give discriminating results. It is also short and easy to mark, and can be interpreted with clarity. This scale might well be used on an experimental basis in other surveys where a number of items need to be marked. Other strengths are the section on items sought and need for help, and search strategy used by patrons. Another advantage is the number of questions of interest to reference that data from this instrument might help to answer. These include questions such as where users are asking their questions, success of those who use reference as compared to those who do not, numbers using the reference collection without assistance, the need for help, and the types of materials requiring the most help. Other questions are related to search strategies most frequently used and sources most frequently consulted, and success at locating different types of materials. A further question is whether difficulty in locating materials, need for help, and success rates vary by class level and majors of users. A possible disadvantage is that questions reported as being asked at reference will probably include both directional and reference. Also, the reference desk area needs to be more clearly defined.

VALIDITY AND RELIABILITY: No information available.

BIBLIOGRAPHIC REFERENCE: Carnegie Mellon University Libraries (1978).

AVAILABILITY: This instrument is available on an accompanying disk under the file name Carnegie.

AUTHOR: Chen, Ching-Chih, and Hernon, Peter

TITLE/NAME OF INSTRUMENT: Information Needs

PURPOSE: To examine information needs of adults 16 years or older.

DESCRIPTION AND EXPERIENCE WITH USE: Information needs reported by respondents were classified in 15 areas, including job related-technical, job getting and changing, consumer issues, household maintenance, education and schooling, recreation, money matters, setting up and running of business, health, salary and benefits, child care, personal relations, transportation, energy, and miscellaneous. Information providers included libraries, own experiences, friends and relatives, personal reading materials, co-workers, television, telephone book, social service, religious leader, doctor or lawyer, business, government agency, and other.

USE: In 1979, residents in six New England states from 2,400 randomly selected households (400 per state) participated in telephone interviews. The respondents explained situations in the past month where they had sought information and a total of 3,530 situations were identified. Situations were classified into 15 categories and information providers were classified into 13 categories.

REVIEW OF THE INSTRUMENT: While this method does not specifically address reference service, it might provide a framework for classifying and studying patrons' information needs and use of different information providers. The instrument was designed with a considerable number of conceptual considerations. Changes in wording could conflict with the conceptual framework of the instrument.

VALIDITY AND RELIABILITY: No information given.

BIBLIOGRAPHIC REFERENCES: Chen and Hernon (1980). Chen, Hernon, Neenan, and Stueart (1979).

AVAILABILITY: The instrument has been published in Chen, Ching-Chih, and Hernon, Peter (1982). *Information seeking: Assessing and anticipating user needs.* New York: Neal-Schuman.

AUTHORS: Christensen, John O., Benson, Larry D, Butler, H. Julene, Hall, Blaine H., and Howard, Don H.

TITLE/NAME OF INSTRUMENT: Evaluation of Reference Desk Service

PURPOSE: To examine the quality of reference service provided by reference student assistants and paraprofessionals who staff reference department desks to relieve professional librarians. It focuses on accuracy of information users received, level of skill student reference assistants used in negotiating patron needs, and degree of satisfaction users felt about service received. As well, the study examines the adequacy of the related training program and ability of student reference assistants to refer users to professional librarians.

DESCRIPTION AND EXPERIENCE WITH USE: The five management study included 1) Patron Survey; 2) Reference Assistant Survey regarding background, work environment, reference training, adequacy of support from department assistant and subject specialists, and job responsibility; 3) Department Assistant Survey regarding education and experience, job responsibilities, work environment, effectiveness of reference service and training, and the role of subject specialists in providing subject expertise; 4) Subject Specialist Survey regarding perceptions of the quality of reference desk service given by student reference assistants and paraprofessionals, reference training provided, and involvement in reference service; and 5) Unobtrusive Question Test, which required factual or bibliographic information, with 15 of 75 questions designed to test question—negotiation skills. The study integrates responses to the five questionnaires, showing comparisons where possible.

USE: Used at Lee Library of Brigham Young University during winter semester 1987 to assess reference service quality by student assistants and paraprofessionals who took on the provision of all reference desk service except for questions referred to appropriate subject specialists.
REVIEW OF INSTRUMENT: The study assumed (Frank, 1984; Courtois and Goetsch, 1984) that paraprofessionals could answer most reference questions and could be trained to refer questions too difficult for them to answer. Extensive investments in training student assistants may not be cost effective given that the accuracy level reported is substantially lower than that reported by Woodard (1989). Woodard suggests it is questionable whether training needed to bring such staff to a higher level is justifiable. Murfin and Bunge (1988a) suggest that paraprofessionals who handle less complex questions and consult other staff more frequently are more effective. Even if the investment in short-term student employees were not a factor, there is not clear data regarding the content of training needed by such staff for reference effectiveness. Considerable time is required to gather and analyze data resulting from administration of the five sections.
VALIDITY AND RELIABILITY: No information is provided.
BIBLIOGRAPHIC REFERENCES: Christensen, Benson, Butler, Hall, and Howard (1989). Evaluative Reports Courtois and Goetsch (1984). Frank (1984). Murfin and Bunge (1988a). Woodard (1989).
AVAILABILITY: This instrument is available on an accompanying disk under the file name Christen.

AUTHOR: Chwe, Steven S. (surname now—1993—spelled "Chweh")
TITLE/NAME OF INSTRUMENT: A Model Instrument for User-Rating of Library Service
PURPOSE: To measure library services, utilizing library users' direct judgment on the present condition of different services and the importance of these services to them. Covers comfort needs, information needs, convenience needs, and cooperation needs.
DESCRIPTION AND EXPERIENCE WITH USE: Intended for public or academic library users but appears somewhat less suited to large academic libraries with many service points. Users are to respond on the basis of their library experiences over time. The survey tends toward evaluation of particular services and units rather than exploring information-seeking behavior. Consists of 54 items. After each item is a one- or two-line description of a service. Each service includes questions concerning condition and importance with seven ratings from minimum to maximum. Comfort needs—eight items, information needs—16 items, convenience needs—21 items, cooperation needs—nine items. "Need Deficiency" is the primary measure and represents the difference between 1) the way users *want* and *need* the service to be (as

measured by importance) and 2) the *present* condition. Demographic variables can be cross-tabulated with need deficiency. Three items were devoted to reference accessibility and adequacy of time given to patrons. These items included asking if enough time was taken with users' questions, if reference hours were sufficient, and if information could be obtained easily by telephone.

USE: Developed but not reported in the literature as having been used by Chwe. Used by Budd and DiCarlo in 1980 at two Louisiana universities. For results see Budd and DiCarlo (1982).

REVIEW OF THE INSTRUMENT: A strong point of this instrument is its comprehensive coverage of a variety of aspects of reference service. Areas covered are quality of answers, subject knowledge of librarians, accessibility, online searching, telephone reference, and the quality of the reference collection. Quality of staff interaction is also covered in regard to attitude, kindness, persistence, willingness, helpful suggestions, promptness, and responsiveness. Questions it will help to answer are: What aspects of reference service are most important to patrons? How well is reference performing in relation to other library services? How important is reference considered to be in relation to other library services? Possible disadvantages are that ratings are based on experiences over a period of time and thus are less objective. Responses of frequent and infrequent users cannot be compared because no frequency of use of reference data is collected. If used in a large library with many service points, the instrument may not provide sufficiently good identification of the reference department. Also, ratings may be inflated in the second category of the seven-point continuum scales.

VALIDITY AND RELIABILITY: No information available.

BIBLIOGRAPHIC REFERENCES: Chwe (1978). Budd and DiCarlo (1982).

AVAILABILITY: This instrument is available on an accompanying disk under the file name Chweh.

AUTHOR: Ciliberti, Anne, Casserly, Mary, Hegg, Judith, and Mitchell, Eugene

TITLE/NAME OF INSTRUMENT: Availability of Library Books

PURPOSE: To identify aspects of library performance where improvement is desirable. Developed for an academic library but could be used by other types of libraries.

DESCRIPTION AND EXPERIENCE WITH USE: First used by Ciliberti in her dissertation (Ciliberti, 1985) and modified from methodology developed by Saracevic, Shaw, and Kantor (1977). As presented here, consists of two different forms, one for patrons to record known-item searches and one for subject searches. The known-item form asks for author, title, and call numbers, and asks, "Did you find the book?" for each item sought. The subject form asks the user to list the subject terms consulted in the catalog, call numbers, whether each item was found, and whether they were either checked out or used in the library. If a book on a subject was found but not utilized in or out of the library, it was assumed that the book was not what was wanted. Each form has a section where library information about each title can be recorded. In connection with this availability study methodology, in a 1985 study Ciliberti used a postcard, which was given to respondents whose known-item or subject searches were successful, to be mailed back after they had examined and evaluated the materials. It had four items, the first addressing motivation (factual information, general reading, learn what's been written, and verify bibliographic information) and purpose (class, personal research, recreation, job requirement, and other), and two satisfaction scales for amount and content of materials. Scales were anchored at each end with unsatisfactory and satisfactory and had five points.

USE: Ciliberti's original dissertation forms have been slightly modified and used in several studies, the first in 1986 in the William Paterson College in New Jersey. A subsequent availability study was done in the same library in 1989 (Mitchell, Radford, and Hegg, 1994).

REVIEW OF THE INSTRUMENT: This instrument has the feature of asking about in-library use or checkout of books found by a subject search. This provides a relatively objective method for judging the success of subject searches. The addition of data on patron academic status and frequency of library use adds meaning and interpretability to the data. Return rate of the postcard that was to be mailed back was 32%. This reflects the difficulty of getting back forms that are to be returned at a later date and may be misplaced or not returned for those reasons. An alternative procedure might be to get agreement for a call-back at a later date. Another possibility might be for the patron to mark the brief form before leaving, indicating his or her degree of satisfaction with the material after a brief examination. Also, for the two satisfaction items, a three-point scale of not satisfied, partly/mostly satisfied, and fully/completely satisfied could be used. Such scales have proved easy for patrons to judge with minimum uncertainty, been easy to interpret, and have provided discriminating results (Carnegie Mellon, 1978; Bundy, 1968).

VALIDITY AND RELIABILITY: No statistics on reliability of this instrument are presented. However, reliability data for known-item availability methodology can be sought in the existing availability literature (Whitlatch, 1978; Palais, 1981). In order to determine whether patron self-report of availability data was a valid method, it was compared to results of researcher-observed patron searches in this same study. No significant difference in results was found, supporting construct validity for the self-report methodology.

BIBLIOGRAPHIC REFERENCES: Ciliberti, Casserly, Hegg, and Mitchell (1987). Ciliberti (1985).

AVAILABILITY: This instrument is available on an accompanying disk under the file name Cilibert.

AUTHORS: Cochrane, Lynn Scott, and Warmann, Carolyn

TITLE/NAME OF INSTRUMENT: Cost Analysis of Library Service

PURPOSE: To determine the full cost for basic library services and identify which were appropriate for fee-based services. Developed for an academic library but could be modified for other types of libraries.

DESCRIPTION AND EXPERIENCE WITH USE: This formula takes into account departmental variables, fixed costs, and library and university overhead. Only the portion of the reference librarian's time spent at the reference desk is charged to the outcome of the reference transaction, and to this is added the cost of fringe benefits. No reference collection costs are added. The costs for maintaining *all* library collections are presumably in a separate budget. Costs for one reference question are then compared to those for one interlibrary loan, one database search, and one user education lecture session.

USE: Used at Virginia Polytechnic Institute and State University in a study begun in 1986.

REVIEW OF THE INSTRUMENT: This method requires minimum reference department data, only number of reference questions, and person hours of desk time. It does require a percent of fringe benefits for the hours of labor, fixed departmental costs, and library overhead and university overhead figures. Disadvantages, on one hand, are that it doesn't take reference collection costs or skill maintenance costs into account. It also does not take into account that all time at the reference desk is not spent in answering reference questions. Nevertheless, it provides a useful method for comparing the costs of labor and overhead for reference service to that of other library services.

VALIDITY AND RELIABILITY: No data available.

BIBLIOGRAPHIC REFERENCE: Cochrane and Warmann (1989).

AVAILABILITY: This instrument is available on an accompanying disk under the file name Cochrane.

AUTHOR: Colorado State University

TITLE/NAME OF INSTRUMENT: Questionnaire for Library Users

PURPOSE: To gather views and opinions from student users of the library in order to plan additional library space best meeting needs of all users.

DESCRIPTION AND EXPERIENCE WITH USE: The two-page instrument consists of 13 questions, largely on the physical environment of the library. Question nine contains six items referring to reference areas as to table space for use of materials, noise level, lighting, materials arrangement, shelf crowding, and locating reference librarians. **USE:** Over 1,900 responses were received for this on-site library use survey. No date is cited.

REVIEW OF THE INSTRUMENT: Users may complete the questionnaire quickly, and the information can be easily tabulated. Yields data to give weight to library funding proposals, as well as revealing user perceptions on the environment. Questions could be modified to suit individual circumstances.

VALIDITY AND RELIABILITY: No information available.

BIBLIOGRAPHIC REFERENCES: Colorado State University (1981).

AVAILABILITY: This instrument is available on an accompanying disk under the file name Colorado.

AUTHOR: Cornell University, Albert R. Mann Library

TITLE/NAME OF INSTRUMENT: Information Sources in Agricultural Research

PURPOSE: To gather data that will guide major changes in services to faculty within the College of Agriculture and Life Sciences. Developed for use in an academic library.

DESCRIPTION AND EXPERIENCE WITH USE: Consists of a 17-item, seven-page questionnaire. Of interest is an item asking respondents to rate the importance to their research of 20 proposed or current services. Importance ratings are in five categories from not important to essential. Each service is described in several sentences. Another item lists five services and asks how they should be funded, with choices of answers to check.

USE: Mailed to faculty in the College of Agriculture Life Sciences, and Human Ecology at Cornell University in 1983. No information is given on return rate and no results are presented.

REVIEW OF THE INSTRUMENT: The item rating potential importance of current or proposed services might serve as a useful model. The item asking who should fund a service is also of interest for a faculty survey on service preferences for the future.

VALIDITY AND RELIABILITY: No information available.

BIBLIOGRAPHICAL REFERENCE: Cornell University (1984).

AVAILABILITY: This instrument is available on an accompanying disk under the file name Cornell.

AUTHORS: Dervin, Brenda, and Fraser, Benson
TITLE/NAME OF INSTRUMENT: "Helps" Users Obtain from Their Library Visits
PURPOSE: To collect data on how library visits specifically helped users in the context of their lives.
DESCRIPTION AND EXPERIENCE WITH USE: Consists of a set of 16 helps. These were 1) got ideas, understandings; 2) planned, decided what, when, where; 3) got skills needed to do something; 4) accomplished or finished something; 5) kept going when it seemed hard; 6) got started or motivated; 7) got confirmation I was doing right thing; 8) got out of or avoided a bad situation; 9) calmed down, or eased worries; 10) took mind off things; 11) felt reassured or hopeful; 12) felt good about self; 13) rested or relaxed; 14) got happiness or pleasure; 15) made contact with others; and 16) felt connected or not alone.
USE: A stratified random sample of Californians 12 or older were selected and contacted by telephone. The final sample included 814 persons. Each recalled his or her last library and was asked the recency of the visit, type of library, purpose for the visit, and materials and services obtained. Users were then asked a set of 16 close-ended questions to determine which of the 16 helps they saw as obtaining from their most recent library visit. Finally, they were asked to tell in their own words what was their most important help. These "most important" helps were coded into the 16 help categories.
REVIEW OF THE INSTRUMENT: While reference services are not specifically addressed in this study, these helps might have application in the study of benefits derived from reference service. These helps have been investigated over 20 years by the authors and colleagues in some 45 studies and are designed to fit all human situations. They were derived from a comprehensive communication theory of human sense-making. They appear to provide a useful starting point for study of the benefits of reference service.
VALIDITY AND RELIABILITY: No information provided.
BIBLIOGRAPHIC REFERENCES: Dervin (1983). Dervin and Fraser (1985). Dervin (1992).
AVAILABILITY: This instrument is available on an accompanying disk under the file name Dervin.

AUTHOR: Donnelly, Anna M.
TITLE/NAME OF INSTRUMENT: Reference Environment Problems Checklist
PURPOSE: To give reference librarians a quick profile/overview of many factors believed to affect quality of service, but which are often outside the practitioner's control at the point of service. May be used by academic, public, and special libraries. Determines staff perceptions of

areas of weakness and strength. May be helpful in cultivating staff development and consolidation, and useful for departmental goal-setting. **DESCRIPTION AND EXPERIENCE WITH USE:** Consists of 11 check-off lists, which comprise a total of 114 individual factors. Each factor is evaluated in three ways: current handling, problem frequency, and service impact. Uses four anchored scales. Covers equipment collection, desk, training, physical, and inter-unit environmental factors. May be completed in one hour, and responses entered in standard spreadsheet software to derive mean averages. Results should be graphed for interpretation.

USE: Completed by 20 libraries 1988-1990 (academic, public, and special); 115 forms returned; administered nationally. Developed by Anna M. Donnelly (St. John's University, NY). Responses from participants: results confirmed known problems and brought unaddressed matters to light; used in management proposals to gain needed improvements; shows staff perceptions of same factors may vary widely. May be used in training and also as a planning and self-evaluation tool. Interinstitutional comparability may not be possible due to the uniqueness of each library's array of environmental factors. Based on subjective staff perceptions, which, although influential in the reference process, do not necessarily reflect objective situations.

REVIEW OF THE INSTRUMENT: Reference units tend by nature to be labor intensive and contain much fragmentation, which is often unified only with great effort. The instrument is meant to provide busy reference practitioners and managers with an uncomplicated tool that will yield a visible profile of elements that frequently pass unnoticed along with their interactive effects.

VALIDITY AND RELIABILITY: A small comparison with three libraries that had also completed the Reference Transaction Assessment Instrument showed 77% similarity on comparable items.

BIBLIOGRAPHIC REFERENCE: Donnelly (1992 June).

AVAILABILITY: This instrument is available on an accompanying disk under the file name Donnelly.

AUTHOR: Duncan, Cynthia B.

TITLE/NAME OF INSTRUMENT: Survey of Actual and Potential Task Participation of Academic Library Reference Personnel

PURPOSE: To develop a checklist of reference-related tasks and to determine by whom these tasks are now being performed and by whom they should be performed. Developed for academic libraries but could be modified for use by other types of libraries.

DESCRIPTION AND EXPERIENCE WITH USE: This study is concerned with performance of nonprofessional tasks by librarians. Ten basic functions were identified: administration and support; bibliographical; cooperative; guidance; information; instruction; public relations; research; selection and evaluation; and maintenance. A task list of 118 items was developed. The final survey instrument was in three segments: 1) descriptive information about reference librarians and their work; 2) task inventory with "does," "should," and an importance index; and 3) a set of 10 interview questions designed to provide insight into reasons for opinions.

USE: Used by the author in a survey of 36 reference librarians in Indiana in 1973. All questionnaires were returned and each participant was then interviewed.

REVIEW OF THE INSTRUMENT: The task list is well developed and organized into broad categories. Study results are particularly useful in gaining perspective on the tasks customarily performed by reference librarians and the importance attached to each of these tasks. The list of tasks *never* performed by reference librarians is also useful. The task list would need to be updated to cover recent developments, particularly in computer and telecommunications technology.

VALIDITY AND RELIABILITY: No data provided.

BIBLIOGRAPHIC REFERENCES: Duncan (1973).

AVAILABILITY: This instrument is available on an accompanying disk under the file name Duncan.

AUTHOR: Durrance, Joan C.

TITLE/NAME OF INSTRUMENT: Reference Interview and the Environment

PURPOSE: To examine the influence of the reference interview setting on the interaction and accuracy, and the librarian's behavior on the success of the reference interview. May be carried out at public, academic, and special libraries. Researchers can examine behavioral impact of external environment on reference staff and patrons, and degree of intrusion into reference transactions.

DESCRIPTION AND EXPERIENCE WITH USE: A five-page data-collection instrument was used over a one-year period for this unobtrusive study, which included questions already available in the literature. A scale of one to five was used. Observers reported on staff activity at initial approach, the question and response, and performance of the library staff as determined by interpersonal behavior, interview/listening skills, and search strategies. Willingness to return to the same staff member (as opposed to accuracy) was the measure of success. Observers included a narrative description of the environment and the interaction. Statistical and text-organizing packages were used to analyze the data.

USE: Under the direction of Joan C. Durrance (University of Michigan, Ann Arbor), graduate library science student researchers gathered information by asking a question or observing interaction between a colleague and a librarian.

REVIEW OF THE INSTRUMENT: Although this study was conducted at a number of institutions, this approach could be replicated in individual institutions using appropriately trained proxies.

VALIDITY AND RELIABILITY: No information available.

BIBLIOGRAPHIC REFERENCES: Durrance (1989). **Evaluative Reports** Burton (1990). Heibing (1990). Stenstrom (1990). Von Seggern (1989).

AVAILABILITY: This instrument is available on an accompanying disk under the file name Durrance.

AUTHOR: Fairfax County Public Library

TITLE/NAME OF INSTRUMENT: Reference Accuracy Study

PURPOSE: To assess telephone information services of the Montgomery County (Maryland) Department of Libraries, the Arlington County (Virginia) Public Library, and the Fairfax County (Virginia) Public Library in terms of quality, quantity, and efficiency.

DESCRIPTION AND EXPERIENCE WITH USE: Answers to the following questions were sought: 1) Are the right answers to questions being given?; 2) Are patrons being treated courteously?; 3) Are correct procedures being followed?; 4) How much time is involved in obtaining answers? a) How long and how often are people put on "hold"? b) Are callbacks made within an acceptable time frame?; 5) What are the roadblocks to good reference service? a) How many different people must the patron deal with? b) How many times must the question be asked?; 6) Are appropriate/correct referrals made to other resources within the system?; 7) What alternatives are offered when no answer is given?; 8) How well/often do staff "escalate" questions (i.e., ask probing or follow-up questions?); and 9) What is the ambiance of the transactions? a) Can the staff member be clearly understood?

USE: The study was planned and implemented and data results analyzed between October 1983 and August 1984 with an unobtrusive test. All study tasks were performed by staff of the three county systems with no new money used to conduct the study. The study took 11 months from planning through data analysis. Twenty-five questions, each with four variations, were prepared with correct answers and reviewed by staff of the three cooperating libraries with a clear concern that they be typical of actual workloads, both in level of difficulty and subject matter. Thomas Childers provided informal guidance and consulting at several points along the way. Questions were telephoned by staff members of the three systems, though no proxy queried his or her own library system. Each system provided one proxy for each of their libraries participating in the study. Calls were made over a five-month period to avoid "on-your-toes" behavior and detection more likely to occur if test was conducted in a short time frame. The questions consisted of 15 ready reference questions divided among library services offered, business, consumer, assignment-related, medical, information and referral, legal, local government, simple factual; five in-system referrals; and five escalator/negotiation divided among business, assignment-related, and other. Each county library system analyzed its own data and no comparisons were made among the cooperating systems. Responses were coded on machine-readable forms for computer processing. This report includes only analysis of the Fairfax County Public Library data. Major recommendations resulting from the study included the creation of a library system information file of facts about system services or resources that should be provided about services, and the development and implementation of a training program for all telephone information services staff to renew and refresh reference interview skills.

REVIEW OF THE INSTRUMENT: Instrument is useful for determining accuracy of answers rather than for patron satisfaction with answers.

VALIDITY AND RELIABILITY: Accuracy results of the study are in line with other unobtrusive telephone information services tests (Childers, 1971—55%; Crowley, 1971—54%; Jirjees, 1983—57%; and Myers, 1983—49%). Results indicated that 56% of the 350 questions asked in the 14 participating libraries were answered completely and correctly, 35% were either answered incompletely or no source was cited for the information given, and 9% were either not dealt with, misunderstood, or responded to with old or wrong information or unnecessary or incorrect referrals. Patrons expressed satisfaction with staff telephone manners for 86% of calls even though only 56% of questions posed were answered completely and correctly. The type of questions sample was too small to allow for generalizations about how particular kinds of questions were handled. It is important, then, not to generalize from the test results to the entire telephone reference service without first examining the degree to which test questions were representative of the mix of questions typically received by the service (Hernon and McClure, 1986b; Whitlatch, 1989).

BIBLIOGRAPHIC REFERENCES: Rodger (1984b). Rodger and Goodwin (1987).

AVAILABILITY: Initial study out of print. Send inquiries to Jane Goodwin, Coordinator, Planning and Evaluation, Fairfax County Public Library, Fairfax, VA 22033. This instrument is available on an accompanying disk under the file name Fairfax.

AUTHOR: Fisher, Harold E., and Weinberg, Ronald
TITLE/NAME OF INSTRUMENT: Training Feedback Questionnaire
PURPOSE: To develop a reliable means of assessing training courses.

DESCRIPTION AND EXPERIENCE WITH USE: "A phone survey was conducted in March 1986 to find out what training evaluation instruments were currently being used by industry. Training managers at several large corporations were contacted and several of these individuals sent copies of what they were using. The results of the survey indicated that none of the organizations had developed an instrument that was both reliable and applicable to all the courses they conduct...The typical instrument was a short quickly constructed, open-ended questionnaire (reaction or happy sheet) that only provided subjective impressions and no data that could be qualified and evaluated." The instrument subsequently developed focuses on two areas: 1) the capability of trainers to get their message across and 2) factors other than the instructor, such as the applicability of material to the trainee's job. Creates two subscales: The Trainer Behavior Subscale and the Participant Experience Subscale. The instrument is comprised of 18 items on a five-point Likert scale. Four open-ended questions are also included. The data are analyzed using correlation techniques.

USE: At Bell Communications Research in New Jersey in 1986-1987, the instrument was pilot tested on 12 individuals from one training course. Then it was tested on 102 trainees from Bellcore.

REVIEW OF THE INSTRUMENT: The questionnaire can provide valuable feedback on usefulness of course materials, specific training exercises, presenter's manner, and time allotted for training. The questionnaire can help identify the trainee's perception of the usefulness of training. Additionally, this form can identify whether there are particular types of trainees for whom training is more effective, assist in identifying whether the problem is amenable to a training solution, and determine changes that can be made to improve the overall training program.

VALIDITY AND RELIABILITY: At this time, no statistical results are available.

BIBLIOGRAPHIC REFERENCES: Fisher and Weinberg (1988).

AVAILABILITY: This instrument is available on an accompanying disk under the file name Fisher.

AUTHOR: Franklin, Hugh, Knittel, Marjorie, and Maughan, Laurel

TITLE/NAME OF INSTRUMENT: Reference Arrangement Survey

PURPOSE: To define problems and possible solutions related to the present arrangement of reference materials in the Kerr Library (Oregon State University, Corvallis). Intended to be completed by professional library staff.

DESCRIPTION AND EXPERIENCE WITH USE: The ten-page survey, dated January 1990, consists of an instruction sheet, 14 evaluative questions on the physical problem areas in the reference

environment, and 21 yes/no questions on possible solutions, with space included for other suggestions. Three potential floor plans are provided. **USE:** After combining the science/technology and the social science/humanities reference areas in the fall of 1988, a Reference Arrangement Task Force was appointed a year later, followed by assessments of the new configuration by 18 Kerr Library reference librarians using the survey. The task force then made recommendations based largely on feedback from 16 of the 18 librarians who completed the survey, which was its primary source of information. Each librarian received another copy of the survey in February 1990 with average ratings and yes/no tabulations provided. Further suggestions were invited at a meeting in March. A number of satisfactory changes in practical physical arrangements resulted through this collaborative effort, especially in the reference desk and index/abstract areas. Floor plans are included in the ERIC document cited below.
REVIEW OF THE INSTRUMENT: The instrument models a logical approach to derive the benefit of wider staff input in the physical reference rearrangement planning process. Although online catalogs are not covered, the approach fills a gap in the literature on reference space utilization on the practical level.
VALIDITY AND RELIABILITY: No information available.
BIBLIOGRAPHIC REFERENCES: Franklin, Knittel, and Maughan (1991).
AVAILABILITY: This instrument is available on an accompanying disk under the file name Franklin.

AUTHORS: Fussler, Herman H., and Simon, Julian L.
TITLE/NAME OF INSTRUMENT: Library Use Study Questionnaire—Revised
PURPOSE: Used in open book stacks to determine the extent of browsing that takes place, as opposed to recorded use, or use which leads to checkout of material. Used to determine the relationship between browsing and recorded use, the value of browsing to the user, and impact of use upon storage decisions.
DESCRIPTION AND EXPERIENCE WITH USE: The brief questionnaire consists of 18 check-off items divided into four areas in which the user indicates how he or she identified the book, where it was to be used, what kind of use was to be made of it, and the degree of value anticipated by using the material. A return box was placed at stack entrance. The questionnaires were placed around the book pages so that any disturbance could be noted if the book was used, even if the forms were not returned. Staff recorded on the completed forms the title, call number, shelf number, date placed in book, and date sheet returned. A new questionnaire was placed in the book within two days of return of

the previous one. Ballpoint pens were taped to half of the forms, in alternate books on the shelf, as a "reward."

USE: Conducted at the University of Chicago 18 October 1959 to 17 April 1960 in monographs and serials in the physics (QC) and general history (D) sections. Of over 2,000 forms placed in books, 654 were returned for physics and 175 for history; 517 forms with pens were returned, and 324 without. A similar study was conducted in 1978 at the Davis and Santa Cruz campuses of the University of California in which Fussler and Simon's original questionnaire was a starting point and adapted to include questions on user status and immediacy of need.

VALIDITY AND RELIABILITY: The authors point out the disparity in their sample sizes, and that user motivation for answering truthfully can introduce bias. Staff shifting of books during the study period was another problem encountered. Books examined and rejected may provide valuable negative information to users, but can't be distinguished from items really useless to patrons in this method. The data cannot be safely generalized to other institutions.

REVIEW OF THE INSTRUMENT: This book-sampling technique permits measurement of touched books and may be adapted to measuring reference use for weeding and storage decisions, as well as determining intensity of use by subject area/type of publication in collection assessment.

BIBLIOGRAPHIC REFERENCES: Anderson (1983). Fussler and Simon (1961). Lawrence and Oja (1980). **Evaluative Reports** Lancaster (1982). Ross (1983). Metz and Litchfield (1988). Ford (1990).

AVAILABILITY: This instrument is available on an accompanying disk under the file name Fussler.

AUTHOR: Gers, Ralph, and Seward, Lillie J. (Seward's surname now—1994—Dyson)

TITLE/NAME OF INSTRUMENT: Model Reference Behavior Checklist

PURPOSE: The study sought to answer two questions: 1) To what degree is a hypothetical user of reference/information services likely to receive a correct answer to his or her question? and 2) What levels of resources and kinds of activities are most likely to lead to desired levels of performance?

DESCRIPTION AND EXPERIENCE WITH USE: The importance of impact of behaviors on performance resulted in development of Model Reference Behaviors Checklist, which if followed should improve reference performance.

USE: The study was conducted during 1983 in 60 libraries in 22 of Maryland's public library systems. Forty questions were asked in each library for a total of 2,400. Questions asked were of two types: direct questions for which a specific answer had to be given and negotiation or escalator questions where librarian probing was necessary to identify each patron's real information need. Ten levels of information received or degrees of correctness were established for judging responses. Each proxy was responsible for only a few test questions and asked the same question in each of 60 study libraries. Proxies also knew the correct answer and sources in which it could be found. Testing was unobtrusive though some reference personnel were aware they were being tested. Proxies were to behave as much like typical library patrons as possible and to complete an evaluation sheet after each reference transaction. Collected data were analyzed using SPSS (Statistical Package for the Social Sciences). Only 55% of the questions were answered accurately. It was learned that resources (volumes, subscriptions, staff, and setting) have a slight influence on reference service performance (level of information received, correctness of answers received); demand (contact and busyness) has a slight influence on performance (but only with regard to type of contact as busyness is the least influential of all variables); and behaviors (negotiation, interest, comfort, follow-up, and length of interview) have a strong influence on performance, with the exception of length of time taken to answer a question, which has little influence.

REVIEW OF INSTRUMENT: The major outcome of this study is evidence of the degree to which librarian reference transaction behavior affects the outcome of the interaction. Subsequent Maryland studies have verified this significant finding even though not all research questions originally posited were answered by the study. The Model Reference Behaviors Checklist has been cited widely as a tool for giving feedback on the use of the model behaviors.

VALIDITY AND RELIABILITY: Individual libraries vary greatly in use patterns so that it would be unwise to assume that data from one library is applicable to another even within the same library system. Because the questions did not result from the experience of each tested library, the use of the study data is limited. The interviewers were not representative of the average library patron, but rather were above average educationally. The proportion of test questions in various categories may not be equal to those in the real world situation of the tested libraries. The fact that 90% of the questions could be answered in seven basic sources suggests a nonrepresentative set of questions.

BIBLIOGRAPHIC REFERENCES: Dyson (1992). Gers and Seward (1985). Isenstein (1991). Stephen, Gers, Seward, Lillie, Bolin, and Partridge (1988). **Evaluative reports** Rodger and Goodwin (1987). Crowley 1985). Whitlatch (1990a, 1990b).

AVAILABILITY: This instrument is available on an accompanying disk under the file name Gers.

AUTHOR: Haase, Richard F.
TITLE/NAME OF INSTRUMENT: Counselor Effectiveness Scale
PURPOSE: To evaluate various characteristics of an individual in an interview situation. Although not designed originally for librarians, it is useful for short-term situations such as the reference interview.
DESCRIPTION AND EXPERIENCE WITH USE: This instrument is a semantic differential scale consisting of 25 pairs of adjectives such as interesting-dull, attentive-inattentive, sensitive-insensitive, nervous-calm, and apathetic-enthusiastic. The scale is a seven-point scale. This range provides a possible score from 25 to 175 on the overall CES instrument.
USE: Originally developed to measure client attitudes toward the counselor. This instrument was used by Crouch (1981). In addition to the 25 items involving librarian communication behavior, Crouch added seven more items that deal with length of the interview, privacy, and librarian movement about the desk. Crouch provided directions which instructed each observer to record his or her assessment of where the librarian fits in between the extreme ends of the scale for each pair of adjectives by placing a check mark in the appropriate space. Observers also noted the time of day.
REVIEW OF THE INSTRUMENT: One problem with this instrument is that it does not deal with specific verbal and nonverbal behaviors that can be taught. One of the pairs is colorful-colorless. It is difficult to see how such pairing could be rated objectively even though the instrument has reported statistical reliability.
VALIDITY AND RELIABILITY: The scale has been tested for validity and reliability, including inter-rater reliability, and has met the statistical standards for these qualities. It can be considered an objective measuring instrument with which an observer could record a measure of the librarian's communication behavior.
BIBLIOGRAPHICAL REFERENCES: Ivey and Authier (1978). Crouch (1981). DeVore-Chew, Roberts, and Smith (1988). **Evaluative Reports** Fine (1984). Michell and Harris (1984).
AVAILABILITY: This instrument is available on an accompanying disk under the file name Haase.

AUTHOR: Halperin, Michael, and Strazdon, Maureen
TITLE/NAME OF INSTRUMENT: Patron Preference for Different Aspects of Reference Service
PURPOSE: To rank in order of importance the various aspects of reference service, including quality, accessibility, helpfulness and attitude, user instruction, and so on. Intended for an academic library, but could easily be adapted for other types of libraries.
DESCRIPTION AND EXPERIENCE WITH USE: Includes a list of 21 items covering quality of answer, wait for service, time taken to

answer, availability of computer searching, reference hours, staff attitudes, interlibrary loan, knowledge of librarians, instruction in library use, availability of printed guides, translation of foreign documents, vertical file, and sex of librarian.

USE: Used by Halperin with 15 students as a pretest before beginning a conjoint analysis study. On the basis of this ranking test, Halperin selected eight of the most important factors to use in conjoint analysis.

REVIEW OF THE INSTRUMENT: This small study illustrates what could be done on a larger scale with simple rankings of aspects of reference service. It should be recognized that it includes only one small group of students and that preferences may vary among different groups of users. It would appear that this method is worthy of replication with a larger sample of users.

VALIDITY AND RELIABILITY: No information available.

BIBLIOGRAPHICAL REFERENCE: Halperin and Strazdon (1980).

AVAILABILITY: This instrument is available on an accompanying disk under the file name Halper1.

AUTHOR: Halperin, Michael, and Strazdon, Maureen

TITLE/NAME OF INSTRUMENT: Reference Service Preferences

PURPOSE: To determine aspects of reference service that were most important to students and to determine how students' background affects their evaluation of reference service. Used in an academic library.

DESCRIPTION AND EXPERIENCE WITH USE: Consists of 16 profile cards with eight factors on each card. Respondents were asked to rank the items 1 to 8 on each card. Aspects to be ranked in the profiles covered 21 factors, including four levels of answers (from complete and accurate to not useful), four levels of database searching (including no searching, free searching, and $3 or $15 searches), two items on interlibrary loan (free or charge), two items on time needed to answer questions (less than 3 minutes or more than 10, two items on hours (14 hours, including weekends and evenings or eight-hour weekdays), two items on knowledge of librarians (very good understanding or not familiar with topic), and two items on wait for service (no wait or ten-minute wait).

USE: This study was carried out with 100 representative Drexel University students sometime prior to 1980. In order to compensate them for their time and effort, all those who volunteered to participate had library fines remitted. Respondents were provided with definitions of terms and given 16 cards and asked to rank eight items on each card in order of preference. Results were then analyzed by a linear version of the computer program MONANOVA.

REVIEW OF THE INSTRUMENT: This study is a good example of how conjoint analysis can yield useful results, in spite of its complexity

and difficulties in administration. The differences between the needs of graduate and undergraduate students are very revealing and would be useful to a reference department. Drawbacks are the critical need to motivate users to respond to this demanding task and the possible need for aid of a statistician and special computer analysis of results.
VALIDITY AND RELIABILITY: No information available.
BIBLIOGRAPHICAL REFERENCE: Halperin and Strazdon (1980).
AVAILABILITY: This instrument is available on an accompanying disk under the file name Halper2.

AUTHOR: Hardesty, Larry, Lovrich, Nicholas P. Jr., and Mannon, James
TITLE/NAME OF INSTRUMENT: Library-Use Instruction Evaluation Instrument
PURPOSE: To evaluate library instruction programs and students' information seeking skills.
DESCRIPTION AND EXPERIENCE WITH USE: Consists of six pretested attitude statements—some relate to reference service: "A person should only ask for help when it looks as if they're not busy" and "Normally a librarian can only help you when you know what you're looking for." Responses are in terms of strongly agree, agree, undecided, disagree, and strongly disagree. Following the attitude statements is the skills test consisting of 20 reference questions. Eight types of library resources are listed as potential answers: catalog, index area, reference area, rotary file of periodical holdings, periodicals reading room, New York Times and Index, government documents, and abstracts. The instrument was developed with the assistance of professors in political science and sociology.
USE: This instrument was given to 162 freshmen at De Pauw University in English composition courses; of these 162, 133 were given library instruction and 29 were treated as a control group receiving no library instruction. All classes were taught by the same instructor. Eight weeks later all 162 students were again given the original test. To establish norms, a sample of 50% of graduating seniors were surveyed, with 95 (60%) returning forms. The mean score for the seniors was 14.8 correct of 20 skills questions.
REVIEW OF THE INSTRUMENT: An updated version of this instrument could be very useful in evaluating students' information seeking skills. Some questions would need to be updated to represent current concerns although questions appear to be representative of students' information needs. The providing of norms for graduating seniors adds to the value of this instrument.
VALIDITY AND RELIABILITY: This instrument is unusual in that reliability has been so thoroughly tested. Validity was judged by the

criterion of face validity, although how this was done is not described in detail. Testing for reliability was done by the test-retest method. Twenty-six questions were pretested with 102 freshmen prior to the beginning of library use instruction. Three weeks later the identical test was administered to the same students and their responses were carefully compared. Items with either a positive or negative trend or with a correlation coefficient of less than .70 were considered unreliable and dropped. In other words, the only items retained were those that were answered by the same person consistently over time. In order to assure that questions themselves were consistent and not too difficult or too easy, only those questions where more than 50% and fewer than 90% answered correctly were considered reliable and retained. As a result of this testing process, six attitudinal and 20 skills questions were retained.

BIBLIOGRAPHIC REFERENCES: Hardesty, Lovrich, and Mannon (1979).

AVAILABILITY: This instrument is available on an accompanying disk under the file name Hardesty.

AUTHOR: Havener, W. Michael

TITLE/NAME OF INSTRUMENT: The Use of Print Versus Online Sources to Answer Ready Reference Questions in the Social Sciences

PURPOSE: To assess the quality of online ready reference searching being done in academic libraries and determine whether the format in which information is stored affects the outcome of the reference transaction. Developed for academic libraries but could be adapted for other types of libraries.

DESCRIPTION AND EXPERIENCE WITH USE: The method used here was testing of participants with their agreement. The author prepared a list of test questions previously asked in academic libraries for which successful online ready reference searches had been done. Sixty-one librarians in randomly selected libraries were mailed this list of questions; one group was asked to conduct online ready reference searches and the other to use print sources to find answers. Participants were also asked to indicate time taken. Answers were returned along with other information about the searchers and the search itself. The investigator then compared the results of online ready reference searches to the results of searches for the same answers in print sources.

USE: Used by the author in 1987 on a sample of 61 experienced reference librarians.

REVIEW OF THE INSTRUMENT: This method might be replicated using these test questions or others characteristic of a particular library (where answers were already known). This might provide one perspective on a reference department's skill in online ready reference searching.

VALIDITY AND RELIABILITY: No information available.
BIBLIOGRAPHICAL REFERENCE: Havener (1988).
AVAILABILITY: This instrument is available on an accompanying disk under the file name Havener.

AUTHORS: Hernon, Peter, and McClure, Charles R.
TITLE/NAME OF INSTRUMENT: Reference Question Tabulation Sheet
PURPOSE: This instrument, contained in *Unobtrusive testing and library reference services*, has as its purpose the gathering by proxies of the response to a simple reference question administered unobtrusively. The testing identifies the accuracy of the information that library staff members provide to users. Unobtrusive testing can indicate the extent to which reference staff are unfamiliar with sources in their own collections and initiate effective and efficient search strategies.
DESCRIPTION AND EXPERIENCE WITH USE: Data gathered with this instrument were used to determine library correct answer fill rate. The form allows the proxy to record the question number and check appropriate boxes for the time of day when the question was presented, whether the answer was correct, and, when applicable, the type of incorrect response and referral. Proxies are also required to provide a written summary of question administration, responses, and staff behavior.
USE: Use of the instrument was reported by Hernon and McClure (1987b). In a study of government documents referral service, Hernon and McClure used this form to record factual and bibliographic test questions. The instrument was used in the administration of an unobtrusive test of reference accuracy in 24 libraries that had separate documents and general reference departments/collections and in two libraries in which general reference received all documents related questions. From March to June 1985, proxies administered 15 test questions at the 26 libraries selected for testing; 13 academic and 13 public libraries participated in the study. Libraries were from different geographical regions: ten libraries were from the West, eight from the South and eight from the Midwest. To ensure the collection of valid data, the researchers discussed the project with the student proxies, conducted training sessions, and coordinated and monitored the data collection process. Once the questions had been administered and responses obtained, proxies completed the Reference Question Tabulation Sheet. The researchers discussed the answers with the students to ensure accuracy, consistency, and completeness in data collection. The researchers also double-checked all responses to ensure consistency and completeness in the reporting of responses. Proxy guidelines included the following: ask the question sincerely and accurately, appear to be conducting research

or writing a paper in which the information is necessary, do not have the Reference Question Tabulation Sheet or the list of questions out in the open during administration. Remember the question and complete the tabulation sheet promptly after question administration has been completed, attempt to ask the question during times of the day in which one could expect to find a professional librarian in the documents or general reference area, ask for government documents librarian or whoever is in charge of the government documents, and attempt to ask the eight questions of these people, and if a library did not have a separate documents department/collection, ask all 15 questions of general reference personnel. The proxies were instructed to use the bottom and the back of the tabulation sheet to add descriptions, comments, notes, or questions regarding each question administration. The researchers reviewed these notes and comments prior to data coding and analysis to ensure that the proxies used consistent tabulation practice. Proxies agreed not to disseminate information about a library's scores. All the data are confidential and will not be linked to an individual library. This instrument was used as part of a true experimental design. Reference performance was measured using the instrument, a training program was provided, and performance was again measured using the instrument.

REVIEW OF THE INSTRUMENT: Instruction for use of the instrument and the training of the proxies were rigorous. The researchers are experienced in reference research using this methodology. The use of this instrument requires substantial knowledge about unobtrusive testing and careful planning. Those who wish to engage in unobtrusive research are encouraged to read carefully Hernon and McClure (1987a). Assumes libraries should deliver answers rather than references or instructions for self help. Unobtrusive testing examines the accuracy of staff answers, although library clientele may consider other factors of equal or greater importance. For example, they may be willing to accept answers that are less accurate but easier to comprehend, or that are more easily accessible. Combining unobtrusive testing with other means of data collection, such as the case study context used by Hernon and McClure (1986a), enables library administrators and researchers to compare various factors and possible interrelationships. Focused questions probing staff performance in a particular area (e.g., knowledge of statistical sources produced by the federal government) may offer a productive basis for identifying staff weaknesses in conducting search strategies. Although proxies are instructed to seek librarians, reference support staff may have answered some questions; unless precautions are taken to insure that only librarians are asked questions, the unobtrusive method generally does not permit separate identification of reference librarians and support staff.

VALIDITY AND RELIABILITY: Extensive work has been done to ensure validity and reliability. The study demonstrated face validity because the researchers had a representative collection of test items and "sensible" methods of test construction and administration. The construct validity of correct answer fill rate has been tested previously and was carefully operationalized (internal validity). The use of this construct and the similarity in findings from the test-retest procedure suggest that the measure, correct answer fill rate, demonstrates both internal and construct validity. Another criterion of validity is the extent to which the study results can be generalized to a population. The general findings from this study support findings from other unobtrusive tests of reference service, which suggests that the criterion for generalizing has been met. To assure reliability through accurate and consistent coding, the proxies followed written procedures for question administration and completed standardized coding forms for each completed transaction. All proxies attended a training session to assure understanding of the procedures and definitions on the coding form, as well as to answer questions about the coding form. The researchers reviewed all responses and comments provided by the proxies (often in their presence to elicit additional information) about individual testing situations in an effort to maintain consistency in the coding. As well, the Kuder-Richardson Formula 20, which assumes different degrees of difficulty on test items, was used to compute the reliability coefficient, which was measured at .83, indicating substantial reliability of responses as a group. Pretests were consistent with this finding. Crowley (1988) notes some inconsistencies in scoring questions as correct or partially correct and observes that test questions may not be representative. Librarians using this methodology may wish to collect actual questions over a period of time to ensure that questions represent actual reference questions received and represent the different types of questions. For an example, see Woodard (1989). Pretesting ensures that questions are representative of the types libraries actually receive. Researchers might identify someone at the test sites to review questions and certify them as representative of those actually received. That person should neither participate in the actual testing nor alert fellow staff members that testing will occur. Research has not determined whether the correct answer fill rate is sensitive to the level of question difficulty or complexity. Questions may not be representative of the full range of questions a library receives. Test questions tend to be of the short answer and simple fact variety, which are easily asked and whose answers are easily evaluated.

BIBLIOGRAPHIC REFERENCES: Hernon and McClure (1987b). **Evaluative Reports** Anderson (1988). Bailey (1988). Benham (1988). Bunge (1987). Childers (1989). Crews (1988). Crowley (1988). Durrance (1989). Stevens (1987). Whitlatch (1989). Woodard (1989).

AVAILABILITY: This instrument is available on an accompanying disk under the file name Hernon.

AUTHOR: Hittner, Amy
TITLE/NAME OF INSTRUMENT: Individual Rating Scale for Communications Skills
PURPOSE: To evaluate attitudes of service, listening skills, "I" language, verbal and nonverbal communication, appearance, self-image, interpersonal relations, and skill in resolving typical library problems.
DESCRIPTION AND EXPERIENCE WITH USE: The scale allows evaluating others in eight areas: empathy, respect or warmth, genuineness or authenticity, self-disclosure, concreteness or specificity, confrontation, immediacy, and potency on a .5 scale from 1 to 5.5.
USE: On 18 December 1980, 33 paraprofessionals participated in a workshop at Mitre Corporation in McLean, Virginia; communication skills were discussed, modeled, role-played, videotaped, observed, and evaluated. On 22 January 1981, 27 paraprofessionals participated in an advanced communications workshop held at the same location. The same form was used in the Communications Skills Workshop and the Advanced Communications Workshop.
REVIEW OF THE INSTRUMENT: Each of the eight areas is described, but no written guidance is given on how the rating scale is to be used or whether the scales are anchored with key words.
VALIDITY AND RELIABILITY: No statistical tests were used to correlate the results of the two scales.
BIBLIOGRAPHIC REFERENCES: Hittner (1981).
AVAILABILITY: This instrument is available on an accompanying disk under the file name Hittner1.

AUTHOR: Hittner, Amy
TITLE/NAME OF INSTRUMENT: In-Service Training Program for Library Paraprofessionals Workshop Evaluation and Pre-Test/Post-Test
PURPOSE: To evaluate a ten-month pilot project designed to instruct library paraprofessionals in basic library skills and to reinforce positive public service attitudes.
DESCRIPTION AND EXPERIENCE WITH USE: Four categories of questions are included. In addition to soliciting descriptions of the participants and their general observations, four questions measure the participants' evaluation of the instruction and methods used in each module and measure the instructor. Participants are asked to rate their levels of understanding before and after the seven workshop modules, which include basic communications skills, advanced communications, basic reference tools, media mania, business reference services, censorship, and basic library skills.

USE: From December 1980 to May 1981, 409 participants from 53 different libraries in northern Virginia attended seven training modules. The program as a whole was evaluated with post-treatment questionnaires. The ten-week course used a pretest and posttest to measure improvement in library skills.

REVIEW OF THE INSTRUMENT: The evaluation is a classic pretest and posttest design which attempts to determine whether training results in improved skill levels. The participants' own evaluation of before and after levels of understanding are accepted instead of more objective data.

VALIDITY AND RELIABILITY: The author states that both designs are weak in that there is no control group nor is there selective randomization. Because the project was a community service pilot project, it was necessary to keep enrollment to a manageable size and is therefore not a representative sample of library paraprofessionals in northern Virginia. Two of the 35 participants did not attend the last session, so they did not complete the post-test. A large number of participants did not respond to all questions. The participants' perceptions of their understanding of specific skills before and after training were summarized. A correlated t-test was performed and results were statistically significant at the .01 level. Their evaluations of the instructors and instructions were summarized and the mean calculated. The author suggests that participants of this program cannot be assumed to be representative of all library paraprofessionals (average participant was a college graduate with a family income greater than $24,000 annually); future programs should consider random selection and control groups to strengthen the experimental design. No effort was made to correlate on-the-job performance with classroom instruction, nor were participants pretested.

BIBLIOGRAPHIC REFERENCES: Hittner (1981).

AVAILABILITY: This instrument is available on an accompanying disk under the file name Hittner2.

AUTHOR: House, R.J., and Rizzo, J.R.

TITLE/NAME OF INSTRUMENT: Anxiety-Stress Questionnaire

PURPOSE: To measure job-induced stress and its possible outcomes.

DESCRIPTION AND EXPERIENCE WITH USE: Consists of 17 statements, which are analyzed in terms of three scales: Job-Induced Tensions (seven items), Somatic Tension (five items), and General Fatigue and Uneasiness (five items). Answers are given in terms of true (two points) and false (one point). Points are added for each scale and averaged. Some of the factors are taken from the *Taylor Manifest Anxiety Scale* in Taylor, Janet A. (1953). A personality scale of manifest anxiety. *Journal of Abnormal and Social Psychology* 48, 285-290.

USE: It was administered to 200 managerial, professional, and technical employees in a single organization. Means reported for the three scales are Job-Induced Tension 1.24, Somatic Tension 1.33, and General Fatigue and Uneasiness 1.25. Various versions have been used since then and are described in Cook, Hepworth, Wall, and Warr (1981). In other uses, overall means of 2.21 are reported for managers, scientists, and engineers, and 2.16 for social service workers.

REVIEW OF THE INSTRUMENT: This instrument has merits in being well designed, having good reliability and validity indications, and being easy to complete. Items are carefully worded to avoid response bias. Norms are available from the original study as shown above.

VALIDITY AND RELIABILITY: Kuder-Richardson internal reliability coefficients from the original study were Job-Induced Tension .83; Somatic Tension .76; and General Fatigue and Uneasiness .72. A 13-item version by another researcher showed a Spearman-Brown internal reliability coefficient of .89 and a test-retest reliability of .79.

BIBLIOGRAPHICAL REFERENCES: House and Rizzo (1972). Cook, Hepworth, Wall, and Warr (1981)

AVAILABILITY: See the article by House and Rizzo (1972).

AUTHOR: Jahoda, Gerald
TITLE/NAME OF INSTRUMENT: Instrument for Search Strategy and Development
PURPOSE: To test search strategy steps of a descriptive model.
DESCRIPTION AND EXPERIENCE WITH USE: The instrument tests the steps in a search strategy model by translating the steps into a series of questions. Steps tested were 1) query negotiation, when applicable; 2) message selection; 3) determination of level of answer required, when applicable; 4) types and sequence of answer providing tools to search; 5) type of answer to provide; and 6) type or types of access points to use. An assumption underlying the model is that reference librarians answer reference queries by matching the query with their perceptions of relevant portions of the bibliographic world.
USE: Reference librarians in 23 science and technology libraries of academic institutions were asked to submit records of answered queries; 435 queries were collected. These queries were used to test the descriptive search strategy model. In addition, for another 20 queries (other than those previously submitted), 23 librarians used the instrument for search strategy development. The model of reference process was revised based on the results of this test. Using similar instruments based on the model of the reference process, Jahoda has also found that library school students have difficulty selecting answers from statistical material. A revised version of the instrument has been used to test 12 queries (Jahoda, Eytes, Lawson, Paskoff, and Pond, 1987).

REVIEW OF THE INSTRUMENT: Reference work is often fast paced and it is difficult to record the entire question, context of question, and interaction accurately. Personal observation by a reference expert using a modified search strategy questionnaire should be considered. The development and use of the instrument has been limited to queries having specific information as the end product.

VALIDITY AND RELIABILITY: Seventeen out of 23 science and technology reference librarians indicated that the original model was not an adequate representation of the reference process. After testing, the model was revised to consist of the following six decision making steps: 1) message selection; 2) selection of type or types of answer providing tools; 3) selection of specific answer providing tools; 4) selection of search headings; 5) selection of answers; and 6) query negotiation and renegotiation.

BIBLIOGRAPHIC REFERENCES: Jahoda (1977). Jahoda, Eyles, Lawson, Paskoff, and Pond (1987). **Evaluative Reports** Bates (1981). Ingwersen (1982). Jahoda (1989). Lynch (1983). Murfin and Gugelchuk (1987). Wagers (1978, 1980).

AVAILABILITY: This instrument is available on an accompanying disk under the file name Jahoda.

AUTHORS: Jensen, Rebecca, Asbury, Herbert, and King, Radford
TITLE/NAME OF INSTRUMENT: Costs and Benefits
PURPOSE: To conduct a client survey to examine user-identified dollar costs and benefits of online searches.
DESCRIPTION AND EXPERIENCE WITH USE: An interview format was developed in which clients were called and asked 1) the estimated costs and gross benefits that the user attributed directly to receiving a particular information package; 2) the type of applications achieved or expected for the technical information received; and 3) the estimated chances of success of the expected applications. The results of applications could be a) number of applications made or will be made; b) information was acquired with less time and cost than for other methods; and 3) economic benefits were or will be realized in improving current applications.
USE: Used at NASA Industrial Applications Center at UCLA in 1977.
REVIEW OF THE INSTRUMENT: This is a good example of obtaining information about the dollar benefits of information from the user's viewpoint. The method of telephone interviews appeared to work well. The authors give tips on cost benefit methodology. They recommend that a benefit survey be conducted some time after the information is received, to allow optimum time for benefits to emerge. They stress the importance of knowing the user's purpose for the search, since

benefits may vary according to purpose. In regard to improvement of service, they recommend obtaining client feedback on a regular basis.
VALIDITY AND RELIABILITY: No information available.
BIBLIOGRAPHIC REFERENCE: Jensen, Asbury, and King (1980).
AVAILABILITY: Those wishing to use this method should consult the article by Jensen, Asbury, and King (1980).

AUTHOR: Joseph, Margaret A.
TITLE/NAME OF INSTRUMENT: Library Survey Form
PURPOSE: To evaluate reference department success in using staff efficiently to serve patrons, with emphasis on institutionally affiliated patrons.
DESCRIPTION AND EXPERIENCE WITH USE: Form is completed by reference staff on duty indicating time of transaction; staff member handling transaction; if query was in-person, by telephone, or in writing; status of patron; question type; subject code; length of help given; type of reference question as directional (subdivided into eight categories) or reference (subdivided into six categories); and space for subject or other comments. A brief written record of each question is also included. All transactions are coded by all reference staff during a *typical* week in fall and spring semesters, first summer session, and following fall semester.
USE: Used in a study conducted by Joseph in 1981 and 1982. Data on almost 1,400 transactions were collected in four *typical* weeks.
REVIEW OF THE INSTRUMENT: Use of this instrument encourages reference staff to establish clearly stated objectives for service and provides a means for analyzing the degree to which some objectives are met. Only some objectives of the reference department are examined through the use of this instrument. Goals such as accuracy of information provided, patron satisfaction, and the ultimate value of the service to individuals are not measured by the simple, inexpensive means reported. Division of labor between librarians and support staff assumes that both are present and that appropriate referrals are made. A substantial amount of time is needed for data entry. Analysis requires the use of computer software (SPSS) and understanding of several basic statistics: Chi-square test of significance and Gamma as a measure of degree and direction of correlation between pairs. Data obtained by a library using this form cannot be generalized to other libraries. However, this instrument could provide a continuous log of questions with type and subject of question, type of patron, and time taken for quick review by staff. The instrument provides a method of collecting reference volume statistics and, at the same time, relating them to other aspects of the reference transaction. This method enables a department to document questions being asked and level of staff answering them. Strong (1980b) has also developed a similar type of transaction log. Data collected through this instrument

could be used to develop test questions for studies of reference accuracy and success.

VALIDITY AND RELIABILITY: Success of this method depends on the degree to which category definitions are understood and correctly reported by all library staff. Self-reporting of question categories by librarians has not resulted in question categories that are valid and reliable (Balay and Andrew, 1975; Cameron, 1976; Strong, 1980a; Kesselman and Watstein, 1987). The question categories have their greatest usefulness as a method of analyzing a collection of *verbatim* reference questions, by grouping and regrouping questions by aspects. Because in this form each question must be put in one category and the categories are not mutually exclusive, librarians will have difficulty placing questions with multiple aspects in a single category. The number of possible categories is also of concern.

BIBLIOGRAPHIC REFERENCES: Joseph (1984).

AVAILABILITY: This instrument is available on an accompanying disk under the file name Joseph.

AUTHOR: Kantor, Paul B.

TITLE/NAME OF INSTRUMENT: Analysis of Availability, Causes, and Behavior for the Reference Process

PURPOSE: To provide an analysis of the reference process which identifies a chain of essentially independent conditions that must be met in order for patrons to obtain the information they seek.

DESCRIPTION AND EXPERIENCE WITH USE: Extends the branching analysis model to reference service by allowing reference librarian to note the apparent behavioral outcome for each encounter: 1) try again; 2) dead end; 3) refer elsewhere; 4) patron gave up; and 5) patron appears satisfied. For each encounter, the librarian also selects one of five causal factors: 1) question not made clear; 2) could not think of source; 3) we don't have the source; 4) source does not have the information; and 5) found the information but patron not satisfied. Of greatest interest to the manager of reference services are the values for "could not think of a source" and "we don't have the source." The former indicates that either the library is receiving inquiries it should not or staff are not well trained to handle present demands. The "we don't have the source" may reveal that either there are important gaps in the library's holdings or the staff are not aware of the extent and power of the library's present collection. A complete analysis involves reviewing the tally sheets (on which some notes about the queries themselves are usually recorded) in collaboration with a knowledgeable colleague or supervisor. The technique relies on the librarian's judgment of success or failure. The librarian may feel under some pressure to present his or her performance in the best possible light. This problem can be reduced but not eliminated by techniques that preserve the anonymity of individual librarians. Thus the category "could not think of a source," which may reflect negatively on the knowledge of the librarian, may be underreported. The collection factor "we don't have the source" may be distorted by incomplete librarian knowledge of the collection. Costs are low. For the 16 libraries combined, the total time for collection of data was less than 50 person hours and for data analysis about 16 hours.

USE: Used by 16 libraries dealing primarily with scientific and technical information. Because the study involves self-selected libraries, the data obtained should not be regarded as norms or standards, particularly because libraries included are from both academic and industrial environments and have differing goals and functions.

REVIEW OF THE INSTRUMENT: To assess the role librarian knowledge ("could not think of a source") plays in failures relative to other factors such as collection, tally sheets should be analyzed by reference experts not handling the transaction. This is important because knowledge failures may be underreported using this instrument.

VALIDITY AND RELIABILITY: Studies based upon review of queries actually received are more indicative of reference performance than studies based upon specially prepared questions. The data collected carry only to the point at which the librarian judges the patron to be satisfied. Patrons judge themselves satisfied in about 75% of the cases that librarians would score patron as appears satisfied.

BIBLIOGRAPHIC REFERENCES: Kantor (1981b). **Evaluative Reports** Kantor (1982). Van House (1989).

AVAILABILITY: This instrument is available on an accompanying disk under the file name Kantor2.

AUTHOR: Kantor, Paul
TITLE/NAME OF INSTRUMENT: Frustration Factor and Nuisance Factor
PURPOSE: To examine the availability of reference service in terms of how often a user approaching the reference desk would have been able to obtain service without a wait.

DESCRIPTION AND EXPERIENCE WITH USE: Developed for academic and special libraries but could be used with all types of libraries. This method involves an availability study lasting one day. A designated person observes the desk at previously selected times and records whether anyone was available to help, number of staff already helping patrons, and number of patrons waiting. The number of observations should be approximately equal to the number of hours reference is open during one weekday. This one-day sample is then extrapolated to give estimated data for a five-weekday period. The primary availability measure derived from this is the percent of these observation periods when someone was free to help. This method has other useful measures including estimated total hours patrons spend waiting for service in one week and estimated desk staff hours *not* occupied in helping patrons. These combined measures create the Nuisance Factor, the measure of patron time spent waiting in proportion to staff time spent helping.

USE: Used by Kantor in his LORCOST study of 50 scientific and technical libraries of different types in 1981. The Frustration Factor and Nuisance Factor study was done by only 13 of those libraries.

REVIEW OF THE INSTRUMENT: Basically this method appears to be a sound one with good potential for use in reference departments. Some modifications that might be suggested are 1) restricting the estimates made on the basis of the one-day sample weekdays (since the pattern of business may differ hour to hour on weekends) and 2) removing the forced choice between "free to serve" and "occupied with other work" (because this could result in erroneous observer judgments). Instead one alternative *"not* occupied helping patrons" could be substituted. One advantage of this method is the short time during which data need to be collected. However, the disadvantage may be the representativeness of the one-day sample. Kantor suggests that these data can be extrapolated to longer periods of time than one week. This should be done cautiously by academic libraries whose business is cyclical—at the most, extrapolating one or two months, and only if reference statistics reveal that the day chosen was reasonably representative of the whole of days in those months in the past. The "Frustration Factor" will supply a rough estimate of accessibility quickly and as such should be useful. Low accessibility times can be identified and linked to a two-hour segment of the day. The "Nuisance Factor," which represents patron hours spent waiting, is extremely useful and usually obtained through a queuing study based on random observation periods over a span of time. A queuing study is usually more representative of different weeks and months. Data will also be more precise because the length of each patron's wait is recorded. A queuing study will also be able to supply such figures as average delay time and maximum delay time. However, as a quick rough estimate the Nuisance Factor also has its merits. Patron delay times that are out of line can be spotted and related to particular two-hour blocks of time. The Nuisance Factor will help to put patron delay time in perspective because no national norms are available for patron delay time. If the Nuisance Factor shows a relatively high percentage of delay time to service time, then the possibility of a problem should be investigated.

VALIDITY AND RELIABILITY: No data available.

BIBLIOGRAPHIC REFERENCE: Kantor (1980).

AVAILABILITY: This instrument is available on an accompanying disk under the file name Kantor1.

AUTHOR: Kantor, Paul

TITLE/NAME OF INSTRUMENT: Measurement of Effort by Simulation

PURPOSE: To study the effort component of a task, such as locating a book, and to determine the difficulties encountered by the user in performing that activity from start to finish. Developed by the author for use in studying patron access in academic libraries. Could be used for other reference activities such as doing a study of patron access to the reference collection.

DESCRIPTION AND EXPERIENCE WITH USE: A particular task or activity selected for analysis must first be broken down into sequential steps such as locating a reference book in the catalog, finding its shelving location, and determining whether it is actually on the shelf. About 35 to 50 titles are chosen at random from the shelf list. Stand-ins for real patrons are selected, using those as naive as possible, newly employed students, and so on. Each person takes a randomly selected title and attempts to locate it, timing each step of the procedure. Methods of analyzing the data are described. A figure can be obtained of the percentage of reference titles actually found by the stand-ins on the shelf. Results can also be used to determine at what stage of the process most problems may be occurring.

USE: None reported.

REVIEW OF THE INSTRUMENT: Using a small sample, this method might provide a way to study patron behavior in finding reference information. Time spent by unaided patrons in finding reference information could then be compared to time spent on the same question by skilled reference personnel, thus establishing a ratio of benefit, in terms of time saved by reference service. If stand-ins were given reference questions, their time might be broken down into steps of selecting an answering source, locating it, and using it.

VALIDITY AND RELIABILITY: To provide the best description, the author suggests that the upper and lower sextiles be used to describe data. For example, with a sample size of 36, the upper one-sixth and the lower one-sixth could be identified at the 90% confidence level.

BIBLIOGRAPHIC REFERENCE: Kantor (1984).

AVAILABILITY: This instrument is available on an accompanying disk under the file name Kantor3.

AUTHOR: King, Geraldine

TITLE/NAME OF INSTRUMENT: Reference Transaction Slip

PURPOSE: To provide useful information for staffing, evaluation of resources, and evaluation and training of personnel. Also useful for training new staff, staff development, and evaluation of individual reference librarians by managers.

DESCRIPTION AND EXPERIENCE WITH USE: The Reference Transaction Slip is composed of the following categories: *Date, Time, Telephone, Author/title, Question, Name, and Tel.No., Address, Barcode, Sources Checked,* and *Total Count. Total Count* is the count of reference questions using National Center for Educational Statistics General Information Survey definitions (Emerson, 1977). The record of work done on the transaction is frequently continued on the back of the slip. Questions take time to record although the form automatically provides the reference practitioner with a handy piece of paper for notetaking on the question and on the progress of the search. Except during initial training periods, when librarians are encouraged to fill out the forms completely and carefully, great latitude is allowed. At any particular time, librarians can be instructed to take particular care in filling out particular parts of the form. Several analyses are possible. For training of new staff or any evaluation of individual work, slips can easily be sorted out by librarian's initials. For finding gaps in resources, slips can be sorted by boxes checked under disposition. Then a librarian must check sorted slips for resource problems. This can be fairly time consuming; suggest emphasizing particular subject areas for a given period of time. A sample of transactions slips can be analyzed. The form requires considerable time to manually sort and analyze. Forms may be modified to collect slightly different data; for example, male/female or adult/student.

USE: The Reference Transaction Slip has been used at Ramsey County Public Library. See King (1982).

REVIEW OF THE INSTRUMENT: Libraries interested in distinguishing between the query originally asked and the question answered may wish to modify the form by replacing the "Question" with 1. "Statement of Query as Actually Answered." 2. "Statement of Query as Originally Received." 3. "Answer and/or Citation Supplied (Jahoda, 1977). To ensure objectivity, questions should be classified into different categories by independent judges. These independent judges should be reference librarians who have not answered the questions. More than one judge should classify questions so that judgments may be checked for internal consistency.

VALIDITY AND RELIABILITY: The system involves a 100% data-gathering system. Every reference question is represented. Librarians must be cautioned to record questions carefully and accurately.

BIBLIOGRAPHIC REFERENCES: King (1982).

AVAILABILITY: This instrument is available on an accompanying disk under the file name King.

AUTHORS: Kirby, Martha, and Miller, Naomi

TITLE/NAME OF INSTRUMENT: Questionnaires I and II for Initial Search and Follow-up Search

PURPOSE: To compare the results achieved by end-users as compared to those of the trained analysts, to provide information for improving training. Developed for a special library but could be adapted for other types of libraries.

DESCRIPTION AND EXPERIENCE WITH USE: The availability of free searches was advertised and two-hour appointments were made with interested users. Users examined manuals and brochures and then performed their own searches on BRS/Colleague/Biomedical databases. Login was done by the search analyst who then left the room and returned after the search was finished. The user then completed the first form reporting the success of his or her search. After interviewing the user, the search analyst conducted a second search. The end-user then completed a second form, reporting how the search analyst's results compared with those of the first search.

USE: Used by the authors at the Medical College of Pennsylvania in 1986. The authors found that initially 71% of end-users judged their searches successful. After seeing the results obtained on these same searches by the trained searcher, only 40% judged their own searches successful. (The earlier high judgment of success by end-users may be due to the inflated ratings which are often associated with two-category scales).

REVIEW OF THE INSTRUMENT: Advantages of this method are that the precise shortcomings of user searches and reasons for failure can be determined, if the user is observed or transaction logs are available. In addition, the success of mediated and unmediated searches can be compared. Also, this method is one of the few available where the user can rate the success of his or her own search and then compare this to the information that could have been found by an expert. This method requires a substantial investment of staff time, but the value of the information gained should well repay the time spent. Another disadvantage is the two-category success scale, which has been prone to inflated ratings (Cuadra, Katter, Holmes, and Wallace, 1967). This, however, could be easily corrected by use of a scale with more categories—for example, three categories: mostly successful, partly successful, and not successful (Carnegie Mellon, 1978).

VALIDITY AND RELIABILITY: No information available.

BIBLIOGRAPHICAL REFERENCES: Kirby and Miller (1985). Kirby and Miller (1986).

AVAILABILITY: This instrument is available on an accompanying disk under the file name Kirby.

AUTHOR: Kramer, Joseph
TITLE/NAME OF INSTRUMENT: Cost Benefit Formula
PURPOSE: To determine the benefits to the corporation of reference service in a special library.
DESCRIPTION AND EXPERIENCE WITH USE: Questionnaires were sent to users of a special library who had received literature searches. They were asked to estimate the amount of time saved. This was then divided by the figure for the amount of time spent on those same literature searches by reference staff. In order to find out how much time was saved on citation and verification questions, a slightly different method was adopted. Users were contacted by telephone, given a citation and verification question that had been previously asked, and questioned as to how much time they thought it would take them to find that information. This total time figure was then divided by the time it had actually taken staff to find the answers.
USE: Used by the author in the Boeing Company Aerospace Group Library from 1967 through 1969 for 24 months.
REVIEW OF THE INSTRUMENT: This method could be useful. Disadvantages are that time saved may not be able to be accurately estimated. As the author pointed out, a time and motion study would probably have resulted in more accurate data. He also notes that there may be some positive bias due to users' fears that if they did not respond favorably support for library service might be cut. Advantages are that time saved is one of the most widely accepted and agreed upon measure of the benefits of reference service and is applicable to reference service in all libraries.
VALIDITY AND RELIABILITY: No information available.
BIBLIOGRAPHIC REFERENCE: Kramer (1971).
AVAILABILITY: Details of this method are available in the article by Kramer (1971).

AUTHORS: Kuhlthau, Carol; Turock, Betty; George, Mary; and Belvin, Robert.
TITLE/NAME OF INSTRUMENT: The Information Search Process: Process Survey and Perception Questionnaire
PURPOSE: To study the ways in which different types of library users who are doing extended projects involving literature searches go about the information search process. To study thoughts and feelings of users at each stage of the process, and to explore the role of mediators in this process.
DESCRIPTION AND EXPERIENCE WITH USE: Consists of two parts: a process survey and a perception questionnaire. The process survey was administered to participants at initiation, midpoint, and closure of the search. The process survey begins with four open-ended

questions exploring project topics and asking who the respondent has previously talked to about the project. The respondent then rates his or her confidence level on a ten-point scale and selects descriptive adjectives from a list which, at this point in the search, expresses feelings, such as frustrated or relieved. In the final section, the respondent is asked to check the state of the information search with alternatives ranging from identifying the topic to completion of the information search. Another item asks respondents to check actions they are performing such as asking a question of librarians, browsing, writing, or taking notes (18 actions). The final item asks respondents to check the intellectual activities they are performing such as organizing ideas, identifying alternative topics, or gaining a sense or direction. The perception questionnaire has been administered to participants twice: before and after the search. This questionnaire has a list of 20 statements about information searching with four responses ranging from almost always to almost never. Ten questions are related to the search process and ten to the role of the mediators. In additions to administration of the questionnaires, librarians also kept diaries of their contacts with each participant.

USE: Sites of the study were 21 libraries in New Jersey: eight school, seven academic (undergraduate students only), and six public (adult users only). Librarians from each site selected up to 30 users, who were beginning extended searches for information for oral or written presentations, to be completed by the end of the 12-week data-collection period. A total of 385 users were surveyed: 59% from school media centers, 28% from academic libraries, and 13% from public libraries; 73% of users were under age 20.

REVIEW OF THE INSTRUMENT: The role of the reference librarian is explored in the different stages of the literature search. Using this method, the role of reference service in the literature search and different types of consultation at each stage of the search might be explored in more depth.

VALIDITY AND RELIABILITY: A three-step search process model—Initiation, Midpoint, and Closure—gained validity, in that this study supported results of previous tests of the six-step model.

BIBLIOGRAPHIC REFERENCES: Kuhlthau (1984). Kuhlthau (1988a). Kuhlthau (1988b). Kuhlthau (1988c). Kuhlthau, Turock, George, and Belvin (1990).

AVAILABILITY: This instrument is available on an accompanying disk under the file name Kuhlthau.

AUTHORS: LAMA-NDCU Committee. Parker, Linda (Chair); Joseph, Margaret; Clark, Bart; and Murfin, Marjorie.

TITLE/NAME OF INSTRUMENT: LAMA-NDCU Experimental Staffing Adequacy Measures

PURPOSE: To help libraries estimate their desk staffing adequacy by comparison of their own data with national norms.

DESCRIPTION AND EXPERIENCE WITH USE: Developed for academic libraries and modified for public libraries. Four items of data are collected for a typical week in the fall quarter: number of reference questions, person hours, hours reference open, and gate count. The measures then formed by various combinations of these items are 1) actual demand—reference questions per person in the library in a typical week; 2) users in the library per reference person hour (potential workload); 3) percent of users in the library who ask reference questions (percent of patrons reached by reference service); 4) reference questions per person hour (workload per hour); and 5) reference questions per hour reference open (maximum demonstrated capacity). After computing these measures a library may compare itself with national norms (Murfin, 1983; Rinderknecht, 1992). Norms for academic libraries are in five size groups by gate count and also by enrollment so that libraries can compare themselves to norms either by gate count or enrollment.

USE: Used in a 1983 study. It was found that desk person hours and enrollment accounted for 71% of variation in volume of reference questions. Revised by the LAMA-NDCU Committee to include public libraries in 1988 and subsequently used again in a pretest. Used again in 1989 in a study of academic libraries of all sizes by Deborah Rinderknecht (1992).

REVIEW OF THE INSTRUMENT: Disadvantages are that these measures need further testing. Advantages are that they do not require a special study and are based on information readily available and thus could be used as a quick screening test for staffing adequacy. The importance of staffing adequacy may increase in the future if it is shown to be related to quality. A study by Woodard has already related the level of desk staffing to quality in the case of an information desk (Woodard, 1989) and other data from both public and academic libraries support this. There is some evidence in regard to use of these staffing adequacy measures that, when users in the library per reference person hour (potential demand/workload) rises above 200, quality may begin to decline (Rinderknecht, 1992). These ratio measurements should be used in conjunction with other methods and viewed as one perspective on staffing adequacy. Even if one does not find the ratio measurements meaningful or chooses not to use them, the simple comparisons of raw numbers for reference questions, desk person hours, hours open, turnstile count, and enrollment, with national norms should be helpful.

VALIDITY AND RELIABILITY: No data available.
BIBLIOGRAPHIC REFERENCE: Murfin (1983). Rinderknecht (1992).
AVAILABILITY: This instrument is available on an accompanying disk under the file name Lama.

AUTHOR: Lange, Janet M.
TITLE/NAME OF INSTRUMENT: San Diego County Library Staff Workload and Reference Training Needs Survey
PURPOSE: To collect data on tasks performed by all library personnel and to determine the amount and kind of reference training needed by San Diego County Library staff. Janet Lange developed the survey for a public library system but it could be adapted for other types of libraries.
DESCRIPTION AND EXPERIENCE WITH USE: Consists of 14 broad categories of work, including reference, children's service, other services, paging, housekeeping, administrative, supervision, public relations, other tasks, and breaks. Within these major categories are numerous subcategories. For example, reference service tasks are broken down into 17 subcategories. All subcategories performed by an individual are checked. Time spent is given only for broad categories. Staff were asked to each keep a diary for one week recording activities every 15 minutes. This diary was then used to complete a record of time spent for each of 14 broad categories. Data are analyzed in terms of percentage of time spent on tasks directly related to reference service for the entire group and for individuals. Also, staff were asked to rate on a five-point scale, with 1=low and 5=high, their need for reference training in 1) knowledge of all kinds of reference services; 2) ability to conduct a reference interview; 3) knowledge of their library's reference collection; 4) knowledge of their library's complete collection; 5) knowledge of reference sources not in their collection; 6) knowledge of how to count reference transactions; and 7) some other aspect of reference services which respondents could specify.
USE: In 1986, 134 respondents were obtained from six groups of San Diego County Libraries.
REVIEW OF THE INSTRUMENT: The diary method was used as a base and the survey was done for only one week, but participants were told that if some activities were atypical, those activities should be adjusted to a more typical portion. The list is intended to be very comprehensive and seems to be a useful compilation of tasks and duties in a public library system which could be modified as needed.
VALIDITY AND RELIABILITY: Little information is given regarding the reliability and validity of the instrument. The author does note, however, that the area staff indicated to need the least amount of

training, knowledge of how to count reference transactions, was indicated by branch managers to be one in which there were numerous confusions. The author notes that while some staff recognize their lack of understanding, others may not recognize that they misunderstood part of the process.

BIBLIOGRAPHIC REFERENCES: Lange (1986).

AVAILABILITY: This instrument is available on an accompanying disk under the file name Lange.

AUTHORS: Lawrence, Gary S., and Oja, Anne R.

TITLE/NAME OF INSTRUMENT: University of California Questionnaire—Library Survey

PURPOSE: To plan for establishing the university's policy on regional compact shelving for infrequently circulated material, data were collected and analyzed for three issues: 1) unrecorded use of material; 2) at-the-shelf discovery (browsing); and 3) user's immediacy of need for material. Also, to test the methodology for data collection.

DESCRIPTION AND EXPERIENCE WITH USE: The library survey questionnaire (placed in books on the shelf) consists of six sections which ask 1) status and institutional affiliation; 2) was this specific book sought? 3) purpose of user's selection of book; 4) what will the user do with the book (i.e., photocopy, examine at desk/table/shelf); 5) if this book were not immediately available how long would user wait for it? and 6) user comments. Multiple uses of volumes might be missed within the three-week checking periods (this time frame was chosen due to budget constraints). Response rate was low (15.7%), but an improved questionnaire could raise this rate of user cooperation. A problem encountered was staff turnover during the administration of the study. Users found it difficult to interpret immediacy of need question, and browsers presented less well-articulated purposes for using books. Reference volumes caused a disproportionate amount of anomalous answers. Long-term patterns cannot be generalized by a short-term study of unrecorded uses.

USE: The study was conducted in 1978 during the spring semester using Fussler and Simon's questionnaire, and following their approach of placing the questionnaires in individual books. This was done in a randomly selected sample group of 5,008 total volumes. After six weeks of testing, the form was redesigned and the study continued. The main libraries and science branches at the Davis and Santa Cruz campuses were the test sites. Stacks were checked at three-week intervals and forms replaced or repositioned as necessary.

REVIEW OF THE INSTRUMENT: Fussler and Simon's earlier similar study had a higher response rate (33%). With the improvements suggested in the California study (adequate publicity, incentives, and

questionnaire simplification) an in-depth analysis of reference book use is possible using this approach and will yield more detailed use information than simple table/reshelving counts. Daily stack monitoring would be feasible in a more focused sample group.
VALIDITY AND RELIABILITY: No information available.
BIBLIOGRAPHIC REFERENCES: Lawrence and Oja (1980).
AVAILABILITY: This instrument is available on an accompanying disk under the file name Lawrence.

AUTHOR: Lawson, V. Lonnie
TITLE/NAME OF INSTRUMENT: Cost Effectiveness Comparison of Two Alternatives
PURPOSE: To determine which method—general library tours or computer-assisted instruction—was the most cost effective. Developed for an academic library.
DESCRIPTION AND EXPERIENCE WITH USE: Effectiveness of both methods was assessed by dividing eight freshman English classes into three groups, one having tours, one CAI, and one no instruction. Pretest and posttests of library knowledge and skills were given to all groups. Costs were figured for librarian and classroom faculty time for the 30 tours given each year. Computer costs were figured for hardware, software, manuals, programming, updates to programming, lab assistants, service, and maintenance. Costs for both methods were prorated for five years.
USE: Used at Central Missouri Sate University in 1987-88 to compare two methods of library orientation.
REVIEW OF THE INSTRUMENT: This method is of interest in that it looks at costs over a five-year period. It provides a good example of the way to carry out a cost effectiveness comparison study. It would have been helpful to have had more information on how effectiveness scores were obtained, along with results and a copy of the instrument used to measure effectiveness.
VALIDITY AND RELIABILITY: No information available.
BIBLIOGRAPHIC REFERENCE: Lawson (1990).
AVAILABILITY: Those wishing to use this method should consult the article by Lawson (1990).

AUTHOR: Lowenthal, Ralph
TITLE/NAME OF INSTRUMENT: Morale Inventory
PURPOSE: To assess the sense of well being, general morale, and job satisfaction of reference staff, and the organizational climate of the reference department.
DESCRIPTION AND EXPERIENCE WITH USE: Consists of a combination of recognized instruments that have been adapted for

reference service. Included are an adapted Maslach Burnout Instrument (permission required from Consulting Psychologists Press for use), the Brayfield Rothe Job Satisfaction Scale, the Purdue Teacher Opinionnaire (permission already obtained), and the Organizational Climate Description Questionnaire (permission already obtained), all in all amounting to 248 items. Respondents mark answers on scales varying from four to seven points, depending on the instrument. Separate special scales have been created, drawn from the tests, for disaffection from patrons, anxiety, stress and tension, and frustration. Other scales are those belonging to the tests themselves and cover depersonalization, emotional exhaustion, personal accomplishment, and autonomy. Further details of how this inventory was developed are included in Lowenthal's (1990) article.

USE: Used in 1987 in a study of 37 public reference librarians in seven public service units in four public libraries. Preliminary indications were that staffs' emotional well being, job satisfaction, and sense of commitment might be major factors in the quality of reference service.

REVIEW OF THE INSTRUMENT: A disadvantage is the length, which may make some librarians reluctant to participate in a study. However, in general longer instruments have been found to have greater reliability.

VALIDITY AND RELIABILITY: An advantage is the use of instruments that already have reliability and validity data available so that confidence can be placed in the results.

BIBLIOGRAPHIC REFERENCES: Lowenthal (1990).

AVAILABILITY: Special knowledge is required for scoring and the confidentiality of each individual's scores must be maintained. Also, validity might be affected if individuals could study questions beforehand. For these reasons, the battery is only available from the author.

AUTHORS: Maslach, Christina, and Jackson, Susan E.

TITLE/NAME OF INSTRUMENT: Maslach Burnout Inventory (MBI)

PURPOSE: To measure burnout in a number of the helping professions.

DESCRIPTION AND EXPERIENCE WITH USE: The instrument is known as the Maslach Burnout Inventory but actual forms are titled "Human Services Survey" to avoid or minimize respondents feeling resentful or fearful about being "tested" for burnout and responding in an untruthful way. The instrument consists of one page of explanations and illustrations and one page with 22 statements of feelings and emotions. Participants are asked how often these feelings occur on a seven-point scale: never, a few times a year or less, once a month or less, a few times a month, once a week, a few times a week, and every day. For scoring, items are combined into scales of emotional exhaustion, depersonalization, and lack of personal accomplishment.

USE: The MBI has been widely used. In the bibliographic reference below, a bibliography of articles describing uses is given.

REVIEW OF THE INSTRUMENT: This is an excellent instrument in all respects. It is short and easy to complete and it does not intrude into respondents' personal lives. It is easy to score and norms for a large population are available. The only disadvantage is that permission must be given and a payment is required. Use of alternative burnout instruments is probably not advisable, because the MBI is so widely used and can be more easily interpreted with benefit of norms for large numbers of persons in different occupations (Smith and Nelson, 1983).

VALIDITY AND RELIABILITY: Reliability coefficients for the subscales are 1) Emotional Exhaustion .90; 2) Depersonalization .79; and 3) Personal Accomplishment .71. Standard error measurement is Emotional Exhaustion 3.80; Depersonalization 3.16; and Personal Accomplishment 3.73. Test-retest reliability in tests separated by two to four weeks was 1) Emotional Exhaustion .82; 2) Depersonalization .60; and 3) Personal Accomplishment .80. All coefficients were significant beyond the .001 level. The test-retest reliabilities for tests separated by one year were 1) Emotional Exhaustion .60; 2) Depersonalization .54; and 3) Personal Accomplishment .57. Evidence for convergent validity, external validity of personal experiences, construct validity, and discriminant validity are presented and discussed in the bibliographic reference below.

BIBLIOGRAPHIC REFERENCE: Maslach (1981).

AVAILABILITY: Contact Consulting Psychologists Press, 577 College Ave., Palo Alto, CA 94306.

AUTHOR: McClure, Charles

TITLE/NAME OF INSTRUMENT: Cost Effectiveness Measures

PURPOSE: To measure the cost effectiveness of traditional desk reference service.

DESCRIPTION AND EXPERIENCE WITH USE: Consists of four measures, three of which are cost-effectiveness measures. The first measure is success or percentage of correct answers. The second is correct answers per staff hour, where staff hours are divided by correct answers. The object of this measure is to obtain the maximum number of correct answers with the least number of reference staff hours. The third measure is reference service delivery rate, where a sample period of time is divided by number of correct answers during that time. This would provide information on how long, on the average, it takes to complete a successful reference question. The fourth measure, cost per correct answer, would be computed by the total cost of reference service for a given period divided by the number of correct answers during that period.

USE: The author did not use these measures. However, a variation of the last method has been used in one study in 1989 (Murfin and Bunge, 1989). Cost per successful reference question was determined by dividing the cost of total time taken in minutes by number of successful questions. REVIEW OF THE INSTRUMENT: These measures seem potentially useful with modification and testing. One difficulty with the measure of correct answers per staff hour is that it would vary by how many questions were asked over a period of hours and would fluctuate with demand. A change in correct answers per hour might reflect changes in demand as well as changes in staff effectiveness. For example, five correct answers for one staff hour might represent high effectiveness and efficiency if six questions were asked, but low effectiveness if 15 questions were asked. Nevertheless, it would reflect output of correct answers per hour, for whatever the reason. This measure would work best in heavy-demand libraries. Research use of this measure in libraries where demand is usually heavy might be very helpful in clarifying the relationship between volume, quality, and cost. This appears to be one of the few measures that takes all three of these into account at the same time.
VALIDITY AND RELIABILITY: No information available.
BIBLIOGRAPHICAL REFERENCE: McClure (1984).
AVAILABILITY: This instrument is available on an accompanying disk under the file name McClure1.

AUTHORS: McClure, Charles R., and Hernon, Peter.
TITLE/NAME OF INSTRUMENT: 1) Academic Library User Ticket; 2) Public Library User Ticket; and 3) Count of In-House Users (User Log).
PURPOSE: To estimate number of users of academic and public Government Printing Office depository library materials (paper copy, microfiche, or map), and describe these users in terms of selected characteristics.
DESCRIPTION AND EXPERIENCE WITH USE: Both the public and academic library user tickets (single sheets) consist of seven sections, five of which were to be completed by the user and two by library staff. User questions cover activity, sex, status, education, and, in case of public library users, occupation. Library staff questions cover how and where reference question was received. The in-house materials user log (hourly counts) permitted including in the overall count user activities requiring no library staff intervention. Data were collected for one week, and could be completed by the user (self-administered), by the user with staff assistance, or by staff member observation. Possible sources of error were noted: staff judgments about the written instructions: misperceptions about the purpose of the study; administration of

instruments (example, giving tickets to persons on a library tour); failure of staff to participate; perceptions of documents and a depository item; reference service failure; duplication of users; documents dispersion; and patron reluctance to participate.

USE: A large-scale study was conducted in the fall of 1988 with 80% of the 1,054 U.S. depository libraries participating. Procedures used might be done on a biennial basis, as a separate survey, and as a case site study. Trend data describing users, nonusers, and uses in all types of depository libraries can be established.

REVIEW OF THE INSTRUMENT: User ticket and log count might serve as simple means, with modifications, to obtain use and user data by limiting collection to reference areas at key periods during the year.

VALIDITY AND RELIABILITY: The development of the instruments was guided by knowledge and findings of previous user studies. Experts reviewed and pretested the instruments, and data coding was accurate and consistent. The characteristics of responding libraries closely matched the academic/public depository libraries' population. Direct assistance was available from the investigators and the advisory board.

BIBLIOGRAPHIC REFERENCES: McClure and Hernon (1989).

AVAILABILITY: This instrument is available on an accompanying disk under the file name McClure2.

AUTHOR: McCue, Janice Helen

TITLE/NAME OF INSTRUMENT: Online Searching in Public Libraries

PURPOSE: To compare and analyze the quality of online searching in public libraries in order to provide understanding of factors that enhance or detract from quality of database searching. Developed for public libraries but could be replicated in other types of libraries.

DESCRIPTION AND EXPERIENCE WITH USE: Using the method of unobtrusive observation, the author presented a single multifaceted question to searchers in 21 U.S. public libraries. The question was designed so that it could be searched in ABI/Inform and National Newspaper Index. These same questions were also searched on the same databases by seven outside experts. The results of both sets of searches were evaluated by panelists on a seven-point system of scoring. Follow-up interviews were then conducted with the online searcher and supervisor to collect information on factors that might have affected quality of results.

USE: Used by the author in a study of 21 public libraries in 1984.

REVIEW OF THE INSTRUMENT: This method might be used for judging the quality of online ready reference searching in a library. It should, however, be used as a research method rather than a tool to measure the quality of online ready reference searching in any particular library since the test questions might not be representative of that library's questions.

VALIDITY AND RELIABILITY: This method, the question used, and the questionnaire to obtain data about the searcher and the library were pretested in two libraries.

BIBLIOGRAPHICAL REFERENCE: McCue (1988).

AVAILABILITY: Those wishing to use this method should consult the book by McCue (1988).

AUTHOR: Miller, Edward P.

TITLE/NAME OF INSTRUMENT: Preference and Feasibility Measure

PURPOSE: To devise a measure that would represent both client preferences and management rating of feasibility of alternative courses of action. Designed for information centers or special libraries.

DESCRIPTION AND EXPERIENCE WITH USE: An experimental measure is proposed in which both client and management ratings are combined. Users are given a ballot where, for example one to three alternatives are given, along with the advantages and disadvantages of each. The user votes *both* yes and no in percentages (summing to 100) on each alternative, according to the strength of the opinion. For example, if the user feels somewhat strongly about an alternative, he or she might vote 80% yes and 20% no. Managers then vote on a percentage of feasibility that this alternative will actually be implemented. Average percentages for alternatives are then compiled for both users and managers. For each alternative the user percentage of yes votes is multiplied times the average manager feasibility rating. Ratings for alternatives are compared and the highest represents the most desirable alternative.

USE: Proposed for use by the author.

REVIEW OF THE INSTRUMENT: Advantages of this method are the ease of obtaining the data and the simple but elegant method of reconciling many shadings of divergent opinion.

VALIDITY AND RELIABILITY: No information available.

BIBLIOGRAPHICAL REFERENCE: Miller (1973).

AVAILABILITY: This instrument is available on an accompanying disk under the file name Miller.

AUTHORS: Murfin, Marjorie, and Bunge, Charles

TITLE/NAME OF INSTRUMENT: Cost Benefit Formula

PURPOSE: To be used with Reference Transaction Assessment Instrument success data to determine cost in staff time in relation to the benefit of patron time saved. Developed for academic libraries.

DESCRIPTION AND EXPERIENCE WITH USE: Benefits to the patron of reference service are described. Time saved by the patron is considered as the unit of benefit and translated into a dollar value. A benefit ratio of seven times cost per transaction or $13 benefit per transaction was postulated. As a negative benefit measure, $12 was subtracted for each unsuccessful transaction on the grounds of inconvenience and frustration experienced by the patron.

USE: Used with Wisconsin-Ohio reference data in 1989.

REVIEW OF THE INSTRUMENT: Advantages are that this measure was considered by a statistician to be promising and appears to have power of discrimination. Disadvantages are that the benefit measure is not founded on research in regard to time saved (other than that of Kramer, 1971) and is experimental in nature.

VALIDITY AND RELIABILITY: No data available.

BIBLIOGRAPHIC REFERENCE: Murfin and Bunge (1989).

AVAILABILITY: This instrument is available on an accompanying disk under the file name Murfin1.

AUTHORS: Murfin, Marjorie, and Bunge, Charles

TITLE/NAME OF INSTRUMENT: Cost in Staffing Time per *Successful* Question

PURPOSE: To be used with the Wisconsin-Ohio Reference Evaluation Program to determine the costs in staff time per *successful* reference question. Developed for an academic library.

DESCRIPTION: This method is meant to be used with the Wisconsin-Ohio Reference Evaluation Program measure of success, but could be used with other success measures. The total time spent in answering reference questions during a particular observation period is divided by the number of questions that were successfully answered.

USE: Recommended by McClure and used by the authors in 1988 to analyze reference question data from 44 academic libraries.

REVIEW OF THE INSTRUMENT: This method is useful if a library has both success data and time-spent data for each question. A warning in regard to this type of cost-effectiveness measure is that it should not be used to make decisions about the *worth* of different types of patrons' questions and questions in different subject areas. The value and worth of an activity and its success should be two separate judgments. A judgment should *not* be made about the worth or value of an activity on the basis of cost-effectiveness analysis.

VALIDITY AND RELIABILITY: No information available.

BIBLIOGRAPHICAL REFERENCE: Murfin and Bunge (1989).

AVAILABILITY: This instrument is available on an accompanying disk under the file name Murfin2.

AUTHORS: Murfin, Marjorie, and Bunge, Charles
TITLE/NAME OF INSTRUMENT: Determining the Full Cost of the Reference Question
PURPOSE: To determine the full cost to the library of one reference transaction. Developed for academic libraries.
DESCRIPTION AND EXPERIENCE WITH USE: This method takes into account reference collection costs, but is based on the premise put forth by Samuel Rothstein that reference questions are not the only output of the reference department. Use of the reference collection by *unaided* patrons should also be credited to the reference department as a separate output. For this reason, only *part* of reference collection costs should be charged to the cost of a reference question. Also, only the time spent at the reference desk actually answering questions should be charged to the cost of a reference question. Figures needed for this method are annual staff salaries, library and university overhead, reference materials budget, contractual and supplies costs, estimation for collection maintenance, volume of reference questions, online searches, lectures/tours, and an estimation of the number of patron and librarian uses of the reference collection per year. Personnel time allocation figures needed are reference questions handled on and off the desk, time spent in reference collection development and maintenance, online searches, lectures, and in nonreference department-related library activities. An illustration of how this works is given for a test library, which supplied many of the above figures.
USE: Used for the anonymous test library only, in 1988.
REVIEW OF THE INSTRUMENT: An advantage of this method is that it attempts to take account of all costs involved in providing desk reference service, including the cost of maintaining the reference collection. It also allocates costs to *other* outputs of the reference department, including maintaining the reference collection for patron use. A disadvantage is that it requires data which are difficult to obtain, such as volume of use of the reference collection by staff and patrons and allocation of staff time. Another disadvantage is that this method is experimental and the example given is illustrative only, since some of the figures used were estimates from other sources rather than from the test library.
VALIDITY AND RELIABILITY: No data available.
BIBLIOGRAPHIC REFERENCE: Murfin and Bunge (1989).
AVAILABILITY: This instrument is available on an accompanying disk under the file name Murfin3.

AUTHORS: Murfin, Marjorie E., Bunge, Charles A., and Gugelchuk, Gary M.

TITLE/NAME OF INSTRUMENT: Reference Transaction Assessment Instrument (RTAI)

PURPOSE: To evaluate library reference question answering effectiveness in terms of the patron's report of success and the library staff member's viewpoint of the same transaction. Developed for both public and academic libraries, but could also be used for special libraries.

DESCRIPTION AND EXPERIENCE WITH USE: The RTAI, a computer scannable instrument, enables libraries to gather data on perception of question answering success from both the librarian and the patron. Consists of a two-part form used to evaluate each reference transaction from both the patron and the librarian viewpoint. The patron form is torn off and given to the patron after a reference question has been asked. The patron questionnaire has 14 questions including "Did you locate what you asked about at the reference desk?" and "Were you satisfied with the information or materials found or suggested?" The library staff member's form contains six questions including type of question, results, special factors, instruction, sources, and question difficulty. Thus, the form allows the library to gather information on the librarian's and the patron's perceptions regarding other factors in the reference transaction situation. Statistical relationships among these various factors may then be calculated and compared with the national norms. Success is judged by patrons reporting that they found exactly what was wanted and are fully satisfied. The librarian portion of the form has an item where a computerized or CD-ROM search can be indicated. Patron report of success for each computerized transaction can then be determined. Online searches by appointment are not evaluated. The RTAI is available (see Availability below) for sample sizes ranging from 100 to 200 or more questions (a minimum of 100 is recommended). An important element is the data analysis service offered. A database of results of tested libraries is maintained and national norms provided. Several complex analyses of the data are possible but might be difficult to do manually. For this reason, libraries are encouraged to use the modest cost data analysis available which will at the same time contribute to the national database. Several questions in the RTAI have been used to develop a measure of intrinsic question difficulty. This measure, called "Question Complexity and Specificity," utilizes the following questions from the RTAI: 1) Wants a number of things; 2) Must be a certain time period, etc.; 3) Relate two subjects; 4) Analysis, trends, pro con, etc.; 5) Concerned with foreign country, etc.; 6) Wants facts and statistics in general; and 7) Smaller item in larger publication.

USE: In order to evaluate the reference transaction assessment instrument, one public and 17 academic libraries ranging in collection size from 56,000 to four million volumes participated in a pilot test (Murfin and Gugelchuk, 1987). By 1988, 33 U.S. academic libraries with collection sizes ranging from 33,000 to over four million volumes had utilized the RTAI (Murfin and Bunge, 1988a). By 1993, this method has been used on an ongoing basis in 67 academic and 83 public libraries across the nation.

REVIEW OF THE INSTRUMENT: This method has the advantage that comparable data are available and it measures an important dimension of success. Patron and library staff success on the RTAI is self-reported. Other methods of assessing success—for example, from the expert viewpoint—should also be used. The findings of Murfin and Bunge are supported by Woodard's (1989) study, which indicates that more accurate answers and referrals are provided when support staff members are able to consult with other staff. The objective measure of intrinsic question difficulty is significantly related to success in answering questions ($X^2 = 15.22$, $p < .0005$). The measure also appears to be quite useful in assessing level of personnel needed to answer complex and specific questions successfully. Libraries that have chosen to use the RTAI are self-selected. The national database of results may not be representative of libraries generally.

VALIDITY AND RELIABILITY: The RTAI has been tested for reliability and validity (Murfin and Gugelchuk, 1987). Validity was arrived at by comparison with previous studies of accuracy of reference service in academic libraries. Murfin and Gugelchuk (1987) found that the number of times a patron found exactly what was wanted on factual questions was 46%. This result was not statistically different than the findings by Myers (49%) and Jirjees (57%) in their unobtrusive studies of academic libraries (Myers, 1983; Jirjees, 1983). Reliability was tested by using an analysis of intercorrelation of multiple, parallel measures to see that the measurements were yielding the same results. The reliability estimate theta computed at the two-cluster stage indicated reliability was .89 for the patron-derived variable cluster and .76 for the librarian-derived cluster. Results using this instrument compare favorably with other instruments/studies. Results indicate that the RTAI is a viable means of testing reference question answering effectiveness. Return rates for the RTAI are generally very high, ranging from a low of 80.0 percent to a high of 97.67 percent. The patron portion of this form has a reliability coefficient of .90 and the librarian form one of .76. Criteria used to measure intrinsic question difficulty level are complexity and specificity. The measure of intrinsic question difficulty level can be no more than a rough approximation of true intrinsic difficulty level because any particular characteristic can vary widely in actual search difficulty. A more discriminating measure in terms of success rates could be developed if it were possible to add additional elements, such as obscurity of the subject and unsuitability to structure of resources. This enriched measure would probably result in lower success rates for intrinsically difficult questions in academic and public libraries but it would also increase the subjectivity of the measure. The original goal was to develop a relatively objective measure of intrinsic difficulty level of reference questions, which would be based on librarian report of the characteristics of reference questions, but at the same time be apart from the librarian's subjective judgment of difficulty level. Questions measuring complexity and specificity were selected on the basis of logic but were included only if empirical evidence showed lower than average success rates in academic libraries. In regard to complexity, the measure appears to represent the major elements of intrinsic complexity in nonfactual questions, including multiple subject; restrictions including on date, period, place, and language; analysis; trends; pro con; and how-to-do-it. Specificity was represented by questions where facts and statistics were wanted and a short answer was not appropriate. However, for specificity the measure does not represent short answer facts because a way could not be found to reliably distinguish common routine short answer factual questions from obscure short answer factual questions; the judgment of obscurity depended too much on the individual rater. When data for all libraries were combined, regardless of sample size, success rates for Complex and Specific Questions as compared to other types of questions were significantly different for academic libraries (55% versus 60%) but not significantly different for public libraries (62.5% versus 60%). Question Complexity and Specificity was significantly related to actual reported difficulty level by librarians both in academic libraries ($X^2 = 175.615$, $p < .0005$) and in public libraries ($X^2 = 147.419$, $p < .0005$). Fully 84% of those questions marked as intrinsically difficult were also marked by librarians as moderate or greater in difficulty. Reference support staff were significantly less successful than reference librarians on Complex and Specific Questions (44.3% versus 59.0%; $X^2 = 10.45$, $df = 1$, $p = .001$). On questions not characterized as complex and specific, there was no difference in success rates between reference support staff and librarians (Murfin and Bunge, 1988a).

BIBLIOGRAPHIC REFERENCES: Murfin and Gugelchuk (1987). Murfin and Bunge (1988a). Binkley and Eadie (1989). Murfin (1989). **Evaluative Reports** Woodard (1989).

AVAILABILITY: This instrument is available on an accompanying disk under the file name Murfin4. The most cost-effective method of utilizing the form is to order copies from Charles A. Bunge, School of Library and Information Studies, University of Wisconsin-Madison, 600 N. Park St., Madison, WI 53706. Price for the forms also includes valuable time-saving services of data processing and printing results. Comparative data from other libraries are supplied as well.

AUTHORS: Murfin, Marjorie, and Harrick, Rosemary
TITLE/NAME OF INSTRUMENT: Murfin-Harrick Reference Survey
PURPOSE: To study patterns of reference source use in relation to class level and status of patrons. Used in an academic library.
DESCRIPTION AND EXPERIENCE WITH USE: Consists of a folded slip of paper with one half to be marked by the patron and the other by the librarian. After a reference question has been asked, the librarian asks the patron to mark his or her class/status and return the slip. After the reference transaction has been completed the librarian then completes the rest of the form, briefly noting the question and any problems, and checking a time category. Sources are divided into four columns: periodical indexes and abstracts, reference books and bibliographies, author catalog, and subject catalog. The librarian jots down an abbreviated source name under the correct column, checks any use of the catalog, and checks if answer was found. Does not have a measure of success or satisfaction.
USE: Used at Kent State University in 1972. A total of 150 reference transactions were surveyed in the sample period.
REVIEW OF THE INSTRUMENT: May be used to study the relationship between type and number of sources used, and the relationship between number and type of patrons (graduate, undergraduate, and so on) and type of question (reference or directional). For example, How do questions asked by freshmen differ from those asked by graduate students? What sources are most frequently used for each different level of patron?
VALIDITY AND RELIABILITY: No data available.
BIBLIOGRAPHIC REFERENCES: None.
AVAILABILITY: This instrument is available on an accompanying disk under the file name Murfin5.

AUTHOR: Murphy, Marcy
TITLE/NAME OF INSTRUMENT: Costing of All Reference Operations
PURPOSE: To generate profiles of departmental functions and fix quick dollar estimates on costs of reference service functions. Developed for an academic library but could be modified for another type of library.
DESCRIPTION AND EXPERIENCE WITH USE: In this method, a two-week study is done, during which time each reference staff member keeps a diary recording the number of minutes spent in each of 105 numbered tasks. Staff are also interviewed and asked for estimates of how much time they spent on various tasks. Staff wages per minute (plus a percentage of overhead) are then multiplied times minutes spent during the sample period for each activity. This total cost is then divided by the

number of transactions handled during this period. In this way, relative costs for reference functions can be determined.

USE: Used in the Air Force University Library in 1973.

REVIEW OF THE INSTRUMENT: The timing in minutes permits data to be more useful for costing purposes because they are more precise. The task list is comprehensive but needs to be updated, revised, and adapted for use in any particular library. It has advantages in that it costs all reference tasks, rather than just reference service at the reference desk.

VALIDITY AND RELIABILITY: Staff agreed that the tasks were representative and the diary and the separate interview method (where each staff member gave percentage estimates of time spent on each task) agreed on major time-consuming tasks. The author suggests that staff estimates of time and tasks might yield sufficient valid and reliable data without additional diary or observed sample studies. Staff had good perceptions of the *percentage* of time spent on different activities. However, their idea of *how often* they performed a task or the exact number of minutes spent was not reliable. Because the costing formula is based on frequency in minutes, it should not be used with estimate data.

BIBLIOGRAPHICAL REFERENCE: Murphy (1978).

AVAILABILITY: This instrument is available on an accompanying disk under the file name Murphy. Reference to the original study might be needed.

AUTHOR: Nowack, Kenneth

TITLE/NAME OF INSTRUMENT: Stress Assessment Profile (SAP)

PURPOSE: To assess stress and health in individuals in the work setting.

DESCRIPTION AND EXPERIENCE WITH USE: The author, a psychologist, is a management consultant and director of Organizational Performance Dimensions. The instrument has a total of 123 items. Items are marked in terms of never, rarely, sometimes, often, and almost always. Results are presented in terms of 14 scales, life events stressors, lifestyle, exercise, rest, hygiene, nutrition, social support, type A behavior, hardiness, positive thoughts, negative thoughts, cognitive avoidance coping, problem-focused coping, and psychological well being. The 15th scale provides an estimate of response bias or accuracy of response.

USE: A number of studies were done in the process of developing the instrument. After the final version of the questionnaire was established, it was given to 621 employees attending management training workshops in the Los Angeles area. It has also been given frequently since then. See bibliographic reference for more details.

REVIEW OF THE INSTRUMENT: This is a well-developed instrument. Advantages are that its validity and reliability have been convincingly demonstrated and that a clear and helpful profile is presented to each employee who completed the questionnaire. The profile covers all 15 scores and comments on the employee's stress profile in relation to the norm, that is, whether the employee was above or below the norm of previously-tested persons on each factor. A possible disadvantage is that in the life events stressors scale stressors are listed and grouped in problem areas of health, work, financial, family, social, and environmental. Items in one group may vary from "never" to "often," so marking for the group as a whole may be difficult. It might be better to list and rate stressors separately. Also positive stressors are not included, as in the Holmes Rahe (Kobasa, 1979) scale. However, the SAP measures the perception of stress, in that participants are asked to consider only experiences that "hassled" or stressed them. Nowack notes that this "perceived" stress approach has been found to account for more variance in psychological and health outcomes than the life events approach, which assumes different levels of stress by the type of event, such as the Holmes Rahe scale.
VALIDITY AND RELIABILITY: The average internal consistency reliability across all scales was .76 with a range from .67 to .93. Criterion-related validity was assessed in a study where 194 respondents completed the SAP, and also completed three other instruments measuring 1) psychological distress—Hopkins Symptom Checklist, 2) physical illness—Greenberg Measure; and 3) psychological well being—Stress Assessment Inventory. These instruments all have demonstrated internal consistency reliability. Multiple regressions for SAP scales with respect to these three instruments indicated that the shared variance ranged from .48 to .78.
BIBLIOGRAPHIC REFERENCES: Nowack (1990).
AVAILABILITY: Contact the author at Organizational Performance Dimensions, 20950-38, Oxnard St., Woodland Hills, CA 91367.

AUTHORS: New York University, Elmer Holmes Bobst Library; The University of California at Riverside Library
TITLE/NAME OF INSTRUMENT: Selected User Survey Items
PURPOSE: To study the outcomes of library users' searches for materials and/or information.
DESCRIPTION AND EXPERIENCE WITH USE: Developed for academic libraries. The first item asks users how successful they were, with four choices: excellent (found everything), good (found most things), fair (found some things), and poor (found few things). The second item asks users whether they were *both* successful and efficient in their searches, and asks for each user's feeling as to his or her own

ability to find materials and information without wasting time and effort. The third item asks whether the user has ever been misdirected from one campus library to another.

USE: The first two items were used by the Bobst Library in a survey given out in classrooms February through March of 1976. Return rate is not known, but returns were obtained from 1,748 students. The third item was given in a survey by the University of California at Riverside in a survey during April and May of 1980. Questionnaires were handed out to users entering the library on a prearranged schedule. Return rate is not given, but 1,584 completed questionnaires were obtained.

REVIEW OF THE INSTRUMENT: One advantage of the first two items is that they appear to have power of discrimination and avoid positive bias. Another advantage is that both success and efficiency can be assessed by the same question. Disadvantages are that data are available from only one library and responses are based on experiences over time, which tend to be more subjective. An advantage of the third item is that it is one of the few attempts in overall surveys to explore referrals from one library to another. Disadvantages are that it does not gain information on how frequently misdirection occurs and it does not identify where the misdirection originated, how much of the user's time was wasted, and the success of the eventual outcome.

VALIDITY AND RELIABILITY: No information available.

BIBLIOGRAPHICAL REFERENCES: New York University (1981). University of California at Riverside (1981).

AVAILABILITY: This instrument is available on an accompanying disk under the file name New York.

AUTHOR: Phipps, Shelley, and Dickstein, Ruth
TITLE/NAME OF INSTRUMENT: Library Knowledge Questionnaire
PURPOSE: To determine the effectiveness of the *Workbook in library skills* by Miriam Dudley in improving library skills of students in beginning English classes.
DESCRIPTION AND EXPERIENCE WITH USE: Consists of a set of 16 questions. Questions were a combination of true or false and multiple choice and were based on skills taught in the *Workbook*. Some additional questions, which were not included in the pretest, were added to the posttest and are reported in the results.
USE: A pretest was given to four English 2 sections and five English 3 sections at the University of Arizona for a total of 280 students who would be using the *Workbook* in library skills over the next six weeks. A control group of four English 2 and four English 3 sections (a total of 207 students) were also given the pretest. Six weeks later after the *Workbook* had been completed a posttest was given to 243 students in the *Workbook* group and 179 students in the control group.

REVIEW OF THE INSTRUMENT: While this instrument is outdated in terms of computer systems, it could be updated and adapted. The skills needed for effective library use are well represented, although the methods by which these skills are attained may have changed with increasing automation of reference resources.
VALIDITY AND RELIABILITY: No information is provided.
BIBLIOGRAPHIC REFERENCES: Phipps and Dickstein (1979).
AVAILABILITY: This instrument is available on an accompanying disk under the file name Phipps.

AUTHORS: Raffel, Jeffrey, and Shishko, Robert.
TITLE/NAME OF INSTRUMENT: Benefit Survey.
PURPOSE: To obtain user feedback on benefits of various aspects of library service as opposed to costs. This information was intended to help in decision making about allocation of library resources.
DESCRIPTION AND EXPERIENCE WITH USE: Intended for use in an academic library. Consists of a four-page set of instructions and a two-page questionnaire. The first page lists 20 alternatives to improve services or save money along with their costs, and gives three columns representing budgets of $200,000, $100,000, and $0. Respondents are asked to check those items they would want to preserve and those they would want to cut under the three different budgetary conditions. The second page asks for demographic data, library use, amount spent on personal books, and money spent on books for courses. Another item lists nine library functions and asks respondents to check those that are significant to them.
USE: This survey was mailed to 700 faculty and students of the M.I.T. Library to obtain information about how library resources should be allocated. Response rate was 40%.
REVIEW OF THE INSTRUMENT: This survey appears to be a cost preference study rather than a cost benefit study, in that users choose according to the benefits and lack of benefits they perceive for each alternative. The survey does not attempt to translate benefits into dollars. While this study is concerned with library services rather than reference services, the method would be adaptable to reference services. This method differs from Halperin and Strazdon's (1980) in that users are asked to reconcile their preferences within budgetary limitations. The complex cost and benefit balancing required here would probably discourage some respondents. However, the cover letter from the library director and the methodology are designed to obtain maximum cooperation. The authors give evidence that respondents understood the choices and responded in a consistent manner. This instrument could be useful in any institution that wished to explore allocation of resources in terms of costs and benefits. It may not be advisable to mail out this type of

cost/benefit survey where respondents must complete a complex task. A low return rate can probably be expected, unless users are reasonably sophisticated and well-motivated.

VALIDITY AND RELIABILITY: No information available.

BIBLIOGRAPHICAL REFERENCE: Raffel and Shishko (1969).

AVAILABILITY: This instrument is available on an accompanying disk under the file name Raffel.

AUTHOR: Reeves, Edward B., Howell, Benita J., and Van Willigen, John

TITLE/NAME OF INSTRUMENT: Activities Performed in the Reference Department

PURPOSE: To apply the concepts and methods of role analysis to determine the perceptions of reference librarians about their tasks. Developed for an academic library but could be adapted for all types of libraries.

DESCRIPTION AND EXPERIENCE WITH USE: An exhaustive task list of 93 tasks was complied and then narrowed to 45 tasks. Each librarian and paraprofessional rated each task on a seven-point scale with regard to 1) importance; 2) interest; 3) complexity; and 4) confidence of staff in ability to perform.

USE: Used at the University of Kentucky Library around 1976. Results were reported for both professional and support staff.

REVIEW OF THE INSTRUMENT: This instrument was designed with the aid of an anthropologist and approaches reference tasks and duties from the standpoint of staff perceptions. For this reason, it should provide a unique dimension in evaluation and be a valuable method for detecting any specific problems staff perceive in these areas and for adjusting staff assignments for maximum effectiveness.

VALIDITY AND RELIABILITY: Using Kendall's Tau, a number of positive correlations were found between groups of tasks.

BIBLIOGRAPHIC REFERENCES: Reeves, Howell, and Van Willigen (1977).

AVAILABILITY: This instrument is available on an accompanying disk under the file name Reeves. Those interested in applying this method should read the article by Reeves, Howell, and Van Willigen (1977).

AUTHOR: Regazzi, John, and Hersberger, Rodney M.

TITLE/NAME OF INSTRUMENT: Queuing Study

PURPOSE: To investigate actual patron delay time at an academic reference desk and to suggest optimum staffing patterns to minimize delay time.

DESCRIPTION AND EXPERIENCE WITH USE: Done in an academic library but could be used in other types of libraries. Regazzi and Hersberger sampled 30-minute peak and nonpeak periods of the day over six months. They recorded for each patron 1) arrival time; 2) time helped; and 3) time left (including those patrons who left before being helped).

USE: Used in a study of the Northern Illinois University reference department in 1978.

REVIEWER'S COMMENTS: Queuing studies have advantages in that they can provide figures on number experiencing delay, number leaving before being helped, average delay time, maximum delay time, and delay time of patrons who leave before being helped. For example, during peak periods Regazzi found an average delay time of 5.86 minutes with the longest delays being 12 to 25 minutes. Another advantage is that samples are usually taken over a span of time so that generalizations can be made about service during that period. In addition, predictions can be made about future outcomes under different conditions. Regazzi's queuing study is particularly noteworthy in focusing on comparisons of peak and nonpeak periods. He found that in order to keep delay time down during peak periods, the time given to each patron was shortened by almost 28%. If the same amount of time had been given as at nonpeak periods, delay time would have risen to a high of eight minutes per person. Data like this highlight clearly the dilemma of peak periods and the tradeoffs between quality and accessibility that must be made. Such data could be very helpful in examining options and working out compromise solutions.

VALIDITY AND RELIABILITY: No information available.

BIBLIOGRAPHIC REFERENCE: Regazzi and Hersberger (1978).

AVAILABILITY: This instrument is available on an accompanying disk under the file name Regazz1. The article by Regazzi and Hersberger (1978) should be consulted for further details of this method.

AUTHOR: Robertson, W. Davenport

TITLE/NAME OF INSTRUMENT: Library/Technical Information Services Survey

PURPOSE: To develop a user-orientated model for setting priorities for services.

DESCRIPTION AND EXPERIENCE WITH USE: Designed to be used in a special science and technology library. Consists of a list of 11 services, including 1) audiovisual material, 2) book and technical report purchases, 3) cataloging, 4) circulation, 5) computerized literature searching, 6) photocopying, 7) interlibrary loan, 8) journal purchases, 9) newsletter, 10) other reference and information services (verifying, indexing, and so on), and 11) physical facilities.

USE: Used at National Institute of Environmental Health Sciences Library in Research Triangle Park, North Carolina, around 1978. A total of 1,200 questionnaires were mailed out to research staff of three organizations of similar size; of these 35% were returned. Respondents were asked to rank the 11 aspects of library service from 1 to 11 in regard to the order they thought the library should follow in allocating personnel and fiscal resources.

REVIEW OF THE INSTRUMENT: This method of ranking is relatively simple and useful and its greatest advantage is in the speed with which a cluster of high and low priority services can be identified. This study is a good example of how this was accomplished. It differs from the study conducted by Halperin and Strazdon (1980) in that each alternative was accompanied by a statement of possible advantages and disadvantages as seen by the investigator.

VALIDITY AND RELIABILITY: No information available.

BIBLIOGRAPHICAL REFERENCE: Robertson (1980).

AVAILABILITY: This instrument is available on an accompanying disk under the file name Robertso.

AUTHORS: Rodger, Eleanor Jo, and D'Elia, George D.

TITLE/NAME OF INSTRUMENT: User Study

PURPOSE: To learn more about the users of the Fairfax County Public Library and to aid in planning in library services.

DESCRIPTION AND EXPERIENCE WITH USE: Intended for public library users. Explores information-gathering behavior of users with responses to be made on the basis of present visit only. This six and one-half-page questionnaire contains 20 items, covering reasons for use of a particular library in the Fairfax system, frequency of use, other library use, physical facilities, importance of visits to the library, and services used within the library. Also included are questions on whether users needed help and asked for it, and on their reasons for not asking for help. Also covers style of use, type of material borrowed, demographic data, and distance and means of transportation, and has an open-ended question on benefits of library use that patrons perceive.

USE: Used in 1984 by the Fairfax County Public Library system. The survey was performed in 20 system branches during one week in March. The return rate was 85%, resulting in 7,375 usable forms.

REVIEW OF THE INSTRUMENT: A strong point of this instrument is the section on need for help and reasons for not asking for help. Questions pertaining to reference that this instrument might help to answer are: "How many use the reference collection? How many library users need help in finding materials and information in the library? How many need help but don't ask for it and why not? How do users in the library gain access to information? What part do helpful staff play in motivating users to come to a particular library in preference to others? A possible disadvantage is that question-answering items are not narrowed sufficiently to identify the asking of *reference questions* of *reference personnel*, but instead investigate the asking of any question of any librarian. Also, this instrument does not provide the user any opportunity for input in regard to any aspect of reference other than use and nonuse. A measure of success or satisfaction has not been used.

VALIDITY AND RELIABILITY: No information available.

BIBLIOGRAPHIC REFERENCE: Rodger (1984).

AVAILABILITY: This instrument is available on an accompanying disk under the file name Rodger.

AUTHORS: Saracevic, Tefko, Kantor, Paul, Chamis, Alice, and Trivison, Donna

TITLE/NAME OF INSTRUMENT: Utility Measures

PURPOSE: To study the user context of questions in information retrieval

DESCRIPTION AND EXPERIENCE WITH USE: Five measures, called Utility Measures, that represent the value of a search, as judged by the user, are given on one page. The first is an anchored "Worth Scale" where the user has five choices, varying from "worth much more than the time it took" to "practically worthless." The second is a five-category anchored scale of user time spent from less than one hour to over four hours. The third scale is a five-category anchored dollar value assigned from "can't assign a dollar value" to over $200. The fourth scale is a five-category scale anchored only at the ends and is called the Problem Resolution Scale. It asks what contribution the information made toward resolution of the research problem, from "substantial" to "nothing contributed." The final scale is a five-category scale anchored only at each end and asks users how satisfied they were from "satisfied" to "dissatisfied."

USE: A study was conducted from 1985 to 1987, where 40 users (48% faculty, 37% graduates, and 15% from industry) each posed a written question related to their research. Thirty-nine paid searchers searched each of the questions nine times (without actual contact with the patron). Number of relevant items received per search as judged by patrons, was considered by the author to be a more sensitive measure than the five other overall utility measures.

REVIEW OF THE INSTRUMENT: Advantages of these five outcome measures are that they are well conceived, appear for the most part to measure distinctly separate concepts, and are comprehensive in covering the values that users assign to online paid searches: value for money spent, value for time spent, solution of a problem, and the emotional feeling of satisfaction. Additional advantages are the indications of construct validity and the face validity of results in terms of traditional knowledge in regard to the importance of knowing the user's purpose for the search. A possible disadvantage is the five-point scale used, with anchoring phrases only at each end of each scale. With this type of scale inflation may occur in the second category. An *anchored* scale might have been more sensitive in revealing differences.

VALIDITY AND RELIABILITY: Indications of construct validity were given when these scales were tested with the cross product ratio method of analysis to compare them with precision and recall, as judged by experts. When users were satisfied and valued results highly, the chances that the searches had high precision increased. Generally, with the exception of time spent, utility of results is associated with high precision.

BIBLIOGRAPHIC REFERENCE: Saracevic, Kantor, Chamis, and Trivison (1988).

AVAILABILITY: This instrument is available on an accompanying disk under the file name Saracev. Other details of this method are available in the article by Saracevic, Kantor, Chamis and Trivison (1988).

AUTHOR: Schwartz, Diane G., and Eakin, Dottie
TITLE/NAME OF INSTRUMENT: Checklist of Reference Skills
PURPOSE: To improve the quality of reference desk service by developing standards for evaluating the performance of reference librarians.

DESCRIPTION AND EXPERIENCE WITH USE: A checklist of reference skills extracts behaviors, skills, and knowledge to evaluate from indicators of service standards. The checklist offers a choice of three levels of performance: 1) always performs at this level; 2) usually performs at this level; and 3) performance needs improvement.

USE: The Reference/Information Services Department at the Alfred Taubman Medical Library at the University of Michigan developed and used the checklist. Prior to 1984, the head of the department bore sole responsibility for preparing performance appraisals. The Checklist of Reference Skills was developed as a part of devising a means by which each reference librarian could participate in evaluation. For a period of four months, two librarians were scheduled to work together at the reference desk on a rotating basis for the two busiest hours of the day. Librarians then were asked to anonymously complete a checklist for every other member of the department. The checklists were submitted to the head of the department, who analyzed the results and met with each individual to discuss the findings. The results were used to prepare the annual merit review and write problem-solving goals for skill improvement. In a second cycle, each librarian used the checklist for self-evaluation, which was compared with one completed by the head of the department. The second cycle was not associated with the merit review process, but was included in the annual performance review.

REVIEW OF THE INSTRUMENT: Despite efforts to emphasize objective factors in the checklist, staff perceived its use by peers as threatening.

VALIDITY AND RELIABILITY: Individuals were not always consistent in evaluation, and thus destructive competition was created when this peer review was tied to merit evaluation.

BIBLIOGRAPHIC REFERENCES: Schwartz and Eakin (1986).

AVAILABILITY: This instrument is available on an accompanying disk under the file name Schwartz.

AUTHOR: Slavens, Thomas P.

TITLE/NAME OF INSTRUMENT: Semantic Differential Scale

PURPOSE: To assess attitudinal changes as a function of exposure to computer technology.

DESCRIPTION AND EXPERIENCE WITH USE: The semantic differential is a seven-step scale having a bi-polar form of verbal opposites defined by adjectives. All adjectives used were pairs identified and studied by Osgood, Suci, and Tannenbaum (1967). Using 20 paired adjectives, students rate their feelings on each of 16 concepts: school, computer, learning, automation, technology, teaching machine, study, University of Michigan, test, programmed instruction, library, browsing, teaching, books, student, and freedom.

USE: The scale was administered to three sections of a reference course at the University of Michigan, two of which used a computer-aided instruction program to simulate reference interviews, and one which did not. A test was given at the end of the semester to determine if any changes in attitudes had taken place.

REVIEW OF THE INSTRUMENT: Semantic differential scales commonly use seven alternatives because it has been found that all of them tend to be used and with roughly equal frequencies (Osgood, 1967); evidence shows that for individual subjects a shift of more than two scale units probably represents a significant change or difference in meaning, and a shift of more than 1.00 to 1.50 scale units in factor score is probably significant. For group data, changes or differences in measured meaning as small as one-half of a scale unit are significant at the .05 level.

VALIDITY AND RELIABILITY: General face validity is high, because the scale obviously differentiates among and clusters concepts much the way most people do spontaneously. There is considerable correspondence found between the semantic differential and instances where subjects determine their own dimensions of judgment, but more data are needed to determine if the semantic differential forces subjects to use unnatural bases of judgment. There is also little evidence to suggest that the semantic differential can accurately predict meaningful behaviors in test situations.

BIBLIOGRAPHIC REFERENCES: Slavens (1979).

AVAILABILITY: This instrument is available on an accompanying disk under the file name Slavens.

AUTHOR: Spencer, Carol C.

TITLE/NAME OF INSTRUMENT: Cost Analysis for Types of Reference Questions

PURPOSE: To determine the cost of different types of reference questions. Developed for a medical library but could be adapted for other types of libraries.

DESCRIPTION AND EXPERIENCE WITH USE: The author defined the elements of reference work as directional, quick facts, biographical, provision of prepared bibliographies, verification, literature search, instructional, consultation, training, tours, and miscellaneous. RAMs or random alarm mechanisms, were set for five to ten alarms per working day for eight reference librarians or 40 observational periods per day. At alarm times staff recorded the activity in which they were engaged.

USE: Used at the National Library of Medicine around 1979.

REVIEW OF THE INSTRUMENT: The RAM method is said to be superior to the diary method because it has "minimal interference with service operations, minimal distortion of collected data, and acceptable reliability at low cost."

VALIDITY AND RELIABILITY: Said by the author to give acceptable reliability at low cost. This method has been frequently used in work measurement.

BIBLIOGRAPHIC REFERENCE: Spencer (1980).

AVAILABILITY: Details of this method are available in the article by Spencer (1980).

AUTHOR: Standera, Oldrich R.

TITLE/NAME OF INSTRUMENT: Cost-Effectiveness Account

PURPOSE: To demonstrate, through use of a case study, how cost effectiveness and cost benefit data can be obtained and recorded for computerized searches in an academic library.

DESCRIPTION AND EXPERIENCE WITH USE: After receiving their search, users were given a feedback card. Each month a cost-effectiveness chart was prepared, summarizing costs (direct and indirect costs, broken down into SDI and retrospective mode, and divided by database used). Cost effectiveness was measured by cost per user and cost per relevant citation. The revenue per profile is used as a measure of benefit per user on the grounds that willingness to pay is an expression of the value of the search to the user.

USE: Used by the author in a case study of an information system prior to 1973 for one month.

REVIEW OF THE INSTRUMENT: This study is of interest in that it presents both cost effectiveness and cost benefit data that can be compiled on a monthly basis. Cost per relevant reference appears to be a good measure of effectiveness. Willingness to pay, however, presents some problems as a benefit measure. Searches are generally priced according to costs rather than demand or willingness to pay.

VALIDITY AND RELIABILITY: No data available.

BIBLIOGRAPHIC REFERENCE: Standera (1973).

AVAILABILITY: This instrument is available on an accompanying disk under the file name Standera. The article by Standera (1973) should be consulted for more details.

AUTHOR: Strong, Gary

TITLE/NAME OF INSTRUMENT: Pattern of Information Requests Survey (PIRS) and User Ticket

PURPOSE: To evaluate and monitor services provided to the public in order to make best use of resources.

DESCRIPTION AND EXPERIENCE WITH USE: Developed for a state library, this instrument evaluates many aspects of reference service in the setting of the library and also explores some aspects of information-seeking behavior. Present-visit-only data are utilized. It consists of two parts, a user ticket given to all those entering the library and a Pattern of Information Requests form, which is filled out by reference staff. The survey was customarily conducted for a one- to three-day period. The user ticket consists of two parts covering demographic information, purpose of visit in terms of materials and services sought, and whether use was for job, school, leisure, or personal need. One question asks whether the material/information being sought was found, and an open-ended item then asks for barriers encountered to be described. The user is *then* asked if the reference department (books, librarians) was used, and if so, to proceed to a separate section of the questionnaire. This separate section asks whether the user asked for help, and if not, why not. Following this, users check on a five-point satisfaction scale appropriateness, completeness, and accuracy of information/materials provided. Availability of staff and materials are also rated on the same five-point scale. During the same period that users fill out tickets, reference staff also complete a Pattern of Information Requests form. This is in the form of a log sheet for recording user status, type of question, sources used, referrals, and whether or not the question was answered.

USE: Forms of this instrument were used at Washington State Library for periodic evaluation, usually quarterly, on a regular basis. The survey forms were generally given out for one to three days.
REVIEW OF THE INSTRUMENT: This instrument evaluates many aspects of reference service in the setting of the library and is used on present-visit-only data. It also explores information-seeking behavior to some extent. One strong point of this instrument is the thorough coverage of reference. It attempts to provide answers for many of the questions important to reference including the following: What are the success rates of library users who do and do not consult reference? How many asked questions in the reference department? How many needed help but did not ask for it and why not? How available are reference staff? What is the satisfaction of users with the staff and with the appropriateness, completeness, and accuracy of information/materials provided? How many used reference materials but did not consult reference? To what extent are needed reference materials available? Other advantages are its suitability for continuing evaluation and the way user tickets are marked in 15-minute blocks of time so that different times of the day can be compared. A possible disadvantage is that there is no way provided to distinguish whether a reference or directional question was asked, so that some responses of asking for help may represent directional questions. Also, some questions asked outside of the reference area may be included. Even though *only* users of reference are asked to complete the last part of the ticket, the questions themselves are not narrowed to reference department experiences. Also, there is no *success* question related specifically to the outcome of the reference transaction, and the five-point satisfaction scales may be subject to positive bias in the second category.
VALIDITY AND RELIABILITY: No information available.
BIBLIOGRAPHIC REFERENCES: Strong (1980a). Strong (1980b).
AVAILABILITY: This instrument is available on an accompanying disk under the file name Strong.

AUTHOR: Strother, Jeanne D.
TITLE/NAME OF INSTRUMENT: Strother's Questionnaire A and B
PURPOSE: To investigate faculty use and awareness of reference works in an academic library.
DESCRIPTION AND EXPERIENCE WITH USE: Questionnaire A, three pages, is intended to determine which older, established reference materials faculty members need; 52 titles are listed under ten categories such as abstracts, bibliographies, and indexes. Questionnaire B, ten pages, asks faculty to indicate their acquaintance with and use of a list of more current reference titles. The instrument uses a checklist style for responses.

USE: The study, completed as a master's thesis, was conducted in the mid-1970s with a population of 26 faculty from the Department of Speech at Ball State University, Indiana. The study was done on an exploratory level and was not strongly conclusive.

REVIEW OF THE INSTRUMENT: The approach is useful to uncover hidden faculty needs, and could easily be updated, especially to include electronic sources.

VALIDITY AND RELIABILITY: Information not available.

BIBLIOGRAPHIC REFERENCES: Strother (1975).

AVAILABILITY: This instrument is available on an accompanying disk under the file name Strother.

AUTHOR: Tagliacozzo, Renata

TITLE/NAME OF INSTRUMENT: Follow-Up Questionnaire

PURPOSE: To assess the outcome of MEDLINE searches

DESCRIPTION AND EXPERIENCE WITH USE: Consists of seven items. The first is a four-category anchored scale: not helpful, moderately helpful, helpful, and very helpful. The second item asks, if helpful, in what way with alternatives of time and effort saved, providing references that might have been missed, uncovering new field, gave feeling of security, and other. The third item asks if any references were missed. The fourth item asks two questions with yes-no answers—if the search was of value for the particular information need. The fifth item is a line-type scale where the user checks from completely useless to very useful. Item six asks how many references were relevant and, of those, how many were useful. Item seven asks about future use.

USE: The questionnaire was developed by the author during her work as associate research scientist at the Mental Health Research Institute, University of Michigan, Ann Arbor, Michigan. In 1973 MEDLINE users in seven information centers were sent a follow-up questionnaire. Return rate was 90% with 904 forms analyzed. It was found that there was a strong positive correlation between the term "helpful" and the term "useful." "Helpful" appeared to be the broader term in that a number marked that a search was helpful but not useful. From the data provided, some 60% found some relevant references. The data suggested that the less knowledge a user has of the subject of the search, the higher the satisfaction.

REVIEW OF THE INSTRUMENT: The author notes that single overall judgments of a service should be looked at with suspicion. This study appears to indicate that "helpfulness" and "usefulness" may not be sufficiently discriminating for use in judging the success of a particular search. Ninety percent found the search to have *some* degree of helpfulness, 80% found it generally to have some usefulness, while the percent who found *some* relevant references was closer to 60%. Utility

measures (Saracevic, Kantor, Chamis, and Trivison, 1988) may be more discriminating measures of success of an individual search. Of particular interest are the items describing the *ways* in which the search was helpful and whether any items were missed.
VALIDITY AND RELIABILITY: No information available.
BIBLIOGRAPHICAL REFERENCE: Tagliacozzo (1977).
AVAILABILITY: This instrument is available on an accompanying disk under the file name Tagliaco.

AUTHOR: University of Arizona Central Reference Department
TITLE/NAME OF INSTRUMENT: CRD Reference Desk Performance Standards/Peer Review Form
PURPOSE: This instrument has been used by reference department staff and the department head for annual personnel evaluations.
DESCRIPTION AND EXPERIENCE WITH USE: There are seven areas of evaluation. Each area is clearly defined. They include communication style with users, both verbal and nonverbal; user interaction at the reference desk; co-worker interaction at the reference desk; and knowledge of collections and personal qualities/traits exhibited at the reference desk towards users and co-workers. There is space for additional comments at the end. A four-point scale is used to rate each of these areas. The four points are defined as seldom, not frequent enough, sometimes, and most of the time.
USE: Rebecca Watson-Boone created the original instrument and modified parts of it in response to staff review and comment. This evaluation instrument has been used over a period of seven years. It has been limited in use to the Main Library of the University of Arizona. Additional revisions are currently underway to reflect other aspects of reference work. A ten-point scale is being tested. The revised version is less oriented toward specific communication cues and takes less time to fill out.
REVIEW OF THE INSTRUMENT: The descriptive detail in this instrument does not leave much to subjective determination, which is good. Under verbal communication, the instrument could add some comment about the use of open-ended questions. Although it has not been used in a research study, it would be useful as a rating tool in this respect as well.
VALIDITY AND RELIABILITY: No statistical measures of reliability have been calculated. Repeated use and refinement of this instrument would suggest validity.
BIBLIOGRAPHIC REFERENCES: None.
AVAILABILITY: This instrument is available on an accompanying disk under the file name Uarizona.

AUTHORS: The University of British Columbia, The University of Colorado, The University of California at Riverside, and The University of Massachusetts
TITLE/NAME OF INSTRUMENT: Selected User Survey Items
PURPOSE: To determine accessibility of reference service.
DESCRIPTION AND EXPERIENCE WITH USE: Developed for academic libraries but could be adapted for other types of libraries. 1) In a survey done by the University of British Columbia, in-library users were asked about their most recent reference encounter, and whether they were able to obtain service immediately, if not, how long they had to wait, and whether they left without having obtained service. 2) The University of Colorado asked users whether they had ever encountered difficulty in locating reference librarians in the reference area. 3) The University of California at Riverside asked users how they felt about having to wait (at the circulation desk). 4) The University of Massachusetts asked reference users for their perceptions of *why* they had to wait.
USE: These questionnaire items have all been previously used.
REVIEW OF THE INSTRUMENT: If the library is already planning to conduct a user study, the user survey method of determining accessibility requires less staff time and outside expertise than a queuing study. The University of British Columbia item, in particular, will give an estimate of those leaving the reference area without having obtained service. It will also give a rough estimate of the total time this group of patrons spent waiting to obtain reference service. The user survey method can also obtain information on patrons' feelings, attitudes, and the degree of inconvenience they suffered due to inaccessibility of reference service. Disadvantages are that in order to learn the *full* extent of inaccessibility, an overall study of all in-library users is needed. These items might be used to survey *only* those in the reference area, but the full extent of inaccessibility might not be discovered this way. Nevertheless, the data might be useful in reflecting perceptions of the most frequent reference users concerning accessibility. The University of British Columbia item is designed to apply to the *one* most recent reference encounter. All of the other items ask for a response based on experiences *over a long period of time.* The present- or one-visit-only method probably gives more precise and less subjective responses, but may be less representative of the total pattern of user experiences over time.
VALIDITY AND RELIABILITY: No data available.
BIBLIOGRAPHICAL REFERENCES: Colorado State University (1981) University of British Columbia (1984). University of Massachusetts. (1976). University of California at Riverside. (1984).
AVAILABILITY: This instrument is available on an accompanying disk under the file name Britcolu.

AUTHORS: University of California at Los Angeles; University of British Columbia; University of California at Riverside
TITLE/NAME OF INSTRUMENT: Selected Items from Overall Library Surveys
PURPOSE: To compare library and/or reference services in regard to importance, preference, and use. These four items were developed for use in academic libraries.
DESCRIPTION AND EXPERIENCE WITH USE: The first item gives a list of six reference services and asks respondents to check all they have found helpful in assisting them to use the library. The second item gives respondents a list of nine services and asks which one was most useful. The third item gives respondents a list of five reference services and asks which ones *would* help increase their knowledge of resources and services.
USE: The first item was part of a survey given to some 772 students in three large undergraduate classes in 1979. The second item was part of a survey where forms were given out to library users and distributed around the campus to 12,000 students and faculty in 1980, with a return rate of 50%. The third item was part of a survey mailed to 1,500 students in 1983, with a return rate of 40%.
REVIEW OF THE INSTRUMENT: These items all illustrate useful ways to obtain information on user preferences for different reference services. The second and third surveys also have an item pertaining to *use* of the different reference services.
VALIDITY AND RELIABILITY: For the University of California at Riverside survey, satisfaction data as reported appear to lack validity because 1) some of the persons who reported never using a service nevertheless gave a satisfaction rating, probably inflating the ratings; and 2) two-category yes-no scales were used and these have been shown to produce inflated ratings.
BIBLIOGRAPHICAL REFERENCES: University of California at Los Angeles (1981). University of British Columbia (1984). University of California at Riverside (1984). Weingart, et al. (1983).
AVAILABILITY: This instrument is available on an accompanying disk under the file name UCLA.

AUTHOR: University of California at Riverside
TITLE/NAME OF INSTRUMENT: UCR Library Services Survey
PURPOSE: To measure awareness of, use of, and satisfaction with library services.
DESCRIPTION AND EXPERIENCE WITH USE: Developed for an academic library. The first section is designed to explore information-gathering behavior and the second to evaluate the performance of particular services. Users' responses are to be based on experiences over

time. Consists of 41 questions, the first 20 of which are concerned with information-gathering behavior and student opinion on particular library issues. Following this 21 different services are listed with columns where the user checks 1) awareness, 2) use in terms of times used per year, and 3) satisfaction in terms of yes or no.

USE: This survey was mailed to all faculty and staff, and to a sample of 500 graduate and 1,000 undergraduate students in 1983. Return rates for the above groups, in order, were 56%, 45%, and 38%.

REVIEW OF THE INSTRUMENT: Services are described with clarity in several sentences and, where necessary, exact location is given in parentheses. Frequency of use data makes it possible to look at perceived patterns of use over time. For example, more weight might need to be given to evaluations of frequent users of a service. These same data on services used and frequency of use could also be used to study information-gathering habits of certain groups of users. Questions it may help to answer are: How aware are users of different library services and areas? How frequently do they use them over a period of time? How well is reference performing in relation to other services? A possible disadvantage is that less objective period-of-time data are used rather than present-visit-only data. Also, there is no success measure and satisfaction is poorly defined on a yes-no scale. These disadvantages could be corrected, however, by making the survey present-visit-only (except for frequency data) and by use of a success scale such as that used by Carnegie Mellon. If period-of-time satisfaction data are desired, the satisfaction scale might be expanded to "completely satisfied, partly satisfied, and unsatisfied." Results also revealed another problem with the satisfaction scale where some respondents rated satisfaction even though they reported *not* having used the service. This might be corrected by removing the "does not apply" column and adding instructions to "mark this item *only* if you have actually used this service."

VALIDITY AND RELIABILITY: No information available.

BIBLIOGRAPHIC REFERENCES: University of California at Riverside (1984). Weingart, et al. (1983).

AVAILABILITY: This instrument is available on an accompanying disk under the file name Ucrivers.

AUTHOR: University of Kentucky Libraries Data Services
TITLE/NAME OF INSTRUMENT: Literature Search Evaluation
PURPOSE: To determine the quality of online searches from the patron viewpoint. Developed for an academic library but could be adapted for other types of libraries.
DESCRIPTION AND EXPERIENCE WITH USE: Consists of a questionnaire of five items to be completed by patrons after having

received online searches. A useful item concerns the user's reason for wanting a literature search.

USE: Used by the University of Kentucky Library Data Services.

REVIEW OF THE INSTRUMENT: Advantages are that the form is concise, well constructed, and could be completed swiftly by patrons. It requests only information which could *not* be obtained from any other source but the patron. It also provides a write-in space for comments beneath each question. Disadvantages are that the two satisfaction scales, one for assistance and one for the bibliography itself, are biased in a positive direction. A three-point scale of dissatisfied, partly satisfied, and mostly satisfied might avoid possible problems with positive bias. Also, more alternatives should be added to the question on the reason for requesting a search, such as database unavailable in printed form.

VALIDITY AND RELIABILITY: No data available.

BIBLIOGRAPHICAL REFERENCE: University of Kentucky Library (1981).

AVAILABILITY: This instrument is available on an accompanying disk under the file name Ukentuc.

AUTHOR: University of Texas at Austin

TITLE/NAME OF INSTRUMENT: Questionnaires for End Users and Intermediaries

PURPOSE: To obtain information from both end-users and intermediary about the various outcomes of searches. Used in an academic library but could be adapted for other types of libraries

DESCRIPTION AND EXPERIENCE WITH USE: Consists of two separate questionnaires, one for end-users and one for intermediaries. These questionnaires were given as part of a test of Search Helper and BRS After Dark. The end-user form asks about the users' familiarity with information sources and microcomputers, about databases used and citations printed. Six specific areas of difficulty are listed for users to check. Five questions attempt to pinpoint areas of difficulty on five-point scales from "easy" to "difficult" in regard to computer interaction and search strategy. Success is judged by asking how they would rate satisfaction on a scale of one to five and what percent of references were relevant. The intermediary portion of the form asks for observations and notes on the patron's search, staff time for each stage of search, and type of help provided. Finally, staff rate users on experience, familiarity with the terminal, ability to use the system, and enthusiasm for searching.

USE: Used at the University of Texas, Austin, in January 1984.

REVIEW OF THE INSTRUMENT: These forms provide a structure for staff observations of end-user searches and for patron report of success and search problems. This method is one of the few which are based on reports of both patrons and intermediaries and these two reports

together should give a good perspective on problems encountered and reasons for failure.
VALIDITY AND RELIABILITY: No information available.
BIBLIOGRAPHICAL REFERENCE: University of Texas at Austin. Library. (1984).
AVAILABILITY: This instrument is available on an accompanying disk under the file name Utexas.

AUTHORS: Van House, Nancy A., and Childers, Thomas
TITLE/NAME OF INSTRUMENT: California Reference Evaluation Form
PURPOSE: To evaluate a reference referral network.
DESCRIPTION AND EXPERIENCE WITH USE: Reference librarians serving as expert judges were provided with documentation for each network referral question, including answers provided and sources cited. For each question, judges completed the rating form. The form permits expert judges to verify the answers reported, using the sources referenced in the documentation or whatever other sources deemed appropriate. Judges also rated the answer on a scale, selecting either complete and correct, partially correct, or incorrect. The study took advantage of a particular characteristic of the California network—that written documentation is available for the vast majority of questions handled. Requires written records of the reference transactions. Collecting these data where records do not already exist by writing down questions and answers at the reference desk may be unacceptably intrusive impacting both on public service and the evaluation. This method can be adapted to other situations by the simple expedient of recording questions and answers. Possibilities for future use of the form would be to identify the determinants of successful reference service. For example, libraries' reference mission or policies could be introduced into the investigation in order to discern differences in performance which may be attributable to differences in reference values from library to library or librarian to librarian.
USE: Five reference centers from California participated in the reference accuracy study. The actual referral transactions were collected and evaluated by a panel of judges.
REVIEW OF THE INSTRUMENT: The form could be modified by using Kantor's (1981b) knowledge, collection, and source categories for researchers to diagnose causes of failure.
VALIDITY AND RELIABILITY: Three judges working independently evaluated each question. The project director, a former reference referral librarian, checked inter-rater reliability by reviewing all questions and judges' comments. Inter-rater reliability was high. Questions evaluated

were selected from actual questions asked of various centers. Evaluation was based on actual verification of answers provided.
BIBLIOGRAPHIC REFERENCES: Van House and Childers (1984).
AVAILABILITY: This instrument is available on an accompanying disk under the file name Vanhous1.

AUTHORS: Van House, Nancy A., Lynch, Mary Jo, McClure, Charles R., Zweizig, Douglas L., and Rodger, Eleanor Jo
TITLE/NAME OF INSTRUMENT: Reference Completion Rate
PURPOSE: This instrument, contained in *Output measures for public libraries*, has as its purpose to define a basic set of output measures that are widely applicable, relatively easy to use, at least partially under library control, comparable across libraries, and easily interpreted by the community. Reference Completion Rate measures the proportion of reference transactions successfully completed in one working day. It is intended primarily for small libraries, medium-sized libraries, regional systems, and state library agencies to use for public library development.
DESCRIPTION AND EXPERIENCE WITH USE: This instrument is part of the Public Library Development program, which includes *Planning and role setting for public libraries, Output measures for public libraries*, and the design and specifications for a public library data service. The output measures themselves are the same as those given in the first edition of the manual in 1982 (Zweizig and Rodger). The second edition (Van House, Lynch, McClure, Zweizig, and Rodger, 1987) revised some methods to make them easier or more appropriate, discussions of each measure were expanded, and information was added on measurement and measurement methods as well as interpretation and use of results. Overall the second edition integrated measurement and evaluation more closely with the process presented in *Planning and role setting for public libraries*. Reference Completion Rate measures transactions successfully completed (in the judgment of the librarian) within one working day. Reference Transactions Per Capita measures the number of reference transactions per person in the community served. Libraries collecting data only for Reference Completion Rate are shown how to calculate their own samples or may use the rule of thumb of a minimum of 100 (preferably 400) completed transactions. More frequently libraries will wish to collect Reference Transactions Per Capita and Reference Completion Rate at the same time during a one-week sample period using a tally sheet. Information and referral requests are considered completed except for referrals to another library which are not considered completed. The reference transaction must be completed within the same working day to be counted. Partially completed questions cannot be counted as completed. The Reference Completion Rate is obtained by dividing the number of Reference

Transactions Completed by the number of Reference Transactions. Suggestions are given on possible ways to increase the Reference Completion Rate including analyzing components of the reference system to identify problems, asking reference librarians regarding troublesome questions and considering possible ways to improve the library's capabilities in those areas, and considering if staff are referring questions when they should.

USE: Seventeen public libraries served as test sites to evaluate the usefulness and practicality of the instrument. The measures were used at Baltimore County Public Library as reported by Van House (1985, 1986).

REVIEW OF INSTRUMENT: Van House (1985, 1986) concluded that the measures, while imperfect, are practical and useful to library managers. This national measure of reference service allows comparisons among departments and branches as well as repeated measures on the same library. It will not yield data on how accurately questions are answered. Instructions for using the measures are detailed. Statistics collected reflect only questions for which patrons ask for assistance. The measure is limited to the library worker's estimate of the completion rates. It is possible that some questions considered completed by reference staff are not actually answered correctly or completely. The measure may tend to overestimate or underestimate the true quality of reference service. Determining the percentage of transactions completed correctly is suggested by the authors for further ways of measurement. Other possibilities include measuring user perception of whether or not a transaction is completed, comparing Reference Completion Rates for departments or branches, and measuring separate Reference Completion Rates for children's and young adult services. Bookmobiles and smaller libraries, which have a high referral rate or a delay in answering questions, may have a lower Reference Completion Rate. It is more useful to compare Reference Completion Rates for the same library over time than to compare with other libraries. Thomas Childers (1983) believes the reference measures do not provide differentiation of various reference activities such as providing answers, bibliographic citations, or bibliographic instruction.

VALIDITY AND RELIABILITY: The authors suggest several cautions regarding reliability and validity. For instance, the methods in the manual should not be adjusted for local conditions as this might affect comparability and accuracy of the data, and local decisions about data collection should be recorded and followed consistently by everyone involved in data collection. Nancy A. Van House (1986) studied the measures for validity and reliability. Using data collected at the Baltimore County (Maryland) Public Library, Van House concluded that the measures in *Output measures for public libraries* are valid. There are problems in reliability with the Reference Fill Rate (now called Reference Completion Rate) due to small sample sizes. She suggests increasing the sample size or analyzing the variable on the system rather than the branch level. Suggestions for analyzing performance on the public library system level (not in the manual) were detailed by Van House (1985).

BIBLIOGRAPHIC REFERENCES: Zweizig and Rodger (1982). Van House, Lynch, McClure, Zweizig, and Rodger (1987). Suburban Library System Reference Service (1986).

Evaluative reports, 1st edition Childers (1983). Van House (1985, 1986). McClure, Zweizig, Van House, and Lynch (1986). Veatch (1982).

Evaluative reports, 2d edition D'Elia and Rodger (1987). Ballard (1989).

AVAILABILITY: The instrument has been published in Van House, Nancy A.; Lynch, Mary Jo; McClure, Charles R.; Zweizig, Douglas L.; and Rodger, Eleanor Jo. (1987). *Output measures for public libraries: A manual of standardized procedures* (2d. ed.). Chicago: American Library Association.

AUTHORS: Van House, Nancy, Weil, Beth, and McClure, Charles R.
TITLE/NAME OF INSTRUMENT: Building Use
PURPOSE: To determine the average number of people in the library or in a particular area at one time.
DESCRIPTION AND EXPERIENCE WITH USE: Developed for academic libraries but could be adapted for other types of libraries. It is suggested that library or area use be surveyed over a two-week period during a moderately or busy time of the year. Observation might be collected at a rate of about 3.3 observations per hour or one observation every 18 minutes, until 400 observations have been obtained. (Avoid sampling on the hour or half hour).
USE: Used in a pretest of a number of academic libraries by the authors. Recommended for use by ACRL.
REVIEW OF THE INSTRUMENT: A disadvantage is that this method requires about 120 person hours available to make observations. An advantage is that a figure can be obtained for total patron activity in the reference area including patrons who use the reference collection or other facilities but do not ask for assistance at the reference desk. This activity figure can then be compared to activity in other library departments. The authors note that this measure can also serve as a service point and facilities use measure. At times of observation the counter can record which part of the reference area is being used, as, for example, persons 1) at the service desk, 2) in the reference stacks, 3) at index tables, and 4) using equipment. The authors suggest that the overall

activity figure for an area can be compared to the number of staff in the area. For example, during evening hours an average of 25 persons are in the reference area as compared to two reference staff on duty.
VALIDITY AND RELIABILITY: The authors warn against using this two-week sample to estimate yearly use. Instead it should represent an estimate of use within plus or minus five points for a typical two-week period.
BIBLIOGRAPHICAL REFERENCE: Van House, Weil, and McClure (1990).
AVAILABILITY: The instrument has been published in Van House, Nancy A.; Weil, Beth T.; and McClure, Charles R. (1990). *Measuring academic library performance: A practical approach*. Chicago: American Library Association.

AUTHORS: Van House, Nancy A., Weil, Beth T., and McClure, Charles R.
TITLE/NAME OF INSTRUMENT: General Satisfaction Survey
PURPOSE: To obtain general information about the nature and outcomes of the user's library visit. More specifically, it is intended to obtain user self-reports of success in carrying out library activities, ease of use of the library, and overall satisfaction with the visit.
DESCRIPTION AND EXPERIENCE WITH USE: Developed for an academic library, this instrument is intended to explore information-seeking behavior and is based on present-visit-only data. The questionnaire has been kept to one page in length in order to encourage user cooperation in returning forms. Users are first asked about their success in carrying out seven activities: looked for books or periodicals, studied, reviewed current literature, did a literature search (manual or computer), asked a reference question, browsed, returned books. Success for each of these activities is measured on a five-point scale anchored with "not at all successful" at one end and "completely successful" at the other end. The second question asks about ease of use of the library, on a five-point scale from "not at all easy" to "very easy." The last question asks how satisfied overall the user was with today's library visit on a five-point scale from "not at all satisfied" to "very satisfied." Concluding questions cover the user's purpose and collect data on class and major discipline.
USE: Pretesting of this instrument took place in 1989 in a number of libraries, including eight libraries at the University of California at Berkeley and three other California academic libraries. Sample data from two social sciences libraries at the University of California at Berkeley are included. Recommended for use by ACRL.
REVIEW OF THE INSTRUMENT: Librarians should adapt the list of uses/services to their libraries. A strong point of this instrument is its

brevity, which should encourage user cooperation. Another strong point is its use of a success scale for each library activity. The success scale is well anchored at each end with "completely" and "not at all." Data from this instrument might help to answer questions related to the success of people using services, such as periodicals and literature searching, and provide information on success rates with and without reference assistance. Possible disadvantages in terms of reference might be that the term "reference question" may not be well understood by patrons and users might perceive that almost any question asked at any place within the library should fall into this category. Pretest data from this instrument indicate that a rather large percentage, 24% of users in the sample, asked reference questions. One possible answer is that users define "reference question" very loosely and this percentage represents the majority of questions asked anywhere in the library. If this is the case, the figure should still be useful in regard to success of question-answering activities in the library in general. A second possibility is that users *are* able to define "reference question" generally as intended and that a considerable number of reference questions are being asked at locations other than the reference desk. Another possible problem may be that the five-point continuum scale may be prone to positive bias in the second category. It is not possible to tell from the pretest data supplied whether or not this might be the case. Again, publication of further data in the future should be helpful in shedding light on the questions raised above.

VALIDITY AND RELIABILITY: No information available at this time.

BIBLIOGRAPHIC REFERENCE: Van House, Weil, and McClure (1990).

AVAILABILITY: The instrument has been published in Van House, Nancy A.; Weil, Beth T.; and McClure, Charles R. (1990). *Measuring academic library performance: A practical approach.* Chicago: American Library Association.

AUTHORS: Van House, Nancy A., Weil, Beth, and McClure, Charles R.

TITLE/NAME OF INSTRUMENT: In-Library Materials Use

PURPOSE: To determine total number of items used in the library but not charged out. For academic and research libraries.

DESCRIPTION AND EXPERIENCE WITH USE: A simple tally sheet designates area or type of material, hour, and totals. The authors suggest the most accurate count is obtained by counting all the materials used in the library at all times or during an entire term, although this may not be feasible.

USE: Information not available. Recommended for use by ACRL.

REVIEW OF THE INSTRUMENT: Could be adapted for use in reference areas with recording by specific subjects.
VALIDITY AND RELIABILITY: Information not available.
BIBLIOGRAPHIC REFERENCES: Van House, Weil, and McClure (1990).
AVAILABILITY: The instrument has been published in Van House, Nancy A.; Weil, Beth T.; and McClure, Charles R. (1990). *Measuring academic library performance: A practical approach*. Chicago: American Library Association.

AUTHORS: Van House, Nancy A., Weil, Beth, and McClure, Charles R.
TITLE/NAME OF INSTRUMENT: Online Search Evaluation
PURPOSE: To obtain user satisfaction ratings for online searches. Developed for academic libraries but could be used in or adapted for other types of libraries.
DESCRIPTION AND EXPERIENCE WITH USE: Consists of seven items concerning the searcher's understanding of the request, thoroughness in selecting databases and searching, and time taken. Outcome is judged by relevance, amount, and currency of material retrieved. The last item of the questionnaire asks for an overall satisfaction rating with that particular search.
USE: Has been pretested in at least ten California libraries in 1988/89. Recommended for use by ACRL.
REVIEW OF THE INSTRUMENT: Designed for online searches by appointment rather than for end-user searches. Nevertheless, questions on amount and currency of materials might be adapted for end-user searching.
VALIDITY AND RELIABILITY: Has been pretested, but results of the pretest, at this date, have not been released.
BIBLIOGRAPHICAL REFERENCE: Van House, Weil, and McClure (1990).
AVAILABILITY: The instrument has been published in Van House, Nancy A.; Weil, Beth T.; and McClure, Charles R. (1990). *Measuring academic library performance: A practical approach*. Chicago: American Library Association.

AUTHORS: Van House, Nancy A., Weil, Beth T., and McClure, Charles R.
TITLE/NAME OF INSTRUMENT: Reference Satisfaction Survey
PURPOSE: Few academic libraries have attempted to quantify the success of reference efforts affected by factors such as size of collections, staff skills, and physical accessibility. This instrument collects user self-reports of outcomes of reference transactions, service experience,

and overall satisfaction with reference services. The survey provides managers with knowledge about user opinions of reference services. While measures were designed for academic or research libraries of all sizes, many are applicable to other types of libraries.

DESCRIPTION AND EXPERIENCE WITH USE: The Association of College and Research Libraries in 1984 established the Ad Hoc Committee on Performance Measures to stimulate librarian interest in performance measures and to provide practical assistance in the conduct of measurements of effectiveness with minimum expense and difficulty. The committee developed specifications and sought an author for a manual on performance measures for academic libraries. Nancy Van House was selected and worked with Beth Weil, Charles McClure, the ad hoc committee, and widely in the profession throughout development of a manual. The Reference Satisfaction Survey instrument is one of two proposed for measurement of reference services in the manual, *Measuring academic library performance.* The manual suggests that academic libraries collect information on total number of reference transactions and user self-reports of satisfaction with reference services. Reference Satisfaction Survey evaluates user perceptions of reference satisfaction with five questions using a five-point scale on relevance of information provided, satisfaction with amount of information provided, completeness of answer, helpfulness of staff, and user overall satisfaction. Two additional questions request information on user status (undergraduate, graduate) and what he or she will be using information for (course work, research, teaching). Detailed suggestions are given on study considerations such as what service desks to evaluate. Implementation requires only basic math. The measures are intended to offer a "snapshot" of performance at a certain point in time. It is recommended that a minimum of 100 (400 is preferred) completed surveys be collected over a one- to three-week period. It is not recommended that data be collected for longer than a three-week period. A response rate of 85% will not be uncommon. Nonreference service desk personnel should distribute questionnaires and persuade users to complete questionnaire before leaving reference area. Surveys can be tabulated manually or by computer yielding information about how users view reference transactions. Suggestions for further use include analyzing data by service point to measure differences in user satisfaction and cross-tabulating answers on status and purpose with satisfaction, or to analyze "unsatisfactory" and "very satisfied" responses as separate groups to discover differences.

USE: All measures were pretested in academic libraries, refined, and retested. Recommended for use by ACRL.

REVIEW OF THE INSTRUMENT: The Reference Satisfaction Survey can be used with relatively minimum effort to collect information on reference performance from user perspectives. It will allow comparisons among departments and branches as well as repeated measures on the same library. It is possible to make comparisons from one library to another as use of the instrument becomes frequent. Comparisons between libraries should be made cautiously as differing types of questions, types of users, and other local conditions may make comparisons questionable. This instrument will not yield data on how accurately questions were answered. The Reference Satisfaction Survey is only the user's estimate of satisfaction rates. The measure is not intended to diagnose the cause of failure for which the reader is referred to such works as Murfin and Gugelchuk (1987) or Hernon and McClure (1987b). Satisfactory reference service depends on many complex variables and reference satisfaction will never be 100%. Reference staff may feel some anxiety regarding the Reference Satisfaction Survey and should be informed prior to implementation. If they understand that only a service is being surveyed, not individuals, it may help them to feel less threatened. Questions 6 (status of user) and 7 (reason for use) would have to be adjusted for use in a nonacademic library.

VALIDITY AND RELIABILITY: The instrument was pretested in a number of academic libraries and experts on library measurement were consulted. The Reference Satisfaction Survey was designed to be valid and reliable if utilized correctly. Libraries are cautioned that changes in method should be made with care as results might be affected and what is measured (validity) may be changed. For results to be consistent measurement methods also must be consistent (reliability). To increase reliability it is recommended that one individual be the final decision-maker on all measurement questions and that all decisions be documented and communicated to everyone who needs to know.

BIBLIOGRAPHIC REFERENCES: Van House, Weil, and McClure (1990).

AVAILABILITY: The instrument has been published in Van House, Nancy A.; Weil, Beth T.; and McClure, Charles R. (1990). *Measuring academic library performance: A practical approach*. Chicago: American Library Association.

AUTHORS: Wessel, C.J., and Moore, K.L.
TITLE/NAME OF INSTRUMENT: SCORE Cost Effectiveness Analysis
PURPOSE: To assess criteria and methods for reference evaluation in a special library.
DESCRIPTION AND EXPERIENCE WITH USE: This cost effectiveness method is meant to be used by a library to check the cost effectiveness of its reference service at intervals over a period of time with a view toward improved operations. In the SCORE method, after a first cost-effectiveness figure is obtained, a library can then attempt to

improve on this figure by raising the quality without increasing cost or, more difficult, lowering cost without decreasing quality. Wessel gives this formula and describes how it was carried out in a special library. The SCOUT method is used to determine the optimum balance between effectiveness and cost. CORE derives unit cost standards for given operations which produce a given quality and GAME is a technique to avoid unnecessary work or excessive delays and to develop time standards.

USE: Carried out in three special libraries in 1969.

REVIEW OF THE INSTRUMENT: This method, similar to availability analysis, attempts to determine the failure rate at each step of the reference process. Once this is done, stages in the process that have high failure rates can be discovered and action taken for improvement. Some time after improvements have been made, the library again tests its cost effectiveness. This method was carried out successfully in special libraries but does not appear in its present form to be well suited to academic or public library reference service. The success of the method depends upon ability to separate a task into stages and to be able to define success or failure at *each* stage. The complete reference process was divided into stages: 1) communication of the need; 2) search; 3) documents identified; 4) user agrees some documents look relevant; 5) some documents arrive in time; and 6) some documents have relevant information. The formula used may present difficulties and some libraries may require assistance in its application.

VALIDITY AND RELIABILITY: SCORE analysis has been widely used in industry.

BIBLIOGRAPHIC REFERENCE: Wessel and Moore (1969).

AVAILABILITY: This instrument is available on an accompanying disk under the file name Wessel. Detailed instructions are available in Wessel and Moore (1969). Assistance in interpretation of this source may be needed.

AUTHOR: Whitlatch, Jo Bell

TITLE/NAME OF INSTRUMENT: Librarian and User Perceptions of Reference Service Quality

PURPOSE: To test a model of the reference service process. Instrument was used as part of a study which reviewed significant theory and research findings concerning service organizations from business, psychology, and sociology.

DESCRIPTION AND EXPERIENCE WITH USE: The instrument consists of twelve sections, six parallel surveys for each reference transaction to be completed by both the librarian and by the user. The librarian completes a Librarian Service Orientation Survey one time at the beginning of the study. With each reference transaction, the librarian completes a Librarian Service Value Scale, a Task Related Knowledge Librarian Survey, and a Librarian Time Spent in the Encounter Survey. Library patrons are asked to complete parallel surveys for each reference transaction evaluated by a librarian. Each scale provides a seven-point range and each section contains several questions. Space is provided for comments. Factors such as satisfaction, relevance, amount of information provided, quality of service provided, enthusiasm, and interest of the reference librarian in answering the reference question are included. Librarians answer questions in which they indicate such matters as familiarity with information sources, if communication with the user is difficult, and degree to which information provided by the user is sufficient and explicit. Questionnaires are coded so that librarian and user questionnaires can be matched for each individual transaction. The Task Related Knowledge Scale measures the degree to which knowledge is incomplete in relation to producing a desired reference outcome. The five measures in the task uncertainty scale are 1) the frequency of use of sources used to answer a question; 2) the question as a new type of problem; 3) the similarity of a question to other questions; 4) familiarity with the subject of the question; and 5) familiarity with the information source used to answer a question. Librarians complete the scale for each transaction sampled.

USE: A study using the instrument was conducted in Fall 1986. A total of 62 librarians from five academic libraries in Northern California sampled 397 reference transactions; 257 library users provided matched responses for analysis of 64.7% of the total transactions. Users who asked questions during the study period were asked to participate in the study when their queries were identified as ones to be sampled. Each librarian kept a separate tally of questions asked and for each fifth reference question, and after the question had been answered, the reference librarian asked the user to complete the user questionnaire. If the user agreed, the librarian made quick notes on the transaction; these notes were to be used later that same day to complete the librarian transaction survey when off the desk.

REVIEW OF THE INSTRUMENT: This field study trades off control over variables for study of real-life situations. Several scales used were developed for this study. They need further testing and improvement to ensure adequate validity and reliability. Data collection was limited to five institutions in one geographic location. This instrument is lengthy and response rate is lower than RTAI (Murfin and Gugelchuk, 1987).

VALIDITY AND RELIABILITY: All instruments were pretested in an academic reference department. Service outcomes were measured by scales adopted from Pearson and Kotler. Service orientation was evaluated using Schneider's measures. Librarian satisfaction was measured by the short form of the General Job Satisfaction Questionnaire by Hackman and Oldham. To assess extent to which individual librarians find doing the job itself rewarding, the Internal Work Motivation scales developed by Withey, Daft, and Cooper for measuring task variety were employed. Each scale was selected because of its demonstrated validity and reliability. As well, Cronbach's alpha (a), the most common of reliability tests for internal consistency, was calculated for each scale. For further information on scales, see Whitlatch (1990b). Six items were developed to test client knowledge and understanding of organizational norms, policies, practices, and procedures. To determine reliability of the various scales, factor analysis was utilized. For socialization, factor 1, with items related to library instruction, was designated training (a =.79) and factor 2, with items related to frequency of library use and understanding of the library system, was designated understanding (a =.67). Feedback scales were developed to assess both extent and quality of feedback. For users, factor 1, with items related to ease and pleasantness of communication and user providing information to the librarian on whether the question was answered, had low reliability (a =.56). Reliability for the two-item scale, ease and pleasantness of communication, was more acceptable (a =.73). Thus, the two-item scale was designated user feedback quality and the item related to the user informing the librarian if the question was answered was treated as a separate variable. Reliability for factor 2, with items related to user participation, was also low (a =.55). Therefore, for this exploratory study, these items were treated as separate variables. For librarians, factor 1, with items relating to ease and pleasantness of communication, sufficiency and explicitness of information, was designated librarian feedback quality (a =.72). Factor 2, with items relating to user participation, was designated librarian judgments of user participation (a = .72). The Task Related Knowledge scale was developed based on data collected in interviews with experienced reference librarians and pretested at San Francisco State University. Internal reliability as measured by Cronbach's alpha is .80, which is considered an acceptable level for research. The scale is based on self-perceptions of librarian knowledge. In assessing the effect of task-related knowledge on reference outcomes, the task-related knowledge measure is most effectively utilized with user reports of reference success instead of librarian reports of reference success. The relationships between librarian perceptions of task-related knowledge and librarian judgments of reference success may be biased because both measures collect data from the same source—the reference librarian.

BIBLIOGRAPHIC REFERENCES: Whitlatch (1987). Whitlatch (1990a). Whitlatch (1990b).

AVAILABILITY: This instrument is available on an accompanying disk under the file name Whitlatc.

AUTHORS: Wilson, S.R., Starr-Schneidkraut, N., and Cooper, M.D.
TITLE/NAME OF INSTRUMENT: Critical Incident Technique
PURPOSE: To study the impact of end-user MEDLINE searches by physicians and other medical personnel on their decision-making process and the ultimate impact of the information on the outcome of the situation that prompted the search.
DESCRIPTION AND EXPERIENCE WITH USE: Consists of two interview schedules, one for Effective Searches (nine questions) and one for Ineffective Searches (11 questions). Below each question is a space for recording the answer. During a 15-minute interview, respondents were asked about searches that were especially helpful in their work or that were unsatisfactory. They were also asked why they did each search, the context and specific questions in mind, what information was wanted and why, how the search was done, what information was obtained, actions taken as a result of having information, and what the end result was for the patient or situation. After these questions had been asked, some other factual data on searches and demographic data were obtained. A sheet with multiple choice answers was provided for uniform coding of factual data. If the respondents agreed, interviews were taped.
USE: A critical incident study was carried out by the National Library of Medicine in 1987 by telephone interviews with 552 physicians and other health care professionals who had been recent end-users of MEDLINE. (almost all searches had been done within the past year and 70% within the last six months).
REVIEW OF THE INSTRUMENT: This is an exemplary use of the critical incident technique and worthy of careful study. The Effective and Ineffective Incident report forms are models of clarity. This technique would appear to be a useful technique for exploring the benefits of reference service. In regard to academic libraries, the impact in regard to course work might correspond to impact on patient care. A possible problem might be some slight difficulty in quantifying benefits. Ineffective searches, particularly in the case of physicians, might be underreported for fear of possible malpractice claims. For public library reference service, Dervin's list of benefits would probably be the most appropriate (Dervin and Fraser, 1985). Another point of importance is that the time that elapses before the interview needs to be sufficient for impact to be known, but not so long that impact is forgotten.
VALIDITY AND RELIABILITY: No data available.
BIBLIOGRAPHIC REFERENCE: Wilson, Starr-Schneidkraut, and Cooper (1989).
AVAILABILITY: This instrument is available on an accompanying disk under the file name Wilson.

AUTHOR: Yocum, James C., and Stocker, Frederick D.

TITLE/NAME OF INSTRUMENT: Survey of Public Library Users

PURPOSE: To obtain data about how much patrons use a particular service and how important they consider it in terms of future development. Developed for use in a public library.

DESCRIPTION AND EXPERIENCE WITH USE: Designed to be used to compare a large group of public library branches. Attempts to explore information-seeking behavior rather than to evaluate particular library departments and services. Based on users' experiences over a period of time. Consists of approximately two pages of questions covering reasons for coming to the library, other libraries used, attitudes toward libraries in general, services of the library being visited, future library use, and demographic data. Services covered include 14 standard services and 13 newer services. Reference assistance is described in three items: 1) special assistance by reference librarian, 2) help from the librarian about where to find it, and 3) help from the librarian about what to read. Users check frequency of use (hardly ever, moderately, always) and future development (reduce or eliminate, keep about the same, enlarge or improve). A form for a field user study of nonusers is also included.

USE: A survey was done of 10,496 library users in 27 public libraries in Franklin County, Ohio, in 1969.

REVIEW OF THE INSTRUMENT: This survey is a good example of the method of asking respondents to estimate their use of services in terms of how often they used the service *when they were in the library*. While it does not give weekly or monthly figures for use, it is a quick and easy method for the respondent, and, in this case, appears to have power of discrimination. It also makes it possible to identify heavy and light users of services. Results in regard to changes and improvements needed in services are revealing. The ranking method used is also a good one, that is, asking only for the *top three* choices in order of importance, making the ranking task easier for the respondent. A strong point of this instrument is its coverage of the importance and use of reference service. Also, an advantage is that this instrument has been tested on a large group of in-library users and the item on "helpful staff" has been found to have power of discrimination. This instrument might help to answer questions concerning the importance of reference in the total picture of library services; the most important motivating factors in library use; and the relationship between reference use and library use. A possible disadvantage is use of period of time data, which are less objective than present-visit-only data. Another disadvantage is lack of a clear success measure. The future directions measure is lacking as a measure of success or satisfaction.

VALIDITY AND RELIABILITY: No data available.

BIBLIOGRAPHIC REFERENCE: Yocum and Stocker (1980).
AVAILABILITY: This instrument is available on an accompanying disk under the file name Yocum.

Secondary Author Index

Since both the "Annotated Bibliography" and the "Summary of Instruments" are arranged by primary author, only secondary authors are included in this index—with citations to the corresponding primary author. Entries in the "Summary of Instruments" are entered in bold type, while the citations to the "Annotated Bibliography" appear in normal type.

Alexander, Carlos — Fisher, Kenneth (1976)
Aluri, Rao — Kaske, Neal K. (1980)
Aluri, Rao — St. Clair, Jeffrey W. (1977)
Anderson, Carol Lee — Fraley, Ruth A. (1990)
Anderson, Fanny — Pings, Vern (1965)
Andrew, Christine — Balay, Robert (1975)
Asbury, Herbert — Jensen, Rebecca
Asbury, Herbert — Jensen, Rebecca (1980)
Atherton, Pauline — Tessier, Judith A. (1977)
Authier, Jerry — Ivey, Allen E. (1978)
Bailey, Catherine A. — Davis, Richard A. (1964)
Belvin, Robert — Kuhlthau, Carol
Belvin, Robert — Kuhlthau, Carol (1990)
Benedict, James — Gal, Cynthia A. (1986)
Benson, James — Clark, Philip M. (1985)
Benson, Larry D. — Christensen, John O.
Benson, Larry D. — Christenson, John O. (1989)
Bloch, T. — Bloch, U. (1981)
Blomquist, Laura L. — Dougherty, Richard M. (1974)
Bolin, Nancy — Stephens, Sandy (1988)
Braunagel, Judith Schiek — Jahoda, Gerald (1980)
Briscoe, Peter — Selth, Jeff (1992)
Brown, Velia — Weingart, Doris (1983)
Bunge, Charles — Murfin, Marjorie (1989)
Bunge, Charles — Murfin, Marjorie (Cost Benefit...)
Bunge, Charles — Murfin, Marjorie (Cost in Staffing...)
Bunge, Charles — Murfin, Marjorie (Determining the...)
Bunge, Charles A. — Murfin, Marjorie E. (1988a)
Bunge, Charles A. — Murfin, Marjorie E. (1988b)
Bunge, Charles A. — Murfin, Marjorie E.
Butler, H. Julene — Christensen, John O.
Butler, H. Julene — Christenson, John O. (1989)
Campbell, Donald T. — Webb, Eugene J. (1966)
Casserly, Mary — Ciliberti, Anne
Casserly, Mary F. — Ciliberti, Anne C. (1987)

Chamis, Alice — Saracevic, Tefko
Chamis, Alice Y. — Saracevic, Tefko (1988)
Childers, Thomas — Van House, Nancy A. (1993)
Childers, Thomas — Van House, Nancy A. (1984)
Childers, Thomas — Van House, Nancy A. (California Reference...)
Clark, Bart — LAMA-NDCU Committee
Cooper, M.D. — Wilson, S.R.
Cooper, M.D. — Wilson, S.R. (1989)
Coutant, Patricia — Budd, John (1981)
Crouch, Wayne W. — Tessier, Judith A. (1977)
Cuff, Renata — Raisig, L. Miles (1966)
Davis, C. Roger — Christiansen, Dorothy E. (1983)
D'Elia, George D. — Rodger, Eleanor Jo
Delmont, Mary K. — Piech, Carlo R. (1986)
Deming, Basil S. — Salenger, Ruth D. (1982)
Dervin, Brenda — Zweizig, Douglas (1977)
DiCarlo, Mike — Budd, John (1982)
DiCarlo, Rebecca — Larason, Larry (1962)
Dickstein, Ruth — Phipps, Shelley
Dickstein, Ruth — Phipps, Shelley (1979)
DuMont, Paul F. — DuMont, Rosemary Ruhig (1979)
Eadie, Tom — Binkley, Dave (1988)
Eadie, Tom —Binkley, Dave (1989)
Eakin, Dottie — Schwartz, Diane (1986)
Eakin, Dottie — Schwartz, Diane G.
Evans, E.G. — Langrish, J. (1972)
Eyles, H.H. — Jahoda, G. (1987)
Fasana, Paul — Mount, Ellis (1972)
Ferguson, Douglas — Matthews, Joseph R. (1983)
Fitt, Stephen D. — Smith, Nathan M. (1982)
Fitzgerald, Dorothy — Haynes, R. Brian (1990)
Fraley, Ruth A.— Katz, Bill (1985)
Fraley, Ruth A.— Katz, Bill (1986)
Fraser, Benson — Dervin, Brenda
Fraser, Benson — Dervin, Brenda (1985)
Fruehauf, Esther, L. — Wender, Ruth W. (1977)
George, Mary — Kuhlthau, Carol
George, Mary — Kuhlthau, Carol (1990)
Gers, Ralph — Stephens, Sandy (1988)
Goetsch, Lori A. — Courtois, Martin P. (1984)
Goldhor, Herbert — Weech, Terry L. (1982)
Goldhor, Herbert — Weech, Terry L. (1984)
Goodwin, Jane — Rodger, Eleanor Jo (1987)
Gorman, K.A. — Daiute, R.J. (1974)

Gothberg, Helen M. — Trautman, Rodes (1982)
Grim, Jerry — Beeler, M.G. Fancher (1974)
Gugelchuk, Gary M. — Murfin, Marjorie E.
Gugelchuk, Gary — Murfin, Marjorie (1987)
Hall, Blaine H. — Christensen, John O.
Hall, Blaine H. — Christenson, John O. (1989)
Halman, Ruth — Weingart, Doris (1983)
Harrick, Rosemary — Murfin, Marjorie
Harris, Roma M. — Michell, B. Gillian (1984)
Harris, Roma M. — Michell, B. Gillian (1987)
Hegg, Judith — Ciliberti, Anne
Hegg, Judith — Mitchell, Eugene (1994)
Hegg, Judith L. — Ciliberti, Anne C. (1987)
Hepworth, Susan J. — Cook, John D. (1981)
Herling, John P. — Beeler, M.G. Fancher (1974)
Herner, Mary — Herner, Saul (1967)
Hernon, Peter — Chen, Ching-Chih
Hernon, Peter — Chen, Ching-Chih (1979)
Hernon, Peter — Chen, Ching-Chih (1980)
Hernon, Peter — McClure, Charles R.
Hernon, Peter — McClure, Charles R. (1989)
Hersberger, Rodney M. — Regazzi, John J. (1976)
Hersberger, Rodney M. — Regazzi, John J. (1978)
Hersberger, Rodney M. — Regazzi, John
Herschman, Judith — Mandel, Carol A. (1983)
Heslin, Richard — Fisher, Jeffrey D. (1976)
Hiebert, Ruth — Weingart, Doris (1983)
Holmes, Emory H. — Cuadra, Carlos (1967 — *Experimental...*)
Howard, Don H. — Christensen, John O.
Howard, Don H. — Christenson, John O. (1989)
Howell, Benita — Reeves, Edward B. (1977)
Howell, Benita J. — Reeves, Edward B.
Ill, Diane — Weingart, Doris (1983)
Jackson, Susan E. — Maslach, Christina (1981)
Jackson, Susan E. — Maslach, Christina
Jakobovits, Leon — Nahl-Jakobovits, Diane (1988)
James, Stephen — Beeler, M.G. Fancher (1974)
Jennerich, Edward J. — Jennerich, Elaine Zaremba (1987)
Jevons, F.R. — Langrish, J. (1972)
Jones, John W. — Haack, Mary (1984)
Joseph, Margaret — LAMA-NDCU Committee
Kantor, P.B. — Saracevic, T. (1977)
Kantor, Paul — Saracevic, Tefko
Kantor, Paul — Saracevic, Tefko (1988)

Katter, Robert V. — Cuadra, Carlos (1967 — *Experimental...*)
Katter, Robert V. — Cuadra, Carlos (1967 — Opening...)
Katzer, Jeffrey — Swope, Mary Jane (1972)
Keable, Ellen Bruce — Schneekloth, Lynda H. (1991)
Kernaghan, Salvinija G. — Kernaghan, John A. (1979)
Kilgour, Frederick — Raisig, L. Miles (1966)
King, Radford — Jensen, Rebecca
King, Radford, — Jensen, Rebecca (1980)
Knittel, Marjorie — Franklin, Hugh
Knittel, Marjorie — Franklin, Hugh (1991)
Kochen, Manfred — Tagliacozzo, Renata (1970)
Koller, Nancy — Selth, Jeff (1992)
Kooiman, Sue — Weingart, Doris (1983)
Lancaster, F.W. — Baker, Sharon L. (1991)
Larason, Larry D. — Steffenson, Martin B. (1978)
Lawrence, Gary — Matthews, Joseph R. (1983)
Lawson, V.L. — Jahoda, G. (1987)
Lawton, Stephen — Auster, Ethel
Lawton, Stephen — Auster, Ethel (1984)
Layton, Frances — LeMay, Moira (1990)
Lin, Nan — Garvey, William D. (1972)
Lindquist, Charles — Whitehead, John (1985)
Litchfield, Charles A. — Metz, Paul (1988)
Littel, Robert David — Kim, Choong Han (1987)
Lovrich, Nicholas Jr. — Hardesty, Larry (1979)
Lovrich, Nicholas P. Jr. — Hardesty, Larry
Ludy, Lorene E. — Van Pulis, Noelle (1988)
Lynch, Mary Jo — McClure, Charles R. (1986)
Lynch, Mary Jo — Van House, Nancy A. (1987)
Lynch, Mary Jo — Van House, Nancy A. (Reference Completion...)
Mahmoodi, Suzanne H. — King, Geraldine (1991)
Malloy, Lois — Weingart, Doris (1983)
Mannon, James — Hardesty, Larry
Mannon, James — Hardesty, Larry (1979)
Marchant, Maurice — Birch, Nancy (1986)
Martin Miles W. — Beeler, M.G. Fancher (1974)
Mason, Joan — Mason, Ellsworth (1984)
Mathews, Eleanor — Arrigona, Daniel
Mathews, Eleanor — Arrigona, Daniel (1988)
Maughan, Laurel — Franklin, Hugh
Maughan, Laurel — Franklin, Hugh (1991)
McClure, Charles R. — Hernon, Peter (1987b)
McClure, Charles R. — Hernon, Peter (1983)
McClure, Charles R. — Hernon, Peter (1987a)

McClure, Charles R. — Hernon, Peter (1986a)
McClure, Charles R. — Hernon, Peter (1986b)
McClure, Charles R. — Hernon, Peter
McClure, Charles R. — Van House, Nancy (Building Use)
McClure, Charles R. — Van House, Nancy A. (1987)
McClure, Charles R. — Van House, Nancy A. (1990)
McClure, Charles R. — Van House, Nancy A. General Satisfaction...)
McClure, Charles R. — Van House, Nancy A. (In-Library...)
McClure, Charles R. — Van House, Nancy A. (Reference Completion...)
McClure, Charles R. — Van House, Nancy A. (Reference Satisfction)
McClure, Charles R. — Van House, Nancy A. (Online Search...)
McGibbons, M. — Langrish, J. (1972)
McKibbon, Ann — Haynes, R. Brian (1990)
Michell, B. Gillian — Harris, Roma M. (1986)
Mielke, Linda — Moore, Carolyn M. (1986)
Miller, Naomi — Kirby, Martha
Miller, Naomi — Kirby, Martha (1985)
Miller, Naomi — Kirby, Martha (1986)
Mitchell, Eugene — Ciliberti, Anne
Mitchell, Eugene S. — Ciliberti, Anne C. (1987)
Montanary, Barbara — Weingart, Doris (1983)
Montanelli, Dale S. — Potthoff, Joy K. (1990)
Moore, K.L — Wessel, C.J. (1969)
Moore, K.L. — Wessel, C.J.
Moult, Gerry — Poulet, Roger (1987)
Murfin, Marjorie — Bunge, Charles (1983)
Murfin, Marjorie — Bunge, Charles (1987)
Murfin, Marjorie — LAMA-NDCU Committee
Murfin, Marjorie E. — Halldorsson, Egill A. (1977)
Nadler, E. — Krulee, G.K. (1960)
Naylor, Alice — Beeler, M.G. Fancher (1974)
Neenan, Peter A. — Chen, Ching-Chih (1979)
Nelson, Carnot — Garvey, William D. (1972)
Nelson, Veneese C. — Smith, Nathan M. (1983)
Newman, G. Charles — Piech, Carlo R. (1986)
Nielson, Laura F. — Smith, Nathan M. (1984)
Nilan, Michael — Dervin, Brenda (1986)
Oja, Anne R. — Lawrence, Gary S. (1980)
Oja, Anne R. — Lawrence, Gary S.
O'Keefe, Robert D. — Kernaghan, John A. (1979)
Parker, Linda — LAMA-NDCU Committee
Parrish, Darlene Ann — Blazek, Ron (1992)

Partridge, Jim — Stephens, Sandy (1988)
Paskoff, B.M. — Jahoda, G. (1987)
Pastine, Maureen — Hernon, Peter (1977)
Perrault, Anna H. — Paskoff, Beth M. (1990)
Pond, M.J. — Jahoda, G. (1987)
Radford, Marie — Mitchell, Eugene (1994)
Ramsden, Michael F. — Haynes, R. Brian (1990)
Reed-Scott, Jutta — Christiansen, Dorothy E. (1983)
Reed-Scott, Jutta — Davis, Roger (1983)
Reynolds, Kathy J. — Allan, Ann (1983)
Rizzo, J.R. — House, R.J. (1972)
Rizzo, J.R. — House. R.J.
Robinson, Judith Schiek — Larason, Larry (1984)
Rodger, Eleanor Jo — D'Elia, George (1987)
Rodger, Eleanor Jo — Van House, Nancy A. (1987)
Rodger, Eleanor Jo — Van House, Nancy A. (Reference Completion...)
Rodger, Eleanor Jo — Zweizig, Douglas (1982)
Roose, Tina — Haack, Mary (1984)
Rosenberg, Lawrence — Tagliacozzo, Renata (1970)
Rubenstein, Albert H. — Kernaghan, John A. (1979)
Ruland, Fred — Murfin, Marjorie (1980)
Ryan, Nancy — Haynes, R. Brian (1990)
Rytting, Marvin — Fisher, Jeffrey D. (1976)
Schlechter, Theordore M. — Campbell, David E. (1979)
Schwartz, Richard D. — Webb, Eugene J. (1966)
Sechrest, Lee — Webb, Eugene J. (1966)
Self, Elizabeth A. — Brehm, Jack W. (1989)
Seward, Lillie — Stephens, Sandy (1988)
Seward, Lillie J. — Gers, Ralph (1988)
Seward, Lillie J. — Gers, Ralph (1985)
Seward, Lillie J. — Gers, Ralph
Shaw, W.M. — Saracevic, T. (1977)
Shishko, Robert — Raffel, Jeffrey
Shishko, Robert — Raffel, Jeffrey (1969)
Simon, Julian L. — Fussler, Herman H. (1961)
Simon, Julian L. — Fussler, Herman H.
Smalls, Mary L. — Jenkins, Barbara Williams (1990)
Smith, Duncan — Shearer, Kenneth D. (1992)
Smith, Meredith — Raisig, L. Miles (1966)
Smith, Nathan — Birch, Nancy (1986)
Smith, Nathan — Elliott, Jannean L. (1984)
Smith, Nathan M. — Markham, Marilyn (1983)
Smith, Nathan M. — Thompson, Mark J. (1980)

Spyers-Duran, Kimberly — Gunning, Kathleen (1993)
Starr-Schneidkraut, N. — Wilson, S.R.
Starr-Schneidkraut, N. — Wilson, S.R. (1989)
Stirling, Keith H. — Markham, Marilyn (1983)
Stocker, Frederick D. — Yocum, James C. (1980)
Stocker, Frederick D. — Yocum, James C.
Stolar, Elaine Culley — Naegele, Kaspar D. (1960)
Strazdon, Maureen — Halperin, Michael (1980)
Strazdon, Maureen — Halperin, Michael (Patron Preference...)
Strazdon, Maureen — Halperin, Michael (Reference Service...)
Stueart, Robert D. — Chen, Ching-Chih (1979)
Suci, George J. — Osgood, Charles E. (1967)
Supinski, Deborah M. — Gal, Cynthia A. (1986)
Tannenbaum, Percy H. — Osgood, Charles E. (1967)
Tomita, Kazuo — Garvey, William D. (1972)
Townsend, David — LeMay, Moira (1990)
Toy, Phyllis — Hatchard, Desmond B. (1986)
Trivison, Donna — Saracevic, Tefko
Trivison, Donna — Saracevic, Tefko (1988)
Turock, Betty — Kuhlthau, Carol
Turock, Betty — Kuhlthau, Carol (1990)
University of British Columbia — University of California at Los Angeles
University of California at Riverside, The — The University of British Columbia
University of California at Riverside — University of California at Los Angeles
University of California at Riverside Library, The — New York University, Elmer Holmes Bobst Library
University of Colorado, The — The University of British Columbia
University of Massachusetts, The — The University of British Columbia
Vandercook, Sharon — Layman, Mary (1990)
Van House, Nancy A. — Childers, Thomas (1989)
Van House, Nancy A. — McClure, Charles R. (1986)
Van Willigen, John — Reeves, Edward B. (1977)
Van Willigen, John — Reeves, Edward B.
Vent, Marilyn S. — Wender, Ruth W. (1977)
Verdin, Jo Ann — Lynch, Beverly P. (1987)
Walker, Cynthia J. — Haynes, R. Brian (1990)
Wall, Toby D. — Cook, John D. (1981)
Wallace, Everett M. — Cuadra, Carlos (1967 — *Experimental...*)
Walsh, Sandra — D'Elia, George (1983)
Warmann, Carolyn — Cochrane, Lynn Scott (1989)

Warmann, Carolyn — Cochrane, Lynn Scott
Warr, Peter B. — Cook, John D. (1981)
Watstein, Sarah Barbara — Kesselman, Martin (1987)
Weber, David C. — Leighton, Philip D. (1986)
Weil, Beth — Van House, Nancy (Building Use)
Weil, Beth — Van House, Nancy A. (In-Library...)
Weil, Beth — Van House, Nancy A. (Online Search...)
Weil, Beth T. — Van House, Nancy A. (1990)
Weil, Beth T. — Van House, Nancy A. (General Satisfaction...)
Weil, Beth T. — Van House, Nancy A. (Reference Satisfaction...)
Weinberg, Ronald — Fisher, Harold E. (1988)
Weinberg, Ronald — Fisher, Harold E.
Wills, Gordon — Oldman, Christine (1977)
Wilson, Constant D. — Wender, Ruth W. (1977)
Woods, Bonnie L. — Thompson, Mark J. (1980)
Wynar, Lubomyr — Murfin, Marjorie (1984)
Zweizig, Douglas L. — McClure, Charles R. (1986)
Zweizig, Douglas L. — Van House, Nancy A. (Reference Completion...)
Zweizig, Doulgas L. — Van House, Nancy A. (1987)

Title Index

Since both the "Annotated Bibliography" and the "Summary of Instruments" are arranged by primary author, the "Title Index" cites the corresponding primary author. Entries in the "Summary of Instruments" are entered in bold type, while citations to the "Annotated Bibliography" appear in normal type.

Academic library development program... — University of North Carolina, Charlotte J. Murrey Atkins Library (1976)

Academic library development programs: Self study. — Carnegie Mellon University Libraries (1978)

Academic Library User Ticket; Public Library User Ticket; and Count of In-House Users (User Log) — McClure, Charles R.

Academic reference service... — Lopez, Manual (1973)

Access and recognition... — Tagliacozzo, Renata (1970)

Accuracy of information provision... — Burton, P.F. (1990)

The accuracy of reference services: Variables for research and implementation. — Crews, Kenneth D. (1988)

The accuracy of selected Northeastern college library reference... — Jirjees, Jassim M. (1983)

Acquisitions, collection development, and collection use... — Kohl, David F. (1985)

Active listening at the reference desk. — Smith, Nathan M. (1982)

Activities Performed in the Reference Department — Reeves, Edward B.

Aggravation quotient: Search time/user time. — Flood, Barbara (1973)

American reference theory and information dogma. — Wagers, Robert (1978)

An analysis of available data on the number of public library reference questions. — Goldhor, Herbert (1987)

Analysis of Availability, Causes, and Behavior for the Reference Process — Kantor, Paul B.

An analysis of questions and answers in libraries. — Hieber, Caroline E. (1966)

An analysis of reference statistics reported in the 1977 Library General Information Survey. — Kaske, Neal K. (1980)

Analysis of tasks performed by reference personnel in college and university libraries in Indiana University. — Duncan, Cynthia B. (1974)

Analytical review of catalog use studies. — Markey, Karen (1980)

Analyzing success in meeting reference department management objectives... — Joseph, Margaret A. (1984)

Analyzing the availability of reference services. — Kantor, Paul (1980)

Annual statistics of medical school libraries in the United States and Canada... — Houston Academy of Medicine (1987)

Answering ready reference questions: Print versus online. — Havener, W. Michael (1990)

Anxiety-Stress Questionnaire — House, R.J.
Applications of operations research models to libraries... — Chen, Ching-Chih (1976)
An approach to the measurement of use and a cost... — Mount, Ellis (1972)
Appropriate settings for reference service. — Pierson, Robert (1985)
Are librarians burning out? — Fisher, David P. (1990)
The Arizona Clinical Interview Rating Scale... — White, Marilyn Domas (1990)
Arranging materials and services in a university library reference area for effective use. — Franklin, Hugh (1991)
The assertive librarian. — Caputo, Janette S. (1984)
Assessment of reference services. — Altman, Ellen (1982)
Automation and job satisfaction among reference librarians. — Whitlatch, Jo Bell (1991)
Availability analysis report. — Palais, Elliot S. (1981)
Availability of Library Books — Ciliberti, Anne
Before the looking glass... — Reeves, Edward B. (1977)
The beginnings. — Gothberg, Helen M. (1986)
Behavioral guidelines for reference librarians. — Rettig, James R. (1992)
Behavioral response to the location of a reference service... — Larason, Larry (1975)
The beneficial library, Cranbrook Institute of Technology... — Oldman, Christine (1977)
Benefit Survey — Raffel, Jeffrey
Bibliography of use studies. — Davis, Richard A. (1964)
Book availability... — Mitchell, Eugene (1994)
Book selection and book collection usage in academic libraries. — Evans, G. Edward (1970)
Budgeting for reference service in an online age. — Anderson, Charles R. (1987)
Building Use — Van House, Nancy
Burnout. — Elliott, Jannean L. (1984)
Burnout: A history of the concept and an analysis of its presentation in library literature. — Blevins, Beth (1988)
Burnout: A survey of academic reference librarians. — Smith, Nathan M. (1983)
Burnout: A survey of corporate librarians. — Smith, Nathan M. (1984)
Burnout: A survey of library directors' views. — Taler, Izabella (1984)
Burnout and public services: The periodical literature of librarianship in the eighties. — Blazek, Ron (1992)
Butler Library displays vital signs... — Piech, Carlo R. (1986)
California Reference Evaluation Form — Van House, Nancy A.
Catalog failure and reference service. — Westbrook, Lynn (1984)
Catalog use difficulties. — Perrine, Richard (1968)
Catch 22: The problem of incomplete evaluation of training. — Newstrom, John W. (1978)

Causes and dynamics of user-frustration... — Saracevic, T. (1977)

CD-ROM stress. — Bunge, Charles A. (1991)

Checklist of Reference Skills — Schwartz, Diane G.

Citizen information seeking patterns: A New England study. — Chen, Ching-Chih (1979)

Client/service provider perceptions... — Whitlatch, Jo Bell (1987)

Collection assessment manual for college and university libraries. — Hall, Blaine H. (1985)

Communication at the user-system interface... — Roloff, Michael E. (1979)

Communication theory's role in the reference interview. — Glogoff, Stuart (1983)

Comparative assessment of patrons' uses and evaluations across public libraries within a system... — D'Elia, George (1987)

A comparison of issues and in-library use of books. — Harris, C. (1977)

Comparison of reference success in Canadian and American libraries... — Murfin, Marjorie E. (1989)

Conflicts in reference services. — Katz, Bill (1985)

Cost Analysis for Types of Reference Questions — Spencer, Carol C.

Cost Analysis of Library Service — Cochrane, Lynn Scott

Cost analysis of library services at Virginia Polytechnic Institute and State University. — Cochrane, Lynn Scott (1989)

Cost Benefit Formula — Kramer, Joseph

Cost Benefit Formula — Murfin, Marjorie

A cost comparison between general library tours... — Lawson, V. Lonnie (1990)

Cost-Effectiveness Account — Standera, Oldrich R.

Cost Effectiveness Comparison of Two Alternatives — Lawson, V. Lonnie

A cost effectiveness formula for reference service in academic libraries. — Murfin, Marjorie (1989)

Cost Effectiveness Measures — McClure, Charles

Cost in Staffing Time per *Successful* Question — Murfin, Marjorie

Cost Per Use of Reference Sources — Anderson, Charles R.

Costing of All Reference Operations — Murphy, Marcy

Costs and Benefits — Jensen, Rebecca

Costs and benefits to industry of online literature searchers. — Jensen, Rebecca (1980)

Costs and effectiveness in the evaluation of an information system... — Standera, Oldrich R. (1973)

Counseling skills applied to reference services. — Peck, Theodore P. (1975)

Counselor Effectiveness Scale — Haase, Richard F.

CRD Reference Desk Performance Standards/Peer Review Form — University of Arizona Central Reference Department

Criteria and methodology for evaluating... — Murphy, Marcy (1978)

Criteria for evaluating the effectiveness of library operations and services...
— Wessel, C.J. (1969)

Critical Incident Technique — Wilson, S.R.

Current trends in the continuing education and training of reference staff. —
Heibing, Dottie (1990)

A cybernetic theory of stress, coping, and well-being in organizations. —
Edwards, Jeffrey R. (1992)

Database Questionnaire — Ankeny, Melvon

Designing an evaluation instrument... — Willett, Holly G. (1992)

Designing optical mark forms for reference statistics. — Hallman, Clark N.
(1981)

Designing training and development systems. — Tracey, William R. (1992)

Determination of continuing medical education needs of clinicians... —
Wender, Ruth W. (1977)

**Determining the Full Cost of the Reference Question — Murfin,
Marjorie**

Developing a model of the Library Search Process... — Kuhlthau, Carol
Collier (1988a)

The development and methodological study of an instrument for measuring
material availability in libraries. — Ciliberti, Anne C. (1985)

Development and testing of a conceptual model of public library user behavior. — D'Elia, George (1980)

Development and testing of a Reference Transaction Assessment Instrument.
— Murfin, Marjorie (1987)

The development and testing of materials... — Slavens, Thomas P. (1979)

The development and validation of the Library Anxiety Scale. — Bostick,
Sharon (1993)

The Development of Franklin County Public Libraries, 1980. — Yocum,
James C. (1980)

The division of a library into books in use, and books not in use... — Eliot,
Charles William (1902)

The ecology of study areas. — Sommer, Robert (1970)

The effect of busy library staff on rate of approach... — McMurdo, George
(1982)

Effective on-the-job training: Developing library human resources. — Creth,
Shelia D. (1986)

An effectiveness measure for information center operations. — Miller,
Edward P. (1973)

The effectiveness of an information desk... — Woodard, Beth S. (1989)

The effectiveness of information service in medium size public libraries. —
Crowley, Terence (1971)

The effectiveness of information service in public libraries... — Childers,
Thomas A. (1978)

The effectiveness of telephone reference/information services... — Myers,
Marcia J. (1983)

The effects of reference librarians' nonverbal communications on the patrons' perceptions... — Devore-Chew, Marynelle (1988)

Effects of the decision making process and related organizational factors... — Marchant, Maurice (1970)

Elmer Holmes Bobst Library: A survey. — New York University (1981)

Estimating the satisfaction of information users. — Tagliacozzo, Renata (1977)

Evaluating bibliographic education... — Werking, Richard Hume (1980)

Evaluating collections by their use. — Lancaster, F. Wilfred (1982)

Evaluating end-user services: Success or satisfaction? — Ankeny, Melvon L. (1991)

Evaluating library-use instruction. — Hardesty, Larry (1979)

Evaluating the competence of information providers. — Michell, B. Gillian (1984)

Evaluating the interview. — Von Seggern, Marilyn (1989)

Evaluating the reference interview... — Michell, B. Gillian (1987)

Evaluating the reference product. — Strong, Gary E. (1980a)

Evaluating training operations and programs. — Smith, Martin E. (1980)

Evaluation of adult reference service. — Weech, Terry (1974)

Evaluation of and feedback in information storage and retrieval systems. — Kantor, Paul B. (1982)

Evaluation of library facilities... — Schneekloth, Lynda H. (1991)

An evaluation of reference desk service. — Christensen, John O. (1989)

Evaluation of Reference Desk Service — Christensen, John O.

Evaluation of Reference Expert... — Gunning, Kathleen (1993)

Evaluation of reference service at the University of Waterloo; 1985. — Binkley, Dave (1988)

Evaluation of the collection. — Bonn, George S. (1974)

Evaluation research in the library and information field. — Childers, Thomas (1989)

Evaluation: The forgotten finale of training. — Parker, Treadway C. (1973)

The everyday information needs of the average citizen... — Dervin, Brenda (1976)

Expanding the repertoire of reference. — Frantz, Paul (1991)

Experience of work: A compendium and review of 249 measures and their use. — Cook, John D. (1981)

Experimental studies of relevance judgments... — Cuadra, Carlos (1967)

An experimental study of the way in which search strategy influences retrieval success... — Tibbo, Helen (1993)

An exploratory study... — Kazlauskas, Edward (1976)

Factors affecting subject catalog search success. — Bates, Marcia J. (1977)

Factors affecting the use of seats in academic libraries. — University of Cambridge Library Management Research Unit (LMRU) (1975)

Factors influencing the effectiveness of question-answering services in libraries. — Lancaster, F. Wilfred (1984)

Factors related to reference question answering success... — Bunge, Charles (1985)
Faculty perceptions of librarians: A survey. — Budd, John (1981)
Fairfax County Public Library user study... — Rodger, Eleanor Jo (1984a)
Fear of talking... — Lederman, Linda Costigan (1981)
FIRO: A three-dimensional theory of interpersonal behavior... — Schultz, William C. (1960)
Follow-Up Questionnaire — Tagliacozzo, Renata
The forgiving building... — Novak, Gloria (1987)
From the mind's eye of the user... — Dervin, Brenda (1992)
Frustration Factor and Nuisance Factor — Kantor, Paul
Fundamental problems of information transfer. — Pearson, A.W. (1973)
Further evidence on response sets and test design. — Cronbach, Lee J. (1950)
General Satisfaction Survey — Van House, Nancy A.
Getting in gear... — Westbrook, Lynn (1988)
The grail of goodness: The effective public library. — Childers, Thomas (1989)
Guide to collection evaluation through use and user studies. — Christiansen, Dorothy E. (1983)
Guide to collection evaluation through use and user studies. — Davis, Roger (1983)
Guide to review of library collections: Preservation, storage, and withdrawal. — Guide... (1991)
Guide to the evaluation of library collections. — Guide... (1989)
Half-right reference: Is it true? — Crowley, Terence (1985)
Handbook of training evaluation and measurement methods. — Phillips, Jack J. (1983)
Hands touching hands... — Fisher, Jeffrey D. (1976)
"Helps" Users Obtain from Their Library Visits — Dervin, Brenda
The hidden agenda in the measurement and evaluation of reference service... — Rothstein, Samuel (1984)
How biomedical investigators use library books. — Raisig, L. Miles (1966)
How libraries help. — Dervin, Brenda (1985)
How to survive in industry: Cost justifying library services. — Kramer, Joseph (1971)
Human aspects of higher technology in special libraries. — Bichteler, Julie (1986)
"I heard you say"... — Gers, Ralph (1988)
If you want to evaluate your library.... — Lancaster, F. Wilfred (1988)
Immediacy... — Gothberg, Helen (1976)
Improving access to library resources... — Dougherty, Richard M. (1974)
Improving reference performance: Results of a statewide survey. — Gers, Ralph (1985)
Improving reference services... — Dyson, Lillie Seward (1992)

Improving the quality of reference service for government publications. — Hernon, Peter (1983)

Individual rating scale for communication skills... — Hittner, Amy (1981)

Individual Rating Scale for Communications Skills — Hittner, Amy

The influence of traditional services on library use. — Kernaghan, John A. (1979)

Information-gathering habits of workers in pure and applied science. — Herner, Saul (1954)

Information need and use studies. — Hewins, Elizabeth T. (1990)

Information Needs — Chen, Ching-Chih

Information needs and uses. — Dervin, Brenda (1986)

Information needs and uses. — Martyn, John (1974)

Information needs and uses in science and technology. — Herner, Saul (1967)

Information resources in agricultural research. — Cornell University (1984)

The Information Search Process: Process Survey and Perception Questionnaire — Kuhlthau, Carol

Information search tactics. — Bates, Marcia J. (1979)

Information services profile, Fairfax County Public Library. — Fairfax County Public Library (1987)

Information Sources in Agricultural Research — Cornell University, Albert R. Mann Library

In-house use of materials in public libraries. — Rubin, Richard (1986)

Initial development of an inventory to assess stress and health risk. — Nowack, Kenneth (1990)

In-Library Materials Use — Van House, Nancy A.

In-Service Training Program for Library Paraprofessionals Workshop Evaluation and Pre-Test/Post-Test — Hittner, Amy

Instrument for Search Strategy and Development — Jahoda, Gerald

The intensity of motivation. — Brehm, Jack W. (1989)

Interface design and user problems and errors... — Puttapithakporn, Somporn (1990)

Interpersonal communication in the reference interview. — Crouch, Richard Keith Chamberlain (1981)

Interpersonal dimensions of the reference interview: A historical review of the literature. — Bunge, Charles (1984)

Introductory training of academic reference librarians... — Stabler, Karen Y. (1987)

An investigation of the relationship of faculty... — Strother, Jeanne D. (1975)

An investigation of the relationships... — Powell, Ronald R. (1978)

Job satisfaction in libraries... — Lynch, Beverly P. (1987)

Job stress and burnout among probation/parole officers. — Whitehead, John (1985)

Keep on learning: Reference breakthrough in Maryland. — Stephens, Sandy (1988)

LAMA-NDCU Experimental Staffing Adequacy Measures — LAMA-NDCU Committee

The lean reference collection... — Nolan, Christopher W. (1991)

Levels of outputs related to cost of operation of scientific and technical libraries. — Kantor, Paul (1981a)

The librarian and reference queries... — Jahoda, Gerald (1980)

Librarian and User Perceptions of Reference Service Quality — Whitlatch, Jo Bell

The librarian of the Northwest. — Naegele, Kaspar D. (1960)

Librarian self-disclosure and patron satisfaction in the reference interview. — Markham, Marilyn (1983)

Librarian subject searching in online catalogs... — Connell, Tschera Harkness (1991)

The library administrator's need for measures of reference. — Runyon, Robert (1974)

Library anxiety... — Mellon, Constance (1986)

The Library Anxiety Scale — Bostick, Sharon L.

Library data, statistics, and information. — Brown, Maryann Devin (1980)

Library design influences on user behavior and satisfaction. — Campbell, David E. (1979)

Library effectiveness in meeting consumers' information needs. — Chen, Ching-Chih (1980)

Library Knowledge Questionnaire — Phipps, Shelley

Library operations research. — Daiute, R.J. (1974)

The library research process... — Kuhlthau, Carol Collier (1984)

The Library Skills Program at the University of Arizona... — Phipps, Shelley (1979)

Library space planning... — Fraley, Ruth A. (1990)

Library statistics of colleges and universities 1982. — Heintze, Robert A. (1986)

Library Survey Form — Joseph, Margaret A.

Library/Technical Information Services Survey — Robertson, W. Davenport

Library use and reference service... — Regazzi, John J. (1976)

Library use and the perceptions of student library users at Southern Illinois University-Carbondale. — Bauner, Ruth E. (1978)

Library use as a performance measure: Its background and rationale. — Burns, Robert W. (1978)

Library-Use Instruction Evaluation Instrument — Hardesty, Larry

Library Use Study Questionnaire—Revised — Fussler, Herman H.

The library's public. — Berelson, Bernard (1949)

Linkages between library uses through the study of individual patron behavior. — Clark, Philip M. (1985)

Literature Search Evaluation — University of Kentucky Libraries Data Services
Literature Search Evaluation. — University of Kentucky Library (1981)
Longitudinal case studies of the information search process of users in libraries. — Kuhlthau, Carol Collier (1988b)
Make training accountable: Assess its impact. — Fisher, Harold E. (1988)
Management of reference information services... — Elcheson, Dennis R. (1982)
Management of student assistants in a public services setting of an academic library. — Frank, Donald G. (1984)
Managing difficult people: Patrons (and others). — Gothberg, Helen M. (1987)
Managing employee performance. — King, Geraldine (1988)
Maslach Burnout Inventory (MBI) — Maslach, Christina
Maslach Burnout Inventory Manual. — Maslach, Christina (1981)
Material availability: A study of academic library performance. — Cilberti, Anne C. (1987)
Materials availability fill rates... — D'Elia, George (1985)
Measurement and evaluation in higher education. — Jordan, Thomas E. (1989)
The measurement and evaluation of library services. — Baker, Sharon L. (1991)
Measurement and evaluation of library services. — Lancaster, F. Wilfred (1977)
The measurement and evaluation of reference service. — Rothstein, Samuel (1964)
Measurement of Effort by Simulation — Kantor, Paul
The measurement of meaning. — Osgood, Charles E. (1967)
The measurement of reference and information services. — Kesselman, Martin (1987)
Measurement of reference transactions... — Murfin, Marjorie (1980)
Measures of user evaluation at two academic libraries: Prolegomena. — Budd, John (1982)
Measuring academic library performance... — Van House, Nancy A. (1990)
Measuring collections use at Virginia Tech. — Metz, Paul (1988)
Measuring library effectiveness... — DuMont, Rosemary Ruhig (1979)
Measuring students' preferences for reference services... — Halperin, Michael (1980)
Measuring the quality of library service: A handbook. — Beeler, M.G. (1974)
Medline searching on BRS Colleague... — Kirby, Martha (1985)
Medline searching on Colleague... — Kirby, Martha (1986)
Metropolitan library users... — Bundy, Mary Lee (1968)
Microcounseling: Innovations in interviewing... — Ivey, Allen E. (1978)
A model instrument for user-rating of library service. — Chwe, Steven (1978)

A Model Instrument for User-Rating of Library Service — Chwe, Steven S.

A model of human responses to workload stress. — LeMay, Moira (1990)

Model Reference Behavior Checklist — Gers, Ralph

Morale Inventory — Lowenthal, Ralph

Municipal yearbook, 1979. — The International City Management Associa tion (1979)

Murfin-Harrick Reference Survey — Murfin, Marjorie

National reference measurement... — Murfin, Marjorie E. (1983)

National reporting on reference transactions, 1976-1978. — Emerson, Katherine (1977)

The necessary and sufficient conditions of therapeutic personality change... — Rogers, Carl (1957)

New measures of user satisfaction with computer-based literature searches. — Tessier, Judith A. (1977)

New norms for reference desk staffing adequacy... — Rinderknecht, Deborah (1992)

Noise in the library: Effects and control. — Eagan, Ann (1991)

Objective performance measures for academic and research libraries. — Kantor, Paul (1984)

Observations of browsing behavior in an academic library. — Ross, Johanna (1983)

Obtrusive versus unobtrusive evaluation... — Weech, Terry L. (1982)

Occupational burnout among librarians. — Haack, Mary (1984)

Occupational perceptions of librarians by high school students. — Bloch, U. (1981)

On browsing... — Morse, Philip McCord (1970)

On the road to STARdom... — Isenstein, Laura J. (1991)

On types of search and the allocation of library resources. — Buckland, Michael K. (1979)

Online access to MEDLINE in clinical settings. — Haynes, R. Brian (1990)

Online data searching as a tool for motivating innovation. — Pitlack, Robert (1980)

Online Search Evaluation — Van House, Nancy A.

Online searching in public libraries... — McCue, Janice Helen (1988)

Online Searching in Public Libraries — McCue, Janice Helen

Online searching: What measure satisfaction? — Sandore, Beth (1990)

Online subject access... — Mandel, Carol A. (1983)

Opening the black box of relevance. — Cuadra, Carlos (1967)

Our competencies defined... — Griffiths, Jose-Marie (1984)

Our real business. — Stenstrom, P.F. (1990)

Output measures... — McClure, Charles R. (1986)

Output measures... — Van House, Nancy A. (1985)

Output measures and library space planning. — Lushington, Nolan (1987)

Output measures for public libraries... — Van House, Nancy A. (1987)

Output measures for public libraries. — Veatch, Lamar (1982)

Output measures for public libraries... — Zweizig, Douglas (1982)
Output measures in libraries. — Van House, Nancy A. (1989)
Output measures, unobtrusive testing... — McClure, Charles (1984)
An overview of sense-making research... — Dervin, Brenda (1983)
Paraprofessionals at the reference desk. — Murfin, Marjorie E. (1988a)
Patron Preference for Different Aspects of Reference Service — Halperin, Michael
Patron preference in reference service points. — Morgan, Linda (1980)
The patrons' side of public library reference questions. — Goldhor, Herbert (1979)
Pattern of Information Requests Survey (PIRS) and User Ticket — Strong, Gary
Patterns in the use of books in large research libraries. — Fussler, Herman H. (1961)
Patterns of information requests at the Washington State Library. — Strong, Gary E. (1980b)
Patterns of information seeking in the humanities. — Wiberley, Stephen E., Jr. (1989)
Peer coaching in a university reference department. — Arthur, Gwen (1990)
Peer performance appraisal of reference librarians in a public library. — King, Geraldine (1991)
Perceived role conflict, role ambiguity, and reference librarian burnout in public libraries. — Birch, Nancy (1986)
Perceptions of the information search process in libraries... — Kuhlthau, Carol Collier (1988c)
Performance appraisal in academic libraries. — Jenkins, Barbara Williams (1990)
Performance measurement and information management. — Cronin, Blaise (1982)
The performance of professionals and nonprofessionals in the reference interview. — Halldorsson, Egill A. (1977)
Performance problems: A model for analysis and resolution. — Allan, Ann (1983)
Personal space and user preference for patterns of carrel arrangement... — Larason, Larry (1962)
A perspective on the evaluation of training and development programs. — Monat, Jonathan S. (1981)
Planned and unplanned scientific communication. — Menzel, Herbert (1958)
Planning academic and research library buildings. — Leighton, Philip D. (1986)
Planning and output measures. — Ballard, Thomas H. (1989)
Potential and reality at the reference desk. — Bunge, Charles (1984)
Practical strategies for evaluating training. — Salenger, Ruth D. (1982)
A prediction study of reference accuracy among recently graduated working reference librarians (1975-1979). — Benham, Frances (1987)
Preference and Feasibility Measure — Miller, Edward P.

Preliminary indications of the relationship between reference morale and performance. — Lowenthal, Ralph A. (1990)

Print, online, or ondisc... — Havener, W. Michael (1993)

Problem solving... — Nahl-Jakobovits, Diane (1988)

The process of answering reference queries... — Jahoda, G. (1987)

The process of answering reference questions. — Jahoda, Gerald (1977)

Professional education and reference efficiency. — Bunge, Charles (1967)

A proposed model of self-disclosure. — Thompson, Mark J. (1980)

The psychological barriers between library users and library staff... — Hatchard, Desmond B. (1986)

Public and academic library reference questions. — Cameron, Dee Birch (1976)

Public library effectiveness... — Van House, Nancy A. (1986)

The public library effectiveness study... — Van House, Nancy A. (1993)

Public Library Use Study — Bundy, Mary Lee

Public library use, users, uses... — Zweizig, Douglas (1977)

Public library users and uses. — Kim, Choong Han (1987)

Public services in research libraries... — University of California at Riverside (1983)

Public services in research libraries... — Weingart, Doris (1983)

Putting values into evaluation. — Poulet, Roger (1987)

Qualitative collection analysis: The conspectus methodology. — *Qualitative...* (1989)

Quality and library collections... — Mosher, Paul H. (1984)

The quality of academic and public library reference service... — Hernon, Peter (1986a)

Quality of data issues in unobtrusive testing of library reference service... — Hernon, Peter (1987a)

The quality of reference: Still moot after 20 years. — Childers, Thomas (1987)

Quantitative evaluation of the reference process. — Kantor, Paul B. (1981b)

Question-negotiation and information seeking in libraries. — Taylor, Robert (1968)

Question-negotiation and information-seeking in libraries. — Taylor, Robert S. (1967)

Questionnaire for library users. — Colorado State University (1981)

Questionnaire for Library Users — Colorado State University

Questionnaires for End Users and Intermediaries — University of Texas at Austin

Questionnaires for end users and intermediaries — University at Texas at Austin Library (1984)

Questionnaires I and II for Initial Search and Follow-up Search — Kirby, Martha

Questions in library and information science. — Swigger, Keith (1985)

Questions negotiation in the archival setting... — Long, Linda J. (1989)

Queues and reference service... — Regazzi, John (1978)

Queuing Study — Regazzi, John
Random time sampling. — Spencer, Carol C. (1980)
Ratio of staff to users... — Slater, Margaret (1981)
Recording of reference/information service activities... — Ciucki, Marcella (1977)
Reference accuracy at the Fairfax County Public Library... — Rodger, Eleanor Jo (1984b)
Reference Accuracy Study — Fairfax County Public Library
Reference and information service... — Wagers, Robert (1980)
Reference Arrangement Survey — Franklin, Hugh
Reference clientele and the reference transaction ... — Weech, Terry L. (1984)
Reference Collection Use Study — Arrigona, Daniel
Reference Completion Rate — Van House, Nancy A.
The reference desk: Service point or barrier? — Larason, Larry (1984)
Reference effectiveness... — Powell, Ronald R. (1984)
Reference efficiency or reference deficiency. — House, David E. (1974)
Reference Environment Problems Checklist — Donnelly, Anna M.
Reference Environment Problems Checklist... — Donnelly, Anna M. (1993)
Reference evaluation. — Westbrook, Lynn (1987)
Reference evaluation manual for public libraries. — Suburban Library System Reference Service (1986)
The reference interview... — White, Marilyn Domas (1987)
Reference Interview and the Environment — Durrance, Joan C.
The reference interview as a creative art. — Jennerich, Elaine Zaremba (1987)
Reference Question Tabulation Sheet — Hernon, Peter
Reference questions—Data from the field. — Bunge, Charles (1987)
Reference Satisfaction Survey — Van House, Nancy A.
Reference service... — Murfin, Marjorie (1984)
Reference service effectiveness. — Whitlatch, Jo Bell (1990a)
Reference Service Preferences — Halperin, Michael
Reference service standards, personal criteria, and evaluation. — Schwartz, Diane (1986)
Reference service upgraded... — Seng, Mary (1978)
Reference services in academic research libraries. — Watson, Paula D. (1986)
Reference services today... — Katz, Bill (1986)
Reference success: Does the 55% rule tell the whole story? — Durrance, Joan C. (1989)
A reference tools database... — Trautman, Rodes (1982)
Reference transaction and end product as viewed by the patron. — Vathis, Alma Christine (1983)
Reference Transaction Assessment Instrument (RTAI) — Murfin, Marjorie E.
Reference Transaction Slip — King, Geraldine

Reflecting on the public library data service project... — Johnson, Debra Wilcox (1993)

Report of the Task Force on Facilities, Space and Equipment — University of California at Santa Barbara, University Library (1986)

Report of the Task Force on Library Service to Undergraduates. — University of California at Los Angeles (1981)

Research and the psychology of information use. — Fine, Sara (1984)

Research in library reference/information service. — Lynch, Mary Jo (1983)

Research in patterns of scientific communication... — Garvey, William D. (1972)

Research in stress, coping, and health... — Edwards, Jeffrey R. (1988)

Research in user behavior in university libraries. — Ford, Geoffrey (1973)

Research on the use of online catalogs... — Lewis, David W. (1987)

Research report on the American public library. — Sager, Donald J. (1982)

Responsible standards for reference service in Ohio public libraries. — Murfin, Marjorie E. (1988b)

Review of methods employed in determining the use of library stock. — Ford, Geoffrey (1990)

Review of output measures for public libraries. — Childers, Thomas (1983)

The role of the academic reference librarian. — Whitlatch, Jo Bell (1990b)

Rules for performing steps in the reference process. — Jahoda, Gerald (1989)

Sampling and data collection methods for a book-use study. — Jain, A.K. (1969)

Sampling by length. — Handley, John C. (1991)

Sampling in-library book use. — Jain, A.K. (1972)

San Diego County Library Reference Service Project Final Report. — Lange, Janet M. (1986)

San Diego County Library Staff Workload and Reference Training Needs Survey — Lange, Janet M.

San Jose State University Library services... — Whitlatch, Jo Bell (1980)

SCORE Cost Effectiveness Analysis — Wessel, C.J.

Search interview technique and information gain as antecedents of user satisfaction with online bibliographic retrieval. — Auster, Ethel (1984)

Search procedures in the library—analyzed from the cognitive point of view. — Ingwersen, Peter (1982)

Search techniques. — Bates, Marcia J. (1981)

Selected Items from Overall Library Surveys — University of California at Los Angeles

Selected User Survey Items — New York University, Elmer Holmes Bobst Library

Selected User Survey Items — The University of British Columbia

Semantic Differential Scale — Slavens, Thomas P.

Service at San Jose State University... — Whitlatch, Jo Bell (1978)

Shelf browsing, open access and storage capacity in research libraries. — Boll, John J. (1985)

Silent majority: Why don't they ask questons? — Swoper, Mary Jane (1972)
Silent messages. — Mehrabian, Albert (1971)
The social context of reference work... — Harris, Roma M. (1986)
Some behavioral patterns of library users... — Trueswell, R.W. (1969)
Some benefits of the online catalog. — Getz, Malcolm (1987)
Some characteristics of reference work. — Cole, Dorothy (1946)
Some effects on library users of the delays in supplying publications. — Stuart, M. (1977)
Stack use of a research library. — Dubester, Henry (1961)
Staff development: A practical guide. — LAMA PAS Staff Development Committee (1992)
Staff resistance to library CD-ROM services. — Giesbrecht, Walter (1991)
Staffing of public libraries. — Great Britain. Department of Education and Science. (1976)
Staffing the reference desk... — St. Clair, Jeffrey W. (1977)
Statewide reference improvement... — Layman, Mary (1990)
Statistical Report. — Statistical... (1988-)
Statistical representation of reference library use. — Lamble, J. Hoskin (1951)
Stress Assessment Profile (SAP) — Nowack, Kenneth
Stress at the reference desk. — Roose, Tina (1989)
Stress in the library environment. — Bube, Judy Lynn (1986)
Stress in the library workplace. — Bunge, Charles A. (1989)
Stressful life events, personality, and health... — Kobasa, Suzanne C. (1979)
Strother's Questionnaire A and B — Strother, Jeanne D.
Student perceptions of academic librarians. — Hernon, Peter (1977)
Student reading characteristics... — Kottenstette, J.P. (1969)
Student Users Survey — Carnegie Mellon University Libraries
Studies of education for science and engineering... — Krulee, G.K. (1960)
Studies of the personality of librarians. — Agada, John (1984)
A study of collection use at the University of Cincinnati Central Library. — Anderson, Paul M. (1983)
A study of information seeking and retrieving. — Saracevic, Tefko (1988)
A study of library use studies. — Tobin, Jayne C. (1974)
A study of reference referral and super reference... — Robinson, Barbara M. (1986)
A study of reference services and reference users... — White, Ruth (1971)
A study of the reference process in a university library. — Murfin, Marjorie (1970)
The study of the research use of libraries. — Stevens, Rolland (1956)
A study of the use of reference materials... — Gitler, Robert L. (1939)
Study of the use of Wayne State University Medical Library, Part 1. — Pings, Vern (1965)
Subject searching in an online catalog with authority control. — Van Pulis, Noelle (1988)

The success case: A low-cost high-yield evaluation. — Brinkerhoff, Robert O. (1983)

Successes and failures of patrons searching the online catalog... — Hunter, Rhonda (1991)

A suggestion for estimating use of the reference library. — Barlow, S.H. (1938)

Summary/analysis: Field responses to the reference referral study report. — Henson, Jim (1987)

Survey of Actual and Potential Task Participation of Academic Library Reference Personnel — Duncan, Cynthia B.

Survey of Olin Library users. — Fisher, Kenneth (1976)

Survey of Public Library Users — Yocum, James C.

Survey of student opinion. — Kent State University Libraries. (1976)

A survey of subject reference questions. — Paterson, Ellen R. (1979)

Survey of the effectiveness of record systems. — University of Cincinnati (1984)

Systematic analysis of university libraries... — Raffel, Jeffrey (1969)

The systematic nature of library output statistics. — Brooks, Terence (1982)

Tailoring measures to fit your service... — Zweizig, Douglas (1984)

Taking the measure... — Moore, Carolyn M. (1986)

Techniques for evaluating training programs. — Kirkpatrick, Donald L. (1979)

Technostress and the reference librarian. — Kupersmith, John (1992)

Telephone information service in public libraries... — Childers, Thomas A. (1971)

Telephone reference questions. — Brown, Diane M. (1985)

Territoriality and the use of library study tables. — Gal, Cynthia A. (1986)

The test of reference. — Childers, Thomas (1980)

Testing for library-use competence. — Bloomfield, Masse (1974)

A time allocation theory of public library use. — Van House, Nancy (1983)

To see ourselves as others see us... — Rodger, Eleanor Jo (1987)

A tool for comparative collection analysis... — Paskoff, Beth M. (1990)

Toward the measurement of organizational practices... — House, R.J. (1972)

Training Feedback Questionnaire — Fisher, Harold E.

Transfer of training: A bibliographic essay. — Carver, Deborah A. (1988)

Try it— you'll like it... — King, Geraldine (1982)

Types of use and users in industrial libraries... — Slater, Margaret (1963)

UCR library services survey. — University of California at Riverside (1984)

UCR Library Services Survey — University of California at Riverside

An unfinished history... — Rothstein, Samuel (1989)

Units of analysis and the individual differences fallacy in environmental assessment. — Richards, James M., Jr. (1990)

University of California Questionnaire—Library Survey — Lawrence, Gary S.

Unobtrusive evaluation of a reference referral network... — Van House, Nancy A. (1984)

Unobtrusive measures... — Webb, Eugene J. (1966)
Unobtrusive studies and the quality of academic reference services. — Whitlatch, Jo Bell (1989)
Unobtrusive testing and library reference service. — Stevens, Norman (1987)
Unobtrusive testing and library reference services. — Anderson, Margaret (1988)
Unobtrusive testing and library reference services [Book review]. — Benham, Frances (1988)
Unobtrusive testing and library reference services [Book review]. — Bunge, Charles A. (1987)
Unobtrusive testing and library reference services. — Crowley, Terence (1988)
Unobtrusive testing and library reference services. — Hernon, Peter (1987b)
Unobtrusive testing and library services. — Bailey, Bill (1988)
Unobtrusive testing: The 55% rule. — Hernon, Peter (1986b)
Urban and suburban public library statistics. — Green, Joseph (1976)
Use and perception of an academic library... — Wood, Fiona (1982)
Use and user studies for collection evaluation. — Brancolini, Kristin B. (1992)
Use and user studies... — Van Heck, Charles, III (1993)
The use of books within the library. — Selth, Jeff (1992)
The use of empirical standards in assessing public library effectiveness... — Strayner, Richard (1980)
The use of general collections at the University of California... — Lawrence, Gary S. (1980)
Use of library facilities... — Potthoff, Joy K. (1990)
Use of Library Services Questionnaire. — University of California at Riverside (1981)
Use of nonprofessionals at reference desks. — Courtois, Martin P. (1984)
Use of personal space in libraries... — Wagner, Gulten (1983)
The Use of Print Versus Online — Havener, W. Michael
The use of print versus online sources to answer ready reference questions in the social sciences... — Havener, W. Michael (1988)
Use of the critical incident technique... — Wilson, S.R. (1989)
Use of the reference service in a large academic library. — Balay, Robert (1975)
Use studies of library collections. — Broadus, Robert N. (1980)
A use study of an academic library reference collection. — Arrigona, Daniel (1988)
User criteria for evaluating the effectiveness of the online catalog. — Nitecki, Danuta (1993)
The user encounters the library... — Steffenson, Martin B. (1978)
A user-oriented approach to setting priorities for library services... — Robertson, W. Davenport (1980)
User-oriented evaluation of information systems and services. — Bawden, David (1990)

User Responses to Online Search Requests — Auster, Ethel
User satisfaction as a measure of public library performance. — D'Elia, George, (1980a)
User satisfaction with library service... — D'Elia, George (1983)
User satisfaction with the online negotiation interview... — Auster, Ethel (1983)
User studies: A review for librarians and information scientists. — Bates, Marcia J. (1971)
User Study — Rodger, Eleanor Jo
User survey... — University of Massachusetts (1976)
User surveys. — User... (1988)
Users of academic and public GPO depository libraries. — McClure, Charles R. (1989)
Using online catalogs... — Matthews, Joseph R. (1983)
Utility Measures — Saracevic, Tefko
Validating a model of the search process... — Kuhlthau, Carol (1990)
The value of information and related systems, products and services. — Griffiths, Jose-Marie (1982)
Wayfinding in the library: Book searches and route uncertainty. — Eaton, Gale (1991)
Wealth from knowledge. — Langrish, J. (1972)
Weeding library collections. — Slote, Stanley J. (1989)
When smart people fail... — Peters, Thomas (1989)
The whole shebang... — Mason, Ellsworth (1984)
Who's giving all those wrong answers?... — Weech, Terry (1984)
Wisconsin-Ohio reference evaluation at the University of Waterloo. — Binkley, Dave (1989)
The Wisconsin-Ohio Reference Evaluation Project. — Bunge, Charles (1983)
Workshop evaluation... — Shearer, Kenneth D. (1992)
Wrong questions, wrong answers... — Tyckoson, David A. (1992)